PENGUIN REFERENCE
The Penguin Dictionary of Marketing

Phil Harris is Professor of Marketing at the University of Otago, Dunedin, New Zealand. He is joint founding editor of the Journal of Public Affairs and a member of ten international journal editorial and advisory boards. He has published over 150 journal articles and conference papers and his books include *The Handbook of Public Affairs* (with Craig Fleisher, 2005) *European Business and Marketing* (with Frank Macdonald, 2004), *Machiavelli, Marketing and Management* (with Andrew Lock and Patricia Rees, 1999) and *Newer Insights into Marketing: Cross-Cultural and Cross-National Perspectives* (with Camille Schuster, 1999).

He is a past chair of the UK-based Academy of Marketing, Fellow of the Chartered Institute of Marketing and Chartered Institute of Public Relations, and member of the Global Marketing SIG Board of the American Marketing Association. He is International Research Director of the European Centre for Public Affairs, and former chairman of its research committee. Before becoming an academic he held marketing positions in the International Chemical and Food Industries and has stood as a candidate for the Westminster and European Parliaments.

He has researched and taught widely in Asia, the Pacific region, Europe and North America, and has been an advisor to a number of business and governmental, energy, utility, media and various not-for-profit organizations.

In early 2009 he will take up the position of Executive Dean, Business, Enterprise and Lifelong Learning and the Westminster Chair of Marketing and Public Affairs at the University of Chester, Cheshire, England.

The Penguin Dictionary of
MARKETING

Phil Harris

PENGUIN BOOKS

PENGUIN BOOKS

Published by the Penguin Group
Penguin Books Ltd, 80 Strand, London WC2R 0RL, England
Penguin Group (USA) Inc., 375 Hudson Street, New York, New York 10014, USA
Penguin Group (Canada), 90 Eglinton Avenue East, Suite 700, Toronto, Ontario, Canada M4P 2Y3
(a division of Pearson Penguin Canada Inc.)
Penguin Ireland, 25 St Stephen's Green, Dublin 2, Ireland (a division of Penguin Books Ltd)
Penguin Group (Australia), 250 Camberwell Road, Camberwell, Victoria 3124, Australia
(a division of Pearson Australia Group Pty Ltd)
Penguin Books India Pvt Ltd, 11 Community Centre, Panchsheel Park, New Delhi – 110 017, India
Penguin Group (NZ), 67 Apollo Drive, Rosedale, North Shore 0632, New Zealand
(a division of Pearson New Zealand Ltd)
Penguin Books (South Africa) (Pty) Ltd, 24 Sturdee Avenue, Rosebank, Johannesburg 2196, South Africa

Penguin Books Ltd, Registered Offices: 80 Strand, London WC2R 0RL, England

www.penguin.com

First published 2009
1

Copyright © Phil Harris, 2009
All rights reserved

The moral right of the author has been asserted

Set in ITC Stone Sans and ITC Stone Serif
Typeset by Data Standards Ltd, Frome, Somerset
Printed in England by Clays Ltd, St Ives plc

ISBN: 978-0-140-51518-3

www.greenpenguin.co.uk

Penguin Books is committed to a sustainable future
for our business, our readers and our planet.
The book in your hands is made from paper
certified by the Forest Stewardship Council.

Dedicated to
Edward Joseph Lumb-Burgess, 1992–2005
Who brought love, happiness and inspiration into our lives

Contents

Introduction

The Penguin Dictionary of Marketing is designed to be used by the modern activist, marketer, practitioner, researcher, stakeholder and student, who would like to know more and wants to own a straightforward A to Z text that explores the core ideas and thinking in the discipline.

Marketing, in one guise or another, continues to have a significant influence throughout every aspect of daily life, whether you agree with its basic premise (of understanding and meeting consumers' needs) or not. Marketing has been driven by our demand to understand modern consumers and their desires for certain products, and to meet those needs profitably. However, there have been many major developments in the last decade and also marketing has been applied to many new areas. Consequently we now recognize that it plays a pivotal role in developing consumer-based provision in public services, in the marketing of politicians, arts and health care and in promoting the causes and issues affecting non-profit organizations. The growth and use of marketing has spawned a significant lexicon of ideas and practice, and this dictionary is an attempt to encapsulate this in a usable but creative and imaginative essence which I hope stimulates the user to explore and develop the subject further.

The growth of marketing activity, and especially service delivery, as a core feature of modern business has meant increasingly that business employment is in one of the key areas of sales, corporate communication, or distribution in the modern economy. As a result university, college-based and part-time education courses have grown substantially, with over five per cent of courses estimated worldwide at these levels having some direct or indirect link to the discipline.

My aim throughout the period of working on materials and definitions for this text was to be selective and to keep the number of terms and ideas that the modern user of marketing needs to know, or at least be aware of, to a realistic minimum. This is for two reasons: first the literature on marketing is substantial and growing, and second I have my own views on marketing, which are my societal and activist leanings. For these I do not make any apologies.

My aim when researching and writing the text was to produce a dictionary which would be sufficiently broadly based to reflect the changing nature of marketing, yet would emphasize some of the key concepts and ideas that have developed over time, underpinning the discipline. Another aim was to ensure that it did not become such a vast edifice that it appeared like a piece of furniture in some ancient library; too large to be removed and used regularly. The book also reflects the development of many of the newer marketing communications media, such as blogs, internet-based social networks and texting, which most books of this nature do not cover, yet which now dominate much consumer thinking and time. I have also used a range of short definitions that hopefully allow information to be easily extracted and used. Selected key ideas or terms are explained in more detail for the benefit of the general reader and enthusiast. The entries vary enormously in length. But I have tried to offer reasonable cross-referencing to aid those using the dictionary merely to obtain definitions, as well as those using the dictionary to obtain explanation. My goal has been to produce a *Dictionary of Marketing* that can be consulted, used as a basic text or dipped into, yet that should keep the reader engaged and interested in exploring the topic of marketing. It also reflects the fact that it is grounded in global marketing having been written by a European, who during its development and completion carried out research and worked in New Zealand, Australia, Russia, Canada, United States, China and the majority of EU states. I hope it reflects some of my own cultural appreciation and therefore meets practitioner, researcher and student needs more effectively.

I have tried to exclude terms of obvious general meaning, such as 'buy', unless there is some particular reason for adding the term to benefit the reader. I have also added a number of methodologies or research theory related terms, as these are frequently employed in the discipline by users and researchers, and it is thus important that all interested in the subject have some basic understanding of them. In selecting which word went in and which I did not include I erred on the side of caution.

Terms from psychology, sociology, statistics, mathematics, computer science, information systems, human resource management, geography, operations research, etc. have been included where they are commonly used in marketing, but the reader is referred to specialist discipline-based dictionaries for further information on terms not widely used in marketing. To supplement the text I provide two appendices of acronyms and websites which I hope the reader will find useful in exploring marketing further.

One difficulty I faced was whether or not to include individuals who had made a significant contribution to the discipline. I decided to stick my neck out and include a range of key influential thinkers in the field, and to display a limited selection of the best of them spread throughout the text. These include figures from business, economics and psychology that have all had a significant influence on the discipline of marketing. Sadly there are many I have not listed, who if the book was longer I would have liked to include. Please forgive me and send in suggestions for the second edition.

The evolution of marketing has broadly been perceived as developing in four stages: production (prior to the 1920s), sales (prior to the 1950s), marketing (since the 1950s) and relationships (since the 1990s). Since the 1950s the discipline has seen significant development in its basic concepts, and the consequent theory development has been taught widely internationally. I outline the major steps in marketing theory development and practice in the table below.

Marketing Paradigm Development

Functionalist	Wroe Alderson. Post WWII functionalism development of general philosophy. Adoption of a Systems Theory approach. Development of basic curriculum i.e. Marketing Concept, Satisfying Customers' Needs, Advertising, 4Ps and Sales Orientation
Managerial	Philip Kotler, Post Cold War managerialism. Move from seller to buyer orientated markets. Customer Orientation, Marketing Management and Curricula Development.
Buying Behaviour	Engel et al./Wind and Webster. Growth in Behavioural Sciences. Development of Consumer Behaviour and Business to Business Marketing.
Relationship Marketing	Len Berry definition. Popularized in 1990s by Gronroos and Gummesson, based on 1930s thinking of Copenhagen Economists. Parallels IMP Group work on Interactions and Networks. Vargo and Lusch's (2004) Service Dominant Logic test variant.

Paralleling these major shifts in thinking, pressures and changes from business and society have led to a major surge in the development of more advanced and consistent marketing techniques and theory, and its application to more complex societal agendas. These developments are outlined in the table below.

School of Thought; Evolutionary Responses to Pressures on the System

1970s Marketing Science	Demand for metrics
1980s Culture & Consumption	Buyer behaviour, consumption patterns, postmodernism
1990s Relationship Marketing	Appreciation of interaction and networks
2000s Societal Marketing	Application to social agendas and policy making

As I finalize this dictionary, it is clear that marketing is being applied to the ever more complex issues within the biosphere and society, which is highlighted by the following terms coming into increasingly common usage: socially responsible marketing, stakeholder marketing and societal marketing. This is evidence that, like the English language, marketing is being commonly used to communicate and address some of the more complex concerns of our modern business and society.

Acknowledgements

There are a number of colleagues and staff who during the writing of this dictionary have inspired me, given me ideas or added to my refinement and development of definitions and I would just like to take this opportunity to thank them. I would like to thank the Department of Marketing at the University of Otago, and the Centre for Corporate and Public Affairs and the Marketing Group at Manchester Metropolitan University for their research support and encouragement. It was greatly appreciated. In particular at Otago, I would like to thank David Ballantyne and Kim-Shyan Fam (now at Victoria University of Wellington) respectively for their definitions on ser-vice-dominant logic and chopstick marketing, which filled in gaps I could not hope to fill, Catheryn Khoo for her advice and work on Generation X and Y and Tim Breitbath for his advice on CSR. Also, Jim Bell of the University of Ulster and of course the musings of the late, great A. Smithee. Special thanks to Colin Dowse and Bruce Newman for their support throughout what became a much larger and more significant research and writing exercise than I had anticipated. For, like the great lexicographer Samuel Johnson, who I used as my guiding star and intellectual mentor, I underestimated how much time it would take to do the work and put together this dictionary. Fortunately my publishers and friends have been very understanding.

When I began the research for *The Penguin Dictionary of Marketing* I read over forty dictionaries, encyclopedias and handbooks written on the subject, and then subse-quently selectively from a range of the major texts and journals in the area. This provided the basic heading list for key entries. In addition, the growth of online sources such as Wikipedia, the CIM, AMA and other websites have been of immense help in providing information and assisting me to construct definitions. The context and research was further underpinned by attendance at a range of international academic, political and trade conferences, and by the consultancy and significant support of many colleagues in the Academy of Marketing, American Marketing Association, Chartered Institute of Marketing, Australian Marketing Institute, Aus-tralian and New Zealand Marketing Academy and New Zealand Marketing Association.

In drawing together the dictionary I have relied upon two people significantly to carry out research and administrative support for me: Heather Ling (née Standeven) in Manchester, who acted as my key researcher and secretary in developing the basic format and research for the text, and Kerry Kirkland in Dunedin at the University of Otago, New Zealand, who rose to the challenge and provided me with very professional and quality support as I completed the manuscript. Without them this work would not have been finished.

I would like to thank the staff at Penguin, who supported me as I developed this dictionary and who have been very patient. Particularly I would like to thank my editor Adam Freudenheim, who has helped support me and has seen this project to completion, and the excellent copy-editing work of David Watson and Ronnie Hanna, who have made the prime text so much more cogent and readable than my earlier draft. Also can I thank Rachel Love and Ruth Stimson at Penguin for their tremendous support in ensuring the final format and style of the dictionary was of such a good standard, this was very much appreciated. In addition, can I thank Martin Toseland, who originally commissioned the work, and Kristen Harrison and Jodie Greenwood, who worked as editors with me during the period spent research-ing and writing the text.

And finally can I thank the person I owe most to, Irene, my wife, for her great patience and support in helping me to complete the dictionary.

I would welcome comments and criticism from readers, particularly any omis-sions you come across. Please send them to me care of the publisher.

THE PENGUIN
DICTIONARY OF
MARKETING

a priori A statement the truth or falsity of which may be known prior to any appeal to experience, e.g. an a priori statement might be 'I exist'. A priori marketing suggests all the thinking is usually done first: the campaign 'design', target-group selection and the creative design, whilst *a posteriori* marketing decisions are made with the benefit of hindsight and with the support of data and information.

AAA (American Academy of Advertising) An organization of advertising scholars and professionals with an interest in advertising and advertising education. The Academy fosters research which is relevant to the field and provides a forum for the exchange of ideas among its academic and professional members. Through the *Journal of Advertising* and the annual conference proceedings, the Academy disseminates research findings and scholarly contributions to advertising education and the profession.

AAAA (American Association of Advertising Agencies) A national trade association, founded in 1917, which represents the advertising agency business in the United States. Its membership produces approximately 80 per cent of the total advertising volume placed by agencies in the US.

Although virtually all of the large, multinational agencies are members of the AAAA, more than 60 per cent of the membership bills less than $10 million per year. The AAAA is not a club. It is a management-oriented association that offers its members the broadest range of possible services, expertise and information regarding the advertising agency business. The average AAAA agency has been a member for more than twenty years.

Aaker, David Regarded by many as the father figure of brand theory development and the creator of AAKER'S BRAND IDENTITY PLANNING MODEL. He has published more than 100 articles and twelve books, including *Managing Brand Equity*, *Building Strong Brands*, *Developing Business Strategies*, *Brand Leadership* and *The World of Brands*. His book *Brand Portfolio Strategy* discusses how to manage a portfolio of brands to optimize business growth. He has been awarded best article awards by the *Journal of Marketing* and the *California Management Review*.

Aaker is Professor Emeritus at the Haas School of Business, University of California, Berkeley and has been awarded four career awards including the 1996 Paul D. Converse Award for outstanding contributions to the development of marketing.

Aaker's Brand Identity Planning Model A strategic brand identity planning model that outlines a fourfold perspective on the concept of a brand. To ensure that a firm's brand identity has texture and depth, Aaker proposes that brand strategists should consider the brand as: a) a product; b) an organization; c) a person; and d) a symbol. Each perspective in his analysis he sees as distinct. The purpose of this system is to help brand strategists consider different brand elements and themes that can assist in clarifying, enriching and differentiating a product identity. He argues that a detailed identity also assists in guiding implementation decisions, allowing you to gain advantage through differentiation.

Aaker cautions that not every brand identity needs to apply or use all or even a selection of these perspectives. For some brands, only one perspective or feature will be viable and appropriate. Each organization should, however, consider all of the perspectives and use those deemed the most important in articulating what the brand should stand for in the consumer's mind.

The four key perspectives Aaker recommends firms take into account in building and developing their branding strategy are:

- *The brand as product.* A core element of a brand's identity is usually its product thrust, which will affect the type of associations that are desirable and feasible. Attributes directly related to the purchase or use of a product can provide functional benefits and sometimes emotional benefits for customers. A product-related attribute can create a value proposition by offering something more like specific features or services, or by offering something better. Aaker argues that the goal of linking a brand with a product class is not to gain recall of the product class when a brand is mentioned, but rather for customers to use to remember the brand when there is a need relevant to the particular product. So car purchase may equal Mercedes.

- *The brand as organization.* This perspective focuses on attributes of the organization rather than on those of the product or service. Such organizational features as innovation, quality, safety and sustainability are created by the people, culture, values and programmes of the organization. Aaker notes that organizational attributes are more enduring and resistant to competitive claims than product attributes. Apple's image as an innovator is undoubtedly at the heart of its brand rather than a particular product.

- *The brand as person.* Like an individual,

a brand can be perceived as having a unique personality. The brand-as-person perspective suggests a brand identity that is richer and more interesting than one based on product attributes. Aaker suggests three ways a brand personality can create a stronger brand: 1) create a self-expressive benefit that becomes a vehicle for customers to express their own personalities; 2) form the basis of a relationship between customers and the brand; and 3) help communicate a product attribute and thus contribute to a functional benefit. As reliable as a Volkswagen very much fits this perspective.

- *The brand as symbol.* A strong symbol can provide cohesion and structure to an identity and make it much easier to gain recognition and recall. Its presence can be a key ingredient of brand development and its absence can be a substantial disadvantage or negative factor. Elevating symbols to the status of being part of the identity reflects their potential power. Aaker highlights three types of symbols: visual imagery, for instance Shell's clam shell; metaphors, for example 'Go to work on an egg'; and the brand heritage – Harrods or Macy's would be good examples.

As suggested by Aaker's elaborate brand taxonomy, brand identity consists of a core identity and an extended identity. The former represents the timelessness of the essence of the brand. It is central to both the meaning and success of the brand and contains the associations that are most likely to remain constant as the brand encompasses new products and is extended into new markets. The extended identity, on the other hand, includes elements that provide texture and completeness. It fills in the picture, adding details that help portray what the brand stands for. A reasonable hypothesis, Aaker states, is that within a product class a larger extended identity means a stronger brand – one that is more memorable, interesting and connected to customers' lives.

aardvark marketing Usually a crude but colourful and vibrant form of hand crafted marketing taking direct expression from the arts and crafts movement. Used extensively by the whole food movement and other alternative product providers, onus is on being low cost and visually bold, slightly coarse and inventive. Aardvark marketing has been applied to market craft goods, designer knitwear, jewellery, organic produce and cultural items. Normally individualistic, very cost effective and widely used in homeopathic medicine, alternative health care and a number of not for profit sector markets such as care communities.

abandonment To give up producing and/ or marketing a product, usually towards the end of its life cycle and/or when it is becoming unprofitable. Also the outcome of rationalizing the product portfolio. Also called product deletion or elimination.

above-the-line communications Marketing relating to marketing expenditure on advertising in media such as the press, radio, television, cinema advertising films and the Internet on which a commission is normally paid to an agency. Often used as a common term to describe an advertising technique which uses primarily mass media to promote brands. Good examples are the Heinz use of mass media to promote baked beans and Procter and Gamble's use of the same media to promote Fairy Liquid. This type of communication is often seen as being conventional in nature and is considered impersonal to customers. It differs from BELOW-THE-LINE COMMUNICATIONS, which believes in less standard advertising-led brand-building strategies such as the use of non-advertising strategies as in public relations, sales promotion, print media, presentations and sponsorship. The ATL strategy makes use of current traditional media: television, newspapers, magazines, radio, outdoor and the Internet, particularly the former.

absolute advantage This argues that a person has an absolute advantage in the production of goods if, by using the same quantities of inputs, that person can produce more of the goods than another person. Thus a country has an absolute advantage if its output per unit of inputs of goods is larger than that of another country. China is often cited as having absolute advantage in labour costs.

absolute income hypothesis A theory proposed in 1936 by the English economist John Maynard KEYNES (1883–1946). It states that consumption is a non-linear function of income and argues that, as income rises, consumption will rise but not necessarily at the same rate. *See also* PERMANENT INCOME HYPOTHESIS; RELATIVE INCOME HYPOTHESIS.

abstract An abbreviated synopsis of a research article, review or any in-depth analysis of a particular subject or discipline. It is most frequently used to help the reader quickly understand a paper's content and purpose. An abstract always appears at the beginning of a document, acting as a summary of the content and an introduction to the work. Abstracts are now frequently accessed online to assess the relevance of the paper to the research being conducted.

ACNielsen An international marketing research firm, established in the United States in 1923 by Arthur C. Nielsen, Sr, in order to give clients objective information on the impact of marketing and sales programmes. Among many innovations in consumer-focused marketing and media research, Nielsen was responsible for creating a unique retail-measurement technique that gave clients the first reliable, objective information about competitive performance and the impact of their marketing and sales programmes on revenues and profits. Nielsen's information gave practical meaning to the concept of MARKET SHARE and made it one of the critical measures of corporate performance. Nielsen also founded the business known today as Nielsen Media Research, the international leader in television audience measurement and other media research services. The company serves the fast-moving consumer goods (FMCG) market by researching market performance and dynamics, solving marketing and sales problems and identifying market growth opportunities.

ACNielsen began expanding internationally in 1939 and now operates in more than 100 countries. It is recognized internationally as one of the leading sources of market research information.

Academy of International Business (AIB) The leading association of scholars and specialists in the field of international business and associated societal activities. AIB was established in 1959 and today has nearly 3,000 members in more than seventy different countries around the world. Members include academics from the leading worldwide academic institutions as well as consultants, researchers and NGO representatives.

Academy of Management (AOM) Founded in 1936 by two professors, the Academy of Management is the oldest and largest scholarly management association in the world. The AOM is a leading professional association for scholars dedicated to creating and disseminating knowledge about management and organizations. Today, the Academy is the professional home for over 16,000 members from across ninety-four countries.

Academy members are scholars at colleges, universities and research institutions, as well as practitioners with scholarly interests from business, government and not-for-profit organizations. Its leading academic journal is the *Academy of Management Journal* and it also produces high-quality research, reviews and comment from practitioners and educators for the international market. Its conference, which is a very substantial international event, is held annually in August in North America.

Academy of Marketing Science (AMS) Founded in 1971, the AMS is a professional scholarly organization offering a range of services, including annual conferences with dissertation and student paper awards. It has over 1,500 international members, known as Fellows of the Academy, who are dedicated to fostering educa-

tion in marketing, advancing the science of marketing and furthering professional standards in the discipline. It publishes the internationally respected *Journal of the Academy of Marketing Science* (*JAMS*).

acceptance sampling A process of sampling designed to accept or reject a product and ensure a high quality finished product. For example, a product quality inspector might examine 1 per cent of items manufactured. On the basis of the number of defects in the sample, the inspector can infer what percentage of defects there will be in the entire production run and whether there need to be any modifications to the production process. Acceptance sampling developed as a process in the Second World War and was used by the military to assess initially which batches of bullets to accept and which ones to reject as they knew they could not adopt this process in the field.

acceptance zone Acceptance in consumer behaviour theory is the degree to which a message is absorbed into an individual's consciousness, unchanged from what was meant by the sender. The acceptance zone lies in the range of opinions a consumer holds that block or bolster acceptance of the message. Acceptance can be blocked or bolstered by strong opinions either contradictory or complementary. There is a tendency for consumers to accept only those products, views and ideas that are consistent with their attitudes, opinions and beliefs.

accidental sample A sample gathered haphazardly, for example by interviewing the first 100 people you come across in your area who were willing to talk to you. This sampling technique makes no attempt to be representative but chooses subjects based on accessibility and immediate convenience. An accidental sample is very different from a random sample, which is invariably a more scientific measure of opinion.

account 1 In sales, usually the term used for a customer INVOICE. **2** In advertising, the term is often used to describe the client of an advertising, marketing, public relations or other agency, that is to say, an organization providing a service in consideration of which an income is derived, hence the term account.

account executive   An executive in advertising, marketing, a public relations agency or other such organization that is responsible for the overall management of a particular client's business. Sometimes known as account supervisor, account manager or account director, the different titles indicating levels of remuneration, responsibility and seniority.

account group   A sub-unit of an advertising agency handling a group of clients or accounts. It can be fully or partly self-contained and often is associated with a particular business area such as health care.

account manager   **1** (advertising) The manager in an advertising, marketing or public relations agency responsible for a particular client's business. The account manager is the member of the account management group whose job it is to see that the objectives agreed upon by client and agency are carried out to the client's satisfaction. They are the key figures in the agency's day-to-day relationship with the client and the person responsible for coordinating the work of all the agency's departments on the client's behalf, from beginning to end.

2 (sales) A sales representative acts as an account manager, arranging contacts between his own (the selling) organization and the buying organizations who are his customers and prospects. Account management has become a key activity for many international businesses, where a multinational business can operate in many countries and continents and require service from one supplier in all its operations.

account planning   The production of an advertising and communications plan by an agency for its client.

accounting   The systematic process of recording, classifying, verifying and summarizing business transactions, and presenting this information in periodic, interpretative financial statements and reports. Modern accounting has its modern origins in renaissance Italy, where both book-keeping and modern banking techniques were developed and put into practice.

accounting ratios   Useful indicators of a firm's performance and financial situation. Most ratios can be calculated and derived from information provided by the organization's financial statements. Accounting ratios can be used to analyze trends and to compare the firm's financial position to those of other firms and usually include the following categories:

• profitability ratios, used to compare the profitability of one company with another or of one company over time;
• liquidity ratios, used to compare the liquidity of one company with another or of one company over time;
• investment ratios, used by potential investors when making investment decisions;
• efficiency ratios, used to compare company efficiency with others or with itself from one year to another.

acculturation   Refers to the complex relationship between culture and consumption patterns. One of the key lessons learned from studying social psychology and global marketing is that cultural variations have a significant impact on the way people view the world and that this ultimately affects behaviour. There is broad agreement within marketing that a person's culture, particularly ethnicity, influences the way consumers perceive and behave. The dramatic demographic shifts that are occurring in the EU and United States act as a catalyst to the study of how intra-country cultural differences affect consumption behaviour. From a marketing perspective, many organizations are discovering that success depends on utilizing opportunities to meet the needs of previously ignored micro cultural groups. Marketers, in order to more effectively reach their target markets, must have an understanding of how intra-national cultures impact product-specific purchases by consumers. The growth of the Hispanic population in the United States and Muslim groups in Western Europe has stimulated marketing and research in this area. Polish shops and food as part of the UK retail scene is a good reflection of acculturation marketing targeting.

acid test ratio A measure of a company's ability to fund its short-term financial obligations. It is estimated by deducting inventories from current assets and then dividing the remainder by current liabilities. It measures the financial condition of a company, which is deduced by working out what would happen if every creditor demanded payment at the same time. *See also* LIQUIDITY RATIO.

ACORN An acronym that stands for 'A Classification of Residential Neighbourhoods'. ACORN is a database which divides up the entire population in terms of the type of housing in which they live. This can be used for various purposes in marketing planning and in designing promotional campaigns. *See also* GEODEMOGRAPHIC TARGETING.

acquiescence bias (yea-saying) A systematic bias caused by some respondents tending to agree with whatever is presented to them. Such a bias may be caused by either respondents or interviewers being overly friendly or supportive during interviews. It has been frequently observed by political candidates when carrying out door-to-door canvassing.

acquisition The purchase of other organizations, or franchise, manufacturing or service rights, as a way of expanding a company's activities or increasing its share of a market. Also may be a means of diversification without the risks associated with the development of a new product; or countering competition with greater certainty than by mounting a direct campaign. *See also* DIVERSIFICATION.

action learning A process in which a group of people come together to regularly assist each other to learn from their own experience. Professor Reg Revans first introduced and coined the term 'action learning' in the coal mines of Wales and England in the 1940s. In Revans's interpretation, the purpose of action learning was not just to promote local action and learning, but to bring about organizational change, and it was mostly used across different organizations. That is, the participants typically came from different situations, where each of them was involved in different activities and faced individual problems. The current practice is more often to set up an action learning programme within one organization. Most commonly the participants are managers, though this is not essential. It is not unusual for a team to consist of people with a common task or problem. There may or may not be a facilitator for the learning groups which are formed. Revans mostly avoided them, but current practice usually adopts this approach.

action plan An action plan describes exactly how strategies are to be implemented. An action plan for the sales promotion of a product over a year would normally show times and places for specific promotions (special sample offers, POINT-OF-SALE displays, COUPONS, TRADE FAIRS to be attended, publicity releases, etc.), together with the amount of money allocated for each activity.

activity-based costing The allocation of costs to the specific activities associated with them rather than by an arbitrary formula. *See also* CONTRIBUTION ANALYSIS.

ad valorem A generic term applied to any tax, duty or levy based on the value of goods rather than on the weight or quantity of them.

ad valorem duty A duty or tax that is levied as a percentage of the value of the imported goods. It also known as a TARIFF.

adaptation The use of a basic idea, as in an advertisement, for another medium, e.g. POSTERS, POINT-OF-SALE. Also the alteration or modification of an advertisement to another shape or size.

adaptive planning (AP) The systematic, on-demand creation and revision of executable plans, with up-to-date options being applied and used as circumstances require. AP grew out of the needs of advanced military planning and is applied in marketing to complex product development and the supply of modern retail business.

adaptive strategy A strategy that emerges through a process of bargaining and consensus and is mainly used by large, often non-profit-oriented organizations that tend to be in the public sector. It is generally recognized that all strategies evolve though a process of adaptation as strategies change in the light of greater information and awareness. *See also* EMERGENT STRATEGY.

added value The increase in value gained by materials, components or other commodities (including labour, for example) as a result of any input, whether processing, assembling, handling, distributing, or any other marketing activity.

adopter categories A classification of users or buyers of a product according to the time of adoption. Everett Rogers in *Diffusion of Innovations* (1962) identified five categories within the adoption curve which he described as conceptualizations based on his own observations of the diffusion process. Rogers's categories are defined in terms of percentage groupings as follows:

- INNOVATORS – first 2.5 per cent of all adopters;
- EARLY ADOPTERS – next 13.5 per cent of all adopters;
- EARLY MAJORITY – next 34 per cent of all adopters;
- LATE MAJORITY – next 34 per cent of all adopters;
- LAGGARDS – last 16 per cent of all adopters.

These definitions are often used to target particular users during the life of a product. An example is that the iPod would have been innovative in 2002, but by 2008 it is being acquired by late-adopting customers (the late majority). The iPhone, which launched in 2007, has targeted innovative customers (innovators). *See also* DIFFUSION OF INNOVATION THEORY.

adoption The process by which consumers accept a new fashion, idea, product, process or service.

adoption curve A line on a graph showing how many consumers adopt or buy a new product at various time periods or points after the launch date. *See also* ADOPTER CATEGORIES.

adshel Form of poster site incorporated into a modern bus shelter, usually of glass or plastic. Adshel is a geneticized trademark and was launched in the UK in 1969 to cover the design, maintenance and installing of bus shelters in the UK. It is owned by Clear Channel and provides this service to 250 local authorities and has joint arrangements providing Adshel products in over fifty countries worldwide.

advance A story that public relations, corporate communications professionals and others send to the news media to announce future meetings, performances, speeches, sports events, conferences and other activities. The prime aim is to tell journalists about the event in an attractive and stimulating way so that they can decide whether or not to attend and report it. Also an amount paid before it is earned or expenditure is made.

advertisement Often used loosely to refer to any persuasive message or slogan forming part of an organization's publicity or promotion. Strictly, the message should be incorporated into a paid-for space or time slot in a periodical or in a television or radio broadcast or on a website. *See also* ADVERTISING.

advertiser Organization or person on whose behalf an advertisement appears and who ultimately picks up the cost.

advertising The promotion of goods, services or ideas through paid communications. It is a form of external communication between an organization

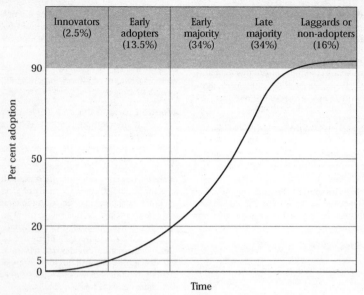

| Innovators (2.5%) | Early adopters (13.5%) | Early majority (34%) | Late majority (34%) | Laggards or non-adopters (16%) |

Adoption Curve

(advertiser) and its target audience, using commissioned and paid-for media such as the Internet, television, radio, magazines, newsprint, billboards and/or public relations. An advertisement normally has two prime components: the message being projected to the potential consumer; and the medium (media) by which it is transmitted. The world advertising industry is dominated globally by six groups: WPP, Omnicom, Interpublic, Publicis, Dentsu and Havas.

advertising agency A business whose role is to provide a service to clients ranging from booking advertising space, designing advertisements and producing them, devising media schedules, commissioning research, providing consultancy and any associated marketing service. More recently many advertising agencies have adopted an integrated marketing communications perspective and can offer services to clients in the area of PUBLIC RELATIONS and PUBLIC AFFAIRS.

advertising brief A formal briefing document passed to an ADVERTISING AGENCY by its client, containing the essential guidelines for a perceived future advertising campaign.

advertising budget A sum of money set aside for spending on an advertising campaign. Sometimes this represents the total sum available to cover all advertising expenditure including overheads. Alternatively referred to as 'advertising appropriation'. *See also* BUDGET.

advertising effectiveness A measure of the extent to which members of a target audience can recall a particular advertising message. *See also* POST-TEST.

advertising impact One of three dimensions used in assessing advertising exposure and its response. The other two are REACH AND FREQUENCY. Impact is a qualitative concept that is difficult to measure precisely, whereas frequency and reach are objective and easier to quantify. Thus impact will vary according to the context in which the advertisement appears.

advertising manager An executive responsible for planning and implementing a company's advertising, and also for managing the advertising department. Alternatively, he or she may be known as marketing communications manager, integrated communications manager, publicity manager, sales promotion manager or marketing services manager.

advertising objectives Specifically, what is to be achieved by an advertising campaign in quantified terms, and over a given time period. *See also* MARKETING COMMUNICATIONS OBJECTIVES.

advertising plan Plan of what key goals an advertising campaign should achieve, how to accomplish those goals, and how to determine whether or not the campaign was successful in obtaining those goals. Advertising plans more recently include full costings of various options and evaluation methods to ensure the plan is achieved.

advertising research The evaluation of the efficiency of an advertisement or of an advertising campaign against the terms of the task or objective it is set to achieve. PRE-TESTING and COPY TESTING examine the likely results, whereas POST-TESTING deals with actual achievements. It is well known that advertising campaigns can win awards for creativity and flair but do the opposite of what the client wanted. The 'New Labour, New Danger' campaign funded by the UK Conservative Party at the 1997 General Election turned people against them and into the hands of those they were supposed to be attacking. *See also* MEDIA RESEARCH.

advertising schedule Programme of planned advertisement insertions, showing detailed costs, timing, nature of media and the bookings to be reserved. *See also* MEDIA SCHEDULE.

advertising space That part of a publication or periodical which is set aside for advertising, as opposed to editorial text and pictures.

advertising standards authority (ASA) A UK self-regulatory body established in 1962, which sets out criteria of acceptability for the advertising industry. Its prime function is to investigate complaints about non-broadcast advertising.

advertising-to-sales ratio The expression of the percentage of advertising expenditure in relation to sales or turnover. Sometimes used as the basis of budgeting in promotional work.

advertorial An advertisement designed to have the appearance of an editorial. The content of an advertorial is heavily influenced and may be written by the advertisers. Examples of advertorials include home improvement, leisure or travel supplements in newspapers or magazines that are designed to attract advertisements from suppliers of relevant goods or services. *See also* ADVERTISING.

advocate A customer who, without any prompting, recommends a particular product.

aerial advertising A persuasive message in the air, e.g. a streamer behind an aeroplane or a slogan on a hot-air balloon. Often used to promote a cause or particular product at a political rally or outdoor sports or leisure event.

aesthetics The philosophical study of taste; the science of the beautiful in nature and art. The term pertains to perception by the senses and appreciation or criticism of the beautiful or art. It is also popularly used as a noun meaning 'that which appeals to the senses'. Aesthetics was established as an independent discipline in the eighteenth century by German philosophers. The word derives from the Greek *aisthetikos*, meaning 'of sense perception'.

affinity card A credit card where a small contribution is made to a specific charity or other organization for every transaction carried out. Universities, charities and various clubs and associations have adopted these, MENCAP, the mental health charity in the UK, has their own with the Co-op Bank.

age cycle The changing of consumer

Alderson, Wroe
(1898–1965)

Generally considered to be one of the most influential people in post-war marketing scholarship and a significant thinker and theorist who did much to legitimize the study of marketing theory and thought. Alderson made major contributions to both the development of a general theory of marketing and to furthering the logical empiricist foundation upon which much of marketing research is currently conducted. Although he died before his academic career was complete, remarkably the traces of his work have continued to influence the wider development of marketing as a discipline.

demand patterns in line with those consumers' age and associated lifestyle.

agency commission An agency's fee for designing and placing advertisements and normally rebated back to the them from the media owner. Historically, this was calculated as 15 per cent of the amount spent to purchase space or time in the various media used for the advertising. In recent years the commission has, in many cases, become negotiable and may even be based on some measure of the campaign's success.

aggregate demand The expression of total demand for goods and services within a national economy, which make up its GDP, usually divided into consumer, industrial, public purchases and exports.

AIDA A mnemonic representing the standard theory of 'Attention, Interest, Desire, Action', denoting the progressive steps of customer reaction in the process of a directed marketing communication. According to this theory, there is a direct and measurable sales response arising from the application of specific marketing communications. It is widely used and dates from the late nineteenth century.

air brush A device which sprays atomized dye or paint in a controlled manner, used for retouching photographs and for producing artwork.

air time The amount of time devoted or allocated to an advertisement on radio or television. It can also refer to actual time of transmission.

allocation The process of breaking down a single quantity of supply into smaller lots or quantities, commonly performed by wholesalers who 'break bulk' by purchasing full truck loads and selling cases or smaller quantities of the product. *See also* BREAKING BULK.

ALT text An HTML attribute that provides alternative text when non-textual elements, typically images, cannot be displayed.

anchor store In a shopping centre, a large and well-known store which acts as an attraction to shoppers, thus benefiting other, smaller, retail outlets.

Andean Common Market (ANCOM) ANCOM was formed under the Cartagena Agreement in May 1969 by Bolivia, Chile, Columbia, Ecuador and Peru. This called for the elimination of all barriers to trade by the end of 1980 and the establishment of a common external tariff. Subsequently Venezuela joined in 1973. Chile withdrew in 1976.

Andean Community of Nations (CAN) Formerly known as the Andean Pact and the ANDEAN COMMON MARKET (ANCOM) and known as the Andean Community since 1997, a trade bloc comprising the South American countries of Bolivia, Colombia, Ecuador, Peru and Venezuela (which is in the process of leaving the bloc). It came into existence with the signing of the Cartagena Agreement in 1969 and its headquarters are located in Lima, Peru. Its objectives include the promotion of balanced and harmonious development of the member countries under equitable conditions through integration and economic and social cooperation.

annual report A document which a company presents to its annual general meeting for approval by its shareholders and/or stakeholders. The report normally includes a profit and loss account and balance sheet, as well as a directors' report and an auditor's report. In the case of multinational corporations, it is usually a quality publication designed for international circulation. Annual reports are increasingly being used to inform other stakeholders, such as employees and shareholding interests, of corporate responsibility activities and standards of corporate governance within the organization.

anonymous product testing Tests in which different basic products are all presented in a common anonymous form, e.g. a plain or unmarked bottle, carton or pack. Sometimes referred to as blindfold testing. The consumer is invited to try the products and suggest what they are. This complements the pseudo product test in evaluating a consumer's ability to perceive intrinsic product differences.

Ansoff matrix *See* GROWTH VECTOR MATRIX.

anti-dumping duties Duties imposed on imported goods when those goods are sold to the importing country at a price which is below the cost of manufacture in the exporting country. They are most frequently charged when imported goods are found to cause or to threaten damage to the economy of the importing country or trade area. They have been used by the American Bush Administration against steel imports from Asia and Europe.

American Academy of Advertising *See* AAA.

American Association of Advertising Agencies *See* AAAA.

American Marketing Association (AMA) Formed in 1937, the leading US association for professionals involved in the practice, study and teaching of marketing. The AMA is one of the largest professional associations for marketers and has over 38,000 members worldwide. It is a NON-PROFIT educational organization

whose publications include *Marketing News* and the internationally highly respected quarterly *Journal of Marketing, Journal of Marketing Research* and *Journal of International Marketing*. It holds two major conferences specifically for educators twice a year: one in February (for research) and the larger annual conference in August, which includes a special 'hiring of staff' section. The AMA defines marketing as 'the activity, conducted by organizations and individuals, that operates through a set of institutions and processes for creating, communicating, delivering, and exchanging market offerings that have value for customers, clients, marketers, and society at large'.

APEC (Asia–Pacific Economic Cooperation) A forum designed to promote trade and economic cooperation among countries bordering the Pacific Ocean. APEC works in three broad areas to meet the Bogor (Indonesia) goals of free and open trade and investment in Asia–Pacific by 2010 for developed economies and 2020 for developing economies; these three key areas are known as the 'Three Pillars':

• trade and investment liberalization;
• business facilitation;
• economic and technical cooperation.

The outcomes of these three areas enable APEC members to strengthen their economies by pooling resources within the region and achieving efficiencies. Tangible benefits are also delivered to consumers in the APEC region through increased training and employment opportunities, greater choices in the marketplace, cheaper goods and services, and improved access to international markets.

Trade and investment liberalization
Trade and investment liberalization reduces and eventually eliminates tariff and non-tariff barriers to trade and investment. Protectionism is expensive because it raises prices for goods and services. Thus, trade and investment liberalization focuses on opening markets to increase trade and investment among economies, resulting in economic growth for APEC member

Armstrong, Scott

Professor of Marketing at the Wharton School, University of Pennsylvania, where he has been since 1968. In addition to teaching in Thailand, he has taught in Switzerland, Sweden, New Zealand, Australia, South Africa, Argentina, Japan and other countries. He founded the *Journal of Forecasting*, the *International Journal of Forecasting*, which he edited, and the International Symposium on Forecasting. A study in 1989 ranked him among the top fifteen marketing professors in the US. Another study named him as the second most prolific Wharton School faculty member during the 1988–93 period. In 1996, he was selected as one of the first six Honorary Fellows by the International Institute of Forecasters. Along with Philip KOTLER and Gerald Zaltman, he was given the Distinguished Scholar Award for 2000 by the Society for Marketing Advances. He coordinates the election polling system Polly vote on his Wharton website and this has been one of the most efficient forecasting tools of US presidential elections.

economies and increased standards of living for all.

Business facilitation

Business facilitation focuses on reducing the costs of business transactions, improving access to trade information and aligning policy and business strategies to facilitate growth and free and open trade. Essentially, business facilitation helps importers and exporters in Asia–Pacific meet and conduct business more efficiently, thus reducing costs of production and leading to increased trade, cheaper goods and services and more employment opportunities due to an expanded economy.

Economic and technical cooperation (ECOTECH)

ECOTECH is dedicated to providing training and cooperation to build capacities in all APEC member economies to take advantage of global trade and the new economy. This area builds capacity at the institutional and personal level to assist APEC member economies and their people gain the necessary skills to meet their economic potential.

appeal The basis of an advertising message or selling proposition or advertising message designed to match a 'customer's want', i.e. the appeal identifies what customers desire and what the product or service concerned can supply.

applet A short programme, usually written in a language such as Java, which can be called down from a web document while the document is processed by a browser. When the applet is called, it is downloaded from the website and runs in the user's computer. The Java language has been designed to allow applets to operate in users' computers without presenting a threat to security.

arm's length agreement An agreement normally made between two parties freely and independently of each other that do not have some special relationship, such as being a relative, close friend or fellow believer of some closed religious groupage. It becomes important in contracts and trade to determine whether an agreement was freely entered into to show that the price, requirements and other conditions were fair and reflect the market value. For example, if a man sells a vehicle to his daughter the value set may not be a true reflection of the market price as it may not have been an arm's length transaction.

arm's length price The price at which a willing buyer and an equivalent unrelated seller would freely agree a transaction or trade.

art director An individual in advertising,

film, publishing, television, Internet or video games charged with the task of overseeing the transforming of a creative idea into a visual form.

artifical obsolescence Annual or regular model changes to cause dissatisfaction among consumers for their existing machines and appliances.

arts marketing One of fastest and most competitive areas of modern marketing as consumer consumption of culture has rapidly increased as a result of the expansion of leisure time and the growth in international tourism. The mass availability and accessibility of the arts has been further stimulated by interest and stakeholder groups and supported by government and international bodies to promote social cohesion in society and has also been seen as part of nation-building on the international scene: the Sydney Opera House, for example, is seen as a symbol of the modern Australia, much as the Eiffel Tower seems to represent Paris and things French.

Arts marketing encompasses such areas as sales of contemporary and 'Old Master' paintings, theatre, opera, modern music, antiques, literature and readings events, popular culture, broadcast media, concerts and music and many more traditional art forms. As a distinct subject the real growth in this area can be traced back to the early 1990s with the establishment of journals, specialist agencies and organizations in this field to market and promote cities and heritage.

In the arts arena marketing's building blocks have been traditionally referred to as the six Ps: product, place, price, processes, promotion and people. These are defined as follows:

Product
The major facilities, goods, or services being offered. The product will vary depending on the organization, for example:

• art gallery: the permanent collection, education programmes, catalogues, research services, any special block-buster exhibits, books, merchandise and souvenirs;
• theatre: the season programme, the timing of performances, the individual plays, the resident actors and special guest performers, the sets, the printed programmes and other merchandise;
• festival: the theme, the major events, the combination and range of activities being offered, the calibre of performers, food, displays, entertainment, stalls and merchandise.

Place
The venue at which the activity takes place. This includes the location, the facilities available, the parking, the comfort and the size of the venue. Again, using specific examples, some of the elements of place include:

• art gallery: the location (city central, suburban, regional), the building, the size of the building, its architecture style, age, decor, level of maintenance, the amenities provided (air-conditioning, lifts, coffee shop, souvenir shop);
• theatre: location, the building itself, the seating capacity, parking facilities, amenities (heating or air-conditioning, comfort of seating), maintenance, decor, condition of facilities, quality of sound, visibility of stage;
• festival: location, access, parking (distance from venue, security, traffic management and control), distance between various venues or events, security and safety, maintenance and amenities (portable toilets, lost children area), quality of sound systems and visibility of stages, access to undercover areas in case of inclement weather.

Price
The prices charged for admission, services, or facilities, or for any other elements of the product (such as printed programmes, food and drinks, parking or souvenirs). Pricing can be a major issue for consumers. Many organizations use pricing policies as a major part of their marketing strategy.

Processes
The procedures which are developed to

provide information, tickets, etc. This includes box office procedures, the use of commercial external ticketing services and the use of free phone numbers and websites for information. Often a customer's experiences during the processing phase can affect their attitude towards the whole event.

Promotion

The way in which information is provided to the potential customers. It includes a wide range of options including advertising, direct selling, publicity stunts, public relations activities and even the Internet. Quality market research can ensure cost-effective promotions which will reach their intended audiences with the right message at the right time.

People

Citizens who appreciate art as part of popular consumption and leisure activity as borrowers, collectors, observers, listeners or users of art. In addition this group includes opinion-formers, art commentators and critics who popularize and promote both art and its support through government and philanthropic donation for major strategic investments and smaller community projects.

artwork The pictorial, illustrative or text part of an advertisement, or publication, in its completed form and ready for production, e.g. a retouched, scanned and masked photograph or alternatively a laid-out notice usually in Adobe or similar format ready for printing or electronic transmission.

Asia–Pacific Economic Cooperation *See* APEC.

aspiration levels Levels which consumers expect or desire to reach in class of product or service, in their aim or ambition to own a prestigious product or brand.

Association for Consumer Research (ACR) A US-based organization which advances consumer research and facilitates the exchange of scholarly information among academia, industry and government worldwide. ACR was founded in 1969 by a small group of consumer behaviour researchers whose informal meeting at Ohio State University led to the vision of a yearly conference devoted to the study of consumer behaviour. Since then, ACR has hosted its yearly conference in the US and brings together researchers, public policy-makers and practising marketers interested in the study of consumer behaviour. In addition it has a number of specialist research groups assessing such complex issues as children's consumption. In addition it hosts meetings in Asia–Pacific, Europe and Latin America annually. Its internationally well-regarded journal is the *Journal of Consumer Research*.

Association of South-east Asian Nations (ASEAN) A political, economic and cultural organization of countries located in South-east Asia. ASEAN was formed on 8 August 1967 by Thailand, Indonesia, Malaysia, Singapore and the Philippines as a non-provocative display of solidarity against communist expansion in Vietnam and insurgency within their own borders. In 1976 ASEAN agreed to a list of industrial projects on which the group would cooperate in the construction of major plants. They also agreed to set up a permanent secretariat. By 1999 Brunei, Vietnam, Myanmar, Laos and Cambodia had joined. The group is working towards the setting-up of a free trade area in which import tariffs on intra-ASEAN trade will be reduced to a maximum of 5 per cent. Similarly there are plans to liberalize intra-ASEAN direct investment by 2010 and foreign direct investment by 2020.

astroturfing Astroturfing is a neologism for structured PUBLIC RELATIONS campaigns in the media and politics that seek to create the impression of being spontaneous (community) behaviour. The term is said to have been used for the first time in this context by former US Senator Lloyd Bentsen and suggests 'artificial grassroots democracy' – hence the reference to astroturf, an artificial grass surface used on sports pitches. The goal of such a campaign is to disguise the efforts of a political or commercial entity as an independent public reaction to some political entity – a politician, political group, product, service or event.

Astroturfing may be undertaken by individuals pushing their own personal agenda or highly organized professional groups with financial backing from multinationals, not-for-profit organizations or even public-sector interests. During the Sunday Retail Trading Campaign in the UK in the 1990s a number of activist events were held in communities which were supposed to be spontaneously supported by local citizens but were in fact funded, planned and staffed by the retail industry. More recently, YouTube has been used as a platform for astroturfing. Examples include parodies of Al Gore as a cartoon penguin consuming the planet, which was sponsored by oil company interests, and fake fifteen-year-old girls in clips advocating or denigrating certain products.

The practice of astroturfing is specifically prohibited by the code of ethics of the Public Relations Society of America and a number of codes of practice adopted across the marketing communications industry.

attention value The extent to which an advertisement can secure the initial attention of a listener, reader or viewer, sometimes expressed in quantitative form in STARCH RATINGS or other content, page or content listening and/or viewing traffic studies.

attitudes Attitudes structure the way customers perceive their environment and guide the ways in which they respond. They are relatively enduring and are useful guidelines as to what consumers may do in certain circumstances. Attitudes are positive or negative views of an 'attitude object': i.e., a person, behaviour or event. In addition people can also be ambivalent towards a target, meaning that they simultaneously possess a positive and a negative attitude.

Attitudes develop on the basis of evaluative responding. For an attitude to form an individual goes through the steps of responding to an entity on an affective, behavioural change and cognitive level (known as the ABC model). The affective response is a physiological response that expresses an individual's preference for an entity. The behavioural change response is a verbal indication of the intention of an individual. The cognitive response is a cognitive evaluation of the entity to form an attitude. Most attitudes in individuals are a result of social learning from the environment. *See also* CONSUMER ATTITUDES.

attributes The features or characteristics of a product which are thought to appeal to customers. A more relevant term than 'product attributes' is 'customer benefits', which may not be the same, as here the product is looked at from the consumer's point of view rather than the seller's. An even more relevant term is 'perceived benefits', since this is the real factor that motivates purchase.

attrition The gradual wearing-away of an individual's loyalty to a product or organization, attributable largely to competitive claims and alternative promotions. This may occur with advancing age but can often be due to a change of behaviour for no very apparent reason.

audience A group of people addressed by any of the media, but usually associated with film, Internet, radio, television or theatre.

audience profile Information on the nature and characteristics of readers, viewers or listeners of advertising media.

audiometer A continuous measuring device for monitoring the use of television sets and hence the size of the television audience.

audit The checking of a company's accounts. Internal audits are checks carried out as part of the company's own controls. When used unqualified the word audit is usually taken to mean an external audit: the examination of accounts by external accountants (auditors) that is required by law. The annual report of a company must be audited and include an auditor's opinion on the accounts. There are legal restrictions on who can carry out an audit.

Audit Bureau of Circulations (ABC) A company that audits the circulation of print publications, to insure that reported circulation figures are accurate. Organizations with this name exist in the UK and the USA and fulfil the same function but are otherwise unrelated. ABC was launched in the UK in 1931 in response to advertiser demand for independent verification of the claims made by the advertising sales teams of newspapers and magazines, especially the national press then known as Fleet Street. ABC holds one of the most renowned brands within the media industry providing circulation figures for newspapers, magazines, B2B publications, directories, leaflets, exhibitions and websites.

augmented product The complete bundle of attributes perceived by, or offered to, an individual buyer. The core product plus all other sources of product benefits, such as service, warranty and image.

Australian Marketing Institute (AMI) This institute represents professional marketers throughout Australia and has established strong links with business, academia and government to become the voice of the marketing profession. It was first established in 1933, and its continued role in advancing the marketing profession has resulted in the emergence of Certified Practising Marketer (CPM) accreditation as a practising reference point, the establishment of a Code of Professional Conduct and the move towards defined practising standards for marketers and marketing metrics for organizations. It holds a number of regional and sectoral conferences in Australia; notable among these is its Government Marketing Conference.

authorized dealer A retail or wholesale outlet which has exclusive rights over the distribution/sale of a product or service in a given geographical region.

autocue A moving written message/script (telepromptor) giving a prompt to a speaker usually in front of a camera or in such a position that the audience is unaware of its presence. It came into popular use through its adoption by President Ronald Reagan in the US and subsequently by Prime Minister Margaret Thatcher in the UK. Autocue is the UK manufacturer of telepromptor systems and was founded in 1955. In 1984 they merged with their US-based partner QTV and now operate worldwide and supply such clients as BBC, Bloomberg, CNN and Fox TV.

autoresponder An email software application that enables Internet users to send automated e-mails when they are not able to respond to incoming e-mail.

avatar Is a computer user's animated or graphic character, cartoon or picture used to represent them in an online forum, web page, Internet game, messenger or social networking system such as Facebook. Avatars have been used extensively in alternative world simulations such as within the 3D virtual world Second Life to represent consumers in virtual marketplaces, resulting in individual buyer types in simulated supermarkets making product choices.

average Usually in marketing refers to the arithmetic mean. The average or central tendency of a set (list) of data refers to a measure of the 'middle' of the data set. The arithmetic mean (or simply the mean) of a list of numbers is the sum of all the members of the list divided by the number of items in the list. If the list is a statistical population, then the mean of that population is called a population mean.

The mean is unfortunately not always the most representative figure as it can be skewed by outlying figures in the series, and, in such cases, other forms of average, such as the mode or median, may be used.

average cost The total cost of production of a given set or group of products divided by the number of products comprising the total in the set or group. Also referred to as unit cost. It is possible to distinguish between long-run and short-run average costs.

average cost pricing A pricing policy where an average price is established over a brand or product range based on average cost.

average fixed cost A measure of cost control, calculated by dividing the total fixed cost of the goods produced by the number of units sold.

average propensity to consume That part of national income devoted, on average, by the nation's individuals to consumption or goods and services. The average propensity to consume is the proportion of income the average family spends on goods and services.

average revenue The total revenue divided by the number of products sold to yield that revenue. In a range of items each selling at the same price average revenue will equal price. Where the range of products is selling at different prices the

average revenue will represent the average price.

average variable cost The number of items produced divided into the total variable costs (total cost less fixed costs). Variable costs – for example, fuel, labour costs and raw materials – change directly with the rate of output. Although the variable costs are likely to be different at different rates of output, the average figure represents the average variable cost per unit. Variable costs may also be referred to as operating costs, on costs or direct costs. *See also* DIRECT COSTS; FIXED COSTS; ON COSTS; OPERATING COSTS.

awareness The movement of an object or idea into the conscious mind. Often a desired objective of an advertising campaign. A principal goal of public relations.

B

B2B (business-to-business) A transaction that occurs between a organization and another organization, as opposed to an exchange involving a consumer. The term may also encompass an organization that provides goods or services for another organization. *See also* B2C.

B2B marketing The marketing of goods and services to organizations. Business-to-business marketing is a concept which encompasses the marketing of business services, industrial products and reseller phenomena with domestic and/or global perspectives. Business-to-business marketing is an important element in the economies of industrialized nations, in some cases accounting for more than half the economy.

B2B marketing differs from business-to-consumer marketing in many distinct ways. B2B purchasing satisfies the needs of the organization rather than the individual consumer. Products purchased by organizations can be included in their final product or may be used to facilitate their activities. Products used by organizations tend to be complex and sophisticated. Custom-built or specially designed products are characteristic of business markets. These products often involve considerable development time and costs. Suppliers of these products require expert skills and become closely integrated with their customers' businesses.

Business customers are more likely to be geographically concentrated. Industries can arise around certain areas and key resources, for example oil and precious metals. If the key resource is personnel, industries can form around pockets of qualified personnel, for example Silicon Valley in the US and the Cambridge Science Park in the UK. Businesses that supply other business tend to locate in the same areas so clusters and networks of industries form. While business markets tend to be geographically concentrated they are also globally orientated. Customers are larger, fewer in number and concentrated in specific areas in the world. Advances in transportation, communications and technology have enabled businesses to compete successfully at a global level. Business buyers are also likely to be more significant in size than individual consumers, which means each business customer is more important to the financial success of the organization.

B2C (business-to-consumer) An exchange transaction that occurs between an organization and consumer, as opposed to a transaction between organizations. The term may also describe an organization that provides products and/or services for consumers.

baby boomer Someone born in a period of increased birth rates, the term is particularly associated with those born in the years 1946 to 1964, during the economic prosperity following the Second World War.

back to back When two commercials for the same advertiser, usually for the same product or for complementary ones, are run consecutively on the same radio or television slot.

backward integration A form of VERTICAL

Bagozzi, Richard P.

An expert in research methodology, its relationship to the philosophy of science and its applications to basic and applied research in management, psychology and the social sciences. Bagozzi's research includes applied research in psychology, marketing, health behaviour, organization behaviour and statistical topics. Much of this work draws upon the theory of action and the theory of mind in philosophy. His ongoing research in marketing looks at brand communities and the effects of social and self-conscious emotions (e.g., pride, empathy, embarrassment, guilt, envy, shame) of salespeople on their coping, adaptive resource utilization, performance and organization citizenship behaviours. He is the J. Hugh Liedtke Professor of Management and Professor of Psychology at Jesse H. Jones Graduate School of Management, Rice University, Texas.

Baker, Michael J.

Seen by many as the father figure of the marketing discipline in UK academe, Baker was Professor of Marketing at the University of Strathclyde until his retirement in August 1999. He has also held positions as dean of the School of Business Administration at Strathclyde, chairman of the Institute of Marketing, president of the UK Academy of Marketing and governor of the CAM (Communication, Advertising and Marketing) Foundation. He was the founding editor of the *Journal of Marketing Management* (UK) and established Westburn Publishing as a publishing outlet for high-quality marketing journal and book publications. An author of over 150 articles and papers, his research interests include marketing strategy; innovation and new product development; country-of-origin effects; and buyer behaviour. He is regarded as one of the great practical editors and proselytizers of marketing and marketing management. He has supervised or examined numerous PhD students in the discipline and these have gone on to hold senior posts at many of the key institutions internationally.

INTEGRATION that involves the purchase of suppliers and/or their supply chain in order to reduce dependency.

balance of payments (BOP) A list, or accounting, of all of a country's international transactions for a given time period, usually taken as one year. Payments into the country (receipts) are entered as positive numbers, called credits; payments out of the country (payments) are entered as negative numbers, called debits. Also, these accounts may be differentiated into two forms: visible and invisible trade. Visible trade is normally seen as manufactured or grown produce whilst invisibles are invariably services, especially financial in the UK's case. Balance of payments are often seen as one of the key indicators of a nation's economic health.

balance sheet A statement of the total assets and liabilities of an organization at a particular date, usually the last day of the accounting period (financial year end). The debit or left side of the balance sheet/statement lists the fixed and current assets while the credit or right-hand side states liabilities and equity; the totals for each part must be equal or balance. The balance sheet is one of the primary statements to be included in the financial accounts of a company.

bandwidth The amount of data that can be transmitted in a given time period over a communications channel, often expressed in kilobits or kbytes per second (kbps). For digital devices, the bandwidth is usually expressed in bits per second (bps), or bytes per second. A modem connection to the Internet is typically 56,000bps (56kbps), a broadband connection can be up to 8 Mbps (megabits) or more. For analog devices, the bandwidth is expressed in cycles per second, or hertz (Hz). Increasingly being seen as of vital importance in multimedia and Internet-based marketing and has the potential to advantage competitors and countries with good bandwidth in fast moving Internet markets. Various states have looked at their bandwith provision on broadband as a way of promoting quality Internet-based business and development.

banner ad An Internet-based interactive ad, which often uses graphic images and sound as well as text. It is placed on a website that is linked to an external advertiser's website. The banner ad is sized so as to appear at the top or bottom of the page.

banner blindness The tendency of web visitors to ignore banner ads, especially large ads, even when banners contain information website visitors are actively seeking.

bar chart or graph A chart with rectangular bars of lengths usually in proportion to the magnitudes or frequencies of what they represent. The bars can be horizontally or vertically oriented. Sometimes the bars are not proportional, often because the chart does not start at zero. Mathematicians will usually indicate a chart that does not start at zero by using a squiggly line near the bottom of the y-axis.

barcode A machine-readable representation of information in a visual format on a surface, normally black ink on a white background to reduce reflectance which affects scanning. Originally barcodes stored data in the widths and spacings of printed parallel lines, but today they also come in patterns of dots or concentric circles and can be hidden in images. Barcodes can be read by optical scanners called barcode readers or scanned from an image by special software. Barcodes are widely used to implement Auto ID Data Capture (AIDC) systems that improve the speed and accuracy of computer data entry.

barriers to competition Factors that limit market competition, usually economic, political, social or technological conditions that restrict the entry of more firms into a market. For instance, in the European state of Belarus access to the marketplace is heavily controlled by the state.

barriers to entry Obstacles in the path of a firm which wants to enter a given market. A barrier to entry may be created, for example, by the fact that current companies in the market have patents so that goods cannot be copied or by the high cost of advertising needed to gain market share. The term also refers to barriers that an individual may face while trying to gain entrance into a profession or trade. It may also, more commonly, refer to restrictions that a firm may face (or even a country while trying to enter an industry or trade grouping). A common barrier is the required amount of investment, especially in industries with economies of scale and/ or natural monopolies.

barriers to exit A factor preventing a company from leaving a market in which it is currently trading. A barrier to exit makes it difficult for a company to pull out of an unprofitable product or service because of factors such as possession of specialist equipment, integration of manufacturing and supply, high costs of retraining the workforce in new skills or because of employee relations. A good example is the chemical industry where many companies have maintained operations because of integrated production facilities in various petrochemical products such as polyethylene to avoid transferring costs to other products.

barter A type of trade where goods or services are exchanged for a certain quantity of other goods or services; no money is involved in the transaction. Barter trade is common among people with no access to a cash economy, in societies where no monetary system exists or in economies

Bartels, Robert
(1913–89)

One of marketing's most prolific scholars whose research covered a broad array of marketing topics, including the marketing-as-a-science debate, theory, meta theory, the nature and scope of marketing, credit management, international marketing, comparative marketing, MACROMARKETING and marketing education, among others.

Bartels's most significant and enduring contribution, however, was his fifty years of ongoing research, from dissertation to last publication, in the area with which his name became synonymous – the history of marketing thought. Although not without criticism, no other work provides such a long view of marketing's past and wide sweep of its sub-disciplines. By tracing the history of marketing thought in twentieth-century America, Bartels nurtured interest in marketing's heritage and established a common knowledge base for generations of marketing students. He was a mentor to a number of marketing students,

suffering from a very unstable currency (as when hyperinflation hits) or a lack of currency.

base line Part of an advertisement or promotional material, usually containing address, company name, logotype and maybe a slogan, situated at the foot of the page.

base salary The annual gross rate before taxation of financial remuneration (pay) that an employee receives and excludes bonuses, employer superannuation contributions and overtime payments.

Bayes Theorem This theory states that recently acquired sample information can be combined with prior personal probabilities, to produce revised probabilities in order to embark on new courses of action which may then, repeatedly, be subjected to further inputs of information and revised.

Bayesian Decision Theory A statistical technique for assisting decision making under conditions of uncertainty. Used primarily for deciding when to implement a decision and what to do when it is made, it provides a framework for alternative courses of action particularly in NEW PRODUCT DEVELOPMENT.

Bayesian probability A probability based on a person's subjective or personal judgements and experience.

BCG (Boston Consulting Group) *See* BOSTON CONSULTING GROUP MATRIX; PRODUCT PORTFOLIO.

BCG matrix *See* BOSTON CONSULTING GROUP MATRIX.

beacon A line of code placed in an ad or on a web page that helps track the visitor's actions, such as registrations or purchases. A web beacon is often invisible because it is only 1 x 1 pixel in size and has no colour.

behaviour In marketing, relates to the actions taken by consumers in their day to day life and specifically to their consumption patterns.

behavioural intention A decision to behave in a particular way based on beliefs about the consequences of such behaviour. For instance, intentions to buy stated in response to market research are notoriously unreliable and should be treated with caution.

behavioural research Research into human behaviour, singly or in groups, particularly in connection with buying or consumption habits and patterns but also concerned with wider aspects of social and organizational conduct.

beliefs The properties and benefits attributed by a customer to a product or service. It does not matter if they are true or false. *See also* BRAND IMAGE; PERCEPTION.

Belk, Russell

One of the most prolific consumer behaviour and marketing scholars in the last two decades. After receiving his PhD from the University of Minnesota in 1972, Belk published his first journal article in 1974 in the *Journal of Marketing Research*. His areas of expertise are consumer behaviour, qualitative research and marketing and development. He is a past president of the Association for Consumer Research and current president of the Society of Marketing and Development. He has received two Fulbright grants (1991–2 and 1998–9) and is a fellow in the Association for Consumer Research and the American Psychological Association. Professor Belk has received several awards for best journal articles, best journal reviewer and best instructor. He is also a recipient of the University of Utah Distinguished Research Award and has published more than 300 books, articles and videotapes.

believability The extent to which an advertising message is accepted as being as credible.

below-the-line communications Advertising media which do not pay commission to advertising agencies buying space or time from them. As a result of the development of web communications and e-marketing this term is less useful as these traditional methods of commission have become eroded. *See also* ABOVE-THE-LINE COMMUNICATIONS.

benchmark 1 A pre-determined standard against which future activity is measured, particularly in market research in order to carry out tracking. **2** A system of investigating 'best practice' for a particular industry. This is then taken up and leads to increased efficiency which impacts upon marketing, giving the company a competitive edge.

Bernoulli process A probabilistic model in which the probability (p) that an event of interest occurs remains the same over repeated observations. That is, p stays the same over time and does not depend on the outcome of past observations. This stationary, zero order model has been used to represent brand-choice behaviour or media-viewing behaviour by individuals.

best-before date *See* USE-BY DATE.

Bernays, Edward
(1891–1995)

Considered one of the most influential figures of the twentieth century and founder of public relations and the architect of the development of the concept of mass consumption. He has also been called 'The Father of Spin' by Larry Tye. Born in Vienna in 1891, Bernays was the nephew of Sigmund FREUD. A controversial figure in the history of political thought and public relations, Bernays pioneered the scientific technique of managing, manipulating and shaping public opinion, which he famously dubbed the 'engineering of consent'. During World War I, he was an integral member of the US Committee on Public Information (CPI), a powerful propaganda apparatus that was mobilized in 1917 to package, advertise and sell the war to the American people as one that would 'Make the World Safe for Democracy'. The CPI has become the model on which marketing strategies for future wars would be based. Bernays used the techniques he had learned in the CPI and incorporated some of the ideas of Walter Lipmann, becoming an outspoken proponent of propaganda as a tool for democratic and corporate manipulation of the population.

Bernays was the first to employ psychological techniques in advertising and is credited with stimulating the development of the mass consumption society in the post-Second World War era.

best practice The superior performance of a system, process or other activity which puts the business organization concerned at an advantage compared with its competitors.

beta binomial model A probability mixture model that is frequently used in marketing to show patterns of brand-choice behaviour or media exposure patterns. These models are used to predict future brand-choice or media exposure patterns based on individuals' past behaviour.

Better Business Bureau (USA) A US organization that works to protect consumers against fraudulent and corrupt business practices, including those used in advertising and sales, by answering customer complaints. Since the founding of the first BBB in 1912, the BBB system has shown that the majority of marketplace problems can be solved fairly through the use of self-regulation and consumer education.

beyond the banner Describes online advertising not involving standard GIF and JPEG banner ads.

bias Anything that produces a systematic error in a research finding. Bias is the difference between the expected value of a sample statistic and the population parameter the statistic estimates. It can also be the effects of any factor that the researcher did not expect to influence the dependent variable.

bidding theory The quantification of purchasing determination and the application of probability theory to arrive at a pricing policy; the numerical expression of relevant factors and their measured likelihood of acceptance at different price levels.

bill 1 An INVOICE, a document requesting payment for goods previously supplied. This presentation of a bill is common practice among restaurants, credit card companies, utilities and other service-providers. The bill for something is the total price of all services and goods received but not yet paid for, and is presented in anticipation of full immediate payment.

2 Short for billboard – a placard or poster in outdoor advertising. **3** An announcement listing persons in a broadcast programme.

bill of entry A document prepared by the shipper for final clearance of imported goods by customs officers. A bill of entry is an account of goods entered at a Customs House, for imports and exports, detailing the merchant, quantity of goods, their type and place of origin or destination.

bill of exchange An old trading term relating to an unconditional written order requiring the party to whom it is addressed to pay a specified sum at an agreed date in the future. Bills of exchange are negotiable documents usually maturing within six months and are often traded and sold at a discount to their face value. They are similar to cheques and promissory notes and widely used in international business transactions, such as grain shipments.

bill of lading A statement of the nature and value of goods and services being transported, especially by ship, along with the conditions applying to their transport. Drawn up by the carrier, the document serves as a contract between the owner and shipper (carrier). The term is derived from the noun BILL, a schedule of costs for services supplied or to be supplied, and from the verb 'lade', which means to fill or load a cargo onto a ship or other form of transport.

billboard (advertising) A large outdoor signboard, usually wooden and/or made of composite construction of plastic and metal, erected close to main traffic flows in cities, and on roads and motorways. Billboards show large advertisements aimed at passing pedestrians and drivers. The vast majority of billboards are rented to advertisers rather than owned by them. They are frequently used to mount major product campaigns or social marketing initiatives like anti-drink-driving campaigns.

bin A container for the bulk display of merchandise at a retail outlet, often used in supermarkets to dispose of goods on special offer. The positioning of the bin to maximize sales is seen as essential and is normally well marshalled by support sales staff.

bivariate analysis A group of statistical methods for analysing the relationship between two variables. Such analysis allows the strength of association or level of differences between the two variables to be measured. *See also* CORRELATION; CROSS-TABULATIONS; REGRESSION ANALYSIS.

black box approach An approach that recognizes that major influences on patterns of behaviour may be unknown or hidden. It works through a process of inference regarding the unobservable variables intervening between observable stimulus inputs and observable response outputs, allowing judgements to be made regarding the nature of the intervening variables, i.e. the contents of the 'black box'. For example, studies of the effects of education on students frequently see schooling as a black box. Characteristics of students starting or leaving are compared and contrasted, without directly considering which parts of the school experience might have produced changes or how they could have been achieved.

black market Black market products are typically illegal. The importing of certain government-restricted items such as human body parts, wild animals, prescription drugs or firearms would be categorized as black market, as would smuggling the goods into the target country to avoid import duties. A related concept is BOOT-LEGGING, the smuggling or transport of highly regulated goods, particularly alcoholic beverages, which became synonymous with the prohibition era in the United States. The term 'bootlegging' is also often applied to the production or distribution of counterfeit, copied or pirated goods, such as fake DVDs, which are often confiscated having been found by anti-fraud services.

blanket coverage Advertising without prior selection of a specific target audience.

bleed An advertisement or printed page which utilizes the entire page area, i.e. the print extends beyond the margin to the edge of the page.

blog A short form for weblog, a personal journal published on the web. Blogs frequently include philosophical reflections, opinions on the Internet and social issues, and provide a 'log' of the author's favourite web links. Blogs are usually presented in journal style with a new entry each day or week. They are used extensively in US election campaigns to get over the key messages, launch stories and issues not covered by conventional media and more recently to launch negative advertising or issue campaigns against candidates. Recently, as blogs and blogging have grown dramatically and attracted growing consumer interest, so the major newspaper groups and broadcasters have developed their own blogs linked to their leading commentators, journalists and pundits which are positioned on their own websites or promoted in their broadcasts to attract and maintain contact with the cyber generation of news and commentary readers and listeners. What separates blogs from other media is the inter-connective nature of the larger blog community. Huffington Post, a liberal leaning blog founded in 2005 by Arianna Huffington and Kenneth Learer, is rated by the UK *Guardian* newspaper as the most influential in the world.

blogosphere The larger community of people who BLOG, and their blog sites.

blogroll A list of links that generally appears along the side of a BLOG page that can be clicked to link to other blogs that the author personally rates or likes.

bluetooth A technology that connects devices wirelessly, over a short range (ten metres). It is particularly useful for mobile phones, for example, allowing a user to speak without holding a handset. The name 'Bluetooth' is borrowed from Harald Bluetooth, the king of Denmark AD 940–985.

blurb A very short summary or a few phrases of promotional text at the end of a creative piece of work. It usually refers to a piece of text used to promote the work and most often refers to the words on the back cover of a book. Blurbs can also been seen on the back of a DVD, CD box covers, LP record sleeves, audio cassette covers, video cassette covers and, increasingly, Internet sites.

A blurb on a book is designed to attract a particular type of buyer and reader. It will normally include a basic idea of contents, comments from well respected reviewers and writers in the field, a biography of the author and a basic summary of the work's originality, relevance and importance. A blurb on an Internet site, such as that on the BBC World News site, gives a basic overview of the site as well as regular newsfeed with features on major news stories. Blurbs can be short phrases to whole pages of text designed to attract readers.

body language The use of body movements or gestures instead of, or in addition to, sounds, verbal language or other forms of communication. *Voluntary body language* refers to movement, gestures and poses made with full or partial intention by a person (i.e. conscious smiling, hand movements and imitation). It can apply to many types of soundless communication. *Involuntary body language* quite often takes the form of facial expression, and has therefore been suggested as a means of being more aware of the emotions of a person with whom one is communicating. One of the most commonly observed gestures is scratching the head, which is supposed to indicate doubt.

bogoff A mnemonic for 'buy one get one free', i.e. a promotional practice where upon purchasing one product another is given to the customer free.

bookmark Just as a paper bookmark is used as a reminder of the page you are on in a book, electronic bookmarks are used to bring you back to a website or another site you may want to return to. The Netscape browser lets you bookmark any site and save the bookmarks in a file you can recall at any time. Bookmarks are pointers – primarily to URLS – built into the various Internet web browsers. Bookmarks have been incorporated into almost every browser since the Mosaic browser and are normally stored on the software client. A folder metaphor may be used for organization and various shareware utilities, and server-side web utilities have been developed to manage bookmarks better, for instance FURL, yet none has gained widespread acceptance. The bookmark within Internet Explorer (and therefore within Microsoft Windows) is called a 'favourite'. As a result of the majority of Internet users using Internet Explorer, the term has become virtually synonymous with bookmark in this respect.

boomerang effect Where the advertising of a product 'A' alienates the consumer by being too 'hard sell' and as a result the customer deliberately buys product 'B'.

bootlegging Originally slang for the concealment of contraband goods (usually bottles of alcohol) inside a boot, the term has come to be applied to the illicit distribution of regulated or copyrighted material. Bootlegging remains a practice in many areas where there is strong regulatory activity or prohibition is in force. Most recently the bootlegging or 'piracy' of CDs and DVDs of music recordings and films has become a major illicit industry on an international corporate scale, exacerbated by the growth in web access and the availability of downloadable music from websites. *See also* BLACK MARKET.

Boston Box *See* PRODUCT PORTFOLIO.

Boston Consulting Group matrix Is widely used in marketing segmentation and product positioning and was developed by Bruce Henderson, the founder of the Boston Consultancy Group (BCG) from his concept of the experience curve which relates unit costs to the cumulative output of a product. He argued that where one producer is further down the experience curve than another and if the products and margins are similar, they will be the most successful.

From this work Henderson derived the

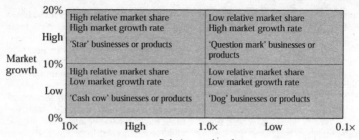

| | | High relative market share
High market growth rate

'Star' businesses or products | Low relative market share
High market growth rate

'Question mark' businesses or products |
| Market growth | | High relative market share
Low market growth rate

'Cash cow' businesses or products | Low relative market share
Low market growth rate

'Dog' businesses or products |

Relative market share

Boston Consulting Group matrix

well-known growth share matrix, often referred to as the Boston Box, which has been used to distinguish between products in a diversified company or organization. Cash cows are those with low growth and high market share which can be used to defend and maintain the product portfolio by generating cash that can be invested elsewhere. Those that are generating sufficient cash for their own long-term development and have high growth and share should be investing in further promotion and research and development and are called Stars. Those that are haemorrhaging cash from the product portfolio/business have limited future because of low growth and poor market share and are referred to as Dogs. And finally those that have high growth but low share will require more investment to become competitive and generate margin or should be divested from the product portfolio and, not surprisingly, are called Question Marks. The BCG matrix has been widely used but there has been some robust criticism of its misapplication leading to corporate disaster by the likes of Scott Armstrong. *See also* PRODUCT PORTFOLIO; ARMSTRONG, SCOTT.

boundary spanning Actions that go beyond a manager's normal area of responsibility especially at the interface between one task area and another. The term is most frequently used in public relations theory to explain the number of overlapping tasks carried out by a practitioner necessary to achieve a given result.

boutique Specifically, a shop specializing in a particular range of merchandise and especially bespoke fashion clothing, accessories and/or jewellery. Generally used in marketing to describe an organization, such as an advertising agency, which specializes in a limited range of activities. The term is widely used to describe a small business offering specialized products and services.

boutique agency A specialized agency which sets out to concentrate on one specific element of advertising services, e.g. creativity, design, images, writing, photography.

BRAD (British rate and data) A monthly index of current advertising rates and mechanical data for virtually every separate media vehicle available to advertisers in Britain. It is traditionally issued as a monthly.

brainstorming A method of creative problem-solving frequently used in product concept generation. Brainstorming normally uses a group of people to creatively generate a list of ideas related to a particular topic, though it can also be done individually. In group brainstorming, the participants are encouraged, and often expected, to share their ideas with one another as soon as they are generated. The key to brainstorming is not to interrupt the thought process. As ideas come to mind, they are captured and stimulate the development of further and better ideas. As many ideas as possible are listed and no criticism or discussion of ideas is allowed until all ideas are recorded. The ideas are then critically reviewed after the brainstorming session.

brand A distinct identity or image – sometimes linked to a specific product – created by an organization and designed to be instantly recognizable by consumers. Its fundamental reason to exist is to ensure that consumers always seek the brand-owner's products or services in preference to those of its competitors. A brand is often intangible and the embodiment of a combination of semiotic and symbolic information associated with an organization, product or service. A brand serves to create and stimulate lingering associations and expectations among products made by a producer. Branding is created with words, logos, graphics and other marketing communication tools and can often be a very complex process. A brand often includes an explicit logo, fonts, colour schemes, smells, symbols or sounds which may be developed to represent implicit values, ideas and even personality. A well-known brand is Kentucky Fried Chicken, which is symbolized by a range of colours and products and the picture of its founder, Colonel Sanders, in folksy American attire used as a logo. BRAND RECOGNITION and other reactions are created by the accumulation of experiences with the specific product or service, both directly relating to its use and through the influence of advertising, design and media commentary.

In accessing a good brand, it should:

- be legally protectable (e.g. Coca-Cola);
- be easy to pronounce (e.g. Shell);
- be easy to remember (e.g. Fairy Liquid);
- be easy to recognize (e.g. Nestlés KitKat);
- attract attention (e.g. BMW Mini);
- suggest product benefits (e.g. Dyson) or suggest usage;
- suggest the company or product image (e.g. Mercedes star motif);
- distinguish the product's positioning relative to the competition (e.g. Aldi).

brand architecture How an organization structures and names the brands within its portfolio. These structures are either mono-lithic in nature where the brand is applied to all products of the organization, such as Cadburys; endorsed, where all sub-brands are linked to the holding company or organization by visual or verbal endorsement such as petrol companies' endorsement of specialist lubricants; and finally, freestanding, where the brand operates as a holding company to endorse each sub-brand: Ferrari is an example which endorses products from computers to perfumes.

brand associations The feelings, beliefs and knowledge that consumers (customers) have about brands. These associations are derived as a result of experiences and must be consistent with the brand positioning and the basis of differentiation.

brand awareness The level of recognition that consumers have of a particular brand and its particular product category.

brand equity A financial measure relating to the estimated value of a brand. The four components of brand equity are considered to be BRAND AWARENESS; BRAND ASSOCIATIONS; BRAND LOYALTY; and perceived brand quality.

brand extension The addition of a new product to a current range under the same brand name in order to benefit from the existing level of awareness and positive perception. A company's use of one of its existing brand names as part of an improved or new product, usually in the same product category as the existing brand. Using the values of the brand to take the brand into new markets/sectors. *See also* HALO EFFECT.

brand image The total of all the impressions the consumer receives from the brand. These include actual experience, hearsay from other consumers, its packaging, its name, the kind of store in which it is sold, advertising, the tone and form of advertising, the media used for advertising and the types of people seen using, buying or recommending the brand. *See also* BELIEFS; BRAND PERSONALITY: IMAGE.

brand leader A product which holds the greatest single share and is the leader of the market. In the Cola market worldwide this has traditionally been Coca-Cola, although its arch rival Pepsi has at times come close to replacing the brand leader.

brand loyalty Is the active support by consumers of continuing to consume a particular brand in the face of competition by other branded substitutes. Such loyalty is often subjective or subconscious. Brand loyalty has been proclaimed by some to be the ultimate goal of marketing (see F. F. Reichheld and W. E. Sasser, 'Zero Defections: Quality Comes to Services', *Harvard Business Review* (September–October 1990)). *See also* LOYALTY MARKETING.

brand management The application of marketing techniques to a specific product, product line or brand involving particular attention to both the intangible and tangible aspects of the brand. This includes setting targets, advertising, packaging, promotions, retailing, and managing all related activities to achieve those targets. The concept was developed by Neil H. McElroy at Procter and Gamble, Cincinnati, Ohio, in 1931. He argued in his famous memo which gave birth to brand management that in addition to having a person in charge of each brand, there should be a substantial team of people devoted to thinking about every aspect of marketing it. This dedicated group should attend to one brand and it alone. Procter and Gamble has become synonymous with quality brand management and has marketed successfully such world brands as Ariel, Bold, Braun, Camay, Crest, DAZ, Duracell, Fairy, Gillette, Head and Shoulders, Lacoste, Lenor, Max Factor, Olay, Oral B, Pampers, Pantene, Pringles, Tampax and Tide. It has the world's largest advertising spend to support its branding and promotion startegy which is expected to reach US $4 billion in 2008.

brand manager An executive responsible for the overall marketing, and particularly promotion, of a specific brand. The job function ranges from a coordination role to one in which profit objectives are built in. The brand manager is sometimes titled product manager, especially in USA.

brand mapping *See* PERCEPTUAL MAPPING.

brand personality The idea that brands have personalities and even character traits has become inseparable with the concept of a brand in the last decade. The purveying and promotion of this personality is usually developed through a planned, long-term ABOVE-THE-LINE advertising and appropriate packaging and graphics campaign. These traits inform brand behaviour both through prepared communication/packaging, etc., and through the people who represent the brand – its employees. This would have been an unusual aspect of brands in the 1960s and this aspect of branding has been termed the changing 'conceptualization' of the brand. However, not all brands have changed conceptually. And, significantly, the nature and role of the brand are linked to the type of marketing style that is followed.

In some markets, transactional style marketing is still preferred and brands may be employed with a 'mechanistic concept' typical of supply-driven markets. The recognition that brands have developed over time, but that different conceptualizations of brands still exist, is significant because the type of conceptualization will arguably influence consumer expectations. As a result, it is likely that consumers value and assess the attributes and characteristics of brands differently according to the type of marketing environment. *See also* BRAND IMAGE.

brand positioning The development of a particular brand's position in the marketplace by emphasizing and enhancing its strengths over other similar products available to consumers. Brand positioning relies on a clear strength or value that a product is seen to have above competitive products by users. *See also* CORPORATE POSITIONING.

brand preference A primary advertising/promotional objective, to establish a situation in which a particular brand is regarded as more desirable than its competitors. A brand preference is a prerequisite of a first sale, whereas brand loyalty is necessary for repeat purchases.

brand properties Actual attributes that collectively make up a brand personality.

brand rationalization Reducing the number of brands on offer, often by making one brand available but providing different labels and packaging and different brand names.

brand recognition The point when a brand is widely known in the marketplace. Brand recognition can be measured by consumer awareness that a brand exists and is an alternative to purchase.

brand reinforcement The bolstering of a consumer's current beliefs in, or attitudes to, a brand. It is a common advertising objective. Also, the brand can be reinforced by the use of strong public relations campaigns designed to project its image into certain critical consumer groups such as children or health workers.

brand share Percentage sales by (or consumption of) a given product or brand related to its total market. Can be expressed in monetary or unit terms and, since these provide different values, should always be defined in terms of the method used to calculate it.

brand value The estimated total worth of a brand, either as a product, group of products or organization, which reflects the value that it would raise if it were sold as a financial asset on the open market. There is debate about whether this value should be included in the company's balance sheet, but a brand's value would certainly be included as an intangible asset (goodwill) in any corporate valuation.

The top global brands based on the author's research and best estimates of value in 2007 are estimated to be:

1	Google	USA
2	GE (General Electric)	USA
3	Microsoft	USA
4	Coca-Cola	USA
5	China Mobile	China
6	IBM	USA
7	Apple	USA
8	McDonald's	USA
9	Nokia	Finland
10	Marlboro	USA
11	Vodafone	UK
12	Toyota	Japan
13	Wal-Mart	USA
14	Bank of America	USA
15	Citi	USA
16	Hewlett-Packard (HP)	USA
17	BMW	Germany
18	ICBC (Industrial & Commercial Bank of China)	China
19	Louis Vuitton	France
20	American Express	USA
21	Wells Fargo	USA
22	Cisco	USA
23	Disney	USA
24	UPS	USA
25	Tesco	UK
26	Honda	Japan
27	L'Oréal	France
28	Pepsi	USA
29	Home Depot	USA
30	Dell	USA

Other significant global brands which are regularly in the top 50 are Deutsche Bank, ING, Carrefour, NTT DoCoMo, Target, Siemens, Banco Santander, Accenture, Orange, BlackBerry, Chase, Nike, Canon, AT&T, Starbucks, Oracle, Intel, Porsche, SAP, Gillette, Yahoo, China Construction Bank, Bank of China, Verizon Wireless, Royal Bank of Canada, HSBC, Goldman Sachs, Samsung, and Mercedes.

branding Establishing in the minds of consumers a knowledge about, and loyalty to, a particular product focused on the brand name, for instance Mercedes, Nike or Shell. Branding produces advantages for a product. The brand name becomes associated with specific benefits, it enables the consumer to recognize the product, it helps to position the product relative to competing brands, and it may help to insulate the product from price competition and to move it more easily through the distribution channel. The primary tool for product branding is advertising although public relations activities, and corporate responsibility campaigns are playing an increasing role. Not all products are branded, however; for the advantages of unbranded products, see GENERIC BRANDS.

break-even The point at which any commercial venture becomes financially viable, i.e. when total expenditure is exactly matched by income, and therefore the point after which a profit begins to be made. This is of particular importance in the launching of a new product where a certain risk investment is necessary; therefore forecasts must be projected before proceeding, as to the circumstances and time within which the breakeven point will be reached. This provides both the information required for policy decisions and a yardstick against which performance can be measured progressively. Hence the expression 'payback period' to denote the time to elapse before all investment costs are recovered and profit will subsequently be generated. *See also* BREAK-EVEN ANALYSIS; BREAK-EVEN PRICING.

break-even analysis The examination of relationships between fixed costs, sales revenue and variable costs to determine the most profitable level of output or the most profitable product mix.

break-even pricing An ambiguous term which is used when discussing pricing objectives. Some writers use it to describe the setting of a price which will recover the manufacturing and marketing costs but not include a profit while others use it as being synonymous with target profit pricing which includes the costs of manufacturing and marketing plus a profit margin.

breaking bulk The function of a wholesaler who buys in bulk and then distributes in small quantities to local retailers. A good example are coal merchants who purchase bulk coal deliveries and then bag for the retail market and smaller deliveries. *See also* ALLOCATION.

British Academy of Management (BAM) Founded in 1986 with the objective of encouraging the development and sharing of knowledge about organizational and management studies. It has also

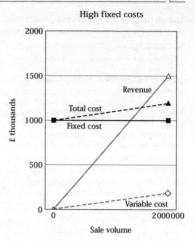

High fixed costs

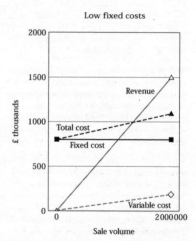

Low fixed costs

Break-even Analysis

declared its aim to act as a forum for the development of an integrated body of management knowledge and encourages future research into the development of management education. Its quarterly journal is the *British Journal of Management*, which has become well established and is widely read by researchers and practitioners. The organization hosts its annual conference in September each year at one of the UK's business schools.

British Standards Institution (BSI) An organization that prepares and publishes standards which specify dimensions, performance and safety criteria, testing methods and codes of practice for a large range of products and processes in most fields of production.

broadband The term comes from the words 'broad bandwidth' and is used to describe a high-capacity, two-way link between an END USER and access network suppliers capable of supporting full-motion, interactive video applications. The term applies to networks having bandwidths significantly greater than that found in telephone networks or systems. Broadband systems are capable of carrying a large number of moving images or a vast quantity of data simultaneously. Broadband techniques usually depend on coaxial or optical cable for transmissions. They use multiplexing to permit the simultaneous operation of multiple channels or services on a single cable. Frequency division multiplexing or cell relay techniques can both be used in broadband transmission.

In addition, the term 'broadband' is often used loosely to refer to high-speed Internet service. The availability of broadband both nationally and globally is causing significant diversity in web-based marketing operations, particularly billing and selling.

Broadcasters' Audience Research Board (BARB) Established in 1981 to provide an industry-standard audience measurement service for television broadcasters and the advertising industry, BARB is a non-profit-making limited company owned by BBC, ITV, Channel 4, Five, BSkyB and the Institute of Practitioners in Advertising. BARB does not undertake audience measurement directly; instead contractors produce audience ratings on its behalf. There are three research companies which hold four audience measurement contracts – RSMB (methodology), Ipsos MORI (surveys) and Nielsen Media Research (see ACNIELSEN) (metering, data collection and processing).

BARB is responsible for providing estimates of the number of people watching television in the UK; there are equivalent organizations throughout most developed countries in the world. This includes which channels and programmes are being watched, at what time, and the type of people who are watching at any one point of the day. BARB provides television audience data on a minute-by-minute basis for channels received within the UK. The data is available for reporting nationally and at ITV and BBC regional level and covers all analogue and digital platforms.

broadsheet Most newspapers in the UK are defined either as broadsheet or tabloid. These are terms which refer to the size of the paper, broadsheet being double the size of tabloid. The term tabloid is traditionally associated with the popular press and concentrates on celebrities, crime, direct political comment, entertainment, gossip and sport. The broadsheet is associated with the quality press and usually places its emphasis on information and analysis with a particular focus on public affairs, international stories, culture and intellectual and traditional commentary. These distinctions are now beginning to break down as publishers of quality newspaper, such as the *Guardian*, the *Independent* and *The Times* in the UK, realize that tabloids are easier to read and hold. The *Guardian* moved to the Berliner format in 2006, which has been adopted by the *Chicago Tribune* and *Le Monde* in France for similar reasons.

The UK press, along with that of Japan, has the highest daily readership in the world: two out of three people read a national newspaper and three out of four read a Sunday newspaper. Britain also has a tradition of reading Sunday newspapers rather than weekly news magazines for an overview of currents issues.

The British and American press are independent but often owned by large media corporations, such as Rupert Murdoch's News International in the UK and US, or the Gannett Group in the US. In the US, as in the UK, there is a distinction between the tabloid (e.g. *USA Today*) and broadsheet (e.g. *The New York Times*), with the major

Brown, Stephen

One of the most influential and provocative marketing thinkers and academics of his generation and is currently Professor of Marketing Research, University of Ulster, Newtownabbey, Northern Ireland. Brown is the highly regarded and influential author of *Postmodern Marketing* (1995) and has been referred to as the 'Antichrist of Marketing' and a 'postmodern provocateur'. He has written or co-edited over fifteen wide-ranging and stimulating texts including (with John F. Sherry Jr) *Marketing* – *The Retro Revolution and Time, Space, and the Market*. Brown's articles have been published in *Journal of Marketing*, *Harvard Business Review*, *Journal of Advertising*, *Business Horizons*, *Journal of Retailing* and *European Management Review*, among others. He held a number of famous retreats at Ulster covering a cornucopia of modern marketing theory and thought and has stimulated a number of critical evaluations of marketing thinking and evaluated such phenomena as Harry Potter, *The Da Vinci Code* and snake oil salesmen.

American quality papers tending to be more liberal in their outlook. *The New York Times* and the *Miami Herald* are two important quality regional papers, but every city of any size has its own newspaper in the US whilst in the UK the press has strong regional daily press with such newspapers as the *Scotsman*, the *Yorkshire Post* and the *Liverpool Post*.

broken lot Goods offered for sale in a smaller than normal quantity. It includes damaged packaged goods where some contents have been lost or removed.

budget An estimate of future sources of income and expenditure including statements of intentions within a given period of time. It can relate to individual parts of the marketing mix, when it may include expenses only, or to the total marketing operation. A budget outlines an organization's financial and operational goals, and so may be thought of as an action plan; planning a budget helps a business allocate resources, evaluate performance and formulate plans.

While planning a budget can occur at any time, for many businesses, planning a budget is an annual task, where the past year's budget is reviewed and budget projections are made for the next three or even five years. The basic process of planning a budget involves listing the business's fixed and variable costs on a monthly basis and then deciding on an allocation of funds to reflect the business's goals. *See also* ADVERTISING BUDGET; MARKETING BUDGET.

built-in obsolescence Sometimes called planned obsolescence, this is the design and construction of a product such that it will automatically fail or otherwise become obsolete after a given period of time. Planned obsolescence has great benefits for a producer in that it means a consumer will buy their product repeatedly, as their old one is no longer functional or desirable. It exists in many different products, including vehicles, light bulbs, buildings (for example in the UK in the 1960s clasp concrete prefabricated buildings were designed for a life of only twenty-five years), software and of course the computer processors that drive them.

bulletin board A virtual 'noticeboard' that allows people to carry on discussions online, read postings, add comments and feedback, upload and download files, etc. without parties being connected to the computer at the same time.

bundling Linking complementary products and/or services together to form a package deal with a lower price/higher value than would be available if the items were purchased separately.

business analysis The stage of NEW PRODUCT DEVELOPMENT where initial marketing plans are prepared, including a tentative marketing strategy and estimates of sales, costs and profitability.

business cycle The business or economic cycle refers to the peaks and troughs seen sequentially in most parts of an economy. The cycle involves shifts over time between periods of relatively rapid growth of output (recovery and prosperity) and periods of relative stagnation or decline (contraction or recession). These fluctuations are often measured using the real gross domestic product. Dramatic shifts in economic activity brought about a number of booms and busts in the nineteenth century. In 2008 there is growing concern that the collapse of certain housing markets in the US and developed world is having a major impact on new building starts and therefore will impact on the business cycle.

business plan A planning document that summarizes the activities of a business for a given period of time. The plan communicates the business elements to lenders and stakeholders, provides the basis for managing the business and indicates how progress can be regularly measured and changes evaluated using such operational management tools as key performance indicators (KPIs). *See also* CORPORATE PLANNING.

business strategy The core aims and direction by which a business aims to achieve its objectives. This is enlarged upon in the business plan. Similarly, each function (e.g. marketing, financial, human resources, production, R&D, etc.) has a set of objectives, strategies and plans. Strategic management is the process of specifying an organization's objectives, developing policies and plans to achieve these objectives and allocating resources so as to implement the plans. It is the highest level of managerial activity, usually performed by the company's chief executive officer (CEO) and executive team. It provides overall direction to the whole company. An organization's strategy must be appropriate for its resources, circumstances and objectives.

button ad A website graphical advertising unit, smaller than a banner ad. Button ads come in a variety of sizes, measured in pixels. There are standards such as 120 x 90, 120 x 60, 125 x 125 and 88 x 31 (micro-button), although non-standard button ads are not uncommon. Whereas banners are often placed at the top or bottom of a page, buttons are often placed towards the middle of a page on the left or right sides. A button exchange is a network where participating sites display button ads in exchange for credits which are converted into ads to be displayed on other sites.

buy classes or buy phases The different sections of organizational purchasing. The simplest is the repeat purchase – buying the same product from the same supplier. This is followed by the MODIFIED REBUY, where the same type of product is purchased from an alternative supplier. Finally, the new buy is a first-time purchase in which a larger number of decision-makers are likely to be involved in the purchase and consequently is a much more complex buying situation. *See also* DECISION-MAKING UNIT.

buy-feel-learn model Suggests that in some situations buyers/customers do not follow the logical learn-feel-buy sequence. The BFL model typically applies to impulse purchasing and/or new brands, where attitudes, knowledge and preference are developed after purchase rather than prior to it. Buying often precedes the creation or reinforcement of feelings about the product. *See also* FEEL-BUY-LEARN MODEL; LEARN-FEEL-BUY MODEL.

buygrids A method where competing products are objectively compared for their attributes and then matched against the specific requirements of a user. The term is used extensively in industrial and B2B marketing.

buy phases P. J. Robinson, C. W. Faris and Y. Wind, in *Industrial Buying and Marketing* (1967), introduced the buygrid framework as a general conceptual model to understand how the buying networks and processes in industrial organizations work. The conceptual framework and ideas have been used extensively in marketing and are now applied to and used in most organizational buying situations. They saw industrial buying not as single events, but as an organizational decision-making process where multiple individuals within a group decide on a purchase. Their framework consists of a matrix of buy classes and buy phases.

The buy classes proposed were:

- *New task*. The first-time buyer who requires and searches for a range of quality information to enable the organization to explore alternative purchasing solutions to their organizational problem. It is suggested that the greater the cost or perceived risks related to the purchase, the more significant the need for information and the larger the number of participants in the buying centre.
- *Modified rebuy*. The buyer wants to replace a product the organization uses regularly with another product. The decision-making may involve plans to modify the product specifications, prices, terms or suppliers, for instance, when managers of the organization believe that such a change will improve quality or reduce costs. In such circumstances, the buying centre will normally only ask for proposals from a limited range of participants which may include the current product supplier thus leading to more rapid decision-making than that incurred in a new task buy class.
- *Straight rebuy*. The buyer routinely reorders a product with no modifications. The buyer retains the supplier as long as the level of satisfaction with the delivery, quality and price is maintained. New suppliers are considered only when these conditions change. The challenge for the new supplier is to offer better conditions or draw the buyer's attention to greater benefits than in the current product offering.

Based on field research, Robinson, Faris and Wind divided the buyer purchase process into eight sequential, distinct but interrelated phases:

1 recognition of the organizational problem or need;
2 determination of the characteristics of the item and the quantity needed;
3 description of the characteristics of the item and the quantity needed;
4 search for and qualification of potential sources;
5 acquisition and analysis of proposals;
6 evaluation of the proposals and selection of suppliers;
7 selection of an order routine;
8 Performance feedback and evaluation.

The most complex buying situations occur in the upper-left quadrant of the buygrid matrix, where the largest number of decision-makers and buying influences are involved. A new task that occurs in the problem-recognition phase (1) is generally the most difficult for management. The buying process can vary from highly formalized to an approximation depending on the nature of the buying organization, the size of the deal and the buying situation.

The relationship between the buyer and seller is initiated in phases 1 and 2. Assessing the buyer's needs and determining gaps between the current and desired situation is vital and can be accessed via preparation and negotiation. Buyers will need quality information and input from sales organizations to be able to make an assessment of their needs now and in the future. Need gaps create the motive behind any purchase. The relationship needs to be developed during phases 3 to 7. Sales staff should be aware that a buyer does not have just functional needs but also psychological, social, knowledge and situational needs as well. These components should be addressed in discussions and meetings in order to obtain commitment. The purchase can be a one-time transaction of a repetitive nature. When there are multiple deliveries, the supplier and buyer must agree on an order routine and invariably a contractual arrangement, which may involve a discount for volume. As buy phases are completed, the process of 'creeping commitment' occurs and reduces the likelihood of new suppliers gaining access to the buying situation. During the performance feedback and evaluation phase, the relationship between the seller and buyer can develop into a longer-term engagement. Buyer loyalty and customer satisfaction are primarily determined by the sales activities during this last phase.

The buy phase model has underpinned much of our contemporary buying behaviour thinking within marketing over the last two decades and has been applied to both tangible and service products.

buy response A particular method of pretesting of consumer perceptions of what represents an acceptable price for a product.

buyer 1 A person responsible for making a final purchasing decision. **2** An executive in a company heading up the overall purchasing function. **3** A department head in a department store. The latter two typically buy items for resale. Wholesale buyers purchase goods directly from manufacturers or from other wholesale firms for resale to retail firms, commercial establishments, institutions and other organizations. In retail firms, buyers purchase goods from wholesale firms or directly from manufacturers for resale to the public. Buyers largely determine which products their establishment will sell. Therefore, it is essential that they have the ability to predict what will appeal to consumers. They must constantly stay informed of the latest trends, because failure to do so could undermine profit potential and the reputation of their company.

buyer behaviour models A way of portraying consumers' buying processes which aid understanding of the buying process. Buyer behaviour models attempt to model the range of influences which affect purchase decisions and show the extent of interaction between influencing variables.

buyer behaviour theories These theories contribute to our understanding of the decision processes and actions of people involved in buying and using products, i.e. consumer behaviour. Developed from disciplines such as economics and psychology, they attempt to take account of various social and psychological influences on buying behaviour. Buying behaviour can be influenced by a variety of external factors and motivations, including marketing activity.

buyer's market A market situation in which excess manufacturing capacity and over-supply of a commodity puts buyers in an advantageous negotiating position as a result of an imbalance between supply and demand. This particularly affects the movement of prices for seasonal goods, like fruit. *See also* SELLER'S MARKET.

buying centre In large industrial and commercial organizations, the team of people at the centre of organization responsible for deciding what products to buy and which companies or organizations to procure them from. Typically in the plastic-processing industry the team would be made up of a buyer, technical manager, engineer and production manager, all being managed and signed off by the CEO. The buying centre will be involved in major purchasing and procurement decisions, involving such things as new machinery, computer systems, energy and utility supply purchases, raw material supplies, and arranging trials and evaluations of new products and suppliers. The more upstream the process, such as oil refining, the larger the buying centre.

buying intention survey A form of attitude measurement designed to predict behaviour from a knowledge of attitudes. The aim is to be able to predict a specific behaviour, such as whether a consumer will purchase a given product, such as a new car, within a certain timescale.

buying motives Factors which set buyer's needs and guide their final selection of the product that best satisfies that need. Are aroused needs, drives, or desires that act as a force to stimulate behaviour intended to satisfy those aroused needs. Perceptions influence or shape this behaviour.

by-product A secondary or incidental product deriving from a manufacturing process or chemical reaction, rather than the primary product or service being produced. One of the by-products of oil refining is naphtha, which is used in producing a range of petrochemical products. A by-product can be useful and marketable, or it can have severe ecological consequences.

byline Line that precedes the text of a story or article and names the writer of the piece. It is called a byline because it tells by whom the piece is written. The term normally applies to journalism, although bylines have been used in advertising copy when the endorser is well known.

C2B (consumer-to-business) The financial interaction, initiated by a consumer, between a consumer and business.

C2C (consumer-to-consumer) An abbreviation for consumer-to-consumer commerce; that is, commerce with no middle business people. The most notable examples are web-based auction and classified ad sites. Most large venues for such models (for example, eBay, Classifieds 2000 and Trademe) are quickly permeated by consumers who participate so actively and regularly that they become small businesses for them. The presence of these quasi-consumers and the obvious businesses that sell through these sites has blurred the distinction between B2C and pure C2C.

cable television A provider of analogue and digital television, radio and Internet services normally via fixed coaxial or fibre-optic cables. There is a high density of cable television usage in urban areas and specific communities and townships where all citizens can be easily connected or plugged into service; it is also widely used in health care and education sectors for provision of programmes and information. The largest cable TV provider in the world is Comcast, based in Philadelphia, USA, with over 40 million users of its services. Cable television has been facing growing competition from SATELLITE TELEVISION systems which are increasingly being seen as a lower-cost and higher-definition alternative.

caching The storage of web files for later reuse at a point more quickly accessed by the END USER.

CAD (computer-aided-/-assisted design) Computer-aided design (CAD) encompasses a wide range of computer-based tools that assist architects, designers and engineers among others in their design activities. It involves both software and specially tailored hardware systems.

call analysis The study of a salesperson's customer calling patterns.

call cycle The frequency with which a salesperson will call upon a particular business account, usually determined by the size and importance of the account to the seller. *See also* COMMUNICATIONS MIX; PERSONAL SELLING.

call to action Advertising phrase or prompt that attracts buyers or users to take an immediate and explicit action. Examples range from 'Click here','Buy now', 'why not call our 800 number to find out more' to 'add to cart'. A call to action is a single focused command to your potential customer.

camera ready Finished artwork or text pages on bromide paper that the printer photographs in order to create printing plates. Also referred to as a complete velox, complete art or glossy. With new technology allowing the creation of printing plates direct from computer files, the camera ready stage of the printing process is becoming redundant.

campaign An organized course of action, planned carefully to achieve predefined objectives. The term can be applied to marketing, advertising, sales, public relations or any part of the promotional mix. The term is also used specifically to describe a product's advertising plan and execution, from development, through production and media placement.

campaign planning An essential preliminary to the execution of an advertising campaign. In practice, individual advertisers' and advertising agencies' approaches to campaign planning vary considerably, but the process should ideally comprise some or all of the following actions: product-market analysis, evaluation of competitive position, client brief, budgeting, selection of target audiences, formulation of creative and media strategies, media buying and scheduling, production, implementation and measurement of effectiveness and evaluation.

cannibalization When the demand for a new product is stimulated at least in part by eroding demand for (sales of) a current product in the market.

canvas A colloquial term meaning to seek or solicit views on a subject. In marketing research it is used with two different and distinct meanings: (a) to conduct a census of a defined population; (b) to identify respondents possessing a particular characteristic from a larger population and so filter them out.

capital The term capital is commonly used in three specific senses: capital invested, capital employed and working capital. Capital invested is the amount of money introduced into the business by the owner and represents their investment in the business. Capital employed is the amount of money being used in the firm. Working capital is the excess of the total current assets over the total current liabilities of the firm (note it is not only the cash available).

capital expenditure Expenditure intended to benefit the future activities of a business, usually by adding to the assets of a business such as the acquisition of manufacturing plant or storage, or by upgrading or enhancing an existing asset.

capital goods Usually seen as one of the four factors of production and consists of machines, plant and buildings that underpin production but excludes raw materials, land and labour. Can also refer to financial assets that are capable of generating income such as patents and bonds.

caption A brief heading or description accompanying an illustration or picture. It is often worded to attract the consumer's attention to a particular product offering.

cartel A group of producers (or producing countries) who enter into a collusive arrangement to regulate pricing, production or marketing of goods by members. The aim of a cartel is to restrict output in order to raise prices; cartel members thereby gain the profit advantages of a single monopoly, but, since they continue to function as separate entities, without the offsetting efficiency gains a monopoly may achieve through economies of large-scale production. Cartels are prohibited by anti-trust laws in most countries; however, they continue to exist nationally and internationally, formally and informally.

cascading style sheets (CSS) A data format used to separate style from structure on web pages.

case study A descriptive, qualitative research method that analyses in great detail a person, an organization or an event. Case studies are found in most applied areas, such as business, law and marketing, and offer insight into practices and tactics. The case study's major advantage is the detail and analysis it provides of a specific person, organization or event. Its major disadvantage is that it cannot be generalized to situations other than the one that was studied.

cash-and-carry Bulk and large-quantity retail or wholesale outlets offering discounted goods and limited or no service. They are particularly popular with small business such as cafés, clubs, restaurants and small hotels.

cash cow *See* BOSTON CONSULTING GROUP MATRIX.

cash flow A measure of cash inflow and outflow from the business. Positive cash flow means more money is coming into the business than is leaving it. Negative cash flow is the converse and one of the prime reasons for businesses going into liquidation. Cash flow is not the same as profitability.

cash on delivery (COD) A system of payment in which goods are paid for on delivery. It safeguards the seller, in that merchandise is not handed over without payment, and the buyer, who takes delivery without any prior financial commitment.

catalogue A publication containing descriptions or details of a number or range of products.

catalogue retailing The sale of goods to the general public through the medium of a catalogue. The range of merchandise may be wide (e.g. Littlewoods) or focused on a specific category of goods such as car accessories. Catalogue retailers usually operate through MAIL ORDER and offer extended credit terms.

catchline Key words that identify the main subject or merchandise in an ad. (The word 'sale' on its own is not considered sufficient as the catchline.)

catchphrase A product slogan in advertising which is so popular that it becomes part of everyday language, at least for a period of time. 'Don't say vinegar … say Sarsons' is the well-known catchphrase of the advertising campaign for Premier Foods' malt vinegar UK branded product.

CATI (computer-assisted telephone interview) An interview, the administration of which is handled specifically by computer-driven software programs. Interviewers enter respondent answers received by telephone directly into the computer memory by means of individual keyboards. CATI has a number of advantages:

- Standardized sampling and call-back procedures can be programmed in the system to ensure consistency of practice and more efficient calling routines.
- Interview questions can be automatically modified to insert information already obtained and to customise and phrase questions to take account of such personal characteristics as gender and marital status.
- Computer-controlled skip patterns permit far more complex interviews than are possible with pen and paper systems. Questions can be designed to vary according to answers given earlier in the interview or even according to random numbers. Complex experiments can be integrated into the survey.
- In using this process data cleaning is a standard benefit, since many potential interviewer errors, such as missed questions or inappropriate skips, are virtually eliminated. Also, apparent discrepancies between responses may be automatically identified for probing during the course of the interview.
- Tabulations and data files are available faster because data entry and most manual editing and data-cleaning steps are substantially reduced or eliminated. In more complex studies, this process can save substantial amounts of time between the completion of interviewing and the start of data analysis.
- It builds in automatic record-keeping, by date, time, sample segment and interviewer, and facilitates both interim and final reports on sampling outcomes and interviewer performance.

cause marketing (cause-related marketing) Marketing that links a product or a company to a charitable cause. The funds that are donated to the charitable cause usually come from a portion of the sales of the product. For example, when a person buys tea from Yorkshire Tea, a portion of the sales profit is donated by the company to support the planting of trees as part of its sustainability cause campaign. Similar examples are Avon Cosmetics' campaign against breast cancer and Mainland Cheese New Zealand's support for the

Yellow Eyed Penguin Trust. In this way, cause-related marketing is an indirect form of corporate sponsorship. It is often used as part of an integrated marketing campaign since it relies on advertising as well as public relations.

celebrity branding Where the name of a celebrity becomes associated with that of a particular product. The aim is that the celebrity can bring glamour or strength to a particular product, and sometimes the brand can bring a particular strength to the celebrity. By wearing the brand the celebrity becomes the face of the brand. The footballer David Beckham became synonymous with Adidas, Pepsi and Vodafone, all distinct and unique products with their own consumers. One of David Beckham's Pepsi commercials features him with Beyoncé Knowles and Jennifer Lopez. Celebrity branding and endorsement has become one of the fastest growth areas of marketing in the early twenty-first century.

celebrity endorsement When an advertisement features a well-known and respected personality who uses a particular product. The celebrity needs to be chosen with care as so to be meaningful to the target group. *See also* ENDORSEMENT ADVERTISING.

centrally determined economy An economy that is planned and controlled by a central administration, as in the former Soviet Union. State authorities, not market forces, determine what sorts of goods and services are produced, in what quantities and how they are priced and allocated. Centrally determined economies are usually contrasted with market economies. Current centrally determined economies include North Korea and Belarus.

Centre for Corporate Public Affairs (Australia) A membership-based organization that acts as a knowledge centre supporting the strategic development of the public affairs function within Australian business and government. The centre comprises major corporations and organizations, many trading internationally, in Asia, Australia and New Zealand. Established in 1990, it is the only organization of its type in the Asia-Pacific region to support, advance and research corporate public affairs as a management function, encompassing government, media and stakeholder relations, corporate social responsibility/corporate citizenship, issues management, internal communications and reputation management.

centrespread A double-page spread at the centre of a publication. Usually regarded as a desirable position since it occupies one continuous sheet of paper, enjoying the advantages both of extra size and prime positioning.

certificate of origin Used to identify source of goods or materials. Useful for economic trading or political reasons, particularly where some privilege is granted in respect of certain producers or where restriction upon movement of goods has been imposed.

chain store One of a number of retail outlets with the same name, owned and managed by one company, with central buying offices and centrally managed marketing, advertising and merchandising. F. W. Woolworth was one of the pioneers of the corporate chain store, opening his first store in Utica, New York State, which failed, and the same year starting a five-and-ten-cent store at Lancaster, Pennsylvania, which led to the development of an international retailing business. The grocery business is increasingly dominated by chain stores – for example Tesco, Sainsbury, Morrison's and Asda (Wal-Mart) in the UK, Wal-Mart, Kroger, Home Depot and Kmart in the USA, and Carrefour in France. Chains may also be formed by voluntary associations of retailers grouped around a wholesaler, such as IGA (USA), Spar (UK) and Tip Top (NZ). The fastest emerging market for retail chains is China, where Wal-Mart, Carrefour and Tesco are active. *See also* FRANCHISE; RETAILING; WOOLWORTH'S.

channel of communication Any particular link between a communicator, e.g. an advertiser, and a receiver, e.g. a potential customer.

channel of distribution Means by which goods pass from the manufacturer or supplier to the END USER (consumer), via distributors, wholesalers and retailers.

chaos theory The study of phenomena which appear random, but in fact have an element of regularity which can be described mathematically. It is used to understand different marketing systems and the impact of technological change.

Chartered Institute of Marketing (CIM) The world's largest professional marketing body, with over 50,000 members in 130 countries. It aims to define the marketing standards that operate in the UK and champions best practice worldwide. Its objective is to develop the marketing profession, maintain professional standards and improve the skills of marketing practitioners, enabling them to deliver exceptional results for their organizations. The CIM provides membership, qualifications and training to marketing professionals around the world. The CIM defines marketing as 'the management process responsible for identifying, anticipating and satisfying consumer requirements profitably'.

chatroom An Internet site where a group of people meet regularly to discuss topics of common interest. Most chats take place in real time (they are synchronous), but it is possible to carry on asynchronous conversations, where the messages are stored for later scrutiny, as with BLOG listings, BULLETIN BOARDS and mailing lists.

cherry picking A buyer selection of only a few items from one vendor's line and others from another line, failing to purchase a complete line or classification of merchandise from one resource. It also sometimes describes a customer's tendency to buy only items on sale.

chi-square test A statistical significance test based on frequency of occurrence. It is applicable to both qualitative attributes and quantitative variables. Among its many uses, the most common are tests of hypothesized probabilities or probability distributions (goodness of fit), statistical dependence or independence (association) and common population (homogeneity).

chief executive officer (CEO) The executive who is responsible for a company's operations and activities. This officer has day-to-day management responsibility and operates to the agreed strategy and plan of the board of directors or trustees.

chopsticks marketing Used predominantly by Chinese, Japanese, Koreans and Vietnamese, chopsticks are a pair of table utensils consisting of two slender sticks originally of bamboo or bone but now frequently of metal or plastic. 'Chopsticks' marketing to East Asian consumers involves knowing and identifying the local customs, traditions, values and the aspects of consumer behaviour they will influence. Success is also dependent on how well a marketer harnesses his or her networks, including government officials, religious bodies, suppliers, distributors and the consumers. A deep appreciation of local consumer cultural values is the key to chopsticks marketing.

circular A piece of printed matter distributed to a defined group of people.

circulation The average number of copies distributed of a print publication. For outdoor advertising this refers to the total number of people who have an opportunity to observe a billboard or poster. The term sometimes is used for broadcast as well, but the term 'audience' is used the most frequently.

citation A citation tells a reader the source for information you have included in your writing, such as your textbook, the lab manual, a reference book or an article published in a journal. A citation should guide the reader to the references, where the reader can find the full bibliographical information on the source.

classified advertising The grouping together of (usually small type-set or semi-display) advertisements into categories or classifications, e.g. 'for sale' or 'situations vacant'.

clearance sale Goods offered at reduced prices to clear surpluses or end-of-season stock. Loss of profit in such sales is balanced by an increase in liquidity, which provides resources for new investment.

clearinghouse A central operation for processing transactions and for collecting, storing and disseminating information. Clearinghouses are frequently used to receive and process payments or cheques. For example, a group of banks might use a clearinghouse to receive cheques and charge cheque amounts against the appropriate accounts. With reference to the Internet a clearinghouse is a service bureau used by Internet marketers to verify the legitimacy of online credit card charges by validating the card number and checking account balances. These clearinghouses may also authorize charges, reconcile and settle accounts and handle charge backs.

click-through An advertising banner or text which is linked to the advertiser's website. When a web user clicks on it with a mouse cursor, he or she 'clicks through' or is redirected to the advertiser's website. Each such event is measured as one 'click-through', also known as 'ad click', and is used as a way of charging the advertiser. When the advertiser scans their log files and detects that a web user has visited the advertiser's site from the content site by clicking on the banner ad, the advertiser sends the content provider a small amount of money as payment for the service. This payback system is often how the content provider is able to pay for Internet access to supply the content in the first place. *See also* BANNER AD; CONVERSION RATE.

click-through rate (CTR) The average number of click-throughs per hundred ad impressions, expressed as a percentage. CTRs typically range from 0.5 per cent for banner ads to 3.0 per cent for text links.

closed-circuit television (CCTV) A television broadcasting system restricted to subscribers and not available to the general public. Frequently used for televising major sporting events in real time. CCTV is now widely used for monitoring the security of private properties, workplaces and public areas.

London is reputed to have more CCTV cameras than any other major city in the world, primarily for security reasons but also to monitor traffic flow. CCTV has played a vital role in providing evidence on many terrorist attacks.

closed-ended questions Those questions that can be answered finitely by either 'yes' or 'no'. Closed-ended questions can include presuming, probing or leading questions. By definition, these questions are restrictive and can be answered in a few words. They are quick and require little time investment. However, there are disadvantages: responses may be incomplete; more time may be required with inarticulate respondents; they can be leading and hence irritating or even threatening to the respondents; they can result in misleading assumptions/conclusions about the respondents' information need; they discourage disclosure. *See also* OPEN-ENDED QUESTIONS.

closure The process whereby individuals will complete or close a stimulus which is incomplete. This tendency is intrinsic to the Gestalt school of psychology, which argues that there is a basic human drive to see things as a whole so that missing information will be supplied by the respondent in order to make the stimulus complete and meaningful. Closure is widely used in advertising both to involve the subject in the advertisement, which encourages learning and retention, and as a means of reminding/reinforcing earlier, more complete manifestations of the ad's message.

club plan selling An arrangement in which a consumer is awarded prizes or granted discount buying privileges by getting new customers to join the club. The club is the group of customers served by the selling organization, and one joins by making purchases. It is regularly used as a technique to promote subscriptions of book clubs and not-for-profit organizations.

cluster analysis A statistical method used to analyse complex data and identify key subgroupings that emerge and share common features and patterns of activity. It is a form of multivariate analysis and widely used in marketing to define different groups and preferences of consumers and users. It is also widely used by pollsters to assess voter attitudes to particular policy positions and the perceptions of party leaders.

co-sponsorship Shared sponsorship of a broadcast programme, cultural or sporting event by two or more non-competing advertisers.

code Any symbol used for classifying marketing data so that it can be processed or analysed in a more convenient way, e.g. for transferring data from a questionnaire to a software system such as Microsoft's Excel or SPSS.

code of ethics A code of practice setting out the ethical standards adopted by an organization and expected of its employees. Well-known voluntary codes of ethics exist in many multinational companies such as Procter and Gamble and are frequently used in the public and not-for-profit sectors.

code of practice Laid-down conditions under which business should be conducted in a particular area of activity. In marketing, perhaps the best known is the Code of Advertising Practice (CAP), but the UK Market Research Society and the Chartered Institute of Marketing also publish codes. Similar codes govern practice in sales promotion (issued by International Chambers of Commerce).

coding A general term used to describe the procedure for classifying objects in terms of some predetermined factor such as age or income level. In market research, it refers to the classifying of data to make it amenable to subsequent analysis. In the case of producers, the BARCODE used in retailing is a

unique number which identifies a product so that it can be processed by EPOS equipment.

cognition An individual's understanding of an object or concept derived from their own perceptions, attitudes, beliefs, learned behaviour and needs (conscious and subconscious).

cognitive consistency The innate human tendency to seek out stimuli that are consistent with one's beliefs and attitudes and to censor or limit one's exposure to those that are inconsistent with the same beliefs and attitudes.

cognitive dissonance A condition first proposed by the psychologist Leon Festinger in 1956. Cognitive dissonance arises from conflicting cognitions. Cognitive dissonance is the perception of incompatibility between two cognitions, which for the purpose of cognitive dissonance theory can be defined as any element of knowledge, attitude, emotion, belief or value, as well as a goal, plan or an interest. It is a state of mental conflict caused by taking an action which is in direct opposition to a particular belief or attitude. In marketing, an example would be pre- or post-purchase anxiety as to the advisability of having made a particular choice, usually for more expensive goods.

cognitive map Is a map of the mental model and belief systems that humans use to make sense of their everyday environment. The technique is broadly based on George Kelly's theory of personal constructs and the phrase is believed to have been first coined by Tolman (1948). It is used extensively in marketing to understand decision-making and to plan retail location strategies.

cohort A group of participants initially identified as having one or more characteristics in common whose activities and development are tracked over time. This term may refer to any group of persons who are born at about the same time and share common historical or cultural experiences. A group of students who are attending and completing a particular course such as an MBA may be termed a 'cohort'.

cold call A personal visit or telephone call to somebody you don't know, or know only slightly, for the purpose of selling that person something.

collateral marketing strategies These occur when a firm's SEGMENTATION strategies accidentally hit the wrong target market as suggested by the late A. Smithee.

colour separation Photographic process whereby the colours in an illustration are filtered to produce a set of three or four negatives from which printing plates are made.

column inch A measurement of an area of display advertising in publications, derived from the width of a column of type multiplied by its depth. Column centimetres now apply in practice.

commercial Advertisement, announcement, spot or message aired on television, radio or Internet which is paid for by an advertiser.

commercial break Scheduled break in television or radio programming for the insertion of commercials.

commercial counterfeiting TRADEMARK and trade name piracy, which may include designs, models and copyrights.

commission 1 The agreed financial share of a transaction accruing to a salesperson or selling agent responsible or initiating or introducing business. **2** A term used to describe the discount allowed to an advertising agency on behalf of clients.

commoditization The process of becoming a commodity. Microchips, for example, started out as a highly specialized technical innovation, priced at a premium and earning their makers a high profit on each chip. Now chips are largely homogeneous: the same chip can be used for many things. Some economists argue that in today's economy the faster pace of innovation will make the process of commoditization increasingly common.

commodity A basic product which is capable of little or no differentiation and so is generally sold purely on the basis of price in accordance with the theory of competition. Agricultural products, raw materials and a number of fabricated products such as chemicals and steel qualify as commodities and call for the addition of value-added services if the supplier is to avoid straight price competition.

communications mix A component of the MARKETING MIX. It includes all techniques available to the marketer which may be put into a mix designed to deliver a message to the target group of buyers, customers or consumers. These techniques can include PERSONAL SELLING, TELE-MARKETING, E-MARKETING, ADVERTISING, DIRECT MARKETING, PACKAGING, SALES PROMOTION and PUBLIC RELATIONS. *See also* CALL PLANNING; INTEGRATED MARKETING COMMUNICATIONS.

communications research Research aimed at optimizing the effectiveness of communications through pre-testing and post-testing of various aspects of the COMMUNICATIONS MIX.

comparative advantage A concept first outlined in the early nineteenth century by David Ricardo in his *Theory of Comparative Advantage*, it describes the ability of a person, company or country to produce a good or service at a lower cost relative to other goods and services. Even though a country may have an absolute advantage over another country, it will still be better specializing in the good or service in which it has a comparative advantage and trading for goods and services it doesn't produce as efficiently. *See also* ABSOLUTE ADVANTAGE.

comparative advertising Advertising that draws attention to one's own product's performance against those of particular competitors in a recognizable form of measurement such as miles per gallon for a car or number of dishes washed for a washing-up liquid. It compares two or more specifically named or recognizably presented brands of the same type of product or service in terms of one or more specific product or service attributes. Direct comparative advertising explicitly names a competitive brand (e.g. Fairy Liquid), and indirect comparative advertising refers to a competitive brand without explicitly naming it (e.g. Brand 'X').

comparative analysis The comparison of quantitative factors relevant to different advertising media or vehicles, based usually on cost factors, taking into account the demographic penetration of different communications or publications.

competition A promotional device whereby prospective purchasers are invited to compete for prizes by submitting solutions to problems along with a required number of 'evidences of purchase'. Competitions nearly always involve tie-breakers in the form of apt descriptions or advertising slogans to adjudicate between winning entries and sometimes to further focus attention on the product, though some competitions offer a multitude of small prizes. These types of competition are usually strictly controlled by gambling legislation.

Competition Commission An independent public body established by the UK Competition Act of 1998. It replaced the Monopolies and Mergers Commission on 1 April 1999. The Commission conducts in-depth inquiries into mergers, markets and the regulation of the major regulated industries. Every inquiry is undertaken in response to a reference made to it by another authority – usually by the Office of Fair Trading (OFT) but in certain circumstances the Secretary of State – or by the regulators under sector-specific legislative provisions relating to regulated industries. The Commission has no power to conduct inquiries on its own initiative.

The Enterprise Act 2002 introduced a new regime for the assessment of mergers and markets in the UK. In most merger and market references the Commission is responsible for making decisions on the competition questions and for making

and implementing decisions on appropriate remedies. Under the legislation which the Act replaces, the Commission had to determine whether matters were against the public interest. The public interest test is replaced by tests focused specifically on competition issues. The new regime also differs from the previous regime, where the Commission's power in relation to remedies was only to make recommendations to the Secretary of State.

There are specialist panels for utilities, telecommunications, water and newspapers. The utilities panel is the specialist panel for gas and electricity inquiries.

competitive advantage An advantage that one firm has relative to competing firms. It usually originates in a core competency. To be really effective, the advantage must be: difficult to mimic; unique; sustainable; superior to the competition; and applicable to multiple situations.

competitive analysis The collection and interpretation of real-world data to yield a deep understanding of the characteristics and dynamics of customers and competitors within a marketplace. It is intended to equip businesses with information to aid in decision-making regarding potential issues and opportunities by providing insight into the nature of their strategic landscapes. It is an integral element of the SWOT ANALYSIS, through which a firm seeks to identify the strengths and weaknesses of rival firms. This includes all elements of the competitors' MARKETING MIX and goes well beyond direct comparison of financial performance indicators.

competitive environment In marketing encompasses the complete range of competitor organizations competing in the same market for a product.

competitive strategy How an organization chooses to compete within a market, with particular regard to the relative positioning and strategies of competitors.

competitor analysis A study of a firm's major competitors. While a firm may have many competitors – especially if it is operating in several different markets – it is very useful to analyse in depth a few close competitors. This will provide insight into those resources that set a firm apart from others and make it a formidable opponent. Some rival firms may have strong brand names or unique technology protected by patents or cost advantages that enable them to achieve superior profits. Large organizations have dedicated departments constantly monitoring leading competitors, whereas smaller firms tend to collect information more informally through meeting customers and suppliers.

competitor mapping This gives information on the characteristics and dynamics of competitors, gives personal insights into the major players, points to inefficiencies in the market ripe for exploiting and advises on optimal market positioning. Competitor mapping helps to indicate which market segments to pursue and how best to position a brand. These maps enable businesses to develop strategies to maximize brands' potential and to help determine which are the right messages to convey to the marketplace.

complementary products Products sold separately but dependent on each other for sales performance.

conative stage Consumer decision-making models suggest that a customer moves from a state of ignorance or unawareness of an organization and its products or services to ultimately making a purchase by passing through three main stages: cognitive, affective and conative. The conative stage is that which elicits some action by the consumer. Action may include information-seeking, product trial and actual purchase of the product or service by the potential consumer. There are marketing techniques available which are more likely to initiate action in the conative stage. These include personal selling, sales promotion and forms of DIRECT MARKETING such as DIRECT MAIL and TELEMARKETING.

concentrated marketing One of three basic marketing strategies (the other two being differentiated and undifferentiated).

A strategy in which a company tries to reach only a single target market. *See also* DIFFERENTIATED MARKETING; UNDIFFERENTIATED MARKETING.

concentration ratio A ratio which shows the range of large organizations that dominate a particular industry or alternatively how the sector is dominated by a number of SMEs (Small to Medium Enterprises). There are a number of ratios used which can be based on turnover, profit margin and capital employed which all aid analysis. The most frequent methods used in marketing are normally variations on the 80:20 principle and market share.

concept testing The process used in marketing to evaluate the effectiveness of a new creative promotion method or new product. This allows for the promotion or product to be refined and target best response rates and markets.

conclusion The final section of a written document, in which the writer ties together what was presented in the passage, summing up the main point, explaining how the thesis was proven and successfully closing the discussion. The conclusion is often the most difficult part to write, and many writers feel that they have nothing left to say after having presented points proving their thesis in the body of the paper. However, the conclusion is often the part of the paper that a reader remembers best and thus must be strong to be effective.

Confederation of British Industry (CBI) The UK's leading independent employers' organization. It represents companies of all sizes and from all sectors of UK business. The CBI's mission is to help create and sustain the conditions in which businesses in the UK can compete and prosper for the benefit of all. It ensures that the government of the day, the European Union and the wider community understand both the needs of British business and the contribution it makes to the well-being of UK society.

conglomerate A company that generally consists of a holding company and a group of subsidiary businesses normally involved in dissimilar markets.

conjoint analysis A statistical method used in market research to evaluate and compare product or service attributes and to discover those most likely to affect buying decisions. It involves the measurement of the collective effects of two or more independent variables (i.e. product attributes, e.g. colour, size, ease of use, cost, etc.) on the classification of a dependent variable ('overall liking', purchase intention, 'best buy', or any other evaluative measurement). The objective of conjoint analysis is to determine what combination of a limited number of attributes is most preferred by respondents. It is used frequently in testing customer acceptance of new product designs and assessing the appeal of advertisements.

conspicuous consumption Term developed by the US sociologist Thorstein Veblen in 1899 in his book *The Theory of the Leisure Class* to define activity by the 'nouveau riche' who made purchases to influence upper-class families and individuals. The phenomenon is not a new one in that throughout history conspicuous consumption has been made to influence others. More recently YUPPIES and footballers are groups that have expressed themselves through conspicuous consumption: they do not need to drive a Ferrari or Maserati but they do so to display their wealth and associated power. The Neiman Marcus catalogue, based in the USA, is famed as one of the leading purveyors of opulent consumption and in 2007 had on offer a private show with Elton John for $1.5 million.

constant (a) A measure or value that remains the same for all units of analysis. (b) A quantity that does not change value in a particular context or setting.

construct validity The extent to which variables accurately measure constructs of interest. In other words, how well are the variables operationalized, and do the operations really get at the things we are trying to measure? How well can one generalize from operations to constructs? In practice, construct validity is used to describe a scale, index or other measure of a variable that correlates with measures of other variables in ways that are predicted by, or make sense according to, a theory of how the variables are related.

consumer Strictly, the ultimate user of a product or service, the person who derives the satisfaction or the benefit offered. The 'consumer' is not necessarily the customer, since there are often 'customers' in the buying distribution chain. Moreover, the consumer is frequently not the person who makes the buying decision; for instance, in the case of many household products, a parent and normally the mother may make the purchase, but consumption or use is by the whole family. 'Consumer' is not normally applied to the purchase of industrial goods and services, where the customer is usually a corporate body and frequently the term END USER is applied. Nevertheless, consumable goods are sold to industry for corporate purposes.

consumer attitudes *See* ATTITUDES.

consumer buyer behaviour The behaviour of individuals when buying goods and services for their own use or for private consumption. The buying and consuming of goods and services roughly involves pre-purchase, purchase and post-purchase stages of consumer buyer behaviour. In most buying situations, consumers progress through a decision-making process that results in various buying decisions in relation to product and brand choice, shop/dealer choice, purchase time, methods of payment, level of service and so on. *See also* CONSUMER DECISION-MAKING PROCESS.

consumer buying power Available discretionary income; the surplus after financial commitments have been met, but including those amounts currently committed via discretionary agreements such as hire-purchase, credit sale or bank loan repayments, which will eventually become available for future expenditure, and excluding taxation, rates and any other obligatory calls upon income that the consumer has no power to evade.

consumer cooperative Cooperatives are member-owned, member-governed businesses that operate for the benefit of their members according to common principles agreed upon by the international cooperative community. In co-ops, members share resources to bring about economic results that are unobtainable by an individual on their own. Most simply put, a cooperative is a business 1) voluntarily owned by the people who use it, and 2) operated for the benefit of its members.

Most food co-ops are consumer cooperatives, which means that retail co-ops are owned by the people who shop at the stores. Members exercise their ownership by patronizing the store and voting in elections. The members elect a board of directors to hire, guide and evaluate the general manager who runs day-to-day operations. All co-ops contain the following elements:

- owned and governed by their primary users (the member-owners);
- democratically governed (one member, one vote);
- they are businesses, not clubs or associations;
- adhere to internationally recognized principles.

Consumer cooperatives are very different from privately owned 'discount clubs', which charge annual fees in exchange for a discount on purchases. The 'club' is not owned or governed by the 'members' and the profits of the business go to the investors, not to members. In a cooperative, the members own the business and the profits belong to the community of members.

The specific goals of a cooperative are determined by its members, but all cooperatives adhere to the principles of cooperation that are based on the practices of the first successful consumer cooperative, founded in 1844 in Rochdale, England. There are consumer, producer co-ops (usually agricultural) and worker-owned cooperatives. There are also housing co-ops, health care co-ops (the original HMOs were co-ops) and financial co-ops (credit unions).

The overall goal of the cooperative movement is to create organizations that serve the needs of the people who use them. Cooperative businesses provide goods and services in a way that keeps community resources in the community. The growth of wholefood retail cooperatives to meet consumer demand has been significant in the last decade in the US and UK.

consumer decision-making process The buying operations and the stages in which a buyer (individual or household) may be involved when making purchases. These stages are usually referred to in complex models of consumer buyer behaviour as problem recognition, information search, information evaluation, purchase decisions and post-purchase evaluation. *See also* CONSUMER BUYER BEHAVIOUR.

consumer durables Goods which are intended for mass markets but are not in fact consumed immediately but have a long-lasting life, e.g. fridges, washing machines, cars, furniture. *See also* WHITE GOODS.

consumer focus group A group of actual or potential users of a product, usually six to eight in number, formed to discuss a topic under the guidance of a moderator, a person who directs and administers the discussion. This is a QUALITATIVE RESEARCH technique and is widely used in NEW PRODUCT DEVELOPMENT and political polling on voter attitudes and perceptions. *See also* QUALITATIVE RESEARCH.

consumer goods Products or merchandise intended for use or consumption by individuals, as opposed to organizations, companies or businesses.

consumer groups Groups comprised of individuals united to address concerns regarding the purchase and use of specific products or services. Consumer groups aim to protect people from unsafe products, false advertising, pollution and other examples of corporate abuse.

consumer learning Most consumer behaviour is gained from experience, and consumer learning can be defined as a trend, change or modification of perceptions, attitudes and behaviours resulting from previous learned experiences in similar situations. The prime stimulus response theories consider learning as the development of behaviour from the result of exposure to stimuli and consequently consumer behaviour is conditioned by that experience. This implies that consumers respond to marketing cues or stimuli as a function of their drives/needs, which determine when, where and how they respond. Cognitive theories view learning as a process of restructuring individual cognitions with respect to specific problems.

consumer magazine Publication both in print and increasingly in electronic media versions for consumers associated with publishing impartial advice, test results and independent reviews on tangible and intangible products such as services and issues that affect the end user.

Well-known consumer organizations that publish these type of magazines include in the UK, *Which?* and in the US, *FDA Consumer* magazine and *Consumer Reports* magazine.

consumer marketing The marketing of goods to individual consumers rather than organizations. Consumer marketing is aimed at the general public and promotes products directly to the consumer rather than via intermediaries.

consumer needs Reference to any desire or requirement a person (consumer) might have, whether existing and perceptible, or latent and unrecognized. The determination and evaluation of consumer needs could be said to be at the root of the MARKETING CONCEPT from which all subsequent activities develop. *See also* CONSUMER WANTS.

consumer panels A sample of consumers that may be used as regular reference point, often asked questions on the same topic and at different points in time. Consumer panels provide a comparison with previous results provided by the same panel, and this is seen as being integral to continuous research. Consumer panels are frequently asked what their purchase preferences are, and this is built into product planning. *See also* FOCUS GROUPS.

consumer perceptions Consumers are exposed to a multitude of stimuli on a daily basis which they endeavour to make sense of through the perception process – which may be defined as the result of interaction between stimuli and individual/personal factors. The perception process is subjective and individuals select, organize and interpret stimuli and information according to their beliefs and attitudes. Selection in the receptive process limits the number of stimuli that consumers comprehend and pay attention to.

consumer preferences Collective consumer scales devised to indicate relative levels of preference for available products and services.

consumer price Accepted retail selling price for a particular type of product or service.

consumer price index (CPI) An index of the average price of goods and services that consumers purchase, used to measure the cost of living or inflation in a particular economy.

consumer profile Household, domestic, cultural and demographic characteristics and details of consumers, including their hopes, aspirations and expectations for the future.

consumer protection The regulations and laws which protect consumers that are now part of most developed countries' legal framework. The legislation has largely been driven by changes in consumer awareness and attitudes.

consumer research The study of consumer attitudes, motives, habits and behaviour in relation to their buying of products and services.

consumer satisfaction The satisfaction of a consumer's wants is an essential part of the marketing operation. Fundamentally, a person buys (acquires) a product or service for the satisfaction it will provide. This may be tangible or intangible (as indeed will be the 'want'), but providing a product gives consumer satisfaction, a main aim of the MARKETING CONCEPT has been fulfilled.

consumerism The influence of the consumer or general public as end users of products or services on the way producers manufacture, source, package or supply products. Consumers exert more pressure on suppliers as they become more environmentally and socially aware. Demand has been rising for products that are high-quality, ethically-sourced and supplied, priced competitively and are safe and increasingly sustainable. Green consumerism is that which is particularly associated with improving and sustaining the environment through putting pressure on producers and suppliers to supply sustainable and biodegradable products.

consumption The process of using consumer products in order to satisfy desires and real or imagined needs so that the products are used up or transformed in such a manner as to be neither reusable nor recognizable in their original form.

consumption function The relationship between total consumption, expenditure and income of the economy. Three broad theories have been suggested to explain variations in aggregate consumption functions: the ABSOLUTE INCOME HYPOTHESIS, the RELATIVE INCOME HYPOTHESIS and the PERMANENT INCOME HYPOTHESIS. It calculates the amount of total consumption in an economy.

contact rate The proportion of times a targeted consumer, voter or user in a household is contacted in a market survey. Rates can vary depending upon access to known telephone numbers; for instance, mobile phones have eroded the representativeness of landline telephone users as a sample size.

containerization Is a system of intermodal cargo transport using standard ISO containers that can be loaded on container ships, railway carriages and road lorries and wagons. There are three standard lengths: 20 ft (6.1 m), 40 ft (12.2 m) and 45 ft (13.7 m). Container capacity (of ships, ports, etc.) is measured in twenty-foot equivalent units (TEU).

Containerization is one of the dramatic methods of storage and transshipment that transformed international logistics and revolutionized freight forwarding and handling in the twentieth century. Malcolm McLean can reasonably claim to be the man who conceived the idea of container shipping to replace the traditional breaking bulk method of handling dry goods. Numerous earlier efforts to ship freight in containers had failed to result in lower costs. McLean realized that to improve efficiency, the container needed to be easily transferable from one method of transport to another as part of a comprehensive system. Containers produced a huge reduction in port handling costs, contributing significantly to lower freight charges and, in turn, boosting trade flows. Almost every manufactured product humans consume spends some time in a container.

content analysis A method of research analysis used to identify the main factors and themes contained within a body of data, usually unstructured qualitative interviews, or in written or broadcast material such as newspapers, magazines and radio and television broadcasts. This method is used extensively to analyse agendas and content in advertising and political campaigns.

content integration In Internet marketing, this refers to the advertising woven into editorial content or placed in a special context on the page, typically appearing on key portal websites and large destination sites. Is also referred to as web advertorial and funded or sponsored content.

contextual marketing An Internet term which refers to showing users adverts based on terms which they have used in an online search. Advanced contextual marketing suggests to the user adverts based upon their usage patterns of a particular website or individual's web-browsing habits. Amazon uses user knowledge to suggest alternative books and goods to purchase; this approach is based upon information gathered from the individual user's activities on the site and previous buying patterns.

contingency coefficient A statistic used to indicate the association between the rows and columns of a contingency table. This is a correlation coefficient between two nominal variables.

contingency plan That part of a marketing plan which attempts to anticipate eventualities, both negative and positive, and to make provision for them. Its sets out an organized, planned and coordinated course of action to be followed when things don't go as planned or if an expected result fails to materialize. The plan contains procedures for emergency response, back-up and post-disaster recovery. See also CRISIS MANAGEMENT.

continuity In advertising continuity normally describes a script for a radio or television commercial or the use of a consistent theme throughout a promotional campaign and can be the continuous, consistent use of an advertising media plan. In direct marketing continuity is a type of sale that comprises a series of sales made over time. A closed-end continuity has a definite number of items to be delivered to the buyer. An open-end continuity has no fixed number of shipments and will continue until the buyer is cancelled for non-payment or withdraws from the continuity programme. For example, encyclopaedias are usually sold as close-end continuities; cookbooks are frequently sold as open-end continuities. Continuity subscribers can stop buying at any time, unlike club members, who must fulfil a member commitment prior to cancelling. However, open-end continuity buyers are much more likely to cancel.

continuous innovation An innovation that does not involve a completely new product such as a computer or light bulb. Rather, new products such as Colgate Whitening Toothpaste or KitKat Bites can be referred to as continuous innovations of an existing product line. See also INNOVATION.

continuous panel A consumer panel that involves participation from the same respondents repeatedly, over time.

contribution analysis A method of estimating the difference between product selling prices and their variable costs per unit, so calculating the extent to which each unit contributes to fixed costs and profits. See also ACTIVITY-BASED COSTING.

control The activity used to ensure that actual results are consistent with those budgeted or planned. Quality control and cost control are obvious examples of situations where the planner will set down clear objectives and standards and then monitor performance to ensure that they are meeting budget and plan. Control also suggests that if results are not meeting targets then remedial action will be taken or else the plan revised to reflect the new conditions.

control group In marketing research, control groups are used as baseline reference points in contrasting and evaluating consumer and user behaviour. For example, marketing researchers assessing the effects of a television advert would divide a group of potential users into two groups and show it to one group and then contrast responses of both groups after the viewing of the ad and assess its effectiveness.

control question A control question is used in a questionnaire as a hidden means of checking the validity of answers to other questions.

convenience goods Those relatively inexpensive, day-to-day items bought by consumers on a regular basis (e.g. food, drink, newspapers, etc). See also FAST-MOVING CONSUMER GOODS.

convenience sample A sample of subjects selected for a study not because they are representative but because it is convenient to use them, for instance when a university academic samples and studies his or her own students. *See also* JUDGEMENT SAMPLING; PROBABILITY SAMPLING; RANDOM SAMPLE.

convenience store A retail outlet the appeal of which is based upon convenience primarily in terms of location, hours of opening and/or the range of products stocked. Frequently purchased consumer goods are bread, milk, newspapers, sandwiches and lunchtime food, etc. Major chains such as Tesco, Marks and Spencer and Sainsbury have opened small specialist units to supply a limited range of food and drink products to meet the growing demand from commuters and office workers in the UK with considerable success.

conversion A positive customer response in response to an advertisement's appeal to purchase or take an appropriate action. A conversion can be a sale, registration, download or donation online, depending on the goal of the particular marketing campaign and the business sector it is operating in.

conversion rate Used for online marketing, this is the ratio of the number of visitors who take a desired action (fill out a form, request information, make a purchase, enter part of a website etc.) to the number of visitors who view the page. The conversion rate is generally given as a percentage. If, for example, twenty people arrive at a certain web page and five request further information (and are therefore considered to be a 'conversion'), then the conversion rate is 25 per cent. The conversion rate is of great significance in e-marketing as it effectively shows the success of the product offering and promotion campaign. *See also* CLICK-THROUGH.

cookie A piece of information sent to a browser by a web server. The browser then returns that information to the web server. This is how some web pages 'remember' your previous visits; for example, an e-commerce site might use a cookie to remember which items you've placed in your online shopping cart. Cookies can also store user preference information, log-in data, etc.

cooperation rate The proportion of eligible respondents who agree to participate in a research study. Rates may vary depending on how partial interviews are considered and unknown eligibility is handled. The cooperation rate can be impacted by the length of the interview, the subject matter and type of person being interviewed.

cooperative An association of persons who join together to carry on an economic activity of mutual benefit, in an egalitarian fashion. The values and principles of cooperation are periodically reviewed and updated by the International Cooperative Alliance, the worldwide apex organization for the COOPERATIVE MOVEMENT. This method is frequently used in the wholefood and organic food businesses.

cooperative movement The cooperative movement in the UK dates from 1844, when the Rochdale Society of Equitable Pioneers was founded as a retail grocery (food) shop by a group of consumers, based on open membership and democratic control. Members shared the profits from the retailing business in the form of dividends calculated from the amount of money each member had spent in the Society's shop. The Rochdale cooperative model spread throughout Europe. In the UK the Co-operative Wholesaling Society, serving an extensive network of retail 'Co-op' shops, is still a significant factor in retailing, with over 2,000 stores, and is in the process of acquiring more and focusing its activities on convenience stores. Some consumer and agricultural cooperatives were established in the USA in the nineteenth century, but the movement did not succeed. In recent years there have been some attempts to re-establish small-scale cooperative retailing. The New Zealand Dairy group of companies was a farmer-owned cooperative which converted itself into the Fonterra company and has over 11,000 farmer cooperative shareholders and controls the leading brand Anchor. *See also* COOPERATIVE.

copy In marketing communications refers to the written text used by advertising, in magazines and newspapers, on websites and as scripts in radio and television programming.

copy brief A detailed statement of aim(s) in relation to the preparation of an advertisement, or series of advertisements, with the purpose of ensuring that copywriters are aware of their purpose and that their submissions may be evaluated by continuous reference to it.

copy test Research conducted for advertising messages to measure the effectiveness before the ad is finalized and launched.

copyright International legal concept granting protection by law to authors, artists, designers, musicians and publishers for their original work. A copyright protects the work from being copied, reprinted, sold or used by someone else without the consent of the owner or owners of the copyright of the work.

copywriter The creator of text, words and concepts for use in advertisements shown or used in news media, magazines, radio, television and websites. Copywriters are usually employed by advertisers, advertising agencies, marketing communication companies and other organizations where advertising is created and developed.

core competency A particular area of skill and competence that is critical to a business achieving a COMPETITIVE ADVANTAGE. The idea of core competencies was first developed by C. K. Prahalad and G. Hamel.

core strategy The means of achieving marketing objectives, including target markets, competitor targets and COMPETITIVE ADVANTAGE.

corporate advertising A form of advertising that covers the corporate vision, core values and organizational culture of an organization. The goals of corporate advertising include building the image of a responsible corporate entity, attracting good talent and reinforcing the corporate mission. Corporate advertising becomes more important during expansion, diversification, mergers and acquisitions and the raising of capital. It has a closer affinity to PUBLIC RELATIONS activity than to marketing. *See also* INSTITUTIONAL ADVERTISING.

corporate brand strategy The name applied to the strategy where the firm uses its name as an umbrella term or brand for all of its products.

corporate communications Strictly, this term is synonymous with PUBLIC RELATIONS. It takes in all communications activities that contribute to the reputation or image of an organization. This is not an end in itself, but must be an integral contributor to the business or corporate objectives. The target audiences or publics might be said to be all those groups of people who have a stakeholding in the business. The term is often linked, incorrectly, with media or press relations, or editorials and publicity.

corporate culture The way the people in an organization behave, or are expected to behave, and which may colour its perception by the outside world. Increasingly, businesses are setting down the culture they would like to apply and then producing a programme designed to achieve a culture change. Corporate culture or organizational culture comprises the attitudes, values, beliefs, norms and customs of an organization. Whereas organizational structure is relatively easy to draw and describe, organizational culture is less tangible and is difficult to measure. Senior management may try to determine a corporate culture. They may wish to impose corporate values and standards of behaviour that specifically reflect the objectives of the organization. In addition, there will be an internal culture within the workforce, who will have their own behavioural quirks and interactions which, to an extent, affect the whole system. *See also* CULTURE.

corporate governance Corporate

governance is the system by which business corporations and not-for-profit organizations are directed and controlled. The corporate governance structure specifies the distribution of rights and responsibilities among different participants in the corporation, such as the board (in not-for-profit, trustees), managers, shareholders and other stakeholders, and spells out the rules and procedures for making decisions on corporate affairs. By doing this, it also provides the structure through which the company objectives are set, and the means of attaining those objectives and monitoring performance. Corporate governance can also be narrowly defined as the relationship of a business organization or not-for-profit organization to its shareholders or stakeholders and more broadly its relationship to society. *See also* ETHICS.

corporate identity The 'message sources' by which an organization develops and enhances the way it is perceived by its various publics. It is commonly thought to refer only to the corporate logo, and its use on letter headings, brochures, uniforms, etc., but equally important are corporate culture, customer care, third-party endorsement and so on.

corporate image The image which is conjured up by mention of a company's name. This can be positive or negative, weak or strong, and it is argued by some that it is the sole purpose of any PUBLIC RELATIONS campaign. Its value is in increasing the propensity to buy, to join a company or organization or to acquire share, and, in general, in facilitating the profitable operation of a business.

corporate logo Company emblems or signs, many of which have become as familiar and powerful as brand names. Leading logos include Royal Dutch Shell's clam shell and Mercedes' three-pointed star in a circle.

corporate mission A short, succinct statement by a company declaring what business they are in and who their customer is. By offering this succinct focus on the core activities and interests of the organization, it provides direction for future corporate development.

corporate planning Setting down of a long-term plan of development in a methodical manner, based upon all the available facts, in relation to the ultimate goals of an organization and the ways it intends to achieve them. Time scales vary from three to ten years (even more in certain industries). Fundamental to the preparation of a corporate plan is the need to define exactly the area of business in which to be operative. A second requirement is that any such plan be flexible, subject to regular updating as events move to change the criteria upon which it is based, and, probably most importantly, regularly evaluated for effectiveness. *See also* BUSINESS PLAN; CORPORATE STRATEGY.

corporate positioning The place occupied by an organization in the minds of its various groups of stakeholders in relationship to other businesses. The criteria for such positioning can be various, such as quality, value for money, innovation, good employment practice, customer care, and so on. *See also* BRAND POSITIONING.

corporate purchasing Buying by an organization rather than a private individual. The implication here is that the buying decision is a 'corporate' one, i.e. made by a number of people, and may consequently be made upon more objective grounds than many consumer purchases. *See also* DECISION-MAKING UNIT; ORGANIZATIONAL PURCHASING.

corporate social responsibility (CSR) Carroll (1999) in his influential article describes the evolution of modern CSR and suggests *Social Responsibility of the Businessman* (1953) by Howard Bowen as the birthplace of the modern CSR literature. Bowen's work argues that modern businesses accumulate considerable power, have far-reaching influence on people's lives and that businesspeople are responsible for the consequences of their own actions in addition to the usual financial performance accounting and associated statements. These views have largely remained the key framework for CSR thinking until today.

However, this approach has also been rigorously criticized and most prominently in the work of neo-liberal economist Milton Friedman (1970), who argued that businesses' focus must be on generating profits for shareholders. In between these two ideological poles, the more practical approach of 'enlightened self-interest' has gained more attention, for example in Bowd, Harris & Cornellison, 2003, and through the policies of the Commission of the European Communities (2002) – which can be summed up as doing well by doing good. Bowen also raises the important question about what 'responsibilities' should be assumed to be included and proposes public policies as the key point of reference and starting point for CSR.

The evolution of the CSR concept has diversified and developed further, most notably on a conceptual basis. Garriga and Mele (2004) provide a useful map of the current CSR territory, and see four dominant lines of thought. Their mapping is based on Parsons' systems theory, whose foundation – entrenched in functionalism – tends to portray static and uncritical description, but has the logical advantage of capturing 'totality' and outlining distinct areas of action within it. The four dominant lines of thought in CSR they see as:

• The *political approach* of focusing on the responsible use of business power in the political arena represented in the idea of (corporate) citizenship where the organization is seen as a citizen with a certain degree of involvement in the community (Thorne McAlister, Ferrell & Ferrell, 2005).

• The *integrative approach* of focusing on the integration of social demands. Here stakeholder theory is outlined as a balance of the interests of the different stakeholders of the organization. An example is Rowley's (1997) CSR analysis from a network point of view which presents the organization's power and influence as a result of the position emerging from the density of the overall stakeholder network and the centrality of the focal organization.

• The *ethical approach* of focusing on the right thing to do. Several approaches aim to achieve 'common good' with either a philosophical, paternalistic-humanitarian, or sustainability ('Brutland Report') background, or following human rights and other international conventions (e.g. UN Global Compact).

• The *instrumental approach* of focusing on achieving economic objectives through social activities. This comprises cause-related marketing and strategies for competitive advantage. Within the former, two ideas can be separated: strategic investment in a competitive context (Porter & Kramer, 2002), and strategies for the bottom of the economic pyramid (Prahalad & Hammond, 2002).

Taking an overview of the CSR research through the lens of the management discipline, Lockett et al. (2006) describe four dominating areas of CSR study, which at the same time capture an accurate picture of where CSR thinking is historically rooted: business ethics, environmental responsibility, social responsibility and stakeholder approaches. Initially and still dominantly thought as a construct to profit-seeking organizations, CSR has been extended as an umbrella construct integrating other forms of organizations (e.g. associations, non-profits), too – Neves and Bento (2005) even suggest the term 'organisational social responsibility'.

Despite efforts to formalize and regulate CSR-related evaluations, measurements and reporting (e.g. ISO 14000, AA 1000, GRI), the concept and its application largely remains dynamic, diverse and context-specific. It has also been criticized as a modern age branding tool, a 'greenwash' of corporate behaviour, boardroom talk, and a public relations invention (Frankental, 2001). However, CSR is no longer a 'fad' or an 'extra option' but describes a deeper change in looking at organizations and their relationships to their stakeholders (Lewis, 2001). It has spread around the world mainly because of governments retreating partly or completely from directly providing public services in several areas (e.g. utilities, health care, education), civil counter-reactions towards economic globalization (e.g. exploitation in supply chains, decay of urban areas) and new tactics used by stakeholder groups to demand organizational transparency and morally balanced corporate action. Several distinctive approaches and applications exist (see Bowd, Harris and Cornelissen, 2003). Guthey, Langer and Morsing (2006) argue that despite the possibility that CSR might be a management fashion, the CSR concept is of value because it has real consequences in the business world. The growing influence of CSR policies (Bowd et al., 2003) and the rise of a respective consultancy industry (Fernandez Young, Moon & Young, 2003) provide strong support for this argument. In the football context, consulting firm Deloitte and Touche (2005: quoted in Holt, Michie, Oughton, Tacon & Walters, 2005) has recommended that clubs integrate CSR management to insure healthy relationships with their communities. On a global level, the world governing body FIFA has created a CSR unit, even so the general moral integrity of the organization and a number of its 'goodwill' activities (e.g. the Goal Programme) remains doubtful (Jenkins, 2006), which links to occasional scepticism about the general idea of CSR and its application.

Realistically, the CSR concept needs to demonstrate its value to managers in order to be a sustainable management concept itself. Consequently, one stream of CSR research is concerned with the rationality of companies to engage in CSR and their likely strategic benefits. The understanding of how and where CSR can contribute to achieve organizational objectives is grounded in what is known as the 'resource-based view of the firm' in strategic management (Fahy, 2000). This approach stresses the value of intangible and interactive assets of a company as the main competitive factors leading to competitive advantages in the marketplace. Adopting the same approach, Freeman (1984) outlined the concept of 'stakeholder management' as a way of thinking and acting for managers who saw themselves confused by the dynamic nature of environmental changes. The author sees CSR as a building block for the stakeholder concept (Freeman & McVea, 2001). On the other hand, the stakeholder concept is referred to as being the most influential in management studies on CSR. Hence, there is a close intrinsic connection between the two concepts. The stakeholder concept itself has since been treated as a foundation for the theory of an organization (Donaldson & Preston, 1995; Post, Preston & Sachs, 2002) and a framework for relationships between business and society (Rowley, 1997).

References and Sources

Bowd, R., Harris, P. and Cornelison, J. (2003), 'Corporate Social Responsibility: A Schools Approach to an Inclusive Definition and a Research Agenda', 10th Public Relations Symposium, Bled, Slovenia.

Bowen, H. (1953), *Social Responsibility of the Businessmen*, New York: Harper & Row.

Carroll, A. (1999), 'Corporate Social Responsibility: Evolution of a Definitional Construct', *Academy of Management Review*, Volume No. 4, pp. 268–96.

Commission of the European Communities (2002), 'Communication from the Commission concerning Corporate Social Responsibility: A Business Contribution to Sustainable Development', Commission of the European Communities.

Donaldson, Thomas and Preston, Lee E. (1995), 'The Stakeholder Theory of the Corporation: Concepts, Evidence, and Implications', *Academy of Management Review*, Vol. 20, No. 1, p. 71.

Fahy, J. (2000), 'The resource-based view of the firm: Some stumbling blocks on the road to understanding sustainable competitive advantage', *Journal of European Industrial Training*, Vol. 24, Nos 2/3/4, pp. 94–104.

Fernandez Young, A., Moon, J. and Young, R. (2003), 'The UK corporate social responsibility consultancy industry: a phenomenological approach', Research Paper Series, International Centre for Corporate Social Responsibility at Nottingham University.

Frankental, P. (2001), 'Corporate Social Responsibility – "A PR invention"', *Corporate Communications: An International Journal*, Vol. 6, No 1, pp. 18–23.

Freeman, E. (1984), *Strategic Management: A Stakeholder Approach*, Boston, MA: Pitman Bowen.

Freeman, R. E. and McVea, J. (2001), 'A stakeholder approach to strategic management' in Hitt, M. A. and Freeman, R. E. (eds), *Handbook of Strategic Management*, Oxford, UK: Blackwell, pp. 189–207.

Friedman, M. (1970), 'The social responsibility of businesses is to increase its profits', *New York Times Magazine*, 13 September 1970.

Garriga, E. and Mele, D. (2004), 'Corporate social responsibility theories: mapping the territory', *Journal of Business Ethics*, 53, pp. 51–71.

Guthey, E., Langer, R. and Morsing, M. (2006), 'Corporate social responsibility is a management fashion. So what?' in Morsing, M. and Beckmann, S. C. (eds), *Strategic CSR communications*, Copenhagen: DJØF Publishing, pp. 39–60.

Holt, M., Michie, J., Oughton, C., Tacon, R. and Walters, G. (2005). The state of the game – the corporate governance of football clubs, Research paper No. 3, Football Governance Research Centre of Birkbeck University of London.

Jenkins, H. (2006), 'Small business champions for Corporate Social Responsibility', *Journal of Business Ethics*, Vol. 67, No.3.

Lewis, S. (2001), 'Measuring Corporate Reputation', *Corporate Communications: An International Journal*, Vol. 6, No. 1, pp. 31–5.

Lockett, A., Moon, J. and Visser, W. (2006), 'Corporate social responsibility in management research: focus, nature, salience and sources of influence', *Journal of*
Management Studies, Vol. 43, No. 1, pp. 115–36.

Morsing, Mette and Beckmann, Suzanne C. (eds) (2006), *Strategic CSR Communication*, Copenhagen: DJØF Publishing.

Neves, J. and Bento, L. (2005), 'Traditional values and the pressure of transformation' in Habisch, A., Jonker, J., Wegner, M. and Schmidpeter, R. (eds), *Corporate Social Responsibility across Europe*, Berlin: Springer, pp. 303–14.

Porter, M. E. and Kramer, M. R. (2002), 'The Competitive Advantage of Corporate Philanthropy', *Harvard Business Review*, December.

Post, J. E., Preston, L. E. and Sachs, S. (2002), *Redefining the Corporation*, Stanford, CA: Stanford University Press.

Prahalad, C. K. and Hammond, A. (2002), 'Serving the World's Poor Profitably', *Harvard Business Review*, September.

Rowley, T. J. (1997), 'Moving beyond dyadic ties: a network theory of stakeholder influences', *Academy of Management Review*, Vol. 22, No. 4, pp. 887–910.

Thorne McAlister, D., Ferrell, O. C. and Ferrell, L. (2005), *Business and Society – a Strategic Approach to Corporate Citizenship*, Boston, MA: Houghton Mifflin.

corporate strategy The means by which the corporate objectives are to be achieved. It will take in and integrate all the various functional strategies, e.g. marketing, human resources, finance, research and development (R&D) and so on. In short, it is a summary of the corporate plan. *See also* CORPORATE PLANNING.

correlation The extent to which two or more items are related to one another. If the changes are in the same direction, then it is a positive correlation. If they are in opposite directions, then it is a negative correlation.

cost-benefit analysis The appraisal of an investment project that includes all social and financial costs and benefits accruing to the project. The techniques adopted in order to evaluate and decide whether a project should proceed.

cost-effectiveness The measure of most

economic activity in achievement of given objectives.

cost-efficiency The relationship between a MEDIUM's (or a MEDIA SCHEDULE's) audience and the cost of using that medium (or media schedule) to reach a specific audience. For broadcast media, 'cost per TARP' (CPT) is the most common measure of cost-efficiency. For print 'cost per thousand' is most often used to measure cost efficiency.

cost leadership strategy A business strategy in which a company tries to provide a product at a lower cost than any of its competitors.

cost per action (CPA) An online advertising payment model in which payment is based solely on qualifying actions such as sales or registrations.

cost per click (CPC) The cost or cost-equivalent paid per CLICK-THROUGH on the web.

cost per contact analysis The cost to an advertiser or promoter to reach 1,000 members of the target audience with a given appeal or message. The cost is normally obtained by dividing the cost of buying a particular media slot by the size of the audience reached in thousands. The costs of reaching the target audience are measured against the number of sales of a product or service.

cost per inquiry (CPI) CPI is used to evaluate the performance of a promotion and is calculated by dividing the promotion costs by the number of inquiries received. A promotion begins to be profitable at the point revenue expected from the inquiry conversions equals or exceeds promotion costs.

cost per thousand (CPM) The cost of reaching an audience on a per-thousand basis. This is used by media planners as a basis for comparison of the cost of advertising in various media. The CPM is calculated by multiplying the advertising costs by 1,000 and dividing the result by the total audience.

cost-plus pricing The most commonly used pricing method where organizations decide the price to charge by looking at their average costs, and simply adding an element of profit margin.

coupons A sales promotion device which tries to persuade buyers/customers to purchase. They may offer a discount on the first or subsequent purchase of a product/service, or they may need to be collected in order to be redeemed against a future purchase or to receive gifts or cash. Coupons are likely to appeal most to the price-conscious consumer. Redemption rates of coupons are traditionally low.

coverage Generally and at its most basic, this term most frequently describes in marketing any statement of how well a media vehicle can reach a particular market segment, expressed as a percentage.

creaming Selling a product range at a higher-than-average price in order to improve quality, whereby it becomes the accepted purchase of the more affluent members of society.

creative director The head of the creative department in an advertising agency. Responsible for the overall creativity of all the contributing personnel such as COPY-WRITERS and visualizers.

credibility The extent to which claims made for a product or firm are believed by its markets. Exaggerated claims may destroy a product's, or even a company's, credibility.

credibility gap The difference between commonly accepted levels of performance and the expectations aroused by extravagant claims on behalf of a person, organization, product or service.

credit rating The systematic rating of customers for creditworthiness.

crisis management A very well developed process and set of public relations techniques that can be used to manage an organization's marketing communications in order to maintain an organization's CREDIBILITY and good reputation after a major incident has occurred that may impact on the organization in a negative manner. Alternatively referred to as disaster management. *See also* CONTINGENCY PLAN.

critical path analysis A planning technique applied usually to a complex project, in which a large number of variables interrelate and where the failure of any one will set back the entire scheme. Any sub-set the timing of which is critical to the whole project is shown thus in advance, usually in diagrammatic form, and the whole series forms a linear sequence (or critical path) from which the minimum project time can be calculated. *See also* NETWORK ANALYSIS.

CRM (customer relationship management) The management practices, methods and technologies used by organizations to manage their relationships with clients. Information stored on existing customers (and potential customers) is accessed, analyzed and used to this end. Automated CRM processes are frequently used to generate automatic personalized marketing based on the customer information stored in the system. Customer relationship management is a corporate-level strategy, focusing on creating and maintaining relationships with customers. Several commercial CRM software packages are available which vary in their approach to CRM. However, CRM is not a technology itself, but rather a holistic approach to an organization's philosophy, placing the emphasis firmly on the customer.

CRM governs an organization's philosophy at all levels, including policies and processes, front-of-house customer service, employee training, marketing, and systems and information management. CRM systems are integrated end to end across marketing, sales and customer service.

A CRM system should:

- identify factors important to clients;
- promote a customer-oriented philosophy;
- adopt customer-based measures;
- develop end-to-end processes to serve customers;
- provide successful customer support;
- handle customer complaints;
- track all aspects of sales;
- create a holistic view of customers' sales and services information.

Cronbach's alpha A test for a model or survey's internal consistency.

crop To eliminate or cut off specific portions of a photograph or illustration.

cross-elasticity of demand Response in demand for one commodity to a change in the price of another, e.g. when the price of electricity increases, demand for less expensive alternatives, possibly gas or oil, increases.

cross-fade To reduce the volume of one form of sound whilst simultaneously increasing the volume of another. Commonly used in radio and audiovisual media such as TV and movies, where the usage of the term extends also to the gradual replacement of one scene by another.

cross-impact analysis A method of analysing the likely impact that predicted developments (technological, social, political, economic) have on each other. The cross-impact matrix provides the structure for accomplishing the analysis.

cross-subsidization The transfer of assets or services from the regulated part of a public utility to its unregulated affiliates in order to produce an unfair competitive advantage.

cross-tabulations A way of presenting data about two variables in table form so that their interrelationships are more obvious. *See also* BIVARIATE ANALYSIS.

cues Weak stimuli not strong enough to arouse consumer action but which may provide motivation and direction in purchasing. For example, cues in shopping are things such as product colour, flavours and distinctive packaging.

culture The habits, behaviour, beliefs, values and customs of a particular society or community. The term can be applied to an organization or a country, and is an important element in developing a marketing strategy. *See also* CORPORATE CULTURE.

cumulative audience The number of different people who tune into a radio or TV channel in a given time period – often over a week.

customer A person or organization actually making the purchasing decision, not necessarily the 'consumer' or 'user'. Legally, a party to a contract for the sale of goods. A customer is not necessarily the same person as the consumer, as a product or service can be purchased by one individual but consumed and used by another, the consumer.

customer care A MARKETING CONCEPT in which everyone in the whole organization is encouraged to think and act with the customer in mind. It has special significance in service organizations.

customer characteristics Any features which may be used to distinguish a customer or group of customers from any other customer or group of customers. These act as the basis for MARKET SEGMENTATION.

customer churn A measure of customer attrition, defined as the number of customers who discontinue a service during a specified time period divided by the average total number of customers over that same time period. For example, churn rate has been an ongoing concern of telephone and mobile phone services in areas where several companies compete and make it easy to transfer from one service to another. Changes in a business's churn rate can provide feedback for a company as it may indicate customer response to service, pricing, competition and so on, as well as the average length of time an individual remains a customer. As such, churn rate is an important business metric.

customer lifetime value (CLV) A commonly used marketing metric that can forecast the profitability of customers during the entire lifetime of the relationship, as opposed to just the profitability of one transaction.

customer orientation The focusing of the company and organization on the customer and meeting their needs profitably, whether commercial or not for profit. In essence the heart of modern marketing theory and good practice, which argues that the customer is paramount and that maintaining a quality relationship over time with them will stimulate growth and reinvestment in the business. In recent years the ability to deal with cutomer complaints, customer retention and relationship management have all been prioritized in successful businesses and reflect a growing movement to be more marketing-orientated and customer-focused. *See also* MARKETING CONCEPT.

customer relations The approach an organization takes to gaining and retaining customers. Putting customers at the centre of the organization is seen by many as an integral part of organizational effectiveness as much as product quality, pricing, distribution and product differentiation are. At one level, customer relations means keeping customers fully informed, turning complaints into opportunities to build customer loyalty as a result of quality responses and generally listening to customers. At another level, being a customer-focused organization means that all company activities, such as design, packaging, communications, costs, production, and after sales support of a product, are being developed around supporting the customer and that all staff and departments within the organization share this vision. This approach is increasingly being more vigorously applied as a quality differentiator by airlines such as Emirates and Singapore Airlines to attract and retain more business and first-class users.

customer relationship management The development of long-term strategic relationships with key customers who purchase products and services. Customer relationship management seeks to increase an organization's sales by improving customer satisfaction ratings.

customer service An element in a company's product policy, since very few products are sold today that have no customer-service element. Customer service is designed to enhance the appeal of a product, often becoming a way of differentiating a product from its competitors. In general, the more technologically complicated a product is, the more important the service component becomes. In the sales of industrial goods and consumer products such as computers and cars, the service component may be at least as important as the product itself to prospective customers. Customer-service offerings take a variety of forms: after-sales service, such as repair and replacement service and/or guarantees; credit; technical advice; ease of contact (toll-free phone numbers); complaints and adjustments policies; maintenance service and contracts; and information services. Where products are leased to customers, service is an integral part of the leasing agreement. Customer service has as its prime objective the establishment of a lasting relationship between buyer and seller.

cut price A price which offers a discount from the recommended or prevailing market price.

cut-throat competition Competition based on predatory pricing under which one competitor will seek to eliminate another or others by cutting prices well below normal levels and to squeeze out competitors from a particular market. Products are often sold for less than they cost to make and distribute in order to achieve this end.

cyberspace A 'virtual' or conceptual meeting place of online networks, databases, e-mail, Internet and any other electronic forums.

cybersquatting The behaviour of a user who acquires a domain name for the sole purpose of reselling it at a higher price.

cyber-stealth marketing Covert attempts using the Internet to boost brand image, to make websites appear more popular than they are or to manipulate search engine listings.

cycle models Cycle models have been used to explain changes in retailing since 1958, when Malcolm McNair (in 'Significant Trends and Developments in the Post-War Period', in A. Smith (ed.), *Competitive Distribution in a Free High-Level Economy and Its Implications for the University*) first proposed the 'wheel of retailing', a four-stage cycle of: (a) innovation; (b) accelerated development; (c) maturity; (d) decline.

D

DAGMAR A well-known marketing acronym used for setting goals and objectives derived from 'Defining Advertising Goals for Measured Advertising Response', which was coined by Russell Colley in 1961. Originally, it was the title of a book advocating the evaluation of advertising effectiveness by communication goals rather than sales. It is a process widely used to establish overall goals for an advertising campaign so that it is possible to evaluate whether the initial goals have been met.

data Information collected by a researcher or any organized information. (Data is the plural term; the singular is datum.) Data are often seen as being quantitative or statistical in nature, but can often be in many other forms, for instance, transcripts of interviews, photographs or videotapes of social interactions. Non-quantitative data such as transcripts or video tapes are often coded or translated into numbers to make them easier to analyse and quantify.

Primary data are data gathered by the researcher in the act of conducting research. Secondary data are documents, records or specimens that have been collected, or will be collected, solely for non-research purposes and are in existence prior to the beginning of the study.

Data should not be confused with information, which is often gained from data manipulation.

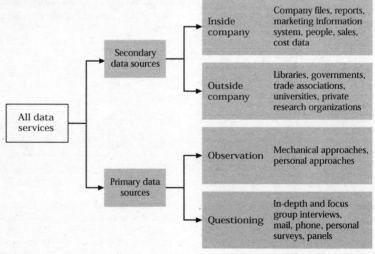

Data

data accuracy The extent which recorded information validly reflects the phenomenon from which it is derived. Inaccuracies most frequently occur from errors of measurement or recording or inadequate transcription.

data analysis The study of quantitative and/or qualitative sets of information to ascertain, establish and evaluate exceptions and trends in consumer or organizational buying behaviour and marketplace patterns. This may involve an assessment of data for current or future problems or opportunities in the marketplace. For instance, the ageing population has a marked preference for automatic gearboxes and assisted steering on the vehicles they purchase; this group has been very effectively targeted by motor manufacturers such as Peugeot-Citroën.

data collection The accumulation of facts and information with a view to inputting it into a database.

data mining Assessing and evaluating a large database until you find a statistical correlation that demonstrates something you would like to assess and possibly prove. The term relates to a class of database applications that look for correlates and patterns in a cluster of data that can be used to predict future behaviour. For example, data-mining software can help retail companies find customers with common demands, such as particular leisure interests. The term is frequently misapplied to describe software that presents data in new ways. True data-mining software does not just change the presentation, but can frequently discover or alert one to previously unknown patterns within the data. Data mining is frequently at the cutting edge of modern marketing, being used for sophisticated retailing consumer assessment by such large organizations as Tesco to give it distinct competitive advantage.

data processing The process normally taken to transform data into something usable carried out usually by a computer and associated software. A term often used to apply for all computer use in business (DP departments) but most frequently used to apply to the production of CROSS-TABULATIONS following data collection.

database A collection of data usually organized for rapid search and retrieval, today usually by personal computer, and frequently a consolidated set of records previously held separately. In electronic records, a set of data, consisting of at least one file or group of integrated files, usually stored in one location and made available to several users at the same time for various applications. One of the most commonly used software packages to store bibliographical research references is Endnote.

database marketing A rapidly increasing form of marketing in which targeted messages and propositions are sent to narrow target groups, a result of detailed information about their characteristics. Direct mail is thus sent to a company's narrowly defined targets based upon data obtained from a database.

decentralization The devolvement of decision-making from the centre or top of an organization to its operational management. In large, multi-complex or transnational organizations decentralization and delegation are often seen as ways which ensure decisions are taken in the local context in which they are to be implemented.

decider A term frequently used to describe a critical decision-maker in buyer behaviour theory. Usually applied to those who are responsible for the final purchase decision within the DECISION-MAKING UNIT (DMU). A term first used to describe the complex buying network associated with purchasing in business to business networks. In major purchase decisions the decider could be the CHIEF EXECUTIVE OFFICER (CEO), purchasing director, technical director or the procurement manager (buyer), but for small purchase decisions the decider may be a junior buyer or a specific member of staff responsible for purchases at that level. The more strategic the purchase the more senior the level of staff involved. *See also* BUYING CENTRE; PURCHASING PROCESS.

decision criteria There are a number of possible decision criteria available for making choices, which invariably involve a staged process. A good example is the four stages most frequently perceived in consumers' purchase decision-making. These are:

- recognizing a need;
- searching for information;
- evaluating alternatives;
- deciding to purchase.

Most theorists recommend that one should seek to maximize the expected utility flowing from a decision. It is usual to express maximum expected utility (MEU) in monetary terms so that the expected value of the transaction becomes the appropriate decision criterion.

decision-making unit (DMU) A group of people who together contribute to a decision on what to purchase. The term was used originally in B2B marketing but is now widely referred to in consumer and service situations, e.g. the multiple household. A DMU usually comprises a SPECIFIER, INFLUENCER, authorizer, GATEKEEPER, PURCHASER and USER. *See also* BUY CLASSES OR BUY PHASES; BUYING MOTIVES.

decision theory An interdisciplinary area of research that focuses its approach on how to select effective ways of making decisions on the basis of evidence. Its origins are in economics but it has increasingly become associated with statistics and hypothesis testing. *See also* GAME THEORY.

decision tree A graphical methodology for exploring the existence and relative merits of alternative courses of action available to a decision-maker to resolve a problem or to reach an effective conclusion to a particular issue. *See also* ISSUES MANAGEMENT THEORY.

decreasing returns These occur when economies of scale cease to operate, because of the counter-acting effect of increasing average costs, and result in a decrease in profitability. *See also* DISECONOMIES OF SCALE.

deductive Conclusions in research derived by reasoning rather than by data gathering; or, research methods using such reasoning. A hypothesis is often arrived at by deduction from a theory or other assumed truth, and the hypothesis can then be tested using INDUCTIVE (data-gathering) research methods.

deflation A persistent price decline in goods and services over a number of months which leads to a decline in the amount of money in circulation within an economy. As a result, production and employment are normally affected negatively and the total marketplace tends to decline. *See also* INFLATION.

delayed gratification The ability of a person to wait for things he or she wants. Those who lack this trait are said to need INSTANT GRATIFICATION and suffer from poor impulse control.

delivery note A paper or electronic document accompanying or advising of a delivery of a product to a buyer. Used as a means of checking delivery and dealing with subsequent claims on quality, shortage, damage, empties, packaging and delivery time.

Delphi technique A research method based on the interactive exchange of ideas and information among a group of experts. Individual views are collected, discussed and debated until participants reach a consensus. Typically questionnaires are used to measure the opinions of participants while minimizing socio-psychological influences by keeping individual responses anonymous. Successive questionnaires are then developed to incorporate feedback from earlier rounds of questioning.

Delphi in ancient Greece was the home of the oracle. People came from all over Europe seeking answers to key questions on the future. The Pythia, or high priestess, was the medium through which the god Apollo spoke. A believer would make a sacrifice and present a question to a male priest. The male priest would then present the question to the Pythia. The Pythia's answers were often used to determine whether farmers planted their fields or whether and when a ruler should go to war.

demand The aggregate total ability, desire and willingness to buy a particular product or service by consumers. Demand is determined by consumers having necessary financial means to be able to make purchases which can also be affected by supply.

demarketing A term that describes attempts to discourage customers and seek to modify demand through differential pricing or the reduction of promotion, price, quality, service, etc.

demo Originally a demo(nstration) disk (vinyl) or tape (reel-to-reel) which contained a sample of music or film footage to promote an artist's offering, campaign or particular work. Now predominantly demos are created on CDs or DVDs or on a digital recording medium such as DAT or pod downloads. The content normally consists of broadcast programmes, announcements, special projects, music promotions or commercials put together by an actor, director, production company, advertising agency or the like to demonstrate the abilities and skills of its owner.

demographic segmentation Dividing consumers into specific groups based on selected categories such as age, sex, location or occupation, so that different groups can be targeted and treated differently. For example, two advertisements or promotions might be developed, one for adults and one for teenagers, because the two groups are expected to be attracted to different types of advertising or promotional appeal, such as a direct marketing appeal of a special offer.

demography Science of social statistics, particularly population statistics, essential to MARKET RESEARCH and effective campaign planning. *See also* SOCIO-ECONOMIC GROUPS.

demonstration Showing the product or service in action. Frequently associated with fitness, household and motor vehicle sales.

deontology Stemming from the Greek word *deon*, meaning duty, deontology is an ethical theory concerned with duties and rights. It is based on acting according to duty or doing what is right, rather than on bringing about good consequences. Immanuel Kant (1724–1804) is the most important deontological theorist.

Department of Trade and Industry (DTI) UK government department, formerly known as the Board of Trade, responsible for all aspects of competition, industry and associated investment policy.

department store A retail outlet traditionally located in the heart of central shopping areas in large urban areas and carrying a wide range of product classes, typically clothing, home furnishings and household goods. In the last decade many department stores have closed, reflecting heavy price competition from shopping centre complexes. The first department store is thought to have been the Bon Marché, which opened in Paris in 1852.

dependent variable A factor the value of which depends on the change the experimenter makes to the independent variable. It is the effect resulting from a scientific investigation. This quantity is plotted along the y-axis of a graph. In experimental design, a dependent variable is a variable the values of which in different treatment conditions are compared.

depreciation The diminution in value of an asset through its use over time. Usually, such reductions in value are charged against the profit and loss account, which spreads the value of the asset over its expected life, in order to show a more realistic cost of operations to the business.

depth interview A one-to-one interview with an individual that explores issues in depth. It is a widely used research technique in interpretive research, where an interviewer meets with consumers individually and asks a series of questions designed to illicit attitudes and thoughts that might be missed when using other methods. The interviewer uses a topic list, which sets out a list of points that should be covered during the interview; their role is to guide the conversation, rather than to ask formal questions. It is sometimes known as an unstructured interview. *See also* QUALITATIVE RESEARCH.

deregulation The process by which government reduces controls and ownership in selected markets, particularly monopoly supply situations such as energy and water utilities, telecommunications, media and financial regulation. The consequences of this approach by government internationally can be seen from the City of London to the new oil companies of Russia.

derivative A financial security, the value of which depends on the value of another underlying asset and is traded by one party to another. The overall value of derivatives is that they reduce risk for one party. Derivatives are normally based on one set of assets such as commodities (minerals, bulk foodstuffs, etc.), stocks, bonds or exchange rates and can include speculation on future trading conditions.

derived demand That demand created by, and arising from, the consumption of a finished good or service, e.g., the demand for aircraft is derived from the consumption of holidays and business travel and in turn influences the demand for metal, plastic, rubber and the technology used to manufacture the product.

design The term covers a wide range of activities – architecture, interior design, graphic design, industrial design and engineering design. All design involves the creative visualization of concepts, plans and ideas and their representation so as to enable the making of something that did not exist before or was not quite in that format or style. Marketing managers tend increasingly to use design as a way of differentiating products and persuading consumers to purchase their products; and customers in turn may require the design to match a particular personal need such as the level of fun it generates at that price level, etc.

design management The management of the visual identity of a company and ensuring that this is expressed consistently throughout the organization. For example, service organizations frequently use visual expressions, such as logos, environment and staff appearance, to convey the nature and quality of the company.

designer products Ostensibly up-market products, created designs by notable people giving an image of prestige or superiority.

desk research Obtaining data, facts and information from sources which are already published (e.g. directories or published research), or which are readily accessible (e.g. sales records), as opposed to field research, which is specific gathered primary data. *See also* DATA.

desktop publishing An in-house function in which computer technology is used to place and position on a screen all the elements of a proposed publication. Its popularity comes from the ease with which changes can be made and thus the economies that are made.

devaluation The reduction of the official rate at which one currency is exchanged for another. Governments regard devaluation as a means of improving the balance of trade, as exports become cheaper for the rest of the world and imports more expensive to domestic consumers. Devaluation may generate inflation and is usually perceived as a temporary tool for curing the economic ills of a country.

diary method A research technique in which respondents keep a regular written record of events such as reading a publication, viewing television or purchasing certain goods.

differential sampling The practice of setting quotas for certain groups within a population that is out of proportion to their representation within that population. For example, roughly half the members of a random sample would be women, but this number could be trebled to pull out a particular issue that impacted particularly upon women, such as availability of child care.

differentiated marketing Also referred to as multi-segment marketing, this is a market coverage strategy whereby an organization appeals to two or more clearly defined market segments with a specific product and particular marketing strategy tailored to each separate segment. Typically differentiated marketing creates more total sales than UNDIFFERENTIATED MARKETING, but it also increases the costs of doing business. *See also* CONCENTRATED MARKETING.

differentiation The modification of a product that allows it to be promoted as a unique brand to a particular segment of the market, or makes it more attractive to the target market. This involves distinguishing it from competitors' products as well as one's own product offerings.

Diffusion of Innovation Theory In his book *Diffusion of Innovation* (1962), Everett Rogers defined diffusion as the process by which an innovation is communicated through certain channels over time around the members of a social system. Rogers's definition contains four elements that are present in the diffusion of innovation process:

- innovation: an idea, practices or objects that are perceived as new by an individual or other unit of adoption;
- communication channels: the means by which messages get from one individual to another;
- time: the three time factors are: (a) innovation-decision process; (b) relative time with which an innovation is adopted by an individual or group; (c) innovation's rate of adoption;
- social system: a set of interrelated units that are engaged in joint problem solving to accomplish a common goal.

The original diffusion research was completed in 1903 by the French sociologist Gabriel Tarde, who plotted the original S-shaped diffusion curve. Tardes's work is highly relevant to marketing thinking today because, according to Rogers, 'most innovations have an S-shaped rate of adoption'. The variance lies in the slope of the S. Some new innovations diffuse rapidly, creating a steep S-curve; other innovations have a slower rate of adoption, creating a more gradual slope of the S-curve. The rate of adoption, or diffusion rate, has become an important area of research to sociologists and more marketers wishing to successfully launch, and more importantly profitably sell, their products.

diffusion process Diffusion is the process by which a new idea or product is spread, accepted and assimilated within a market or industry. The rate of diffusion is the speed at which the new idea spreads from one consumer to the next. Adoption is similar to diffusion except that it deals with the psychological processes an individual goes through, rather than an aggregate market process. *See also* PRODUCT INNOVATION.

digital coupon A voucher or equivalent coupon unit of value that exists electronically, and can be exchanged at a website retailer or conversion site via email or text messages for discounts on products or complete goods.

digital Darwinism The Internet commerce philosophy that suggests that the development of Internet businesses is governed by the same basic principles as Darwin's theory of evolution and that those that adapt the most effectively to their environment will be the most successful.

digital radio Over-the-air broadcast or cable radio that uses a compressed digital format for transmission. Digital radio effectively increases the capacity of a transmission channel. It also can accommodate data as well as audio transmission.

digital television (DTV) The term includes all elements of digital broadcasting, including high- and standard-definition television, data casting and multicasting. Analogue television, which was developed in the 1940s, receives one continuous electronic signal and is being phased out progressively around the world (Britain is due to complete this process by 2012). In contrast, DTV works on the same principle as a computer or a digitally recorded compact disk. It uses binary code, a series of ones and zeros, rather than a continuous signal. Data can be compressed to provide four, five or more channels in the bandwidth required for one channel of analogue television. In a number of countries government has set a date for the end of analogue broadcasts thus stimulating the adoption of DTV as a preferred broadcast medium.

direct costs Any charge which can be directly allocated to a cost centre or cost per unit. The costs incurred, in addition to fixed costs, as a result of manufacturing a product or providing a service. Direct costs are made up of direct material, direct labour and direct manufacturing or servicing costs. *See also* AVERAGE VARIABLE COST.

direct mail The sending by mail, fax or electronic mail of promotional communications addressed to targeted specific potential customers. Can be used as part of a marketing communications strategy with other mediums such as advertising, sales and public relations to support the promotion. *See also* DIRECT MARKETING; TELEMARKETING.

direct marketing A specific form of marketing that attempts to send its communications directly to consumers using addressable media such as post, Internet e-mail and telephone text and messaging. Direct marketing differs from regular promotion in that it directly targets the consumer rather than using some third-party medium to promote a consumer behaviour.

This form of marketing is particularly attractive to marketers as its results can be measured by counting the number of sales per thousands of postings. Although used successfully by many standard commercial and not-for-profit organizations, it has also been widely used by those on the Internet selling pornographic materials and enhancing drugs which have given it a bad name. While many marketers like this form of

marketing, it is sometimes criticized for generating unwanted solicitations, which are sometimes referred to as JUNK MAIL and SPAM. *See also* DIRECT MAIL; TELEMARKETING.

Direct Marketing Association (DMA) Founded in 1917, the US-based Direct Marketing Association is the leading global trade association of business and NON-PROFIT ORGANIZATIONS using and supporting DIRECT MARKETING tools and techniques. The DMA advocates industry standards for responsible marketing, promotes relevance as the key to reaching consumers and provides research, education and networking opportunities to improve results throughout the entire direct marketing process. The DMA has more than 4,800 corporate, affiliate and chapter members from the US and forty-six other nations, and its membership includes over fifty companies listed in the Fortune 100.

The Direct Marketing Association UK is Europe's largest trade association in the marketing and communications sector. The DMA was formed in 1992, following the merger of various like-minded trade bodies, forming one UK organization to protect the direct marketing industry from legislative threats and promote its development.

direct response advertising An advertising strategy in which special techniques are used to invoke an immediate response (not necessarily instantaneous) rather than a delayed one. *See also* DIRECT RESPONSE MARKETING.

direct response marketing A rather loosely interpreted term, often conflated with 'direct marketing'. Strictly, however, it refers to marketing in which purchasing is made directly involving the manufacturer or supplier and the customer, without going through the intermediary of a retail outlet. The offer of goods is not just by means of direct mail and/or telephone, but also by press, television, radio and web advertising. In direct marketing, the marketer contacts the potential customer directly, but in direct response marketing the customer responds to the marketer directly. The most common form today is INFOMERCIALS, which try to achieve a direct response via television presentations. Viewers respond via telephone or the Internet with their credit card details. Other media, such as magazines, newspapers, radio and e-mail, can be used to elicit the response, but they tend to achieve lower response rates than television. Order forms or coupons in magazines and newspapers are another type of direct response marketing. Mail order is a term that describes a form of direct response in which customers respond by mailing a completed order form to the marketer. *See also* DIRECT RESPONSE ADVERTISING.

direct selling A form of selling without retail outlets, distributors, wholesalers or any type of middlemen whereby the producer sells direct to the user or ultimate consumer. Direct selling offers many advantages to the customer, including lower prices and shopping from home. Potential disadvantages include the lack of after-sales service, an inability to inspect products prior to purchase, lack of specialist advice and difficulties in returning or exchanging goods. It can include both personal contact with consumers in their homes (and other non-store locations such as offices) and telephone sales initiated by a retailer.

directional matrix Developed by H. I. Ansoff (*Corporate Strategy: An Analytic Approach to Business Policy for Growth and Expansion*, 1965), this matrix is based on two dimensions: markets and technologies, both of which are subdivided into 'new' and 'existing'. Whilst this framework is criticized as overly simplistic, it is useful when formulating specific development strategies. The quadrants are:

• Market penetration: existing products are introduced into existing markets. The aim is to increase sales volume through higher market share or greater per capita consumption.
• New product development: products developed from new technologies are introduced into existing markets.
• Market development: existing products are introduced into new markets.
• Diversification: products developed from new technologies are introduced into new markets.

See also GROWTH SECTOR MATRIX.

directory A reference book published annually or more frequently which sets out a complete list of individuals, members of a profession, companies, products or services in a particular field. Alternatively a compilation of websites reviewed and organized by human editors into useful categories and topics, similar to the organization of the Yellow Pages. Examples of web directories are the Google Directory, About. com and the Open Directory Project.

discount A reduction in the face value price offered to a customer. Discounts are normally used to persuade customers to purchase when they would normally not do so. Winter and Summer Sales are normally special offerings of discounted standard seasonal products whose stocks need to be reduced substantially by heavy discounting.

discount store A retail store that offers merchandise for sale at lower prices than conventional stores that sell merchandise at list prices or suggested retail prices; also sometimes referred to as a discounter or discount outlet.

discounted cash flow An accounting management method used for evaluating investment projects involving the calculation of present value. As money in the business is worth more than that earned at a future date, the method is used to calculate the present value of earnings of specified future times (by discounting the flow of expected earnings at chosen rates) and to compare it with capital investment required to obtain such earnings.

discretionary income The part of household net income which remains after fixed expenditure such as mortgage or loan repayments. It represents a challenge for all organizations to be able to persuade buyers and customers to spend a greater

Positive and negative cash flows

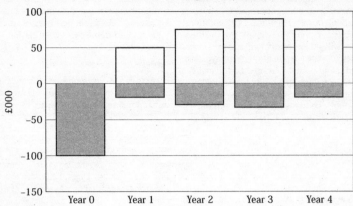

Discounted Cash Flow

proportion of their discretionary income than hitherto on a particular product or service.

discriminant analysis A multivariate statistical technique that identifies weighted combinations of variables which allow discrimination between groups or users.

discriminant validity The assessment of validity of a measure by showing it does not correlate with measures of other concepts.

discrimination test A form of product test in which the objective is to discover whether one product is perceived to be different from, or preferred to, an alternative offering. It may be carried out by expert panels which monitor production quality or formulation changes.

discussion The purpose of the discussion in a report or thesis is to interpret results, that is, to explain, analyse and compare them. The discussion states whether or not the results from the procedure fully support the hypothesis, do not support the hypothesis or support the hypothesis but with certain exceptions. Specific data – with direct evidence from the laboratory or from market research that either support or reject the hypothesis – are identified in paragraph form. Outcomes from results are used to identify the particular data that led to the judgement about the hypothesis. This is the point at which the researcher stands back from the results and talks about them within the broader context set forth in the introduction. It is perhaps the most important part of the report because it is where the researcher demonstrates that he or she understands the experiment beyond the level of simply doing it.

discussion board A location on the Internet where users can post and read messages. Discussions boards are known by many names, including BULLETIN BOARD, discussion group, discussion forum, message board and online forum. Discussion boards are often used to share and discuss information and opinions about specific topics or interests. There are literally thousands of discussion boards available on the Internet with a wide range of topics.

diseconomies of scale The point at which the gains from the economies of scale have ceased to make a difference and the average costs of production and/ or marketing begin to rise, thus leading to a decline in the overall economy of the product. *See also* DECREASING RETURNS.

display advertising (1) Printed advertising that is located throughout a publication and that utilizes size, colour illustrations, photographs and various decorations and typography to attract the reader's attention. (2) Freestanding advertisement designed for exhibition in traffic areas, such as retail stores, public buildings, terminals and the like.

display bin Used in POINT-OF-PURCHASE advertising, a display bin is an open container for small items in a supermarket or retail outlet. It is designed in such a way that customers can handle, inspect and assess the merchandise contained within, in the belief that, once a customer has the goods in hand, a purchase will result.

display card An advertisement printed on a card or sheet of poster board and then attached to a store display. Usually a display card will announce special sales such as two for one or a special price for a discounted item.

display case A particular type of display used in POINT-OF-PURCHASE advertising where the merchandise is in an enclosed container. Alternatively, a portable case carried by a salesperson and opened to display the products they are selling.

display pack A pack which, in addition to performing a 'packaging' function, also serves as a means of displaying the product at the point of sale.

disposable income The total amount of income a consumer has left after paying government taxes and receiving all benefits and allowances from the state This income is available for the consumer to spend in the marketplace as reflects their needs.

disproportionate sampling The deliberate use of different sampling rates for the collection of market research data, for instance, high levels of an ethnic group, young people or high incomes. This can be used to ensure there is limited sampling error and to ensure the sample is representative of particular groups that otherwise might not appear in the sample. This is very important in sampling for opinion polls where often the behaviour of certain

income or ethnic groups in a particular area can be crucial to target for electoral success but may be hard to access in general sampling situations which have not built in quota sampling.

disruptive technology This is a term which refers to the way specific technology can change fundamentally the rules and operations of business and society at large. The major technology to change our way of communication and trading in the past decade has been the widescale availability of the Internet as a new sphere for exchange and thus marketing. It has thus disrupted rational methods of business and led to the development of E-MARKETING and E-COMMERCE.

dissonance-attribution model In consumer learning theory, consumers will attempt to reduce COGNITIVE DISSONANCE after a purchase by gathering positive information about the product and ultimately attributing the purchase to good judgement rather than the influence of peers, family members or salespeople. This model follows classic dissonance – purchase occurs under force or spontaneously, the consumer develops an attitude after trial and then seeks and/or consumes information to support their attitude. According to M. L. Ray et al. ('Marketing Communications and the Hierarchy of Effects', in P. Clark (ed.), *New Models for Mass Communication Research*, 1973), dissonance attribution is likely to appear when involvement levels are high but PRODUCT DIFFERENTIATION or alternative identification are extremely low. *See also* DISSONANCE-REDUCTION STRATEGIES.

dissonance-reduction strategies Behaviour designed to reduce cognitive dissonance following purchase and the acquisition of more information by reading advertisements, brochures, consumer reports. *See also* COGNITIVE DISSONANCE; DISSONANCE-ATTRIBUTION MODEL.

distribution The pivotal marketing function of delivering products to consumers of goods. Although some manufacturers can and do sell direct to consumers and users, practical considerations require most to use a distribution system composed of wholesalers and retailers. These intermediaries carry out critically important marketing activities, such as buying and selling, sorting and storing, transporting and financing products as they move from producer to consumer.

distribution centre A centrally located storage complex or warehouse, usually highly automated, which acts as a focal point for the distribution of various goods where bulk deliveries can be broken up into appropriate quantities and mixes and sent to customers within the catchment area served by the centre. In many industries, such as the petrochemical and oil industries, the distribution centre may be used by a number of producing companies who will call off supplies from the various product tanks located in the storage complex.

distribution channel *See* CHANNEL OF DISTRIBUTION.

distribution network The network of organizations performing the functions necessary to move goods or services from manufacturer to END USER. The channel can be simple when producers sell direct to consumers or can consist of one or more intermediaries such as agents, importers, exporters, repackagers, wholesalers and retailers. The form and complexity of the channel depends on the product, the customers for the product and their geographical location. *See also* CHANNEL OF DISTRIBUTION; MARKETING CHANNELS.

distributor A firm which buys and sells on its own account but which deals in the products of certain specified manufacturers. Common business areas where special representation, stocking and service facilities are required are automotive, building, chemical and electrical industry products.

distributor's brand A brand name used by a retail outlet. Generally referred to as 'own label' or private label goods, distributor's brand products are competitively priced and are intended to promote outlet loyalty, rather than brand loyalty.

diversification A strategy in which an organization introduces itself to products and/or target markets not previously in its ambit of experience. *See also* INTEGRATION.

divestment strategy A planned strategy where a product line (or a product division of a business) is sold so as to limit either real or anticipated losses. The resources behind that product line or division are redirected into other company products or divisions or alternatively returned to investors.

DIY 'Do It Yourself'. It is used as a label for shops specializing in the supply of construction, repair, decorative or assembly goods or materials mostly used by skilled artisans but made available in convenient quantities for people wishing to do the work themselves. DIY now refers to the practice of fabricating or repairing things on one's own rather than purchasing them or paying for professional repair.

dodo Marketing term derived from the extinct bird and describes a product with a poor market share of a contracting market. Thus 'as dead as a dodo'.

dog *See* BOSTON CONSULTING GROUP MATRIX.

domain name The text name corresponding to the numeric IP address of a computer on the Internet. While it is possible to reach computers on the Internet by using the IP address, IP addresses are not easy to remember. The domain name lies to the right of the @ sign in an Internet address. Domain names are an important branding tool for a business. Businesses are thus keen to protect their trademarks by acquiring their appropriate domain name(s). Clearly, domain names such as Amazon.com have significant economic value.

door drops Unaddressed leaflets, magazines and samples, or other promotional material, delivered by hand to a consumer's door, letter box or postbox.

door-to-door survey A survey administered by face-to-face interviews with respondents gained through talking to them on their doorstep. One of the earliest forms of market research techniques but

Drucker, Peter Ferdinand
(1909–2005)

Influential management author, educator and thinker. From 1971 to his death in 2005 he was the Clarke Professor of Social Science and Management in the Peter Drucker and Masatoshi Ito School of Management at the Claremont Graduate University, California. Drucker's career took off as a leading management thinker in the 1940s, when his writings on politics and society gained him access to the internal workings of General Motors, then one of the largest manufacturing companies in the world. In Europe he had been fascinated with the problem of authority and he shared this fascination with Donaldson Brown, the key figure behind the administrative controls at GM. Drucker was invited to conduct what has come to be called a political audit. The resulting book, *The Concept of the Corporation*, popularized GM's multidivisional structure and led to numerous articles and consulting engagements and additional books.

Drucker was a prolific author, and his books include *The Practice of Management, The Effective Executive, Managing for Results, The Age of Discontinuity, Managing Discontinuity, The Manager and the Organization, Managing for Tomorrow* and *The Concept of the Corporation*. He continued to act as a consultant to businesses and NON-PROFIT ORGANIZATIONS well into his nineties.

---

has fallen into decline because of telephone and Internet surveys and the fact that the survey approach has frequently been used as a ploy by door-to-door salespeople and fraudsters.

Dow Jones Index One of the world's best-known financial share indexes, the Dow Jones reflects the average stock prices for the thirty leading US industrial stocks. The Dow Jones Industrial Average (NYSE: DJI) is one of several stock market indices created by *Wall Street Journal* editor and Dow Jones & Company founder Charles Dow. Dow compiled the index as a way to assess the performance of the industrial component of America's stock markets. It is the oldest continuously running US market index.

downsizing The reduction of the size of a company or organization through lay-offs in order to cut labour costs. Downsizing can occur at any time, but becomes epidemic in difficult economic times. The industrial chemical conglomerate ICI plc has downsized over the last two decades to fewer than 20,000 employees from a highpoint of 200,000.

drive time In radio broadcasting, the time during which many listeners are driving to or from work.

drop-out rate The number of online survey respondents who start but do not complete an Internet-based survey. These respondents may have dropped out of the survey because of its design, lack of relevance to the respondent, length of survey and boredom factor.

Where a survey is well targeted and relevant to the respondent then drop-out rates are much lower. Rewards for completing the survey, pleas from leaders of sector to complete questionnaire, ease of completing survey and user friendliness of text and server capacity are all critical factors that can influence the drop-out rate.

dumping Exporting goods at a price lower than the price a company normally charges on the domestic market. Governments in the importing country may levy anti-dumping duties, designed to offset the actual or potential injurious effects of dumping practices.

durable goods Consumer goods which have a life expectancy of more than three years are normally classified as durable, while those with a life expectancy of between six months and three years are usually referred to as semi-durable. Consumer goods with a life of less than six months are consequently regarded as non-durable.

dustbin check A survey at consumer level to establish purchases over an agreed period according to brand and pack. Empty containers are retained in a bin known as a dustbin.

DVD (digital video disc; digital versatile disc) A high-density double-sided compact disc that can store up to 17 gigabytes of digital data – roughly the equivalent of twenty-four CDs. The popularity of DVDs has rapidly risen, with Nielsen Media Research reporting that 85.9 per cent of US television-owning households owned a DVD player in 2006. In the same year total sales of DVDs via rental and home purchase in the US market totalled 1324.7 million units, with the film *Pirates of the Caribbean: Dead Man's Chest* being the top-selling item at 14.4 million units.

It uses MPEG2 compression to encode 720:480p resolution, full-motion video and Dolby Digital to encode 5.1 channels of discrete audio. The disc can also contain PCM, DTS and MPEG audio soundtracks. The DVD has become the dominant form of storage for movie and multimedia concert materials in the last decade.

dyadic relationship A relationship between two parties in which both have the power to influence the other. Any encounter, interaction or relationship between two groups, organizations or people is referred to as a dyad. This is frequently used in marketing as a theoretical concept to help explain and explore the complex linkages and interactions between different buyers and sellers of products or services.

E

e-commerce Also known as 'electronic commerce' and 'e-business' this refers to the buying and selling of goods and services in different business sectors via commercial and non profit exchanges using new, electronic technologies. A transaction might involve online order taking, online payment and online delivery (as with electronic confirmation of an insurance policy). The most common e-commerce transaction is that of EFTPOS.

For online retail selling, the term e-tailing and Internet marketing are also used.

e-governance The application of ICT to enhance access to information and delivery of government services. E-governance can improve dramatically efficiency, effectiveness, transparency and accountability of informational and transactional exchanges within government, and between government agencies and citizens and businesses. Governments need to ensure that they involve the whole population, in particular by ensuring that the largest possible numbers of citizens have access to, and are educated in, the use of computers. E-governance when effectively developed can lead to greatly improved citizen involvement in the governmental decision-making process.

e-mail (electronic mail) The exchange of messages and computer files between computers that are connected to the Internet or some other computer network. Most e-mail messages usually contain text, but non-text files, such as graphical images and sound files, can be sent as attachments. E-mail accounts for a significant percentage of the total traffic over the Internet, with the dominant language being English. *See also* E-MAIL MARKETING; SPAM.

e-mail marketing A form of direct marketing which uses E-MAIL as a means of communicating messages to business, fundraising or not-for-profit organizations. It has proved to be a popular medium for direct marketers, primarily because of its relatively low cost, but also because customer responses can be generated rapidly. When sent to customers who have given their permission to receive such marketing material, e-mail marketing can be a very effective targeted marketing communications tool. However, when performed without permission, or used to send inappropriate messages, the result is e-mail SPAM, which most Internet users and administrators consider an abuse of network resources and a nuisance. Spam is prohibited by the appropriate-use policies of nearly all Internet service providers and increasingly is the subject of laws and regulations aimed at curbing the practice nationally and internationally.

e-marketing The utilization of Internet communications and particularly the World Wide Web to market goods or services and achieve objectives. It is the strategic process of creating, distributing, promoting and pricing goods and services to a target market over the Internet or through other digital tools.

e-zine An electronic magazine, delivered via a website or an e-mail newsletter.

early adopter One of the five terms

originally proposed in Everett Rogers's DIF-FUSION OF INNOVATION THEORY. In NEW PRODUCT DEVELOPMENT there is a general theory which allocates different risk tolerances to particular consumers of goods, and one of the earliest clusters of users is termed early adopters, whilst the first to purchase are termed INNOVATORS. The innovators and early adopters are critical to the launch of a new product. If initial efforts are targeted at these groups, limited resources will be well spent as they become product champions. For example, many music groups and performers begin their careers and launch their products in the college circuit market. This is because college students are target market influencers, and many fit the definition of early adoptors and innovators. *See also* ADOPTER CATEGORIES.

early majority One of the five terms originally proposed in Everett Rogers's DIFFU-SION OF INNOVATION THEORY. The early majority is a term used to identify consumers who make up to approximately 34 per cent of purchases and who are usually innovative but cautious and follow the lead of EARLY ADOPTERS of products. These consumers and users wait to see if the product will be adopted by society and purchase only when they see that this has happened. The early majority usually have some status in society. *See also* ADOPTER CATEGORIES.

Eastern Europe Defined economically and politically as that part of the European landmass which covers the Baltic States, Belarus, Moldova, Russia and the Ukraine. The term was widely used in the West till 1992 to cover all European countries that were previously under Moscow's control. The concept of Eastern Europe was greatly strengthened by the domination of the region by Communism and more specifically the Soviet Union after the Second World War. The terms Central Europe and the Balkans are now applied to many of these former Soviet satellite states.

ecology Increasingly the critical factor stimulating the development of the sustainable marketing movement, ecology is the branch of biology covering the study of the relationships between all living organisms and the environment and particularly the totality or pattern of interactions between different bio-systems. This view encompasses all plant and animal species and their unique contributions to a particular habitat and the natural balance. The sustainability and inter-connectedness of the natural biosphere is very much enshrined in a number of leading ecology-driven concepts and movements such as carbon credits, the Kyoto protocol on CO_2 emissions, sustainable travel and energy initiatives, which are all stimulating the development of renewable and responsible marketing campaigns.

econometric model One of the tools that economists use to forecast future developments in the economy. It is used to measure past relationships between variables such as consumer spending and gross national product, and then to forecast how changes in some variables will affect the future course of others. Before economists can make such calculations, they need what is termed an economic model, or a theory of how different factors in the economy interact with one another. The most common model is that linking household expenditure to business output.

economic forces Those environmental forces which determine the economic environment and so directly influence total demand.

economic growth The increase in value of the goods and services produced by a defined economy over a given period of time, which is normally measured and reported quarterly and on an annual basis. It is often seen as the key indicator of the increase in wealth of a particular state or region. It is usually measured as the percentage rate of increase in real GROSS DOMESTIC PRODUCT (GDP). Economic growth leads to increases of incomes of consumers and therefore sustained improvements normally in the quality of life of individuals. There are major debates about the levels of economic growth that are desired or required in economies for them to sustain themselves, but it is normally taken as a good thing provided it is sustainable and takes account of impacting on other economies that are less successful.

economic infrastructure The services and social capital of an economy that supports the flow of goods and services between buyers and sellers. Infrastructure can include such assets as airports, ports, power systems, railways, roads, telecommunications and utilities among others.

economic life The period during which a machine or device works economically or profitably.

economies of scale An economic term referring to the benefits derived from the reduction of average costs resulting from larger-scale production. These economies of scale are seen to stem from the increased specialization of labour as the volume of output increases, for instance, declining unit costs of materials, better utilization of labour and management, acquisition of more efficient equipment and greater use of by-products.

economies of scope An economic theory stating that the average total cost of production decreases as a result of increasing the number of different goods produced. Economies of scope are possible when specialized inputs (for example, new machinery, improved quality of the labour force or new technology) can be shared among different production processes – as, for example, when civil and military aircraft can be produced across the same business operation.

ecosystem A term that has its ancestry in the biological sciences. An ecosystem is a self-sustaining system, the members of which benefit from each other's participation via symbiotic relationships. As it is used in marketing, an ecosystem can be viewed as a business network of interactions where the relationships established across different industries become mutually beneficial and self-sustaining. Silicon Valley, California, for example, contains the entrepreneurs, venture capitalists

needed to fund it, software designers and Stanford University (birthplace of Google and Yahoo! etc.) which supplies the additional intellectual expertise needed to develop innovative and creative ideas and technologies.

Once a business ecosystem is established and is able to take first-mover advantage, it becomes very difficult for other regions to emulate it or catch up. The region exhibits network effects and is able to establish lock-in, since the collective costs of many moving out of the region (i.e. if another region tried to incentivize a large move) would be prohibitive and in addition it starts to draw in additional resources both in terms of physical and human capital. Thus current members have a clear incentive to remain, and new would-be entrepreneurs, venture capitalists and students interested in this industry have a significant incentive to relocate to this region.

eco-terrorism The threats and acts of violence (both against people and against property), sabotage, vandalism and intimidation committed in the name of environmentalism. The most common form of eco-terrorism has been the illegal release of animals used for fur production or in animal testing. Activities have also included contaminating supermarket foods and violent attacks on scientific research personnel and institutes.

ECR (efficient consumer response) The improvement of product introduction and the promotion, replenishment and storage of goods throughout all parts of the supply chain to increase customer service, especially in FAST-MOVING CONSUMER GOODS and particularly evident in retail marketing, especially in apparel goods.

edit To review a piece of writing, marking and correcting grammatical, spelling and factual errors. The editing process also often includes shortening or lengthening articles to fit the available space and writing headlines and subheads. More recently this has been extended to include computing, the Internet and photography and can refer to the editing of audio, film or video files to remove certain sections or rearrange the order to enhance the story or to create a particular sequence of images or sounds.

editorial A published or broadcast expression of opinion presented by the editor, publisher, manager or owner of any medium.

editorial advertisement *See* ADVERTORIAL.

effective demand Demand backed by purchasing power.

ego A term borrowed from psychology, indicating an individual's conception of him- or herself, which often has an influence over his or her purchasing behaviour patterns.

ego-superego concept The determination of how individuals seek satisfaction within the bounds of conscience based on moral and ethical conduct. The ego, superego and id are the three divisions of the psyche in psychoanalytic theory and separate mental activity into three energetic components:

1 The *ego* is the organized conscious mediator between the internal person and the external reality.
2 The *superego* is the internalization of the conscious extenuated by rules, conflict, morals, guilt, etc.
3 The *id* is the source of psychological energy derived from instinctual needs and drives.

Although there are varying views on the origins of ego psychology, most place its beginnings with Sigmund FREUD's 1923 book *The Ego and the Id*, in which Freud introduced what would later come to be called the *structural theory* of psychoanalysis.

Elaboration Likelihood Model (ELM) A model of attitude formation and change that proposes that the process by which attitudes change depends upon the message recipient's level of motivation. According to this model, when motivation is high, the message recipient will pay attention and respond to the quality of message arguments, and when motivation

is low, the message recipient will be more responsive to peripheral elements of the message (e.g., music, spokesperson attractiveness, etc.).

elasticity In economics, the measure of the responsiveness of one variable in response to another variable.

elasticity of demand Demand is considered elastic when a decrease in price results in an increase in total revenue. It is inelastic when the reduction results in a decrease in total revenue. Unit elasticity means volume increases sufficiently to compensate for loss of revenue. Zero elasticity is the term used to define a change in price where no change in demand results. *See also* THEORY OF DEMAND.

electronic funds transfer at point of sale (EFTPOS) An electronic transfer system that allows sales transactions to be directly debited from the customer's bank account at the sales point via a debit card and scanning device, which allows the consumer to charge a particular account, such as current or savings. The selling organization using EFTPOS. Additionally, a petrol station or supermarket can also offer cash facilities to customers, where a consumer can then withdraw cash alongside their purchases. EFTPOS is sometimes also referred to as Point of Sale (POS) terminals or payment terminals and is the preferred way of processing credit cards, debit cards, cheques, smart chip cards, electronic benefits transfer (EBT), and other electronically-submitted transactions in a developed mass retail environment. The sales person will swipe the customer's card through the terminal or key-in payment information and the terminal arranges for the deduction and transfer.

electronic point of sale (EPOS) The electronic systems that are used by retailers, i.e. modern tills and associated systems. Their basic functions include scanning BAR-CODES or RFID tags to identify products, scanning credit or debit cards and cash handling. EPOS systems not only handle both cash and card transactions but they can also connect to a network, which

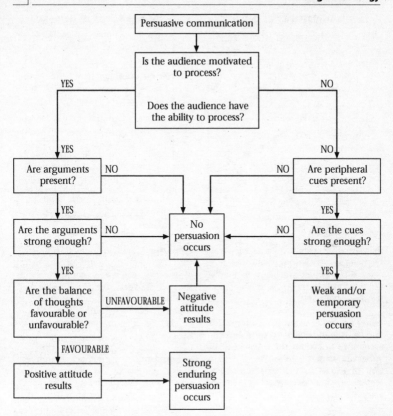

Elaboration Likelihood Model

means that information on sales becomes instantly available. This is useful both for providing management with information for decision-making and for improving logistics and stock control.

ELMAR (ELectronic MARketing) A moderated electronic mail and Internet-based information service for marketing academics and others interested in the study and teaching of marketing. The primary language of ELMAR is English. ELMAR is a free service supported by the AMERICAN MARKETING ASSOCIATION (AMA), which provides hardware, software and programming support.

embargo The prevention of the physical movement of trade, originally specific to ships but now used in a much broader economic sense. Embargo is also used in the marketing context as a ban, particularly with regard to the release of information until a specified time and date. It can also be an international diplomatic act in which a nation or group of nations such as the United Nations (UN) bans its citizens or members from trading with a particular country or group of countries.

emergent strategy A strategy that is not pre-planned, but is rather realized in the absence of intentions, or in an unexpected form. Emergent strategies are a result of adaptation, and due to the uncertainties

Low elasticity of demand

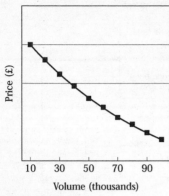

High elasticity of demand

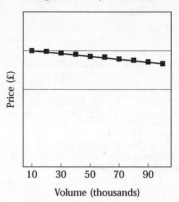

Elasticity of Demand

that surround organizational decision making there are very few pure deliberate strategies: all strategies are likely to involve some blend of intention and adaptation. *See also* ADAPTIVE STRATEGY.

emic An insider's view of a culture. Most frequently found in ethnography, an 'emic' account of behaviour uses native explanations and concepts to provide a description of behaviour in terms meaningful (consciously or unconsciously) to the actor. *See also* ETIC.

emoticon A combination of keyboard characters designed to convey the emotion associated with a particular facial expression. The simplest forms represent basic attitudes, positive in the case of :) and negative in the case of :(. Emoticons are typed as a string on a single line and usually located at the end of a sentence; most need to be read sideways. They are now frequently used as sign-offs in e-mail and text messages on mobiles and have become an integral part of an individual's personal marketing communication. The smiley figure is the most popular use of the emoticon in use today.

emotional appeal The appeal of advertising to desires rather than to logic, economy or utility.

empathy Identifying oneself completely with the problems and aspirations of others. It is often used in connection with the necessity for a salesperson to see their task through the customers' eyes and to establish reciprocity with them and can be very effective in concluding business agreements.

empiricism Any approach to research that relies heavily on observation and experiment; also, the belief that only such an approach yields true knowledge. It is used extensively as the prime method to underpin market research.

empty-nesters A term commonly used to describe middle-aged or older couples whose children have grown up and 'left the nest' to live on their own. This group often looks to sell a larger house and buy a smaller one. Marketing specialists would target this group because of their perceived high level of disposable income.

encoding The mapping of a set of characters (letters, logograms, digits, punctuation, symbols, control characters and so on) to numeric values (called code points) that can be used by computers.

end-aisle display A promotional device to put on show a particular offer in the form of a display at the end of an aisle in a supermarket.

end user The person who ultimately consumes or uses a product or service. He or she may or may not be the original or final purchaser of products. In both consumer and organizational markets end users can have a significant influence on the purchasing decision.

endogenous variable An inherent part of the system being studied the value of which is determined within that structure. Put differently, a variable that is engendered by other variables in a causal system. It is generally contrasted with EXOGENOUS VARIABLE.

endorsement advertising An advertising strategy that uses personalities as a device to increase the credibility of a particular message. These may be celebrities, experts, typical users or wholly anonymous third parties; what they have in common is that they endorse the advertised product or service either explicitly or implicitly by their presence in the advertisement.

Engel's Law An axiom noting differences in consumer spending patterns at different income levels, as observed by Ernst Engel in a paper published in 1857. Engel noted that the percentage of income families spent on food declined as their income level rose. The percentage of income spent on clothing and housing remained constant, and the percentage of income spent on recreation, education luxuries and savings programmes rose. Though 150 years old, Engel's Law is still valid today.

entrepreneur Widely used term in marketing and business developed from the French word *entreprendre* (to undertake), an entrepreneur is used as the common term to describe somebody who is prepared to take up risks to develop a business or product. An entrepreneur is usually seen as an individual who has the drive, energy, enthusiasm, organizational skills and tenacity to build a business and have the ability to pull together all the features of the organization to achieve profit and long-term success. Sir Richard Branson of the Virgin Group is often cited as being one of the leading entrepreneurs of his generation.

entry barriers Factors that limit the flow of new entrants into profitable markets, for example, direct government restrictions in the form of an import tariff. A less direct example would be large ECONOMIES OF SCALE in relation to the size of a market, which would require an entrant to enter at a large size and create a consequently large addition to industry output. In that case, a potential entrant might forgo entry into a market in which incumbents are making large profits because the entry itself would substantially drive prices down and cause losses for the entrant.

environment Within the marketing concept and planning process normally seen as the surroundings in which an organization operates, including air, water, land, natural resources, flora, fauna, humans and their interrelationships.

environmental analysis The study of market conditions, particularly culture, lifestyle and purchasing patterns and behaviour.

Environmental Protection Agency A US agency whose purpose is to enforce federal laws protecting human health and the environment and conduct environmental research that reduces risks to human health and adverse impacts on the environment. The EPA influences US and global policies concerning environmental and natural resources as they pertain to human health, economic growth, energy, transportation, agriculture, industry and international trade.

environmental scanning This is described as a form of business radar 'to scan the world systematically and signal the new, the unexpected, the major and the minor' (Brown and Weiner, *Supermanaging*, 1985, p. ix). Environmental scanning is used extensively in marketing to position the business and enable it to look ahead and thus be in a position to manage its response to change successfully. A good example is the way some carmakers have developed sustainable motor vehicles which can run on alternative, less or renewable energy while others are not expecting the need for the fuel economy to go away. This has had a major impact on Chrysler, Ford and GM's ability to respond to a changed market.

The key components of environmental scanning are seen by Coates (*Issues Identification and Management*, 1985) as:

• detecting scientific, technical, economic, social and political trends and events important to the institution;
• defining the potential threats, opportunities or changes for the institution implied by those trends and events;
• promoting a future orientation in the thinking of management and staff.

In marketing, environmental scanning, like ISSUES MANAGEMENT, is seen as a way of forecasting what future trends, issues and stakeholder thinking will impact upon the organization and its market positioning and interface.

environmental threat Any factor in the market, external to the marketing organization, that has the potential to damage or reduce demand for the product or service being marketed.

environmentalism A concern for the preservation of the natural environment as exemplified by the green or environmental movement. It is a social movement which seeks to influence the political process by lobbying, education, activism and setting an example in order to protect natural resources and ecosystems. Recent concerns about the impact of global warming and food quality scares in developed countries have stimulated a growth of interest and support for this movement. Other issues of concern for the environmental movement are pollution, species extinction, waste reduction, recycling and genetically engineered crops. Environmentalism has had a major impact on marketing thinking and practice, which is stimulating a growth in socially responsible marketing.

environmentalist A person, usually one of an organized group, devoted to the protection of the environment against such hazards as pollution, effluent, industrial development, etc.

epistemology Literally, 'the study of knowledge'. That branch of philosophy concerned with the nature and criteria of knowledge. Methodological debates in the social and behavioural sciences are often the result of differences of opinion about epistemological issues and often raise epistemological questions.

equilibrium price The price at which supply equals demand and there is no tendency to change, upwards or downwards.

ergonomics The study of workplace design and the physical and psychological impact it has on the employee. Ergonomics is about the fit between people, their work activities, equipment, work systems and environment to ensure that workplaces are safe, comfortable and efficient, and that productivity is not compromised.

ERM (exchange rate mechanism) A system introduced by the then EUROPEAN COMMUNITY (EC) in March 1979 as part of the EUROPEAN MONETARY SYSTEM (EMS) to reduce exchange rate variability and achieve monetary stability in Europe. This was adopted ahead of EUROPEAN ECONOMIC AND MONETARY UNION (EMU) and the introduction of a single currency, the EURO, which took place in January 1999.

The ERM was based on the concept of fixed currency exchange rate margins, but with exchange rates variable with those margins. Before the introduction of the Euro, exchange rates were based on the ECU, the European unit of account, the value of which was determined as a weighted average of EU participating currencies.

A grid of bilateral rates was calculated on the basis of these central rates expressed in ECUs, and currency fluctuations had to be contained within a margin of 2.25 per cent either side of the bilateral rates (with the exception of the Italian lira, which was allowed a margin of 6 per cent).

Determined intervention and loan arrangements protect participating currencies from greater exchange rates fluctuations.

EROR (expected rate of return) The anticipated mathematically predicated return derived from assets employed or invested. Pension fund investments to changing cover market conditions will suggest a range of expected rates of return over time, given projected trends in stock markets and other investments.

escalator clause A provision in an agreement that allows for automatic adjustments in payments based on an economic index that neither party controls. Typical escalator clauses provide for increases in wages based on rises in the cost of living index, or higher rent or other charges based on high fuel or maintenance costs.

ESOMAR (European Society for Opinion and Marketing Research) Based in Amsterdam, the Netherlands, ESOMAR is an international body which was founded in 1948 to represent established marketing and market research specialists. It stands for the highest possible standards – both professionally and technically – and hosts a range of training and information events throughout Europe.

ethical pricing The pricing of a product, whether it is service or product which has inelastic demand, where there is pressure or regulation on the seller to provide the product at a given price. This is particularly evident in pharmaceutical product markets where producers and licensees are often required to supply at a given price. In the wider context the ethics of pricing is regularly being debated and of course in the supply of anti-AIDS drugs to Africa has resulted in direct intervention and pressure from the developed world on producers.

ethics From the ancient Greek *ethos*, meaning 'arising from habit', this major branch of philosophy is the study of value or morals and morality. It covers the analysis and employment of concepts such as right, wrong, good, evil and responsibility. It is divided into three primary areas: *meta-*

ethics (the study of the concept of ethics), *normative ethics* (the study of how to determine ethical values), and *applied ethics* (the study of the use of ethical values). When applied to professions or government this normally refers to a code of professional standards, such as the Standards of Public Life for Government and the Chartered Institute of Marketing Code of Conduct in the UK, containing aspects of fairness and duty to the profession and the general public.

ethnic marketing Hispanics and African-Americans comprise more than a quarter of the total US population, and their numbers continue to grow. If current trends continue, by 2050, close to half of the population in the US will be non-white, and nearly a quarter of it will be Spanish-speaking, with every Texan city being predominantly Hispanic. With demographic shifts in ethnic populations comes greater economic clout for minorities. In the US, the combined buying power of Hispanics, African-Americans and Asians now exceeds one trillion dollars – an all-time high – and is expected to keep climbing. Furthermore, many of these minority consumers are young, for instance, about one-third of all Hispanics and African-Americans in the US are currently age eighteen or under. In Australia, France, New Zealand and the UK, among others, similar ethnic populations are increasing and provide a marketing opportunity for those companies that appeal to minority groups.

ethnic media Specific media that targets a particular ethnic group; for instance Hispanic magazines, radio and television in the US which provide information and marketing opportunities to reach a part of the national population which is anticipated to be a quarter of the population by 2050. Ethnic media is well established in many states and can provide a quality way to market products to a particular segment of the market which would be less successful using conventional media.

ethnocentricity The perception of the world based on one's own cultural or ethnic group perspective. The term was developed by William Graham Sumner of Yale, a social evolutionist and Professor of Political and Social Science, who proposed that it reflected somebody seeing their own group as the centre of everything. Thus anyone that did not conform to that perception was an alien to your common culture or identity. Used extensively within marketing to target various ethnic consumers who may have specific segment needs.

ethnographic research Any of several methods of describing social or cultural life based on direct, systematic observation, such as becoming a participant observer in a social system or interaction. *See also*: PARTICIPANT OBSERVATION.

ethnography Any of several methods of describing social or cultural life based on direct, systematic observation, such as being a participant observer in a particular group activity. Ethnography is widely used to study patterns of consumption and has its early origins in the observation and analysis of animal behaviour. Ethnographers employ a wide range of methods of data gathering, including, documents, diaries, pictures, verbal transcripts and video, to underpin their understanding. *See also* GOFFMAN.

etic An outsider's view of a culture. The search strategy through which the emphasis is on an anthropologist's rather than a local's interpretation and explanation of culture. *See also* EMIC.

euro The common currency of most of the members of the EUROPEAN UNION (EU), the exceptions being Denmark, Sweden and the United Kingdom. The euro was introduced in January 1999 for non-cash transactions, with paper notes and coins put into circulation January 2002. The euro was developed to strengthen and integrate the EU economies and to facilitate international commerce. The EMU nations (see EUROPEAN ECONOMIC AND MONETARY UNION) represent an economy which rivals the US as the world's largest free-trade single currency. The euro is controlled by

European Central Bank (ECB), which sets interest rates and monetary policy. The symbol of the euro is €.

euro-marketing On 1 January 1993, the EUROPEAN UNION (EU) formally became a single market, wherein people, goods, services and money were allowed to move around as freely as within one country. Euro-marketing refers to the marketing of goods and services in the different socio-economic, cultural and legal-political environments of Europe at national and regional levels.

European Advertising Standards Alliance (EASA) A NON-PROFIT ORGANIZATION founded in Brussels in 1992 to bring together advertising self-regulatory bodies across Europe, to promote and support advertising self-regulation, to coordinate the handling of cross-border complaints and to provide information and research on advertising self-regulation.

European Centre for Public Affairs (ECPA) Founded in 1986 at Templeton College, Oxford, ECPA is a NON-PROFIT ORGANIZATION under English law. It is run by an executive director and supported by a small staff.

The ECPA has particular expertise in public affairs practice in the EUROPEAN UNION (EU). It works closely with the European Commission, the European Parliament and the Presidency of the EU and national governments of the Union to develop understanding of the evolving process of governing Europe. Civil servants are taught on programmes specifically designed for their needs, but the ECPA also has a long tradition of teaching them in the company of corporate and civil society participants to the mutual benefit of all three categories. The ECPA is a pioneer in the establishment of best practice in corporate, social and environmental responsibility and undertakes benchmarking studies on corporate public affairs.

European Community (EC) The European Community was founded in 1957 under the Treaty of Rome to work towards the regulation of European international trade. Originally it began as a post-war initiative between six countries pooling control over coal and steel to guarantee a more peaceful future for Europe. The EC included the European Coal and Steel Community (ECSC), the EUROPEAN ECONOMIC COMMUNITY (EEC) and the European Atomic Energy Community (Euratom). Its agreements aimed to unify and integrate member nations by establishing common economic policies including the elimination of tariffs and other trade restrictions among members and the establishment of uniform tariffs for non-members.

The Single European Act 1986 committed the EC to the complete unification of its internal market and the free movement of goods, people and capital. This led to the Maastricht Treaty of 1992, which created between EC members the new Treaty of Economic Union (EU) comprising a EUROPEAN ECONOMIC AND MONETARY UNION (EMU) and a Political Union. The Treaty came into effect in 1993, and at this time the name European Community (EC) was replaced by EUROPEAN UNION (EU).

European Currency Unit (ECU) A composite currency unit made up of the currencies of the member countries of the European Union. *See also* ERM (EXCHANGE RATE MECHANISM).

European Economic Community (EEC) The name given to the customs union consisting of twelve member states: Belgium, France, West Germany, Italy, Luxembourg, the Netherlands, the United Kingdom, the Republic of Ireland, Denmark, Greece, Spain and Portugal. It has now developed into the EUROPEAN UNION (EU).

European Investment Bank (EIB) The EUROPEAN UNION's financing institution, established under the Treaty of Rome in 1957. The task of the Bank is to contribute towards the integration, balanced development and economic and social cohesion of the member countries. The EIB raises on the markets substantial volumes of funds, which it directs towards financing capital projects meeting the objectives of the Union.

Outside the Union the EIB implements the financial components of agreements concluded under European development aid and cooperation policies. The Bank's aims are to help to stimulate development in less-favoured regions, to modernize or convert industries, to help to create new activities and to offset structural difficulties affecting certain states. In 2005 it raised €40 million to fund projects, with most of its funds being raised in the international capital markets. As it is a NON-PROFIT ORGANIZATION, its rates closely parallel those of the world capital market.

European Monetary System (EMS) The system by which members of the EUROPEAN UNION (EU) cooperate on monetary matters to achieve exchange rate stability.

European Economic and Monetary Union (EMU) A currency union of all participating member countries of the EUROPEAN UNION (EU), where a single currency, the EURO, will replace individual country currencies. A programme for the establishment of monetary union was agreed under the Maastricht Treaty in 1992. The European Economic and Monetary Union consists of three stages coordinating economic policy and culminating with the adoption of the euro, the EU's single currency. EMU came into full operation with the replacement of twelve national currencies with the euro on 1 January 2002. The United Kingdom and Denmark have opt-outs exempting them from the transition to the third stage of the EMU. The ten new countries that acceded to the European Union in 2004 all intend to enter the third stage and adopt the euro within the next ten years.

European Union (EU) On 11 December 1991 the Maastricht Treaty, officially known as the Treaty of the European Union, was ratified by members of the EUROPEAN COMMUNITY (EC), and the European Union came into existence. Two new areas, justice and home affairs and a common foreign and security policy, were added to the existing remit of the EC, and the so-called three pillars of the Union were established. This expanded European cooperation from economic and commercial into monetary, security and judicial matters.

Maastricht created the blueprint for economic and monetary union and defined the three stages of EUROPEAN ECONOMIC AND MONETARY UNION (EMU) which eventually led to the single currency and set out the convergence criteria or economic tests that member states have to pass. Citizens of the member states were given European citizenship and the right to move and live in any EU state and vote in European and local elections in any country.

The European Union is the framework for economic and political cooperation between twenty-seven European countries. Together, these twenty-seven members of the EU now form the largest economy in the world. A key activity of the EU is the establishment and administration of a common single market, consisting of a customs union, a single currency (adopted by thirteen of the twenty-seven member states), a Common Agricultural Policy and a Common Fisheries Policy. The EU manages cooperation on issues such as the environment, transport and employment and wields increasing influence in defence and foreign policy. The EU has five declared objectives:

1 to promote economic and social progress;
2 to assert the identity of the European Union on the international scene;
3 to introduce European citizenship;
4 to develop an area of freedom, security and justice;
5 to maintain and build on established EU law.

Several institutions have been set up to ensure the effective functioning of the European Union. The most important include the Council of the European Union, the European Commission, the European Parliament, the European Court of Justice and the European Central Bank.

The EU current member states at the beginning of 2008 were: Austria, Belgium, Bulgaria, Cyprus, Czech Republic, Denmark, Estonia, Finland, France, Germany, Greece, Hungary, Ireland, Italy, Latvia, Lithuania, Luxembourg, Malta, Netherlands, Poland, Portugal, Romania, Slovakia, Slovenia, Spain, Sweden and the United Kingdom. Croatia, Macedonia and Turkey are all candidates for future entry to the EU. *See also* EUROPEAN ECONOMIC COMMUNITY.

events marketing A promotional activity in which an organization stages an event to which customers and prospects are invited, e.g. a private exhibition, a concert, a sports fixture or a competition.

ex officio By virtue of office.

exchange A transaction by which goods, services or money are traded for other goods, services or money. Exchange is the central concept in marketing, as long as it is voluntary. The expected result of exchange is that benefit will accrue to both parties.

exchange controls Restrictions imposed by the central bank or other government authorities on the convertibility of a currency or on the movement of funds in that currency.

exchange rate This refers to the rate at which one currency may be exchanged for another or for gold. A floating exchange rate exists when the rate is not fixed but is allowed to find its own level in trading markets.

exchange value This refers to the rate at which a particular currency can be exchanged for the parity equivalent in another currency or gold.

exclusion clause A term in a contract that seeks to restrict the rights of the parties to the contract by excluding a specific aspect or feature, such as the right of resale to third parties.

exclusivity A contractual agreement which allows an organization or particular party exclusive rights to conduct a particular business activity or service. Examples would be an exclusive franchise for a luxury car brand or for the launch of a new product over a period of time.

exit barriers The economic, emotional and strategic infrastructure and operational aspects of a business that force organizations to stay in a particular market or activity even when there are declining or negative returns on investment. An example of this is that the major chemical companies in the EU in the 1990s were all making losses on petrochemical products, especially bulk commodity plastics, but did not want to withdraw from the market as this would give another competitor advantage and increase their costs of their total production. Major sources of exit barriers include: specialized assets; fixed costs of exit; emotional barriers; government and social restrictions; and strategic interrelationships.

exogenous variable A variable entering from and determined from outside the system being studied. A casual system says nothing about its exogenous variables; their values are given, not analysed. For example, if we were studying the relationship of hours spent practising to score in an archery contest the subjects' dexterity and strength might be related to their scores but would be exogenous variables for the purposes of our study. *See also* ENDOGENOUS VARIABLE.

expectancy value (EV) The most widely used model of attitude (generally attributed to Martin Fishbein); it suggests that one's attitude is a summary of everything believed about something weighted by the importance attached to those beliefs.

expectations Benefits or satisfactions which the consumer hopes to receive through consumption of particular goods or services. The failure of a product to live up to the consumer's expectations will invariably lead to its commercial failure.

experience curve A graph representing the inverse relationship between the total value-added costs of a product and an organization's experience in producing and marketing it. The experience curve is used to depict the way a product's total unit costs will decline due to the impact of the advantages of the economies of scale.

experience effects The reduction in costs associated with increased production arising from (a) labour efficiency; (b) work specialization and method improvement; (c) new production processes; (d) better performance of equipment; (e) changes in the resource mix; (f) product standardization; (g) product innovation and redesign. The combined effects of experience are usually described in terms of an experience curve.

experimental design The art of planning and executing an experiment. The greatest strength of an experimental research design, resulting largely from random assignment, is its internal validity. The greatest weakness of an experimental design may be external validity, as it is often inappropriate to generalize results beyond the laboratory.

experimental effect A type of confounding effect that occurs when different experimenters working on the same experiment administer different treatments or conditions.

experimental group A group of respondents in a market research experiment who receive some treatment or stimulus in an experiment. This group of respondents is then contrasted with a control group which has not received such a treatment/ stimulus and another which has received alternative stimulus or treatment.

experimental research Research procedures which attempt to indicate the presence and/or extent of causal relationships, typically by random assignment of cases to experimental conditions.

experimentation The process of testing a hypothesis by collecting data under controlled, repeatable conditions.

exponential growth New products or services exhibit a pattern of exponential growth when they are first introduced to the market. This is characterized by slow initial growth of sales accelerating as the product becomes better known by the market, then finally slowing down as the market becomes saturated and most purchases become a repeat or replacement decision.

exponential smoothing Statistical techniques in time-series data used to give more weight to more recent data. Exponentially weighted averages are used to accomplish this.

export agent A selling agent or agency which specializes in representing its customers and their products in a particular overseas market or markets.

export marketing Marketing goods or services in a country other than one's own. *See also* INTERNATIONAL MARKETING.

export rebate A system of repayment to exporters of certain taxes which have been charged on raw materials, fuel, etc. used in the manufacture of exports.

exports The sales of a country's goods and services overseas. In economics, an export is any good or commodity, shipped or otherwise transported out of a country, province, town to another part of the world, typically for use in trade or sale.

extensive distribution Making a product as widely available as possible. It is usu-ally associated with MARKET PENETRATION and is the opposite of SELECTIVE DISTRIBUTION.

external audit The collecting and analys-ing of information on the different aspects of the environment within which the organization is operating, with a view to identifying threats to, and opportunities for, an organization. *See also* SWOT ANALYSIS.

external validity The degree to which findings in a particular study can be rele-vant to other markets and situations. This is of particular importance in marketing where products and promotions are tested and need to be rolled out nationally to the wider marketplace. *See also* GENERALIZABILITY.

extraneous variable Variables in a regression or factor analysis that are super-fluous to the model-building in progress. Researchers usually try to control for extra-neous variables by experimental isolation, by randomization or by statistical tech-niques such as analysis of covariance.

extrapolation Inferring values by pro-jecting trends beyond known evidence, often by extending a regression line.

face-to-face selling Personal selling, usually on a one-to-one basis, i.e. involving a personal meeting between buyer and seller in which each can state a case and/ or hear the other's point of view.

facing The front of a carton which can be seen when stacked upon a shelf in a shop or supermarket.

factor A person acting for another as an agent.

factor analysis A statistical technique reducing large data sets to the smallest number of 'factors' required to 'explain' the pattern of relationships in the data. It is used in the social sciences and in marketing, product management, operations research and other applied sciences that deal with large quantities of data.

factoring Similar to invoice discounting, but in this instance the FACTOR takes on responsibility for credit control, debt collection and credit risk. The organization purchases the accounts receivable (invoices) from a client. An advance payment is given that is between 70 and 90 per cent of the total value of the receivables. A small fee is charged, and the remaining balance is released upon receipt of payment for all invoices. The exact percentage will vary from industry to industry and from firm to firm.

factory outlet Stores owned and operated by manufacturers through which they sell branded merchandise at a discount. In addition to surpluses on normal manufacturing runs they are also used for disposing of discontinued lines, particularly the previous season's products and seconds.

fad A fashion that is taken up with great enthusiasm for a brief period of time; a craze.

fade in In broadcast, to gradually increase the video or audio signal so that a picture emerges on the screen from black or bank space, or sound volume increases from an inaudible or low level to audible or loud sound.

fade out In broadcast, to gradually decrease the video or audio signal so that an image on the screen slowly changes to black or empty space, or the sound volume slowly diminishes so that it becomes almost or completely inaudible.

fair trade The fair trade movement promotes international labour, environment and social standards for the production of traded goods and services. The movement focuses in particular on exports from the Third and Second Worlds to the First World. Standards may be voluntarily adhered to by importing firms, or enforced by governments through a combination of employment and commercial law. Proposed and practised fair trade policies vary widely, ranging from the commonly adhered-to prohibition of goods made using child or slave labour to minimum price support schemes such as those for coffee. NON-GOVERNMENTAL ORGANIZATIONS also play a role in promoting fair trade standards by serving as independent monitors of compliance with fair trade labelling requirements. Fair trade products have emerged as major product lines in the twenty-first century, with many major retailers such as Marks and Spencer, Sainsbury, Tesco and others groups stocking a range of coffees and tea labelled as fair trade.

Fair trade can also refer to consumer rights and fair contracts. Office of Fair Trading is a common name for an organization that aims to protect these interests and/or to facilitate a fair and ethical marketplace. Governmental and non-governmental organizations with this name exist, for example, in the United Kingdom and Australia.

family brands A name or symbol used to identify and promote a number of different, related or branded products.

family life cycle A description of the stages of family life based on demographic data. This has been useful in defining the demand for certain goods and services, since each stage in the family life cycle has distinguishable needs and interests. The six stages in the cycle are: **1** young single people; **2** young couples with no children; **3** young couples with their youngest child under six years; **4** couples with dependent children; **5** older couples with no children at home; **6** older single people.

fast food A food that is delivered to the customer fast and is normally considered inexpensive and has the ability to be eaten at the consumer's convenience either in a serviced restaurant area or as takeaway meal. Fast food has come to be associated primarly with those organizations with franchised restaurant operations such as Burger King, McDonald's, KFC (Kentucky Fried Chicken) and Pizza Hut amongst many others. Although the noodle and wok stalls of Asia and fish and chip shops of Australia, New Zealand and the UK have many of the same attributes.

The modern history of fast food is associated with the hamburger, as the first fast food outlets in the US primarily sold hamburgers to their clientele. Fast food has often been blamed for leading to poor diet and obesity which has stimulated much issue group interest. More recently a number of the major multinational companies have introduced low-calorie and healthy options to their menus. *See also* SLOW FOOD.

fast-moving consumer goods (FMCG) This term refers to wide range of frequently purchased consumer products that have a quick shelf turnover and relatively low price and don't require a lot of thought, time and financial investment to purchase. Examples of FMCGs include soft drinks, tissue paper, toiletries and other non-durables such as glassware, bulbs and batteries. Three of the largest and best-known examples of fast-moving consumer goods companies are Nestlé, Unilever and Procter & Gamble. Examples of FMCG brands are Coca-Cola, Pepsi and Mars. *See also* CONVENIENCE GOODS.

fax A system for the electronic transmission of images over telephone lines from one fax machine to another. An abbreviated form of 'facsimile'.

fear appeal Advertising that attempts to create anxiety in the consumer on the basis of fear, so that the consumer is encouraged to resolve this fear by purchasing or using the product or service. A common example are TV commercials showing car crashes and reminding drivers and passengers to use their seat belts.

feasibility study A preliminary study undertaken before the real work of a project starts to ascertain the likelihood of the project's success. It is an analysis of all possible solutions to a problem and a recommendation on the best solution to use.

Federal Communications Commission (FCC) An independent United States government agency, directly responsible to Congress. The FCC was established by the Communications Act of 1934 and regulates interstate and international communications by radio, television, wire, satellite and cable. The FCC's jurisdiction covers the fifty states, the District of Columbia and US possessions. The FCC is directed by five commissioners appointed by the president and confirmed by the Senate for five-year terms. The president designates one of the commissioners to serve as chairperson. Only three commissioners may be members of the same political party. None of them can have a financial interest in any Commission-related business.

Federal Food and Drug Act *See* FOOD AND DRUG ADMINISTRATION.

Federal Trade Commission (FTC) A US government agency created in 1915 under the Federal Trade Commission Act of 1914 the purpose of which is to protect the system of free enterprise and competition in the interests of a strong economy. In the words of the Section 5 of the Act, the FTC is responsible to 'promote free and fair competition in interstate commerce in the interest of the public through prevention of price-fixing agreements, boycotts, and unfair and deceptive acts and practices'. The FTC is empowered to investigate interstate and foreign commerce as well as to take legal action to enforce the laws that fall under its jurisdiction. In the advertising industry, the FTC's role is to prevent fraudulent or deceptive advertising and unfair trade practices.

feedback Audience response from which advertisers can glean information about how well the advertising message is received, the environment in which it is received and the temperament and attitude of the consumer upon its reception.

feel-buy-learn model Advertising can create feelings for products prior to purchase through trailing the product, but learning about the product attributes does not occur until after the purchase. This happens, for example, when it is not easy or possible to describe a product or service using words; instead pictures or images are used to invoke feelings in the potential customer's mind in the hope that such feelings will lead to a purchase. Examples include perfume, travel, aspects of entertainment and leisure activities. *See also* BUY-FEEL-LEARN MODEL; LEARN-FEEL-BUY MODEL.

field research Market research under-

taken outside the business using observation or surveys with questionnaires.

field sales force The staff allocated by a sales manager to assist and/or persuade prospective customers to buy a product or service. The field sales force is normally employed on a day-to-day basis outside the sales office.

field sales manager The first-line supervising executive of the sales force who is responsible for organizing, research, planning and implementing sales policies in the field.

fieldwork Research collected in the marketplace as against data collected via experiments or conceptualization. The use of quality fieldwork is essential in exploring the complex consumption patterns that are essential to understand in marketing in order to satisfy consumer demand. *See also* DESK RESEARCH.

FIFO Literally 'First in, First Out'. A policy for rotating stock to ensure that the oldest stock is always consumed first.

file sharing Peer-to-peer technology that allows one user of the Internet to access files of another user of the Internet through a public directory. Before the advent of the World Wide Web, this was the primary form of Internet information sharing, through public (and private) FTP sites. It has now emerged as a methodology for sharing digital files across the web. Napster pioneered this, distributing music files. File sharing is coming under increasing regulatory scrutiny for copyright reasons.

filter A question in a survey designed to isolate a subgroup to which further questions will exclusively be directed.

financial planning Assessing a business's financial situation, determining its objectives and formulating financial strategies of how to achieve them. Financial planning should become a continuous activity where the plan is reviewed regularly and performance measured against specific devised targets.

financial services retailing The

distribution of financial services via branch distribution networks. The key approaches and concepts of retail marketing have been heavily adopted by most types of financial institution that have a direct interface with the consumer market.

financial year The twelve-month period used by an organization to serve as a fixed time span in which to meet its operational goals – revenue, profits, etc. It is frequently not the same as the calendar year: many organizations choose, for example, to operate a financial year which keeps in step with the government's fiscal year.

finder's fee A fee paid to an individual or company whose function is to bring together the parties involved in a business deal. The finder will often serve as an intermediary until the deal is completed. The fee is usually based on either a percentage of the profit created by the transaction or the value of the deal, but it may also be a flat rate paid by one or all of the parties involved. It is most frequently used in the advertising industry and industrial and military procurements.

firewall A piece of software or hardware designed to serve as a barrier to exclude outside intruders, typically those on the Internet, access to internal content. Companies often adopt firewalls in order to keep their internal communications private (intranets and extranets). Firewalls can also sometimes prevent those behind the firewall communicating with websites on the Internet that require cookies for the transaction.

fiscal policy The use of government spending and taxation, as opposed to monetary policy (interest rates and money supply), to try to influence the level of economic activity. An expansionary fiscal policy means lower taxes and higher government spending. The effect of these policies would be to encourage more spending and boost the economy. Conversely, a fiscal policy is used to raise taxes and cut spending.

five forces model The model used by

Michael Porter in *Competitive Strategy* (1980) to describe competition and has become internationally accepted and used as one of the key theoretical models applied on a daily basis in strategic marketing. Porter argues that there are five forces that determine industry attractiveness and long-run industry profitability. These five dominant competitive forces he describes as the:

1 threat of new market entrants;
2 threat of substitute products;
3 bargaining power of suppliers;
4 bargaining power of buyers;
5 intensity of rivalry.

fixed costs Costs that a company incurs in making goods regardless of how much it is producing. A firm that manufactures plastic pipes has to pay for the cost of its factory and machines whether it makes one pipe or 10,000. *See also* AVERAGE VARIABLE COST; ON COSTS.

flagship stores The largest stores belonging to firms which are leaders in their category. Marks and Spencer, for example, has a pivotal position in many leading shopping centres in the UK. Such firms are considered vital to ensure the success of new shopping developments, such as the Trafford Centre in Northern England, which has managed to attract the flagship stores of Harvey Nichols and Selfridges. Flagship, originally a naval term, has crossed over into common parlance, where it means the most important or leading member of a group.

flame An aggressive, inflammatory or hostile electronic message sent in an e-mail or to a chatroom; also, the act of sending such a message. Flaming is always aggressive, related to a specific topic and directed at an individual recipient.

flexible manufacturing systems The integration and arrangement of several production operations that use advanced process technologies to form a self-contained 'micro-operation', which is capable of manufacturing a whole component. A distinct feature of such systems is the use of numerical control, automated loading and unloading and movement of components between work stations, often using robotics. This is usually coordinated by a centralized computer-driven production and quality control system.

fluff A mistake in speech, usually on radio or television, made in such a way as to be obvious to an audience.

flyer An inexpensive promotional item, commonly comprising one sheet of paper, printed on one or both sides and used as a handout or a direct mailing piece.

FMCG *See* FAST-MOVING CONSUMER GOODS.

FOB *See* FREE ON BOARD.

focus group An increasingly popular qualitative research tool pioneered in the 1940s and 1950s by Robert K. Merton, who called it the 'focused group interview'. The basic technique involves having about a dozen people engage in an intensive discussion focused on a particular topic. It has been used extensively in market research among potential customers, and in planning political campaigns and tracking voter support of core policies and decisions by Bill Clinton and Tony Blair amongst many others. *See also* GROUP DISCUSSION.

focus strategy In this strategy a firm concentrates on a select few target markets. It is also called a focused strategy or niche strategy. It is hoped that by focusing marketing efforts on one or two narrow market segments and tailoring the MARKETING MIX to these specialized markets, a firm can better meet the needs of that target market.

follow-up Sales contact, telephone call or letter sometimes but not always as a result of an expression of interest by a PROSPECT and usually after his/her receipt of an initial promotional piece.

font The typographer's name for the complete selection of type of one size and face. A font will include all twenty-six letters in the Roman alphabet (including upper case and lower case as well as small caps), the numbers from 0 to 9, punctuation marks and some commonly used symbols, such as the ampersand (&) and pound sign (£).

Food and Drug Administration (FDA) The US federal government agency responsible for the protection of consumer rights in the administration of the Pure Food and Drug Act of 1906, which prohibits shipment of adulterated foods and drugs, and the Pure Food, Drug and Cosmetics Act of 1938, which attempted to clarify the legislation of 1906. The FDA functions as a division of the Department of Health and Human Services and monitors the safety and purity of foods, drugs and cosmetics, and also the labelling of these products. The administration has the additional authority to ban these products when necessary as well as to regulate their contents and packaging.

Although the jurisdiction of the FDA is actually in the area of the content, packaging and labelling – as distinguished from advertising – of foods, drugs and cosmetics, the term labelling has been held to include advertising that appears in the places where these products are sold. Therefore, advertisers whose products are in these categories must pay careful attention to the packaging and labelling restrictions and requirements in their advertising.

footage In film and video, footage is the raw, unedited material as it has been recorded by the camera, which usually must be edited to create a motion picture, video clip, television show or similar completed work.

footfall The number of people visiting a shop or a chain of shops during a particular period of time. Footfall is an important indicator of how successfully a company's marketing, brand and format are in bringing people into its shops. Footfall is an indicator of the reach a retailer has, but it needs to be converted into sales, and this is not guaranteed to happen. Retailers such as Marks and Spencer have struggled to turn good footfall into high sales.

Trends in footfall do help investors to understand how a retailer's sales growth (or decline) is happening. Investors may want to know whether sales growth is due to an increase in the number of people entering the shops (footfall) or more success at turning visitors into buyers (which can be seen by comparing footfall to the number of transactions). Sales growth may also come from selling more items to each buyer (compare number of transactions to sales volumes), selling more expensive items (an improvement in the sales mix), or increasing prices. Which of these numbers is disclosed varies from company to company, but investors should look at whatever is available.

forecast An estimate for predicting future market circumstances. Most forecasting is based upon extrapolative research techniques which extend past and current trends forwards as a basis for setting targets and budgets for future levels of activity.

forecasting Predicting future events on the basis of historical data, opinions, trends and known future variables.

forum An online community where visitors may read and post topics of common interest.

Forums can be useful for anyone doing business online, both in terms of reading the content and actively participating in the discussions. Reading a forum's archives can be a good way to obtain a basic knowledge about a topic, and it also provides a historical perspective on trends and opinions. Participation, whether as a member, moderator or owner, can help one achieve recognition within a business community and may even generate highly qualified business leads. Forums differ, however, in their treatment of self-promotion; some disallow any hint of self-promotion, some are geared specifically towards self-promotion, and many fall somewhere in between, limiting URLs to an off-the-page member profile.

forward buying contract An agreement between a buyer and a seller, calling for the delivery of a specified amount of a product or service on a particular date or within a particular time period. It is also usually an agreement on a specific price for the commodity. It is used to control and hedge risk, for example currency exposure risk (e.g. forward contracts on USD or EUR) or commodity prices (e.g. forward contracts on oil).

forward purchasing Buying quantities in excess of current needs to ensure continuity of supply and/or volume discounts from the seller.

four Ps *See* MARKETING MIX.

frame A list of the population of interest that is used to draw the sample in a survey.

franchise A trading agreement, most often between a supplier and a retail outlet, where cooperation and support, often in the form of promotional facilities, are provided to the retail outlet by the supplier as part of a contractual arrangement in return for a guarantee of sales income. It is a distribution device of growing importance, particularly for service industries. The largest contemporary franchise chain worldwide is McDonald's.

free alongside ship (FAS) When all charges are met by the exporter up to the point of delivering to the ship.

free gifts Promotional gifts. These can be in the form of mail-in (where prospective customers are invited to send for a gift); on-pack (a gift attached to product at point of sale); or on-pack offer (where purchasers are invited to send for the gift, usually with evidence of a minimum purchase).

free on board (FOB) When all charges are met by the exporter up to the point where goods are loaded on board the transit vessel.

free sample A means of encouraging the trial of a product, particularly of new consumer goods. Free samples are a means of reducing PERCEIVED RISK and generally apply to FAST-MOVING CONSUMER GOODS.

free trade The ability of people to undertake economic transactions with people in other countries free from any restraints imposed by governments or other regulators. It is measured by the volume of imports and exports. World trade has become increasingly free in the years since the Second World War. A fall in barriers to trade, as a result of the General Agreement on Tariffs and Trade (GATT) and its successor, the WORLD TRADE ORGANIZATION (WTO), has helped stimulate this growth. *See also* COMPARATIVE ADVANTAGE; FREE TRADE AREA; FREE TRADE ZONE.

free trade area A designated group of nations that has agreed to eliminate all tariffs and duties that restrict trade between them. *See also* FREE TRADE; FREE TRADE ZONE.

free trade zone A particular region or part of a country where duties and taxes are reduced to stimulate economic development and trade and encourage companies to do business there. A good example is the Ras Al Khaimah (RAK) Free Trade Zone in the Emirates which is marketing itself as one of the most effective and environmentally friendly free trade zones in the Gulf region. It markets itself as 'a truly Positive and Stress free zone'. Its prime free trade zone features are seen as:

- allowing 100 per cent foreign ownership;
- 100 per cent income and corporate tax exemption;
- 100 per cent capital & profit repatriation;
- long-term renewable leases;
- strategic location with access to over 1.2 billion consumers;
- transparent laws and regulations;
- promotion centres in Dubai and Abu Dhabi;
- simple and fast application procedures;
- state-of-the-art communication facilities;
- excellent seaport and international airport facilities;
- easy international access;
- abundant energy supply;
- marketing support services.

See also COMPARATIVE ADVANTAGE; FREE TRADE; FREE TRADE AREA.

freebie Slang term used to describe any free promotional item, e.g. pens, diaries and notepads, given to the trade or an agent.

freefone A telephone service whereby calls made to a business or organization are charged to that organization rather than to the caller. In the UK freefone numbers often have the dialling code 0800.

freelancer A self-employed person working in a profession or trade in which full-time employment is also common. The word comes from 'free lance', a term apparently invented by Sir Walter Scott, the nineteenth-century writer, to refer to a medieval mercenary, a knight who was not attached to any particular lord and could be hired for a given task. Fields where freelancing is especially common include journalism and other forms of writing, computer programming and graphic design, consulting, and many other professional and creative services.

freepost A postal service provided by various postal authorities whereby a person sends mail without affixing a stamp, and the recipient pays the postage when collecting the mail.

freesheet A regional or local weekly or monthly newspaper distributed free of charge door-to-door in a defined geographical area as opposed to a 'paid-for title'.

freeware Software that may be passed on to additional users at no charge. It is either in the public domain or is copyrighted but made available at no charge to anyone who wants a copy. Freeware is often confused with shareware, copyrighted software that may be freely copied and distributed by users but that requires payment from each new user.

freight forwarders Organizations specializing in assisting manufacturers of goods to export their products to overseas markets. 'Freight forwarders' have specialist knowledge of distribution services available in various parts of the world. They are familiar with the customs and excise requirements of the importing countries and handle all the documentation to assist in the export/import procedures.

Freud, Sigmund
(1856–1939)

Austrian neurologist and the founder of the psychoanalytic school of psychology, based on his theory that human development is best understood in terms of changing objects of sexual desire; that the unconscious often represses wishes (generally of a sexual and/or aggressive nature); that unconscious conflicts over repressed wishes may express themselves in dreams and 'Freudian slips'; that these unconscious conflicts are the source of neuroses; and that neurosis could be treated through bringing these unconscious wishes and repressed memories to consciousness in psychoanalytic treatment.

frequency The number of times an advertising message is presented within a given time period. It can also be used to describe the average number of times a commercial or advertisement has been viewed per person (or per household) during a specific time period. The idea of frequency is the same throughout all of the possible advertising media choices. Frequency, along with REACH, is an important concept in the planning of an advertising media schedule. It is calculated by dividing the total possible audience by the audience that has been exposed at least once (reach or cumulative audience) to the particular time segment (in broadcast) or publication in which the advertising message appears. It can also be used to describe the number of times a particular type of event occurs or the number of individuals in a given class or category.

frequency curve The graphical expression of a continuous frequency distribution.

frequent shopper programme A reward system for a retailer's best customers, the ones with whom it wants to form long-lasting relationships.

fringe accounts Low-profit customers making marginal contributions to a supplier's turnover and therefore liable to least service or even closure in times of financial stringency.

fringe area A zone just outside of the range of a broadcasting station in which signals are weakened and distorted.

full-cost approach A pricing policy which is also known as absorption costing. Full-cost approach pricing aims to cover all costs, both direct and indirect, which is added to the required profit contribution. The approach is often criticized for failing to take into account the fact that a price that fails to cover all such costs may still make a positive contribution to profitability as long as its price is greater than variable costs.

futures Contracts specifying the future date for delivery or receipt of a particular amount of a specific tangible or intangible product. The commodities traded in futures markets include stock index futures; agricultural products like barley, maize, wheat and beef cattle; metals such as copper and tin; and financial instruments. Futures are used by businesses as a hedge against potential unfavourable price changes and by speculators who hope to profit from such changes.

futures market A market dealing in options on bonds, shares, foreign currencies or commodities.

G

G8 The Group of Eight (G8) consists of Canada, France, Germany, Italy, Japan, Russia, the United Kingdom and the United States. Together, these countries represent about 65 per cent of the world economy. The G8 is the most influential group of developed countries in terms of its role in the setting of policy in the international financial system. The hallmark of the G8 is an annual political summit meeting of the heads of government with international officials, though there are numerous subsidiary meetings and much policy research. The presidency of the G8 rotates among the member states annually, with the new president assuming his or her position on 1 January. The country holding the presidency hosts a series of ministerial-level meetings leading up to a mid-year three-day summit with the heads of government and is responsible for the safety of the participants. The ministerial meetings bring together ministers in topics such as health, law enforcement, labour, development, energy, environment, foreign affairs, justice and interior affairs, terrorism and trade to discuss issues of mutual or global concern.

Gallup Organization (The) An organization that provides market research and consulting services around the world. It has subsidiary operations in more than twenty countries, covering 75 per cent of the world's GNP, and publishes the Gallup Poll, a widely recognized barometer of American opinion.

As a pioneer pollster, the company founder, Dr George Gallup, determined that, in seeking the truth, that is, the actual 'will' of the people, his guiding principle would be professional independence and detachment from vested interest. To ensure his independence, and therefore his objectivity, Gallup resolved that he would undertake no polling that was paid for or

---

Galbraith, John Kenneth (J. K.)
(1908–2006)

A Keynesian economist (see KEYNES) and a leading proponent of twentieth-century American liberalism and progressivism. His books on economic topics were bestsellers in the 1950s and 1960s. During the Second World War, at the America Office of Price Administration, he headed the wartime price-control activities and was later a director of the US Strategic Bombing Survey and of the Office of Security Policy, receiving the Medal of Freedom and the President's Certificate of Merit for his work. He was American Ambassador to India from 1961 to 1963 and later Paul M. Warburg Professor of Economics at Harvard University. Professor Galbraith was well known as a major contributor to leading American journals and reviews, and edited the 100-volume Harvard Economic Studies. His books include *A Theory of Price Control*, *American Capitalism*, *The Affluent Society* (which held its place on the best-seller lists for some thirty weeks), *The Great Crash 1929*, *The Liberal Hour*, and *The New Industrial State*.

sponsored in any way by special interest groups such as the Republican or Democratic parties.

Historically, Gallup has measured and tracked the public's attitudes concerning virtually every political, social, and economic issue of the day, including highly sensitive or controversial subjects. Although Gallup has typically conducted its polling activities in collaboration with various media organizations and, on occasions, with worldwide associations and academic institutions, these polls have always been carried out independently and objectively.

game theory The study of winning strategies for parties involved in situations where their interests conflict with each other. In other words, game theory studies choice of optimal behaviour when the costs and benefits of each option are not fixed but depend upon the choices of other individuals. It was developed by John von Neumann (1903–57), who built a solid framework for quantum mechanics. He also worked in game theory, studied what are now called von Neumann Algebras and was one of the pioneers of computer science. Game theory has applications to real games (cards, chess, etc.), economics, commerce, marketing, politics and military strategy.

gap analysis The methodical tabulation of all known 'consumer wants' of a particular product category, together with a cross-listing of the features of existing products which satisfy those wants. Such a chart shows up any gaps that exist and thus provides a pointer as to where new products might find an unfulfilled demand.

gatekeeper A key influencer who actively acquires and disseminates information from both external and internal sources. A gatekeeper can also be those in control of the flow of information and can choose to accept or reject a piece of information for public consumption. Newspaper publishers, editors and reporters, television producers, press secretaries, government spokespersons, radio station owners and broadcasting executives have all been cited as examples of media gatekeepers. The term can also be applied to the pivotal role in the buying/decision-making process and the guarding and filtering-out of unwanted offers of products and associated services.

gateway A computer or router on a network that is the connection point to the Internet. This is the device that usually has the dedicated line, such as a T-1 line, connected to it. If a computer has Internet access, it must have a gateway in its network configuration (unless a proxy server is being used).

GATT (General Agreement on Tariffs and Trade) An international agreement signed in 1947 by numerous countries to liberalize trade by the reduction and removal of tariff barriers and quota restrictions. The agreement has no legal force but has had considerable influence in post-war economic development. The GATT was created by the Bretton Woods Conference and is generally considered the precursor to the WORLD TRADE ORGANIZATION (WTO). The GATT was part of a larger plan for economic recovery after the Second World War which included a reduction in tariffs and other international trade barriers.

The agreement was signed by twenty-three countries on 1 January 1948. This first version, developed in 1947 during the United Nations Conference on Trade and Employment in Havana, Cuba, is referred to as 'GATT 1947'. In 1994, GATT was updated ('GATT 1994') to include new obligations upon its signatories. One of the most significant changes was the creation of the WTO. The seventy-five existing GATT members became the founding members of the WTO on I January 1995. The other fifty-two GATT members joined the WTO in the following two years. Following the founding of the WTO, twenty-one new *non*-GATT members have joined and twenty-eight are currently negotiating membership.

gearing The ratio of one's own money to borrowed money in an investment. Fol-

Positive gearing is when one borrows to invest in an income-producing asset, and the returns (income) from that asset exceed the cost of borrowing. Negative gearing is when one borrows to invest in an income-producing asset and the cost of borrowing exceeds the returns (income) from that asset.

gender analysis The study of the differences in women's and men's roles and access to, and control over, resources. It is a tool for improving understanding of how differences between men and women influence their opportunities and problems and can include the identification of challenges to participation in development. It is a subset of social analysis, the study of human differences and their social impacts. *See also* GENDER SEGMENTATION.

gender segmentation The segmentation of a market on the basis of gender. *See also* GENDER ANALYSIS.

General Agreement on Tariffs and Trade *See* GATT.

General Electric Company In 1878 Thomas Alva Edison invented the carbon filament incandescent lamp and formed the Edison Electric Light Company. By 1890, Edison had organized his various businesses into the Edison General Electric Company. The Thomson-Houston Company and the various companies that had merged to form it were led by Charles A. Coffin, a former shoe manufacturer from Lynn, Massachusetts. As these businesses expanded, it became increasingly difficult for either company to produce complete electrical installations relying solely on their own technology. In 1892, these two major companies combined to form the General Electric Company, which, with the combined patents of the two former businesses, occupied a dominant position in the electrical industry.

Several of Edison's early business offerings are in fact still part of GE, including lighting, transportation, industrial products, power transmission and medical equipment. Today General Electric has eleven technology, services and financial businesses with more than 300,000 employees in 160 countries around the world.

generalizability The extent to which one can come to conclusions about one thing (often a POPULATION) based on information about another (often a sample). *See also* EXTERNAL VALIDITY; SAMPLING.

Generation X A particular consumer group who are also known as Gen X. The term originated from the title of a 1991 novel by Douglas Coupland. It refers to the generation of individuals who followed the post-war BABY BOOMER generation and were born between 1964 and 1984. They have also been referred to as 'baby bust' because they are significantly smaller in population size than the baby boomers. X is a mathematical formulation to identify the unknown and hence symbolizes the mystery of what these individuals are like. The general characteristics of Generation X are their cynicism and pessimism, frequently seen as being a result of unstable family backgrounds and circumstances and/or the impact of insecure political situations during their lifetime. Hence they tend to reject authority and are highly sceptical of designer labels and major corporations. They can be divided into three groups: college and graduate students, young professionals and married couples. Entrepreneurship is significant amongst members of Generation X, and they are highly mobile employees. Extreme sports and adventure tourism are seen as having developed in answer to the demands of Generation X.

Generation Y A term designating the generation born immediately after GENERATION X. It is only one of several terms used to describe roughly the same group of people, born in the 1980s and the 1990s. There is, however, no consensus as to the exact range of birth years that constitutes 'Generation Y', nor whether this term is specific to North America, the Anglophone world or people worldwide.

The world of Generation Y includes computers, high-speed Internet, CDs,

DVDs, mobile phones, digital cameras and iPods. Hence, they represent a unique demographic group, one that is highly conversant with technology and media-savvy. Corporations and marketers are very cautious of this group as they have very different characteristics from BABY BOOMERS and Generation X. Attributes commonly associated with Generation Y are optimism, idealism and confidence. They also have purchasing power, by having either part-time work or parents who have established themselves financially (75 per cent have working mothers and thus dual household incomes). They are also children of baby boomers who are inheriting wealth from their retiring parents. This is the generation that can afford the best things in life. Because of this and the size of this population, Generation Y is predicted to be the next most powerful demographic force after baby boomers and is receiving a lot of attention from researchers and practitioners.

In attempting to define and characterize generations, demographers often rely on the experience of formative national events as one tool of demarcation. Generations are shaped by their childhood experiences and then defined by their early-adulthood actions, when each generation can consciously adopt or reject the attitudes or actions of prior generations. Notably, the experiences of the moon landing, the assassination of President Kennedy and the 1960s social revolution are key events that demarcate the formative years of the baby boomer generation.

Several such events have been used as ways of defining Generation Y.

- The fall of the Soviet Union and the First Gulf War in 1991 are both midway events for members of Generation Y, as many members were old enough to remember these events as children, but many had not yet been born.
- The widespread use of personal computers and the Internet is an event shared by the majority of Generation Y. Internet use took off during the period 1996–2001, and most members of this generation spent at least part of their youth with a home computer and Internet access. Members of this generation use the Internet as a tool for socializing more than previous generations.
- The date of the 11 September attacks is often proposed as an end-point for the generation. Those that were not yet born in 2001 and those that were otherwise too young to remember and/or understand the events of that day (those born in or after 1997) would thus be grouped into Generation Z, as they would have no memory whatsoever of the twentieth century and any of the pre-digital technologies still around in the 1990s. People who were still in school (or had recently graduated) at that time would be called Generation Y. Such interpretations, of course, remain disputed.

As with previous generations, many problems began to surface as Generation Y grew up:

- Under-age drinking and illicit drug use is still prevalent among high school and college-age members of Generation Y. In urban areas, rave culture was known for its influence on Ecstasy usage. Marijuana, methamphetamine, cocaine and inhalants seem to be most favoured. However, statistically, today's teens are less likely to smoke, drink, do illegal drugs, get pregnant, commit a crime or drop out of college than their counterparts in the 1970s.
- Childhood obesity is another health problem that has plagued Generation Y, and X before them. In response, many local school boards have started to remove junk food from school cafeterias in an effort to reverse this trend.
- Members of this generation are facing higher costs for higher education than previous generations.

This generation was the first to use or witness the following technology from an early age:

- the Internet, especially the World Wide Web, in a more prolific form for the general user ('consumer'-friendly) rather than the technically oriented (about 1995 onwards);
- PCs with modern operating systems and mouse-based point-and-click systems requiring fewer keyboard skills (late 1980s onwards);
- sophisticated computer graphics in many video games, animated movies and television shows (late 1980s to mid-1990s) and the related non-keyboard interfaces;
- mobile phones (late 1990s onwards);
- instant messaging (late 1990s onwards);
- DVDs (1997 onwards);
- digital audio players (Mp3 players), especially Apple's iPod (2001 onwards);
- broadband Internet (early 2000s);
- digital cameras (late 1990s);
- robotic and digital pets (1990s and 2000s);
- camera phones (early 2000s).

generic brands Products distinguished by the absence of a well-known brand name. They may be manufactured by less prominent companies, or sold by supermarkets as their own brand. Generally they imitate more expensive brands, competing on price. Generic brand products are often as good as the branded product, though not necessarily, and many are made on the same production line. However, the quality may change suddenly in either direction with no change in the packaging if the supermarket changes the supplier for the product. Also known as house brands or home brands, in the United Kingdom they are often referred to as own brands.

generic term/name Brand names that have come to be adopted as the general descriptive term for a product, often as the result of extensive promotion, e.g. Hoover, Biro, Linoleum, Lux.

genetically modified *See* GM.

geodemographic targeting Identifying an audience by its location and demographic characteristics. *See also* ACORN.

geodemographics Segmenting consumers by where they live. Geodemographic neighbourhood classification systems have been in operation since the mid-1930s and widespread commercial applications really only began in the late 1970s and early 1980s, principally with the launch of the PRIZM system by the Claritas Corporation in the United States and MOSAIC and MONICA in the 1990s particularly in the retail sector. Since that time, cluster systems have been adopted by most major consumer marketers, including financial institutions, retailers and automotive manufacturers throughout North America, Europe and the rest of the world.

geometric mean The nth root of the product of all the members of a set of positive data, where n is the number of members. For example the square root of two scores, the cube root of three scores and so on. The geometric mean of a data set is always smaller than or equal to the set's arithmetic mean (the two means are equal if and only if all members of the data set are equal).

gestalt theory A holistic, process-oriented, dialogical, phenomenological, existential and field theoretical approach to human change with the centrality of contact, awareness and personal responsiveness and responsibility. Primacy is given to the uniqueness of the individual. The person is never reduced to parts and structural entities but viewed as an integrated whole with the innate potential of growth and mature self-expression.

Gestalt theory first arose in 1890 as a reaction to the dominant psychological theory of the time, atomism. Atomism examined parts of things with the idea that these parts could then be put back together to make wholes. Atomists believed the nature of things to be absolute and not dependent on context. Gestalt theorists, on the other hand, were intrigued by the way our mind perceives wholes out of incomplete elements.

The importance of the gestalt theory is nowhere more clearly demonstrated than in the media, where context and demographics must be understood. In the television and advertising industry, it is asked *how* this message will be seen, heard or read by customers and *how* this customer will be motivated to action.

gestation period The length of time which elapses between an initial inquiry for a product and the placing of an order. It is more often applied to capital goods, where it can amount to several years.

gift voucher A special incentive to purchase, usually involving money off against next purchase of the qualifying brand or providing an opportunity for a special purchase.

GIGO syndrome An acronym for the well-known phrase 'Garbage In, Garbage Out', which emphasizes that the output of a system or analysis is directly dependent upon the quality of the data inputs to that process or analysis.

gimmick Attention-getting device used in advertising a product or service, also called a 'hook'. A gimmick can be in the form of unusual or contrived words or expressions in the copy, a unique or novel display device, pictures or headlines that do not actually relate to the message, a novel giveaway or any other unusual form of promotion for a product or service.

global marketing Marketing on a worldwide scale reconciling or taking commercial advantage of global operational differences, similarities and opportunities in order to meet global objectives.

global markets Markets for products that are global in nature and not territorially constrained. National borders are not significant barriers to the conduct and organization of economic activity. Originally global markets existed for commodity goods; however, GLOBALIZATION has created a worldwide marketplace for a myriad of goods and services.

global products It has been suggested by PricewaterhouseCoopers among others that a global product is one which is available and has brand names that are universally recognized in at least three of the continents. Examples of products which have brand names that are universally recognized in much of the world but not all of it are: BP, Calvin Klein, Coca-Cola, Ferrari, Guinness, Hilton, Kentucky Fried Chicken (KFC), Land Rover, Mercedes, McDonald's, Nike, Nokia, Shell, Starbucks and Vodafone. A number of marketers speculate that in the near future the world's markets will be dominated by global branded products because of the productive and marketing capability of large transnational corporations.

global strategy A coherent, overarching strategy for the parts of the world in which an organization operates. A global strategy tends to be seen as synonymous with a standard strategy across international markets.

globalization The growing integration of economies and societies around the world and the erosion of national boundaries for economic purposes. Globalization has been one of the most debated topics in international economics and marketing over the past few years. Rapid growth and poverty reduction in China, India and other countries that were poor twenty years ago has been a positive aspect of globalization. Despite a world population increase from 1.8 billion to 6.0 billion, and despite giant political upheavals and wars, real average income per person has at least quintupled over the past century. Globalization has also generated significant international opposition over concerns that it has increased inequality and environmental degradation.

glut When the supply of a good is greatly in excess of demand, leading in turn to a substantial fall in price.

GM (genetically modified) Genetically modified (GM) and genetically modified organisms (GMOs) are terms heavily associated with foods that are genetically engineered to produce some desired effect, such as pest resistance, larger yields, different flavours or colours and varieties which are deemed to benefit the marketplace such

Goffman, Erving
(1922–82)

A leading ethnographer of the twentieth century best known for his theories suggesting that routine social actions, such as gossip, gestures and grunts, indicate that people naturally strive to formulate identities. Amongst his best-known works are *The Presentation of Self in Everyday Life*, 1959, *Asylums Essays on the Social Situation of Mental Patients and Other Inmates*, 1961 and *Frame Analysis: Essays on the Organisation of Experience*, 1974.

as for instance an apple with no pips. GM crops have been under widespread criticism from environmental groups for being unnatural and restricting the natural gene pool and renewability of sustainable agriculture. In turn, GM products have been widely promoted by companies such as Monsanto and major governments as a way of alleviating food shortages and pestilence. GM foods have been called Frankenstein foods by environmentalists.

goal A well-used synonym for business objectives or aims to be achieved by a business, organization or individual.

gondola A form of racking or shelving carrying displays of goods with aisles on either side in a self-service shop, retail unit or supermarket.

goods An economic term widely used to describe any objects desired or required by consumers and organizations in the market.

goods on approval Goods, usually of a durable character, provided for a period of trial prior to a purchasing decision and returnable in the absence of such a decision.

goodwill The value of a business to a purchaser over and above its net asset value.

Google The world's most popular search engine, located at www.google.com.

googling To use the GOOGLE search engine to explore the web for answers to questions and ideas typed into the search screen of the website. In addition to standard searches Google now have other variants of its site and search capabilities for specialists such as Google academic, which allows detailed research searches by academics. In addition the user can also customize their Google site for their own particular needs and tastes by choosing weather reports, news items or any other categories of information.

government market Also known as the public sector, the government market is a group of consumers composed of national and local government units. The government market in total accounts for the greatest volume of purchases of any consumer group in most countries. Although government purchases comprise a wide range of products such as food, military equipment, office supplies, buildings, clothing, public services and vehicles, selling to this market typically involves a great deal of paperwork, financial constraints, bureaucratic barriers and awareness of specific political sensitivities.

government relations A growing part of public relations dealing with local, national and international government relationships, often dealt with within an organization under the heading of corporate affairs, or public affairs.

graphical representation The human eye has evolved to be extremely good at analysing and recognizing patterns. Graphical representation can be used in data analysis to critically examine plots of the data. Statisticians have developed various methods for visualizing samples of both univariate and multivariate data. An early example of the use of this technique in action was Florence Nightingale (1820–1910), who had been an enthusiastic mathematician since her schooldays. When she began working as a nurse in the Crimean

War (1854–6) she quickly saw that the death rate among soldiers would wipe out the army in no time. But it wasn't the war itself that was killing the soldiers at the rate of 40 per cent per month in the first winter, it was the conditions of hygiene that the soldiers lived in. Eighteen months later the death rate had been reduced to 2 per cent per month. Florence Nightingale became a leading figure pressing the government of the day to improve conditions for their armed forces. She developed statistical techniques, working with the leading medical statistician of the day, Dr William Farr, to refine various charts and diagrams for presenting information.

Today there are a number of standard statistical and graphic representational packages available to the researcher and presenter such as Excel. Some of the most common forms of graphical representation are vertical bar graphs, horizontal bar graphs, histograms and pie charts.

graphics Visual elements used to create images for print publications, videos, and websites. The term graphic is often used in a generic sense and can include a wide variety of visual elements associated with the design and creation of printed materials, such as photographs, illustrations, drawings, clip art and typefaces. Graphics are a powerful way to communicate in today's visually oriented society. Most publications need strong, dominant visual elements to make them more interesting to the reader. Graphics can accompany copy to help attract attention, unify a look or theme, convey special meaning and add impact; they can express ideas, create a mood or image or enhance the attractiveness of a piece.

green marketing A form of marketing in which particular attention is given to products and packaging that are biodegradable, sustainable and/or recyclable. The term has also been applied to the marketing of products which have wholly or partially been produced from recycled materials, e.g. writing paper. It is associated with environmental and organic marketing and has more recently been focused on renewable energy such as the use of wind farms and solar energy in place of fossil fuels.

green movement An international social movement linked to consumerism which is concerned about the impact of consumption on the natural environment and particularly the use or destruction of non-renewable resources. Alternative energy sources and transport, pollution and waste disposal and recycling are high on the 'green' agenda. In some countries like Australia, Germany and New Zealand the green activists have formed political parties and have a growing impact on government policy through coalitions in government and pressure group and lobbying activity on sustainability issues.

green products Products which will not cause damage to the environment in either manufacture or use, e.g. recycled paper, CFC-free aerosol products. A good example of green product manufacture is Green Products Alliance in Vermont, USA, which is a consortium of manufacturers and marketers who make and sell natural personal care products. They operate a network for companies who believe that socially responsible business practices can help to create a sustainable economy and ecosystem. Member companies work together to lower raw material, marketing, advertising and public relations costs through cooperative projects and group buying power. Membership is free. Marketing and distribution opportunities are on a project-by-project basis. All products are subjected to a rigorous set of standards as to what is considered natural.

green tax A form of pollution control where a tax equal to the marginal external cost of pollution is charged on output.

greenwash The distribution of misleading information or statements by an organization or person to conceal its abuse of the environment in order to promote a positive public eco friendly image of its self. In 2008 the environmental group Greenpeace launched a website called 'Stop Greenwash' to 'confront deceptive greenwashing campaigns, engage companies in debate, and give consumers and activists and law-makers the information and tools they need to ... hold corporations accountable for the impacts their core business decisions and investments are having on our planet'.

Gresham's Law This states that bad money drives out good, i.e. where two coins with identical face value have different bullion content, the more valuable coin will be taken out of circulation. A similar situation may often happen in marketing, where inferior goods can create a poor market reception for sound goods.

grey market 1 The older population segment (fifty-five and over), also known as the third age, which is growing in affluence and is of increasing interest to many marketing operations. People in this population segment are also referred to as grey panthers or silver surfers.
2 A term used to describe the distribution of branded goods to unauthorized dealers. The stock is made available as a result of non-authorized over-production by manufacturers, the availability of excess stock because of poor sales performance or the actions of rogue agents, distributors or stockists. Most of the leading international fashion brands have faced this problem, notably Benetton, Burberry and a number of other international garment suppliers. Grey market goods are normally new and should be distinguished from second-hand goods. Particular target markets have been fashion wear, pharmaceuticals and cameras in the past decade.

grocery A retail outlet offering a wide range of consumable household goods such as foodstuffs, beverages and cleaning materials. Alternatively, a collective noun used to describe such merchandise itself.

gross circulation The total of credited circulations in groups of media – newspapers, magazines etc. – without discounting for any duplication or errors.

gross domestic product (GDP) A region's gross domestic product, or GDP, is one of several measures of the size of its economy. The GDP of a country is defined as the market value of all finished goods and services produced within a country in a given period of time. Until the 1980s the term GNP, or GROSS NATIONAL PRODUCT, was used.

gross margin The difference between the cost or purchase price and the selling price for a particular piece of merchandise. *See also* GROSS PROFIT.

gross national product (GNP) The value of a country's final output of goods and services in a year. The value of GNP can be calculated by adding up the amount of money spent on a country's final output of goods and services, or by totalling the income of all citizens of a country including the income from factors of production used abroad. *See also* GROSS DOMESTIC PRODUCT.

gross profit The value of the difference between the cost of purchase of a product and its selling price, i.e. without allowance for overheads, promotion or other expenses. *See also* GROSS MARGIN.

gross sales The total amount of money received by a business in a specified period before any deductions for costs, raw materials, taxation, etc.

grounded theory A research methodology in which the researcher collects data about a subject without any preconceived ideas concerning its content or structure. It is a general methodology for developing theory that is grounded in data systematically gathered and analysed. The theory develops and evolves during the research process due to the interplay between the data collection and analysis phases. It is important to note that the result of a grounded theory study is the generation of a theory consisting of a set of plausible relationships proposed among concepts and sets of concepts. This differs from other ethnographical methods, where often the information is presented with little detailed comment from a researcher.

group discussion A research technique in which a group of people is encouraged to express freely views and opinions on a selected subject. This might relate to the message contained in an advertisement or any other component of a campaign upon which a viewpoint is sought. Group discussions are frequently used as a means of determining both overt and subconscious attitudes and motivation, and discussion may range widely around the topic, with a controlling psychologist ensuring that the topic is fully explored. The recorded proceedings are then subjected to further analysis. This technique is used extensively in assessing new products and trends in many consumer behaviour situations and political campaigns. *See also* BRAINSTORMING.

growth-share matrix A graph designed by the Boston Consulting Group (often called the Boston Box) that classifies all of a company's strategic business units (SBUs) and measures the performance of a company's products. *See also* BOSTON CONSULTING GROUP MATRIX.

growth stage The phase in the product life cycle when sales of a particular item begin to increase rapidly and start generating profits. At this stage it is important to have adequate supplies of the particular product or to attract in alternative suppliers.

guarantee A promise, especially in writing, that something is of specified quality, content or benefit, or that it will provide satisfaction or will perform or produce in a specified manner.

guerrilla marketing Unconventional marketing intended to get maximum results with minimal resources.

habitual buying The practice by a customer of always buying the same product, particularly where there is little or no difference between one brand and another in terms of price, product or availability.

haggle A term used to describe bargaining and/or wrangling over an item for sale historically in a market or souk (Arab commercial quarter) with a trader. The term is now used most commonly to describe the tough negotiating of contracts, prices, terms, etc. or other forms of intense trading.

hall test A popular term used to describe a research activity in which passers-by are invited into a public hall or other such place in order to answer questions. It is used to evaluate advertising, new products, brand images and so on.

halo effect The cognitive bias in which the assessment of an individual quality serves to influence and bias the judgement of other qualities. For example, attractive people are often judged as having a more desirable personality and more skills than someone of average appearance. In brand marketing, a halo effect is one where the perceived positive features of a particular product have enhanced the overall appeal of a broader brand. It has been used to describe how the iPod range has had positive effects on perceptions of Apple Computer's other products.

Similar to the halo effect is the 'devil effect' (or 'horns effect'), where one weak point or negative trait influences everything else, as when an individual judged to have one poor trait is subsequently judged to have many poor traits.

handbill A small, printed advertising sheet or flyer distributed by hand.

handout Is something given freely or distributed *gratis* (without compensation). It can refer to materials handed out for presentation purposes or to a charitable gift, among other things.

hard copy Information printed on paper in contrast to being electronically displayed on a personal computer screen.

hard goods Durable consumer goods such as furniture, washing machines, TVs, etc., as opposed to soft goods which have a textile base. Hard goods are products with a relatively long useful life.

hard sell A description of the behaviour and particular style of a salesperson in which the potential purchaser is placed under extreme pressure, bombarded with information and pushed to purchase a particular product.

harvesting strategy A planned programme for withdrawing a product from the market at a maximum profit. All non-essential costs are eliminated, such as promotion, and the product is just allowed to decline.

hawthorne effect A tendency for respondents in a piece of research to behave in a different way if they are aware of being observed. This might be to respond in the way they feel they are expected to respond, or indeed the very opposite.

headhunter An independent employment service or individual that searches out personnel usually for specific high-level business executive positions, formally known as an executive search agency, company or consultancy. Headhunters are generally used by organizations that are looking outside their present staff to fill key senior positions. An example of a major headhunting company is London-based Saxton Bampfylde Hever, who have been involved in finding senior personnel in the arts, business, government and higher education industries internationally.

headline A headline is the text at the top of a newspaper article or web page, indicating the nature of the article below it. Headlines may be written in bold and in a much larger size than the article text. Headline conventions include normally using the present tense, omitting forms of the verb 'to be' in certain contexts and removing the articles 'a' and 'the'. Most newspapers or web news providers such as the BBC use a very large headline on their front or opening page, outlining what they perceive as the key story of the day.

heavy user Consumer whose purchases of a product are larger than average.

hedging In finance, a hedge is an investment that is taken out specifically to reduce or cancel out the risk in another investment. Hedging is a strategy designed to minimize exposure to an unwanted business risk, while still allowing the business to profit from an investment activity. A long hedge involves buying futures contracts to protect against possible increasing prices of commodities. A short hedge involves selling futures contracts to protect against possible declining prices of commodities.

heterogeneous Mixed or diverse. The term is used to describe groups, samples and populations with high variability.

heteroscedasticity A situation in which there are considerably unequal variances in the dependent variable for the same values of the independent variable in the different populations being sampled and contrasted in a regression analysis or an ANOVA. From *hetero*, meaning other or different, and *scedasticity*, meaning tendency to scatter. Heteroscedasticity is the direct opposite of HOMOSCEDASTICITY.

heuristic programming A branch of artificial intelligence that uses heuristics, or common-sense rules drawn from experience, to solve problems. This is in contrast to algorithmic programming, which is based on mathematically provable procedures. Heuristic programming is characterized by programs that are self-learning and get better with experience. Heuristic programs do not always reach the very best result but usually produce a good result. Many expert systems use heuristic programming.

heuristics A problem-solving technique in which the most appropriate solution is selected using a range of key rules. Heuristics are rules of thumb people follow in order to make judgements quickly and efficiently. People use heuristics judgement to deal with the large amount of social information with which they are faced on a day-to-day basis.

hierarchical organization An organization in which power and responsibility are clearly allocated to individuals according to their relative standing or position. Good examples are the Catholic church, the judiciary, public services, royal families and military services.

hierarchy of effects model This is a model of marketing communication which proposes seven stages through which the buyer/customer passes from unawareness of a product or service to purchase: unawareness, awareness, knowledge, liking, preference, conviction and purchase. The basic idea of the hierarchy of effects model was proposed by R. J. Lavidge and G. A. Steiner ('A Model for Predictive Measurements of Advertising Effectiveness', *Journal of Marketing* (1961)). In their view, consumers do not switch from uninterested individuals to convinced purchasers in one instantaneous step. Rather, they approach the ultimate decision through a process or series of steps in which the actual purchase is but the final step. This is the reason why the hierarchy of effects model has been considered a 'stair-step and linear' model.

hierarchy of needs model *See* MASLOW'S HIERARCHY OF NEEDS.

high-involvement model An advertising medium that requires active involvement on the part of the consumer. Print media are generally considered to be high-involvement models, since the consumer must be an active participant in the sense that he or she must read in order to gain information.

high-involvement products Products for which the buyer is prepared to spend considerable time and effort in searching. This is because of the risks involved in making the wrong choice. Consumers are likely to be highly involved in purchasing products such as homes and computers and be more aware of performance, financial, safety, social, psychological or time consequences. For example, if one were to buy a car, one would be investing a fair amount of money in it, and hence the risk of making a loss if one made a bad decision would be high. Hence one would go through a process of looking at many cars, collecting information, etc. before deciding about which car to buy. *See also* LOW-INVOLVEMENT PRODUCTS.

high-street retailing Retail activity in traditional shopping areas of town, city, urban and suburban locations. Over the last decade there has been a movement of large retailers to develop out-of-town stores which has fuelled debate concerning the future vitality and viability of high street retailing. This has focused many local government organizations to focus on retail retention and regeneration strategies to maintain this sector within their local economies.

histogram *See* BAR CHART OR GRAPH.

historical trend A pattern revealed through the analysis of current and historical data, for instance of customer visits, complaints, sales or market growth. The use of this analysis allows the organization to focus activities on the most lucrative parts of the market.

hit A request for a file from a web server. It is often used as a measure of attractiveness of a website or its content.

hit list Names of prospective customers, usually held by a sales person, who then sets out to convert them into actual customers.

hit rate The rate at which sales calls are converted into actual sales, expressed as a percentage. It is also now associated with website usage and is a means of measuring the number of visits to a particular site.

hoarding A wooden structure, or large outdoor advertising signboard, used to carry advertisements. It is also known as a billboard.

hold-over audience Listeners or viewers who stay tuned to a station after having heard or seen a particular programme.

hologram A special effect three-dimensional picture as used on credit cards for instance. A true hologram is created optically with laser light. Holograms are created by projecting half of a laser light beam directly on to an object as well as on to a photographic plate, which also receives the other half of the beam directly. The interference pattern created on the plate replicates the image or object in three dimensions. Holograms are very difficult to copy or simulate without sophisticated, expensive equipment and much expertise. They are used for security and aesthetic purposes on ID, credit cards and passports, etc., and are very effective for authentication of genuine articles or protection against forgery. They are generally much more expensive than other security features, depending on the manufacturer, but may be needed for birth certificates, some licences and immigration papers.

home audit The regular measurement of product purchases and in some cases consumption using a panel of households. It is regularly used in testing new developments

Hofstede, Geert

A world-renowned expert on the inter-actions between national cultures and organizational cultures. Hofstede has authored several books including *Culture's Consequences*, *Cultures and Organizations* and *Software of the Mind*. He was Professor of Organizational Anthropology at the University of Limburg, Maastricht, in the Netherlands until his retirement.

Hofstede demonstrated that there are national and regional cultural groupings that affect the behaviour of organizations, and that are very persistent across time. He identified five dimensions of culture in his study of national influences:

- Power distance: the degree to which the less powerful members of society expect there to be differences in the levels of power. A high score suggests that there is an expectation that some individuals wield larger amounts of power than others. Countries with high power-distance rating are often characterized by a high rate of political violence. A low score reflects the view that all people should have equal rights. Latin American and Arab nations are ranked the highest in this category, Scandinavian and German-speaking countries the lowest.
- Individualism v. collectivism: the extent to which people are expected to stand up for themselves or alternatively act predominantly as a member of the group or organization. Latin American cultures rank the lowest in this category, while the US is the most individualistic culture.
- Masculinity v. femininity: masculine cultures value competitiveness, assert-iveness, ambition and the accumulation of wealth and material possessions, whereas feminine cultures place more value on relationships and quality of life. Japan is considered by Hofstede to be the most 'masculine' culture, Sweden the most 'feminine'. The US and UK are moderately masculine.
- Uncertainty avoidance: the extent to which a society attempts to cope with anxiety by minimizing uncertainty. Cultures that score highly in uncertainty avoidance prefer rules (e.g. about religion and food) and structured circumstances, in these cultures employees tend to remain longer with their present employer. Mediterranean cultures and Japan rank the highest in this category.
- Long- v. short-term orientation: a society's 'time horizon', or the importance attached to the future as opposed to the past and present. In long-term-oriented societies, thrift and perseverance are valued more; in short-term-oriented societies, respect for tradition and reciprocation of gifts and favours are valued more. Eastern nations tend to score especially highly here, with Western nations scoring low and the less developed nations very low; China scores the highest and Pakistan the lowest.

Hofstede was the first to analyse cultural differences systematically and apply them to business management, and his work has made managers in international companies more sensitive to cultural differences as they affect both employees and customers in a globalizing economy.

in products such as cereals, detergents, personal products and shampoos. Data may be collected by means of diaries, interviews, regular visits and even dustbin checks.

home market The market of the geo-graphical area or country in which an organization's headquarters are based.

home page The page designated as the main point of entry of a website (or main page) or the web page that comes up when a

Holbrook, Morris B. ('The Cat')

The W. T. Dillard Professor of Marketing in the Graduate School of Business at Columbia University who, since 1975, has taught courses in Marketing Strategy, Sales Management, Research Methods, Consumer Behaviour and Commercial Communication in the Culture of Consumption. His research has covered a wide variety of topics in marketing and consumer behaviour with a special focus on issues related to communication in general and to AESTHETICS, SEMIOTICS, hermeneutics, art, entertainment, nostalgia and stereography in particular. His books include *Consumer Research: Introspective Essays on the Study of Consumption*, *Daytime Television Game Shows* and *The Celebration of Merchandise: The Price Is Right*.

browser first connects to the Internet. Typically, it welcomes visitors and introduces the purpose of the site, or the organization sponsoring it, and then provides links to the lower-level pages of the site. In business terms it is what grabs the attention. If a company's home page downloads too slowly, or it is unclear or uninteresting, they may well lose a customer.

homeostasis A state of physiological balance within the individual. For example, a lack of fluid leads to the uncomfortable sensation of thirst. The individual seeks products, such as soft drinks, that reduce the ensuing tension to return to a state of physiological balance or homeostasis.

homogeneous Generally, the same or similar. Used to refer to POPULATIONS and samples that are similar and consequently have low variability.

homoscedasticity **1** Homogeneity of variances. **2** A condition of substantially equal variances in the dependent variable for the same values of the independent variable in the different populations being sampled and compared in a regression analysis or an ANOVA. From *homo*, meaning same or equal, and *scedasticity*, meaning tendency to scatter. Parametric statistical tests usually assume homoscedasticity. If that assumption is violated, the results of those tests will be of doubtful validity. *See also* HETEROSCEDASTICITY.

horizontal integration When an organization moves to acquire its competitors or make some other form of strategic association. *See also* VERTICAL INTEGRATION.

horizontal market A market which meets a given need of a wide variety of industries, rather than a specific one. The opposite of VERTICAL MARKET.

hotline A telephone line that gives quick and direct access to a source of information or help. It allows customers and concerned citizens to seek information or express opinions to businesses, government agencies and NON-PROFIT ORGANIZATIONS. Originally, businesses set up free phone numbers to cater for those customers who had hitherto written letters to obtain information or express concerns. Astute businesses were among the first organizations to realize that all customers might wish additional information about products and services, so hotlines were established to make it easy for a customer to call an expert to seek advice on the use of a product or to solve a problem relevant to a product or service, such as might occur with an insurance policy. Government organizations and non-profit organizations soon recognized the virtue of this kind of constituent contact and built it into their service delivery process.

HTML (hypertext mark-up language)
The basic language used to write web pages. Is consists of a set of codes that are displayed over a web browser. It is a guide for the browser with instructions on how the page is set up and where and how text and graphics should be placed. HTML is a mark-up language and not a full-blown

Hunt, Shelby D.

One of the great thinkers and writers on marketing theory. He is a past editor of the *Journal of Marketing* (1985–7) and author of *Foundations of Marketing Theory: Toward a General Theory of Marketing* and *A General Theory of Competition: Resources, Competences, Productivity, Economic Growth*. He has written innumerable articles on competitive theory, macromarketing, ethics, channels of distribution, philosophy of science and marketing theory. Hunt is currently the Jerry S. Rawls and P. W. Horn Professor of Marketing at Texas Tech University, Lubbock, Texas, USA.

For his contributions to theory and science in marketing, he received the Paul D. Converse Award from the American Marketing Association in 1986, the Outstanding Marketing Educator Award from the Academy of Marketing Science in 1987, and the American Marketing Association/ Richard D. Irwin Distinguished Marketing Educator Award in 1992. His current research interests are marketing theory, marketing ethics, marketing strategy and competition theory.

programming language so is therefore essentially static in nature. Originally defined by Tim Berners-Lee, the inventor of the World Wide Web, HTML is now an international standard.

human capital A form of specialist capital (resources that can produce income) that exists within persons rather than externally to them. Education, organizational knowledge, skill and strength are good examples of human capital.

human resource management The structured policies, plans and processes for the effective management of employees. Specific areas of interest include: (a) employee recruitment and selection; (b) staff training and development; (c) employee reward, appraisal and evaluation processes; and (d) internal communications. Generally, the aim has been to instil employee commitment – to create shared values, encourage innovation, promote flexible and adaptable behaviours, foster communication and shift emphasis away from control of employees to autonomy and empowerment. One of the largest professional organizations in this area is the Chartered Institute of Personnel and Development based in the UK, which is increasingly operating internationally to promote quality standards in this area.

hype In broadcast, special promotional activities in programming presented by a station or network in order to attract a large audience and therefore generate higher audience ratings for a particular time period. It can also be applied to the extreme promotion of a person, idea or product.

hypermarket A store that combines a supermarket and a department store, usually built on the outskirts of a town. The result is a gigantic retail facility that carries an enormous range of products under one roof, including full lines of fresh groceries and apparel. Some of the largest hypermarkets can be seen on the French Channel coast selling duty-free goods to returning British travellers. Proximity to border crossings, transport hubs such as airports and railway interchanges are also prime locations for major hypermarkets.

hypothesis A term used to describe a proposal intended to explain certain facts or observations. A hypothesis is a tentative theory about the natural world and/or a concept that is not yet verified but that, if true, would explain certain facts or phenomena. Thus a scientific hypothesis that survives experimental testing becomes a scientific theory.

hypothesis testing A means of interpreting the results of a clinical trial that involves determining the probability that an observed treatment effect could have occurred due to chance alone if a specified

HYPOTHESIS were true. The specified hypothesis is normally a null hypothesis, made prior to the trial, that the intervention of interest has no true effect. Hypothesis testing is used to determine if the null hypothesis can or cannot be rejected.

icon A graphical on-screen representation of a software program, function, menu item, hardware peripheral, etc., used extensively in GUI applications, e.g. the icon for the 'File Manager' utility in Microsoft Windows is a 3-D representation of an office filing cabinet. In addition sometimes used as a term to refer to a leading international brand or personality such as Cartier in jewellery and Jonah Lomu in rugby union football.

ICT (information communications technology) The use of computer-based information systems and communications systems to process, transmit and store data and information. Includes any communication device such as radio, television, mobile phones, computer hardware and software, satellite systems and so on, as well as the various services and applications associated with them, such as videoconferencing and distance learning.

idealism A wide range of philosophical doctrines and perspectives methodologically important for their belief that the mind and its own ideas are the ultimate source and criteria of knowledge.

identity theft The stealing of information about a person that allows a second person to assume the identity of the first. Essentially this only requires knowledge of very limited information, including a national insurance or ID number. While most identity theft still occurs through the traditional means of scouring household waste for documents containing personal information, the threat of theft over the Internet is a growing concern for e-commerce. It can occur as data are in transit (for a transaction), or data stored on a company's site are stolen, or from PHISHING activities. Theft can also occur via GOOGLE hacking (i.e. documents that are available on the Internet that should not be available, but are easily found via search engines).

ideology A system of beliefs held by a group that tends to serve the interests of that group. In research reports, one generally reserves the term 'ideology' for positions one dislikes and positions seen as intransigent and not grounded in scientific rationale or reason.

image In common usage, an image (taken from the Latin *imago*, or picture) is an artifact that reproduces the likeness of some subject, usually a physical object or a person. In marketing it most frequently refers to the consumer perception of a brand, organization, retail outlet, etc. It is made up of two separable but interacting components, one consisting of the attributes of the object, the other consisting of the characteristics of the user. *See also* BRAND IMAGE.

IMP (Industrial Marketing and Purchasing) Group An academic group formed in the 1970s by researchers originating from the Universities of Uppsala, Bath, UMIST, ESC Lyon and the Ludwig Maximilian's University (Munich). Leading figures have included Malcolm Cunningham, Hakan Hakansson, David Ford, Geoff Easton, Evert Gummesson, Lars-Gunner Mattson and Kris Moller among many others.

The IMP Group developed a dynamic model of buyer–supplier relationships in industrial markets (the interaction model) and illustrated its applicability through comparative studies of buyer–supplier relationships within and across a number of European countries (France, Germany, Italy, Sweden, the UK). The main conclusion of these pan-European studies was that buying and selling in industrial markets could not be understood as a series of disembedded and serially independent transactions. Instead, transactions could only be examined as episodes in often long-standing and complex relationships between the buying and selling organizations. These relationships seemed to be fairly stable when studied over long periods of time but turned out to very dynamic when looked at in more fine-grained detail. The results of these studies were published in two books which are still widely used and cited.

The IMP Group is now embedded in a wider community of researchers concerned with industrial marketing and purchasing. Since 1984 the Group has organized an annual conference that has become an important meeting place for all researchers sharing an interest in inter-organizational relationships and networks.

impact The force with which an advertising or promotional message registers in a person's mind.

imperfect competition Any form of competition which does not conform with the definition of perfect competition. It is used to describe competition between many suppliers where the emphasis is on differentiation and non-price competition. In economic theory, imperfect competition is the competitive situation in any market where the conditions necessary for perfect competition are not satisfied.

Forms of imperfect competition include:

- monopoly, in which there is only one seller of a good;
- oligopoly, in which there is a small number of sellers;
- monopolistic competition, in which

there are many sellers producing highly differentiated goods;
- monopsony, in which there is only one buyer of a good;
- oligopsony, in which there is a small number of buyers.

There may also be imperfect competition in markets due to buyers or sellers lacking information about prices and the goods being traded, or to a time lag in a market.

imports Goods that are produced abroad but purchased for use in the domestic economy.

impression An ad delivered by a server to a user's browser. It is also known as an exposure. The number of impressions determines the cost of online ads in CPM pricing models.

impulse buying Spur-of-the-moment decisions to buy, made at the time of purchase. Goods which are apt to be bought impulsively, for example magazines, chocolate or flowers, are usually placed close to the point of payment. Goods which are often bought routinely, like cereals or shampoos, may also be subject to impulse buying. The regular brand may be passed over if another catches the consumer's eye or is the focus of a sales promotion.

in-depth interview An extended interview, usually on an individual basis, in which the interviewer explores a topic in considerable depth. The interviewer may follow an unstructured approach, using a list of pivotal issues to remind them of the key issues to be explored, or a semi-structured approach with a more detailed checklist of questions. It can sometimes be referred to as a 'depth interview'.

in-house This describes activities conducted within a business as against those contracted out to a specialist supplier.

in-pack premium A premium included in the packaging of another product (e.g., buy a can of shaving cream and get a free razor in the same shrink-wrapped package). The term package enclosure is also used.

in-store promotion Promotional activity located within a sales outlet.

incentive Any factor (financial or non-financial) that provides a motive for a particular course of action, or counts as a reason for preferring one choice to the alternatives. Incentives can be classified according to the different ways in which they motivate agents to take a particular course of action. One common and useful method subdivides incentives into three broad classes:

- Remunerative incentives (or financial incentives) are said to exist where an agent can expect some form of material reward – especially money – in exchange for acting in a particular way, for example offering salesmen bonuses, commission and/or prizes.
- Moral incentives are said to exist where a particular choice is widely regarded as the right thing to do, or as particularly admirable, or where the failure to act in a certain way is condemned as indecent. A person acting on a moral incentive can expect a sense of self-esteem and approval or even admiration from his or her community; a person acting against a moral incentive can expect a sense of guilt and condemnation or even ostracism from the community.
- Coercive incentives are said to exist where a person can expect that the failure to act in a particular way will result in punitive measures being taken against him or her (or his/her loved ones) by others in the community – for example, the inflicting of pain or punishment, imprisonment or the confiscation or destruction of possessions.

incentive marketing The function of providing special additional reasons for making a purchase, such as tactical pricing, competitions, premium offers, prizes and interest-free credit. It is also known as consumer promotions.

income The money that is received as a result of the normal business activities of an individual or organization. For example,

for individuals income usually means the gross amount on their pay slips, i.e. the amount before any tax and other deductions have been made by their employer.

Internationally, the accounting term income is synonymous with the term revenue. One of the best accounting definitions of income is the one used by the International Accounting Standards Board: 'Income is increases in economic benefits during the accounting period in the form of inflows or enhancements of assets or decreases of liabilities that result in increases in equity, other than those relating to contributions from equity participants' (IFRS Framework, F.70).

incrementalism The notion that public policy and/or social change is usually brought about through small, piecemeal alterations. Called 'salami tactics' by William Safire, incrementalism is said to be typical of pluralism, where the many veto groups make it difficult to enact major synoptic change.

Independent Television Commission (ITC) The statutory body responsible from 1991 to the end of 2003 for the licensing of commercially funded television stations in the UK and for regulating both programme and advertising content. The UK government, in a policy paper, declared its intention to merge the ITC with the Radio Authority, the Office of Telecommunications and the Radiocommunications Agency. This merger, under the Communications Act 2003, took effect on 29 December 2003. Most powers of the ITC are now exercised by the Office of Communications (Ofcom), making some powers – and the ITC itself – defunct.

independent variable A variable which is manipulated or selected by the experimenter to determine its relationship to an observed phenomenon (the DEPENDENT VARIABLE). In other words, the experiment will attempt to find evidence that the values of the independent variable determine the values of the dependent variable (which is what is being measured). The independent variable can be changed as required, and its values do not represent a problem requiring explanation in an analysis, but are taken simply as given.

index **1** A summary statistic which condenses a large amount of data into a single, readily understandable number which can be compared over time and related to the original base number, e.g. the RETAIL PRICE INDEX, the DOW JONES INDEX. **2** In publishing, a detailed list, usually arranged alphabetically, of the specific information in a publication. **3** In economics, a single number calculated from an array of prices and quantities.

indexing A statistical term describing a method of standardizing the base for comparative data in a time series, usually equating the initial measure to 100 and then expressing all other data in exact relation to that base, e.g. the index of wholesale prices in any year by comparison with a base year of 100 might stand at 92 or 108 to indicate a fall or rise of 8 per cent respectively. *See also* PRICE INDEX.

inductive Using statistical methods to form generalizations by finding similarities among a large number of cases. Inductive characterizes a reasoning process of generalizing from facts, instances or examples. *See also* DEDUCTIVE.

industrial advertising The advertising of products or services to industrial, commercial or business organizations. This often involves industrial or technical products but can refer to the advertising of any goods or services which might be made by any such organization as opposed to advertising directed at consumer markets.

industrial buying behaviour The factors and motivations which go into organizational purchasing. *See also* DECISION-MAKING UNIT (DMU); BUYING MOTIVES.

industrial goods Goods and services purchased by industrial buyers for use in the production of their own goods and services or in the conduct of their business. Industrial goods can be broadly classified as equipment, raw materials and services.

industrial marketing *See* B2B MARKETING.

industrial marketing research The specialist research of industrial markets, which focuses on organizational buying behaviour and the way network transactions are conducted in these B2B marketplaces.

industrial selling Selling to industry for industrial consumption, e.g. catering or fuel products, but more usually goods required for further production, e.g. raw materials and machinery. *See also* B2B MARKETING.

inelastic demand *See* ELASTICITY OF DEMAND.

inertia selling Goods delivered to a PROSPECT upon a sale-or-return basis without the previous consent or knowledge of the prospect.

inferential statistics Statistics that allow one to draw conclusions or inferences from data. Usually this means forthcoming conclusions, such as estimates, generalizations, decisions or predictions about a population on the basis of data describing a sample.

inflation An economic phenomenon in which decreasing purchasing power of a currency is caused by a persistent tendency of prices to rise, often sharply. *See also* DEFLATION.

influencer A person in a business who has an effect on buying decisions and helps the purchasing manager decide which products to buy.

infomercial A television home commercial that runs as long as an average TV show (approximately 28 minutes). The term infomercial is made up of the words information and commercial. Infomercials, sometimes known as TV shopping or viewer promotional programming, are normally shown outside prime viewing hours such as late at night, early in the morning and Saturday and Sunday morning on the main TV networks. Infomercials are designed to stimulate a direct response from viewers to purchase a particular product over the telephone in a given time period for certain financial benefits. Thus, place your order in the next hour and be amongst the first to receive the ... Infomercials are normally part of the promotional mix used in DIRECT RESPONSE MARKETING.

information systems (IS) 1 The equipment and facilities that collect, process, store, display and disseminate information. This includes computer hardware and software and communications, as well as policies and procedures for their use. **2** A system, whether automated or manual, that comprises people, machines, and/or methods organized to collect, process, transmit and disseminate data that represent user information.

INFORMS (Institute for Operational Research and Management Science) The largest professional society in the world for professionals in the field of operations research (OR). It was established in 1995 with the merger of the Operations Research Society of America (ORSA) and the Institute for Management Sciences (TIMS). The society serves the scientific and professional needs of OR educators, investigators, scientists, students, managers and consultants, as well as their organizations. It publishes twelve scholarly journals that describe the latest OR methods and applications and a membership magazine with news from across the profession. It organizes national and international conferences for academics and professionals, as well as members of the society's special interest groups. It serves as a focal point for OR professionals, permitting them to communicate with each other and reach out to other professional societies, as well as the varied clientele of the profession's research and practice.

initiator The individual who first recognizes a felt need and initiates the buying process.

inner wrap An advertising message that is printed on the plastic bag which wraps the Sunday newspaper package of comics, magazines and advertising inserts.

innovation The process of converting knowledge and ideas into better ways of doing business or into new or improved products and services that are valued by the community. The innovation process incorporates research and development, commercialization and technology diffusion. As all products normally have a life cycle which dictates that, at some point, their usefulness will decline, innovation is an essential ingredient to long-term development of commercial enterprise, and its absence must lead to the decline of the enterprise itself. *See also* CONTINUOUS INNOVATION.

Innovation-Adoption Model A model developed by Everett Rogers in *Diffusion of Innovations* (1962), who postulated a number of stages through which a targeted buyer or customer passes, from a state of unawareness, through awareness, interest, trial, to purchase/adoption. *See also* DIFFUSION OF INNOVATION THEORY.

innovator One of the five terms originally proposed in Everett Rogers's DIFFUSION OF INNOVATION THEORY. A consumer who is first within the market to adopt an innovation. Advertisers can optimize the cost effectiveness of a new product advertising campaign by targeting innovators and EARLY ADOPTERS. *See also* ADOPTER CATEGORIES.

input Information entered into a computer for processing, as from a keyboard or from a file stored on a disk drive. Normally used as a noun or an adjective, the word is often also used as a verb meaning to enter information.

inquiry The initial request from a prospective buyer or user for information, often following some form of advertising or sales promotion, usually with a particular purchase in mind or under consideration. *See also* SALES LEAD.

insert Piece of sales promotional material placed into the pages of a publication, either loosely or bound in.

inside covers Premium positions in a magazine, the inside back and the inside front.

instant gratification A term ascribed to

consumer behaviour associated with 'free spending' and the philosophy of 'buy now, pay later'. *See also* DELAYED GRATIFICATION.

Institute of Direct Marketing (IDM) Europe's leading professional development body for direct, data and digital marketing. Founded in 1987, the IDM is an educational trust and registered charity and is the internationally recognized leading body for the professional development of direct, data and digital marketing. As a global provider, the IDM acts as an expert partner to individuals and companies worldwide.

Institute of Export (IE) A registered charity whose mission is to enhance the export performance of the United Kingdom by setting and raising professional standards in international trade management and export practice. This is achieved principally by the provision of education and training programmes.

institutional advertising Advertising undertaken for whole industries rather than individual corporations, e.g 'Eat More Fruit'. *See also* CORPORATE ADVERTISING.

integrated marketing The bringing-together of all marketing communications so as to have common or complementary messages, themes, visual identity, response mechanisms and timing. Also, to inter-relate with the sales force and other elements in the marketing plan. The rationale is that, by so doing, the outcome will be synergistic.

integrated marketing communications A management concept that is designed to make all aspects of marketing communication such as advertising, sales promotion, public relations and direct marketing work together as a unified force over time, rather than permitting each to work in isolation.

integration A strategy aimed at increasing profit and/or sales turnover and/or market share by acquiring other companies in related fields. There are three forms of integration: backward integration, whereby a company acquires one or more of its suppliers; forward integration, in which some part of the distribution is taken over; and, finally, the most common form – horizontal integration, in which acquisition of some of the competition takes place. *See also* ACQUISITION; DIVERSIFICATION.

intellectual capital The knowledge assets of an organization. Knowledge assets include the internal knowledge employees have of information processes, external and internal experts, products, customers and competitors. Intellectual capital includes internal proprietary reports, libraries, patents, copyrights and licences that record the company history and help it plan for tomorrow.

intellectual property (IP) An internationally used umbrella term for the various legal entitlements which can be attached to intangible forms of property such as inventions, patents, broadcasting and performing rights, trademarks and copyright. The holder or owner of these legal entitlements is generally entitled to exercise various exclusive rights in relation to the subject matter of the IP. The term intellectual property reflects the idea that this subject matter is the product of the mind or the intellect, and that IP rights may be protected at law in the same way as any other form of property ownership.

interaction approach This approach was first introduced in 1982 by the IMP (INDUSTRIAL MARKETING AND PURCHASING GROUP), who became actively involved in a joint research project, based in international markets, which saw the buyer–seller relationship as pivotal to the whole basis of industrial marketing and consequently what has come to be called B2B marketing. It marked a turning point in industrial marketing theory and thought as no longer was the MARKETING MIX considered to be the only active partner in a relationship.

interaction effect The joint effect of two or more independent variables on a dependent variable. Interaction effects occur when independent variables act in combination on dependent variables. The presence of statistically significant inter-action effects makes it difficult to interpret main effects.

interactive television (ITV) Television programming that allows viewers to par-ticipate in some way. This may involve vot-ing for who should be eliminated from a contest, picking the next action on a pro-gramme or choosing from a menu of con-tent options. For the experience to be truly interactive, the viewer must be able to alter the viewing experience (e.g. choose the camera angle from which to watch a foot-ball match) or return information to the broadcaster. The return signal from homes (the 'return path' or 'back channel') may be via a touchtone telephone, the web or directly over a two-way cable system.

Interbrand's Brand Equity Model When seen as a corporate marketing asset a brand is a symbol of the expected future profits of a company and the key issue for marketers and investors is how do you cal-culate the value of that brand. Interbrand is a UK-based branding consultancy which has led the way in defining a consistent and workable methodology for brand strength assessment and publishes an annual table of the best-performing brands. Its criteria for brand value includes future business prospects of the brand and the brand's market environment, as well as consumer perceptions. Interbrand's seven core criteria consist of the following:

- *Leadership*. A brand that leads its mar-ket sector is more stable and powerful than other market entrants. This criter-ion reflects ECONOMIES OF SCALE for the first-place brand in communication and distribution, as well as the prob-lems also-rans have in maintaining dis-tribution and avoiding price erosion.
- *Stability*. Long-lived brands with iden-tities that have become part of the fab-ric of the market – and even of the culture – are particularly powerful and valuable.
- *Market*. Brands are more valuable when they are in markets with growing or stable sales levels and a price structure

in which successful firms can be profit-able. Some markets, such as consumer electronics, are so rife with debilitating price competition that the prospects of any brand being profitable are dim.
- *International*. Brands that are inter-national are more valuable than national or regional brands, in part because of economies of scale. More generally, the broader the scope of a brand, the more valuable it is.
- *Trend*. The overall long-term trend of the brand in terms of sales can be expected to reflect future prospects. A healthy, growing brand indicates that it remains contemporary and relevant to consumers.
- *Support*. Brands that have received con-sistent investment and focused support are regarded as stronger than those that haven't; however, the quality of the support should be considered along with the level of support.
- *Protection*. The strength and breadth of a brand's legal trademark protection is critical to the brand's strength.

There are a number of brand assessment methods but Interbrand's method has tended to set the standard for the industry.

internal audit An internal audit is the part of the marketing audit which involves the examination of the internal operations, strengths and weaknesses of an organization.

internal marketing An essential ingredi-ent of RELATIONSHIP MARKETING, in which all employees are regarded as being in market-ing, the only difference being as to whether they are in customer-facing positions or providing a service to those who are.

internal validity The extent to which the results of a study, normally an experiment, can be attributed to the specific treatments rather than to the problems found in the research design. In other words, internal validity is the degree to which one can draw valid conclusions about the causal effects of one variable on another. It is highly dependent upon the extent to which extraneous variables have been controlled by the researcher.

International Advertising Association (IAA) A global partnership of advertisers, advertising agencies, the media and other related services, headquartered in New York City, whose objective is to establish a common platform for building and sustaining the prestige of the advertising profession and to serve as spokespersons against unwarranted attacks on members, provide information on advocacy, regulatory and constitutional issues affecting the marketing communications industry and maintain a list of recommendations for international advertising standards and practices for the benefit of its membership. Founded in 1938, the IAA's network includes more than 3,600 individual members in 92 countries and accounts for 99 per cent of the world's advertising expenditures.

The IAA sees itself as the one global organization committed to fighting unwarranted regulation on behalf of all those engaged in responsible commercial speech and to act as an advocate for freedom of choice for individuals across all consumer and business markets. The IAA champions advertising as a force for growth in all free market societies. Advertising revenues ensure an independent, pluralistic, affordable media with competing channels of information for consumers, which ensure that individuals have choices. The IAA is uniquely positioned to intercept emerging cross-border trends before they become obvious and to provide marketing communications professionals with an international, multi-industry forum for the global exchange of knowledge, best practices, professional development, intelligence, experience and ideas.

International Association of Business Communicators (IABC) An international information association of communications professionals with a worldwide membership of over 13,700 persons from nearly sixty countries. It came into being in 1970 as a merger between the American Association of Industrial Editors and the International Council of Industrial Editors, and was joined in 1974 by Corporate Communications Canada. IABC is 'dedicated to fostering communications excellence worldwide, to help communicators contribute to their organization's goals, and to being a model of communications excellence itself'. Its headquarters are in San Francisco, and it has chapters in 109 cities and twelve district or regional offices throughout the world. It offers a wide range of member services including a programme to become an Accredited Business Communicator, workshops, conferences, publications, resources for research, career planning and referrals and attempts to promote better understanding of the professional communicator's role.

International Bank for Reconstruction and Development *See* WORLD BANK.

international marketing Conducting a marketing operation simultaneously in a number of countries but with a strong degree of regional and central coordination. *See also* EXPORT MARKETING.

International Monetary Fund (IMF) An institution arising from the Bretton Woods Agreement in 1944, the fund being established from 1946. Its primary object is to maintain and stabilize international rates of exchange. It is also expected to provide facilities for arranging multilateral clearing systems and to help to eliminate restrictions on international trade. The IMF is often used by countries as a world bank, particularly when facing balance of payment difficulties, each country having drawing rights against present and anticipated contributions to the fund.

international standard book number (ISBN) An internationally utilized numeric code allotted to books for the purposes of identification and inventory control. The International Standard Book Number, or ISBN (sometimes pronounced 'is-ben'), is a unique identifier for books, intended to be used commercially. The ISBN system was a nine-digit code created in the UK in 1966 by the bookseller and stationer W. H. Smith and originally called Standard Book Numbering or SBN (a term used until 1974). It was adopted as international standard ISO 2108 in 1970. From 1 January 2007, ISBNs have been thirteen digits long. Each edition and variation (except reprints) of a book receives its own ISBN. *See also* INTERNATIONAL STANDARD SERIAL NUMBER (ISSN).

international standard serial number (ISSN) An ISSN is an eight-digit serial number used to identify a print or electronic periodical or journal publication and became the common international standard in 1975.

ISSN codes are similar in concept to INTERNATIONAL STANDARD BOOK NUMBER (ISBN) codes, which are assigned to individual books. ISSN codes are allocated by a network of ISSN national centres, usually located at national libraries and coordinated by the ISSN International Centre based in Paris.

international trade The exchange of products and services across national boundaries. Although more recently and with the growth in world trade it has come to mean trade across and with a number of states. *See also* AIB and SMITH, ADAM.

internationalization The distinction between internationalization and localization is subtle but important. Internationalization is the adaptation of products for *potential* use virtually everywhere, while localization is the addition of special features for use in a *specific* locale.

For successful localization, products must be technically and culturally neutral. Effective internationalization reduces the time and resources required for localization, improving time-to-market abroad and allowing simultaneous shipment. In other words, internationalization abstracts out local details, localization specifies those details for a particular locality.

In software markets internationalization (often shortened to I18N, an abbreviation of 'I - eighteen letters – N' for ease of communication) is the process of planning and implementing products and services so that they can easily be adapted to specific local languages and cultures, a process called localization (also abbreviated to L10N).

Internet The publicly accessible global network of interconnected computer networks which is based on transmitting data by packet switching using the standard INTERNET PROTOCOL (IP). It is made up of a 'network of networks' consisting of millions of smaller national networks of academic, business, consumer, government and not-for-profit networks that provide a platform information and data exchange that supports everyday communications and associated media such as electronic mail, blogging, file transfer, online chat, and the whole World Wide Web. The highest penetration rates of the Internet are in North America and Europe, with Asia showing very rapid growth in the last decade. The Netherlands and Norway have some of the highest usage rates in the world with over 85 per cent of their population regularly using the Internet.

Internet Advertising Bureau (IAB) A global not-for-profit association founded in 1996 and devoted exclusively to maximizing the effectiveness of advertising on the Internet. The IAB is the only association dedicated to helping online, interactive broadcasting, e-mail, wireless and interactive television media companies increase their revenues.

The IAB objectives are:

- to increase the share of advertising and marketing dollars that interactive media captures in the marketplace;
- to organize the industry to set standards and guidelines that make interactive an easier medium for agencies and marketers to buy and capture value;
- to prove and promote the effectiveness of interactive advertising to advertisers, agencies, marketers and press;
- to be the primary advocate for the interactive marketing and advertising industry;

- to expand the breadth and depth of IAB membership while increasing direct value to members.

Internet protocol (IP) The communications protocol which underpins the Internet, which allows large computer networks all over the world to communicate with each other efficiently. The IP address is the numerical address that is used to identify a network interface on a specific network or sub-network. Every computer or server on the Internet has an IP address. It is a unique number consisting of four parts separated by dots. For example, 167.207.1105.1. The address is made up of two pieces of information: the network portion, known as the IP network address; and the local portion, known as the local or host address.

The IP address can also be used to help determine where a web browser is located. This enables sites to present content specific to the location of the browser. For example, Amazon is able to present amazon.co.uk content to browsers who are accessing the site from the UK. Sites can also restrict access to a range of IP addresses; for example, Google is able to limit IP addresses originated in China to google.cn. Similarly, sites can present unique content to individual IP addresses based on previous activity with that IP address. This helps customize the user's computer access point and is being used very successfully as a sales and marketing platform to e-buyers.

Internet service provider *See* ISP.

interpretivism An approach to research that holds that we can have knowledge of the world only through our interpretations of it, for example classificatory schemes (such as the classification of animal species into mammals, insects, birds, etc. Given this, we cannot know the 'true' nature of the object world, separate from our perception of it.

In the interpretivist's methodology, the key is to understand, not to explain and predict, as in the naturalist's methodology. As a method, understanding must begin from the presupposition that there is at least some common ground between the researcher and the researched.

- Human behaviour is affected by knowledge of the social world.
- The social world does not 'exist' independently of human knowledge.
- Human life can only be understood from within. It cannot be observed from some external reality.
- Social life is a distinctively *human* product.
- Human beings, or the human mind, are the purposive source or origin of meaning.
- The human subject is equipped with elements of mind or of consciousness not derived from experience. It is a subject equipped to know, a subject that is the source of ideas.

interval scale (or level of measurement) A scale or measurement that describes variables in such a way that the distance between any two adjacent units of measurement (or 'intervals') is the same, but in which there is no meaningful zero point. Scores on an interval scale can meaningfully be added and subtracted, but not multiplied and divided.

interview The process of eliciting information from an individual (respondent) or group in a census or survey, either face to face, by phone, video link or over the Internet.

interview protocol A list of questions and instructions used to ask research questions. It is used as a guide and prompt system when interviewing subjects.

interviewer bias Opinion or prejudice on the part of an interviewer which is displayed during the interview process and thus affects the outcome of the interview. In research interviews, it is essential that the interviewer conducts the interview with total objectivity, so that respondents are not influenced by any outside biased questioning, factor or source in their responses.

intranet A private network inside an

organization that conforms to the same standards as the Internet but that is only for use inside the organization. Its websites may look and act exactly like those found on the Internet, but the intranet will only be accessible to those members or employees who have authorization and the security protocols to use it. Like the Internet, an intranet is used by its members to share information.

introduction stage The stage in the product life cycle when the new product is first introduced into the market.

introductory offer An offer, such as a discount or free gift, made to interest consumers in the purchase of a new product, or a product that has been changed or improved and is being reintroduced.

invention A new idea or way of doing things or a product which has not been tested in practice.

inventory A list of units of goods and their value kept for trade by a merchant. The valuation may be used in financial accounting and the planning of the stock units. Of Latin origin, this term is more widely used in the US; the UK term most frequently used is 'stockholding'.

invisible assets A major source of competitive advantage in that such assets largely reside in the skills of individuals and other intangible factors like reputation, image, corporate culture, etc. Because they are invisible they are difficult to benchmark and even more difficult to replicate.

invisible trade Items such as freight, insurance and financial services that are included in a country's balance-of-payments accounts (in the 'current' account), even though they are not recorded as physically visible exports and imports.

invoice A commercial document issued by a seller to a buyer, indicating the products, quantities and agreed prices and taxes paid for products or services that the seller has already provided the buyer with. An invoice indicates that, unless paid in advance, payment is due by the buyer to the seller, according to the agreed terms.

involvement In marketing, involvement, and specifically consumer involvement theory, is a method to understand the behaviour and psychology of your target customer audience. There are other methods, but few so simple and insightful. Involvement refers to how much time, thought, energy and other resources people devote to the consumption and purchase process. The emotional/rational scale is a measure of reason vs impulse, desire vs logic, passion vs prudence. These can be broken down into the following levels of involvement associated with particular purchases:

High involvement/rational. In this category you find expensive business purchases: anything relating to the technological infrastructure, the office location and lease, as well as the company health insurance plan. On the consumer side, high involvement/rational purchases tend to be linked to high cost. This category can include financial services and products, the purchase of a home or car, as well as major appliances and electronics.

High involvement/emotional. Organizational purchases that fall into this category might include office design, advertising and staff recruitment. For individual consumers, high involvement/emotional purchases can include jewellery, weddings and holiday travel plans. In some societies the selection of a husband or wife will fall into this group; as can the purchase of a house, car or boat. Again this depends on the culture of the individual consumer and how much purchasing power they have. Advertising in this category tends to focus on visual and emotional appeals, giving individuals and groups visual details with music.

Low involvement/rational. These are purchases made out of habit, which require limited thought, such as basic supermarket and stationery purchases. Here the typical role for advertising is to get people to sample or switch to an alternative product and break the automatic habit of spending their money with the competitor. So, special offers, coupons and other incentives as well as ways to differentiate or re-position the product. Over-the-counter medicines tend to fall into this category. But pain relievers, cough syrups and similar products, especially those for children, can be more emotionally driven. In that case, see the LI/E below.

Low involvement/emotional. The gratification we get from these products is emotional or sensual, but momentary – it doesn't last a long time. So we don't spend significant time thinking about the purchase of, for example, movies, sweets, an entertaining magazine, or a birthday card; perhaps selecting a restaurant for a special occasion. The advertising challenge here tends to be the promise of pleasure, of gratification and of personal hedonistic benefit. Strong brand positioning can strengthen this offering especially when in a crowded product category.

IPO (initial public offering) The offering of stockholding in a particular company through the launch and trading on a particular public stock market to the public. NASDAQ is a popular market for e-commerce-related companies in the US.

ISDN (integrated services digital network) A form of of circuit-switched telephone video-conferencing system, thus the phrase 'integrated services digital network'.

island display A self-standing unit in a retail outlet, typically a supermarket, in which goods are presented in an eye-catching way in order to attract extra sales.

ISP (Internet service provider) A business or organization that sells to consumers access to the Internet and related services. Usually for a monthly or yearly fee, the Internet service provider will provide a software package that enables the user to gain access to the Internet, provided the user has a personal computer with a modem.

Internet service providers include AOL (America On Line), BT Internet (UK) and Telstra (Australia). ISPs also serve large companies by providing a direct connection from the company's own network to the Internet.

issues management theory The use of issues, analysis and strategic responses so that organizations can adapt, respond and thereby proactively maintain mutually beneficial relationships with various constituencies. At its most basic, issues management is the public relations specialization encompassing an organization's efforts to monitor and communicate with various publics about a public issue. Issues management theory suggests that, while responsiveness is positive, early identification of such issues and change made proactively, rather than reactively, are important to reputation.

J

JavaScript A trade mark of Sun Microsystems and scripting language developed by Netscape to enable web authors to design interactive sites. Although it shares many of the features and structures of the full Java language, it was developed independently. JavaScript can interact with HTML source code, enabling web authors to spice up their sites with dynamic content. JavaScript is endorsed by a number of software companies and is an open language that anyone can use without purchasing a licence. It is supported by recent browsers from Netscape and Microsoft, though Internet Explorer supports only a sub-set, which Microsoft calls Jscript.

jingle A short song, mainly broadcast on radio and sometimes in television commercials, usually mentioning a brand or product benefit. It normally contains a memorable slogan and is set to an engaging melody. An effective jingle is constructed to stay in one's memory (colloquially, 'ringing a bell'). People often nostalgically remember a jingle decades later, even after the advertised brand has ceased to exist. The most common form of a jingle is a radio station's on-air musical or spoken station identity. The first known jingle was produced in the US for the cereal Wheaties in 1926. Memorable jingles have included probably the most globally well-known Diet Coke, 'Just for the taste of it', through to 'Nuts, whole hazlenuts, Cadbury's take 'em and they cover them in chocolate'.

JIT *See* JUST-IN-TIME.

job enrichment The attempt to make jobs more rewarding and less monotonous for the individual worker. Procedures used may include job enlargement (including more responsibilities in the job) or job rotation (allowing the worker to move from one job to another at specific intervals).

joint venture In defining joint ventures it is useful to differentiate between equity joint ventures and non-equity joint ventures. Equity joint ventures are often seen as 'traditional' joint ventures which are created when two or more parties (partners) join forces to create a new incorporated company in which each has an equity position. Thus each partner expects a proportional share of dividends and representation on the board.

Harrigan (1985) in her analysis sees joint ventures as 'separate entities with two or more active businesses as partners', with the emphasis being on the development of the child – a corporate 'entity created by partners for a specific activity' and normally over a fixed renewable period of time. Equity joint ventures can thus be defined as involving two or more legally distinct organizations (the parents) each of which invests in the venture and actively participates in the decision-making activities of the jointly owned entity.

The use of the parent/child metaphor for understanding joint ventures and their development is a good one which is widely used and can be extensively developed, to make sense of what is a difficult concept to comprehend. Using the atomic family as a metaphor one can explore and assess the corporate relationship and its direction. Is it a marriage of convenience? Have the partners entered into a formal contractual relationship, perhaps an equity joint venture (marriage) which could result upon consummation and other partnerings in the birth of a number of other joint ventures (as children)?

Or is the joint venture just the result of one brief alliance between the two parents which gave birth to an unwanted new corporate child. It was good at the time, but it is unwanted now, as the partners do not get on. Could it be adopted or fostered by somebody else?

If the relationship is a stable one, how is the child nurtured, educated and developed? Is it starved of funds and good staff or given these freely in quantities which will enable it to make its own way in the world and achieve full independence from its parents? Will it be allowed to enter adulthood and be responsible for its own actions rather than the parents controlling it and restricting its independence? Will the child eventually grow and challenge the parents' actions?

Contractor and Lorange (1988) explore the development of non-equity joint ventures and see them as agreements between partners to cooperate in some way, but do not necessarily see them leading to separate legal corporate entities. In non-equity joint ventures, like for example the Euro Tunnel contractor Trans Manche Link which was made up of four partners, the norm is to have carefully defined contracts setting down rules, regulations, formulas governing the allocation of tasks, costs, penalties and revenues. Contractor and Lorange give three examples which involve different levels of risk and return for the partners:

i) Exploration consortia, which often involves the sharing of costs out of the venture once a successful formula has been developed and marketed. Many offshore oil exploration ventures adopt this risk/profit-sharing approach.

ii) Research partnerships, where in contrast costs may be allocated by an agreed mechanism, but the revenue of the company is dependent on what each partner does with the formulation. This is commonly used as a mechanism for effective shared pharmaceutical research. The cost of such activity can be very punitive and the outcomes not always marketable.

iii) Co-production agreements, where each partner's costs are a function of its own efficiency in producing its part, while revenue is a function of the successful sales of the major partner. This has frequently been used in agreements in automotive and aerospace markets.

With non-equity joint ventures, rewards for each firm are dependent upon the level of profits earned and there is a reasonable degree of inter-organizational dependence, much as there is with equity joint ventures. In terms of financial benefits, it can also be seen that the use of joint ventures offers much scope for parent companies to keep borrowings, losses and returns on capital off the main balance sheet and thus trigger asset and profit growth.

All other types of cooperative agreements, such as contracting, franchising and licensing, may be considered as contractual arrangements where reward is determined by profits generated and inter-organizational dependence is low to negligible. Thus the term 'joint venture' is frequently used as a catch-all to define a number of commercial arrangements and relationships, some fairly loose, whilst others are characterized by formal equity stakes and linkages to third parties. Christelow (1987) suggests a very broad definition of joint-ventures: 'Joint ventures are co-operative forms of organisation between independent parties who could otherwise engage in competition or have competitive potential.'

This definition does not specify the necessity for creating a separate entity and can therefore include marketing agreements and teaming arrangements. Lyons (1991) suggests in analysing STRATEGIC ALLIANCES that there are four potential domains: technological, industrial, commercial and financial. Thus cooperations and joint ventures can be formed on the basis of any combination of these domains.

The ability to do more through SYNERGY is also a factor, as organizations need to pool resources to compete and meet the needs of the global customer. Joint ventures can be a very effective way of putting two or more organizations together to create something greater than the sum of the two parts by synergy. The development of Airbus Industries, a result of four partners pooling their expertise and resources to create a world-class EU-based commercial aircraft supplier from a much smaller base, shows the great benefits of synergy. Technology, engineering, marketing, finance and modern management have been put together from various countries and industries into one group which through synergy has developed this business.

The benefits of synergy are difficult to bring about and test managers to the full in many cases. The experience of acquisitions and mergers is not good as there seems little benefit from synergy in many cases as very often the two or more organizations do not fit together very well and they are certainly not complementary. This can result in failure on a grand scale, as can be seen in the poor results and declining profits of merged groups which have attracted corporate predators who then acquire them and dismember them.

The prevailing management style has been decentralization in the last two decades, to counter poor mergers. However, synergy, through putting together companies to make something more successful on a global scale, is now becoming a necessity of international business life. Crompton (1990) observes that some organizations are now too decentralized to benefit from the synergy of their product portfolios, and as a result competitive advantage in their industries is being lost. He argues that some businesses need restructuring 'to exploit potential shared resources, where these give competitive advantage (e.g. by creating a distribution company or upstream component manufacturing unit)'.

The criticisms of joint ventures are numerous and a prime one is that they are often unstable because of partners and risk of business and have normally only a short corporate life before becoming part of some other group or being broken up. Also, in some countries like China and India they are commercial arrangements with the state where 51 per cent is controlled by the government and the rest by the foreign partner and that technology and INTELLECTUAL PROPERTY are often lost by the non-indigenous partner. Even given these difficulties, such joint ventures can be highly successful for both corporate entities, for example the Shanghai-Volkswagen Company which is a 50:50 joint venture aims to supply 20 per cent of the Chinese car market by 2010.

Sources and References

Christelow, D. B. (1987), 'International joint ventures: how important are they', *Columbia Journal of World Business*, Vol. 22, No. 2, Summer, pp. 7–13.

Contractor, F. J. and Lorange, P. (eds) (1988), *Cooperative Strategies in International Business*, Lexington, MA: Lexington Books.

Crompton, R. (1990), 'The Return of Synergy', *Long Range Planning*, Vol. 23, No 5, pp. 122–4.

Harrigan, K. R. (1988), 'Strategic Alliances and Partner Asymmetries', *Management International Review*, Vol. 28, pp. 53–72.

Harris, P. and Dodd, M. (2004), 'EVC (1986–94): The European PVC Industry and the Creation of The European Vinyls Corporation (EVC)' in Harris, P. and McDonald, F., *European Business and Marketing*, London: Sage.

Harris, P. and Harris, I. (2004), 'EVC (1995–2002): Joint Venture, The Amsterdam Stock Market Flotation and Acquisition by INEOS' in Harris, P. and McDonald, F., *European Business and Marketing*, London: Sage.

Killing, J. P. (1982), 'How to make a global joint venture work', *Harvard Business Review*, May/June, pp. 120–7.

Lorange, P. and Roos, J. (1991), 'Why some strategic alliances succeed and others fail', *The Journal of Business Strategy*, Vol. 12, No. 1, pp. 25–30.

Lyles, M. (1988), 'Learning among joint venture sophisticated firms,' in Contractor, F. J. and Lorange, P. (eds), *Cooperative Strategies in International*

Business, Lexington, MA: Lexingon Books.

Lyons, P. (1991), 'Joint-ventures as strategic choice – A literature review', *Long Range Planning*, Vol. 25, No. 1, pp. 90–9.

judgement sampling A procedure in which a researcher makes a judgement that a CONVENIENCE SAMPLE (e.g. volunteers) might be similar enough to a RANDOM SAMPLE that it could make sense to use statistical procedures designed for use on random samples. Selecting a sample according to the researcher's judgement of how representative it is is only recommended when a PROBABILITY SAMPLE is impossible or not practical.

junk mail Unsolicited mail such as letters, pamphlets, special offer brochures, catalogues and questionnaires issued by commercial organizations, political parties or charities, which may or may not be addressed to named individuals at the particular address. Junk mail has become highly despised by both consumers and environmentalists and given rise to the growth in use of 'no junk mail' stickers

on letter boxes. The main deliverers of junk mail are private and public postal services, which receive revenue per delivery. *See also* SPAM.

just-in-time (JIT) A management philosophy and inventory strategy implemented to improve the return on investment of a business by reducing in-process inventory and its associated costs. The process is driven by a series of signals, or Kanban, that tell production processes to make the next component. Kanban are usually simple visual signals, such as the presence or absence of a component on a shelf. New stock is ordered when stock reaches the reorder level. This saves warehouse space and costs. JIT can lead to dramatic improvements in a manufacturing organization's return on investment, quality and efficiency when implemented correctly. However, one drawback of the JIT system is that the reorder level is determined by historical demand. If demand rises above the historical average planning duration demand, the firm could deplete inventory and cause customer service issues.

K

keiretsu A Japanese term which describes a set of companies with interlocking business relationships and shareholdings.

key account The term account here refers to a pool of interactions and transactions between a customer and a supplier with respect to a specified set of offerings. As some accounts are more important than others, they may be termed 'key accounts'

Keynes, John Maynard
(1883–1946)

One of the most respected economists of the century who was so influential an entire school of modern economic thought bears his name. Many of his ideas were at the time of publication deemed revolutionary, and almost all are controversial. In fact Keynes's economics acts as a benchmark against which virtually all economists who came after him can be measured.

Keynes was born in Cambridge and went to King's College, Cambridge, where he earned his degree in mathematics in 1905. After graduating, Keynes took a post in the civil service in Britain. While there, he collected the material for his first book on economics, *Indian Currency and Finance*, in which he described the workings of India's monetary system. He returned to Cambridge in 1908 as a lecturer, then took a leave of absence to work for the British Treasury. By 1919, he was the Treasury's principal representative at the peace conference at Versailles after the First World War. He subsequently resigned because he thought the Treaty of Versailles was over-harsh in forcing non-sustainable reparations on the defeated Germans. He then returned to Cambridge to resume teaching. At the 1944 Bretton Woods Conference, where the INTER-NATIONAL MONETARY FUND (IMF) was established, Keynes was one of the architects of the post-war system of fixed exchange rates.

Keynes's *The General Theory* revolutionized the way economists thought about economics. It was path-breaking in several ways. The two most important are, first, that it introduced the notion of aggregate demand as the sum of consumption, investment and government spending. Second, it showed (or purported to show) that full employment could be maintained only with the help of government spending. Economists still argue about what Keynes thought caused high unemployment. Some think that Keynes attributed unemployment to wages that take a long time to fall. But Keynes actually wanted wages not to fall and advocated in *The General Theory* that wages be kept stable. A general cut in wages, he argued, would decrease income, consumption and aggregate demand. This would offset any benefits to output that the lower price of labour might have contributed.

Little of Keynes's original work survives in modern economic theory. Instead, his ideas have been endlessly revised, expanded and critiqued. Keynesian economics today, while having its roots in *The General Theory*, is chiefly the product of work by subsequent economists.

Kotler, Philip

Arguably the most well-known exponent of marketing management, principles, concepts and practices in the international arena. His work contributed to the legitimacy of the marketing discipline during a critical period in the discipline's history. A prolific author, he has published over 100 articles in leading journals, in areas such as marketing planning and control and marketing in not-for-profit, social and health-care contexts. His textbook *Marketing Management: Analysis, Planning, Implementation and Control* is the most widely used marketing textbook in graduate schools and his *Principles of Marketing* is often seen as the bench mark text for undergraduate marketing teaching.

Kotler is Professor of International Marketing at the Kellogg Graduate School of Management, Northwestern University, and has consulted for such companies as IBM, General Electric, AT&T, Honeywell, Bank of America and Merck. He has also advised governments on how to develop and position the skills and resources of their companies to compete globally.

because of implications for either or all parties. Good key account management has been seen as pivotal to success in many food manufacturer or wholesale markets where these particular customers provide the majority of sales.

keyword tag A META TAG used to help define the primary KEYWORDS of a web page.

keywords Keywords (normally not more than ten at a time) appear on the first page beneath the abstract of a research journal article, such as in the *Journal of Marketing Management*, and sum up the key terms and issues discussed in the work. These sets of keywords help online researchers to investigate articles and current thinking in a particular field of research or enquiry.

More recently the term has been commonly used to describe a key term typed into a web-based SEARCH ENGINE, such as GOOGLE, to illicit information or set off an inquiry.

kickback An illegal, secret payment made in return for a referral which resulted in a transaction or contract. Unlike a discount, which is a reduction in the selling price, a kickback is a payment to the individual and so may be regarded as a bribe and an unethical practice. Well-known cases of kickbacks have been reported in political scandals for contracts. Also used as a term to describe the dangerous pressure build-up at a well head which could lead to an explosion and fire.

kiosk A free-standing unit, usually in a retail store, which contains promotional material or selling information. It may or may not be staffed.

KISS principle 'Keep It Simple, Stupid'. This principle is generally considered one of the golden rules of selling and marketing and more recently web design and online business.

knocking copy Advertising material which denigrates rival products in the marketplace.

KPI (key performance indicator) Financial and non-financial metrics used to quantify objectives to reflect the strategic performance of an organization. KPIs differ depending on the nature of the organization and the organization's strategy. They are used in Business Intelligence to assess the present state of the business and to prescribe a course of action and are frequently used to 'value' difficult-to-measure knowledge-based factors such as the benefits of leadership development, engagement, service and satisfaction. KPIs are typically tied to an organization's strategy (as exemplified through techniques such as the Balanced Scorecard). The act of monitoring KPIs in real time is known as business activity monitoring.

L

laggards One of the five terms originally proposed in Everett Rogers's DIFFUSION OF INNOVATION THEORY. Laggards are traditionally orientated users of products, caring for the old ways and often critical of new ideas and innovation. These consumers will only accept a new idea or product if it has become mainstream or part of accepted tradition. *See also* ADOPTER CATEGORIES.

laissez faire An economic and political doctrine taken from the French, meaning to leave alone or to allow to do. It is a doctrine that opposes economic interventionism and taxation by the state beyond that which is perceived to be necessary to maintain peace, security and property rights. This philosophy suggests governmental involvement in business should be kept to a minimum, consistent with a basic level of legal protection regarding breaches of contract, safety measures and fair dealing.

The laissez-faire school of economic thought holds a pure or economically liberal market view, that the free market is best left to its own devices and that it will dispense with inefficiencies in a more deliberate and quick manner than any legislating body could. The basic idea is that less government interference in private economic decisions such as pricing, production, consumption and distribution of goods and services makes for a better (more efficient) economy.

late majority One of the five terms originally proposed in Everett Rogers's DIFFUSION OF INNOVATION THEORY. The late majority are those adopters who buy a new product some time after its introduction, often because of difficulties in sourcing the original product for which it is a substitute. The fourth group to adopt a new product; they represent about 34 per cent of a market. *See also* ADOPTER CATEGORIES.

lateral thinking A concept developed by the Maltese-born Cambridge mathematician Edward de Bono which is of particular relevance to the idea-generation stage of NEW PRODUCT DEVELOPMENT and marketing problem solving. According to de Bono, lateral thinking is a way of using the mind, a deliberate process, a general attitude, which may make use of certain techniques to generate alternatives, new ideas and solutions to problems when necessary. The techniques that apply lateral thinking to problems are characterized by the shifting of thinking patterns away from orthodox, entrenched or predictable thinking to new, radical or unexpected ideas. There are a number of mental tools or methods that can be employed to bring about lateral thinking. These include:

- Random entry: randomly choose an object or a noun from a dictionary and associate that with the area you are thinking about.
- Provocation: declare the usual perception or way of operating out of bounds, or provide some provocative alternative to the usual situation under consideration. Prefix the provocation with the term 'po' (which stands for provocative operation) to indicate that the provocation is not necessarily a valid solution

or a good idea but instead is there to act as a stimulus to move the thinking process along to where new ideas can be produced.

• Challenge: simply challenge the way things have always been done or seen, or the way they are. This is done to highlight that there is nothing wrong with the existing situation, but in challenging the norm one can explore outside the existing area and come up with new ideas.

The following anecdote is provided by de Bono (*New Think: The Use of Lateral Thinking in the Generation of New Ideas*, 1967) as a good example of the use of lateral thinking. A merchant who owes money to a moneylender agrees to settle the debt based upon the choice of two stones (one black, one white) from a money bag. If his daughter chooses the white stone, the debt is cancelled; if she picks the black stone, the moneylender gets the merchant's daughter. However, the moneylender 'fixes' the outcome by putting two black stones in the bag. The daughter sees this and, when she picks a stone out of the bag, she immediately drops it on to the path full of other stones. She then points out that the stone she picked must have been the opposite colour of the one remaining in the bag. Unwilling to be unveiled as dishonest, the moneylender must agree and cancel the debt. The daughter has solved an intractable problem.

launch To introduce a new product or service on to the market with some special campaign or activity.

law of demand The theory that the higher the price, the lower the demand, and vice versa. With some goods, e.g. luxuries, the very opposite happens, as it does with any other goods or service where a pre-purchase evaluation is difficult. In this case, price is taken as a measure of quality, e.g. perfume or a seminar. *See also* DEMAND.

law of diminishing marginal utility The situation that arises when the consumption of an additional unit adds less satisfaction for the consumer than that obtained from the immediately preceding unit.

law of diminishing returns An economic 'law' which states that, while extra units of input critically increase output, perhaps more than proportionately, the rate of return will flatten out, increasing by steadily smaller amounts until ultimately more units of the same kind will have a negative effect. For example, $X spent on advertising may bring a return of $Y in sales, but twice the amount spent, $2X, may bring only $1.5Y; the rate of return has fallen even though the overall amount of return has increased.

law of statistical regularity The rule that samples taken from a large group of a test population tend to reflect the characteristics of the group, and any anomaly can be resolved by comparing different or larger samples.

law of supply and demand An economic principle describing the interrelation between demand, supply and price. As demand increases, a higher price can be charged, which in turn will encourage an increase in supply. Similarly, an increase in supply will tend to depress prices. In marketing practice this law has to be viewed with caution since in certain cases a high price is taken as being indicative of high quality, in which case an unduly low price may lead to a low demand.

layout The arrangement of printed text and illustrations on a page within a document.

lead **1** A selling opportunity where an expression of interest has already been made by a future customer. **2** The first sentence of a news story, which should concisely reveal the story's basic events and provide an introduction to the details given in the rest of the story.

lead time The period of time required to prepare for a certain stage of, or introduction of, a particular project. For instance, the lead time in introducing a new product is the time it takes for research, development, market research, sales planning and

Levitt, Theodore
(1925–2006)

An American economist and professor at Harvard Business School. Levitt was a monumental and iconoclastic figure in the field of marketing who influenced generations of both scholars and practitioners with his ground-breaking, carefully crafted, always provocative and often controversial books and articles. He was also editor of the *Harvard Business Review* and is credited with transforming the magazine from an academic periodical into a more accessible publication that focused on important ideas and practices that influenced a readership comprised of top business leaders.

In 1960 his article entitled 'Marketing Myopia' was published in *Harvard Business Review*. Its theme is that the vision of most organizations is too constricted by a narrow understanding of what business they are in. It exhorted CEOs to re-examine their corporate vision and redefine their markets in terms of wider perspectives. It was successful in its impact because it was, as with all of Levitt's work, essentially practical and pragmatic. Some commentators have suggested that its publication marked the beginning of the modern marketing movement.

He is widely credited with coining the term 'globalization' through the article he wrote for the *Harvard Business Review* entitled 'Globalization of Markets'. Although the term 'globalization' was in use well before (at least as early as 1944) and had been used by economists as early as 1981, Levitt popularized the term and brought it to the mainstream business audience.

By the time he retired from Harvard in 1990, Levitt was considered one of the School's living legends, a seminal scholar who had radically altered marketing both as a practice within corporations and industries and as a field of academic inquiry.

the tooling-up of the production and distribution process.

leading question A question which is constructed in such a way that it illicits the 'correct' or desired answer from the respondent, e.g. 'Are you happy with that?' Answers to such questions are of doubtful and dubious validity and therefore introduce bias into the data collected.

learn-feel-buy model This model proposes that consumers first learn about the product or service by reading, viewing and understanding an advertisement or by being the recipient of other forms of marketing communications. Consumers not only learn what benefits the product or service may have but may also develop positive feelings about it. In turn this may stimulate the potential customers and consumers to buy the product or service and to develop loyalty towards it in the longer term. *See also* BUY-FEEL-LEARN MODEL; FEEL-BUY-LEARN MODEL.

learning curve The tendency to learn how to do something more efficiently the more often you do it. The concept is widely used in manufacturing when the focus is on the unit cost of production, but it can be applied to other sorts of learning as well, for instance the way in which a new manager learns a new role or task for the first time.

leasing A practice in business whereby a firm may, for period of time, obtain the use of a piece of equipment or other plant without purchasing it.

less-developed countries Countries with low average incomes averages per capita, relatively under-developed infrastructure and poor human development indexes when compared to the global norm. The term has tended to edge out earlier ones, including less-refined adages such as the 'Third World'. It is now declining in regular usage and is being replaced by less degrading and more favourable terms such as the 'developing' and/or 'emerging' world.

Levy, Sidney

One of the main contributors to marketing and consumer behaviour in the twentieth century and a significant figure among marketers today. He saw well before others the value of doing research on BRAND IMAGE, symbolism and cultural meaning in marketing and broadening the MARKETING CONCEPT. Levy was able to achieve these insights by questioning the prevailing assumptions of the day and taking an interdisciplinary perspective to solve what he saw as marketing problems. At the start of Levy's career, marketing viewed the consumer as a rational, utility-optimizing individual. The purpose of business was to create superior quality while pricing competitively.

Levy believed this led toward narrowly conceived, static and ultimately unrealistic portrayals of products and human behaviour. Understanding consumers had less to do with the question 'Do I need this?' and more to do with the questions 'Do I want it?' or 'Do I like it?' Levy sought to demonstrate that purchases were made on grounds that his colleagues thought were insubstantial. He questioned the prevailing economic wisdom of the time: 'The ideal market is like a Heaven – perfect but dull; the real one is the human one on Earth, fraught with emotion, striving, and the symbolic investments that make us care about what and how we market to and from others.'

letter of credit A financial document issued by one bank generally to a correspondent bank instructing it to pay money to a third person, e.g. to an exporter who has shipped goods and has documents which he/she can present to the bank to prove it.

level of service The quality of a company's service to its customers over a period of time. Level of service is notionally quantifiable as the percentage of orders (or volume of goods) which can be supplied on time to meet the customers' demands, whether from stock or from current production.

leverage 1 The process of incurring debt in order to continue or expand the scope of a business operation. An enterprise is said to be highly leveraged if it relies heavily on debt financing (borrowing) as opposed to equity (investor) financing. **2** An additional benefit which accrues to an individual or organization by virtue of their position or relationship, e.g. ownership of a raw material in scarce supply, entitlement to landing times at an international airport.

licensing In marketing, normally refers to giving permission to sell or manufacture a product. A legal arrangement transferring the rights to manufacture or to market a product. Such an arrangement, also known as franchising, is usually formalized by a contract in which there is a consideration, perhaps in the form of a regular fee, or of a commission or royalty. For the licensing company, it represents a means of expanding demand from new markets without incurring a high speculative investment. For the licensee, it reduces the need to generate NEW PRODUCT DEVELOPMENT, facilitates lower setting-up and operating costs and thereby diminishes the degree of business risk. *See also* FRANCHISE.

lien The right of a seller to hold goods in possession when the price is not paid, even when not the owner.

life cycle The pattern of demand for a product after it is first introduced, involving: growth, stabilization for a period, then decline and finally disappearance. Whilst demand curves differ in rates of change, shape and time span, the life cycle hypothesis states that all products have both a beginning and an end. This dictates the need for NEW PRODUCT DEVELOPMENT; the order of time scale determines the intensity with which such development takes place. *See also* PRODUCT LIFE CYCLE.

lifestyle The way a person (or a group) lives. This includes patterns of social relations, consumption, entertainment and dress. A lifestyle typically also reflects an individual's attitudes, values or worldview. Having a specific 'lifestyle' implies a conscious or unconscious choice of one set of behaviours over others. In business, lifestyles provide a means of targeting consumers as advertisers, and marketers endeavour to match consumer aspirations with products.

lifestyle analysis The development of market profiles from LIFESTYLE measurements based on demographic information as well as ratings of consumers' activities, interests and opinions, to give a broader, more three-dimensional view of customers.

Likert scale Attitude measurement used in research, where, in place of a numerical scale, answers are given on a scale ranging from complete agreement on one side to complete disagreement on the other side, with no opinion in the middle.

limit pricing When a firm adopts predatory pricing policies by lowering prices to a level that would force any new firms entering the industry to operate at a loss. This allows the firm to sustain a monopoly position in a market.

limited distribution The distribution of a product only to specific geographic locations or to specific outlets, retail chains or stores.

limited liability A form of business organization under which the liability of the shareholders is restricted to the full nominal value of the shares that they own.

line extension A new variation of a product or service sharing the same essential characteristics as the parent, but offering a new benefit, such as flavour, size, package type, etc.

lineage A standard method to describe CLASSIFIED ADVERTISING space in a newspaper or magazine: a count of the number of column-wide lines an advertisement occupies. Display advertising is sold by the column-centimetre or by fractions and multiples of a page.

linear programming A mathematical research method used in marketing for solving practical problems, for instance the allocation of packaging or production resources on a particular product line using linear functions where the variables involved are subject to constraints. Linear programming has inspired many of the central concepts of optimization theory, such as duality, decomposition and the importance of convexity and its generalizations. Likewise, linear programming has become heavily utilized in global marketing and the operations of major businesses as it can be used as a very efficient system to run models which can suggest how income is maximized or costs minimized and a product allocated for maximum profit.

link rot When web pages previously accessible at a particular URL are no longer reachable at that URL due to movement or deletion of the pages.

liquidity The ease with which something can be bought or sold (converted to cash) in the marketplace. A large number of buyers and sellers and a high volume of trading activity are important components of liquidity. Depth, or the ability of the market to absorb either a large buy or a large sell order without a significant price change in a security, is also crucial to the liquidity of the market.

liquidity ratio The total monetary value of cash and marketable securities divided by current liabilities. For a bank this is the proportion of total assets which are held in the form of cash and liquid assets. The liquidity ratio measures the extent to which a corporation or other entity can quickly liquidate assets and cover short-term liabilities, and therefore is of interest to short-term creditors. *See also* ACID TEST RATIO.

list price The price at which manufacturers recommend retailers sell a good. The list price is often reduced at the point of sale by the retailer to promote sales.

literature review A systematic survey and interpretation of the research findings (the 'literature') on a particular topic, usually designed to prepare for further research on the subject. The literature review is often done a second time to help one interpret unexpected results. A META-ANALYSIS is a literature review in which the completeness of the survey is stressed and statistical techniques are used to summarize the findings.

literature search A thorough exploration of all information published about a given topic. It is a core foundation to any research thesis.

livery In the marketing context, such elements of corporate identity as corporate colour schemes, symbols and uniforms.

Lloyd's of London Lloyd's is the world's leading specialist insurance market. Like all markets, it enables those with something to sell – underwriters providing insurance coverage – to make contact with those who want to buy – brokers, working on behalf of their clients who are seeking insurance. It is an incorporated society of private insurers in London, established in one of the city's coffee houses in 1688. It serves as a meeting place where multiple financial backers or 'members', individuals (traditionally known as 'Names') or corporations, come together to pool and spread financial risk. Lloyd's is not an insurance company. It is a marketplace made up of members who can provide insurance and underwrite. As the oldest continuously active insurance marketplace in the world, Lloyd's operates effectively as a market regulator, setting rules under which members operate and offering centralized administrative services to those members.

Lloyd's covers some of the world's most complex and specialist insurance risks – from oil rigs to celebrity body parts, from major airlines to the world's biggest banks and sporting events. Lloyd's conducts business in more than 200 countries and territories worldwide and covers eight of the world's top pharmaceutical companies and fifty-two of the world's top banks; 90 per cent of FTSE 100 companies and 93 per cent of Dow Jones companies have insurance at Lloyd's.

lobbying The professional practice of advocating not-for-profit, private or public-sector interests to legislators. Its prime aim is to influence the governing bodies to amend or frame legislation, decision-making and regulation to their advantage. The terms PUBLIC AFFAIRS or GOVERNMENT RELATIONS are often used as synonyms for lobbying. The golden rule of lobbying is usually to get involved early and preferably at the thinking stage ahead of the development of legislation. Lobbying and associated public affairs work have been one of the fastest-growing areas of modern marketing in the twenty-first century.

Lobbying is heavily regulated in the US, partially so in the UK and increasingly so within the EU. There are distinct differences between lobbying in the US, the EU, Australia and New Zealand, China and India, reflecting the different cultural and societal traditions of nation states. The best practitioners of lobbying suggest good preparation, early involvement in the policy-making process and the application of issues management techniques to key business areas of an organization are the essence of best practice in the area. The former Head of Public Affairs of Rio Tinto, Michael Shea, has commented, 'Good lobbying is like growing asparagus, you wished you had started two years ago.'

Public affairs is usually practised by integrated corporate communications companies and specialist public relations groups and is basically limited to information gathering (monitoring legislation and politics) and influencing public opinion through the means of PUBLIC RELATIONS and campaigns. Government relations, however, means directly influencing the legislative process and the legislator to highlight legal or economic problems and concerns regarding a certain draft legislation or proposed directive or regulation. This is still primarily carried out by specialized lobbying firms, corporate in-house departments or large multinational law practices. Most small and medium-sized companies do not have their own government relations department, but handle these as part of their corporate communications function or choose to employ external consultants. A large multinational company, however, will have extensive contacts with government every day at a number of levels and in relation to a range of issues. To achieve this end, they usually have a government relations department or lobbyist to coordinate the firm's relations with government. It therefore implies that large organizations and groups are better organized and resourced to apply strategic lobbying to gain competitive advantage. Only federations of small businesses and interests are able to have a similar impact.

logistics A tool for getting resources, like products, services and people, where they are needed and when they are desired. It is difficult to accomplish any marketing or manufacturing without logistical support. It involves the integration of information, transportation, inventory, warehousing, material handling and packaging. The operating responsibility of logistics is the geographical repositioning of raw materials, work in process and finished inventories where required at the lowest cost possible.

Logistics as a concept is considered to have evolved from the military's need to supply themselves as they moved from their base to a forward position. The *Oxford English Dictionary* defines logistics as: 'The branch of military science having to do with procuring, maintaining and transporting material, personnel and facilities'. Logistics as its own concept in business evolved only in the 1950s. This was mainly due to the increasing complexity of supplying one's business with materials and shipping out products in an increasingly globalized supply chain, calling for experts in the field.

In business, logistics may have either internal or external focus, covering the flow from originating supplier to end user (see SUPPLY CHAIN MANAGEMENT). The main functions of a logistics manager include purchasing, transport, warehousing and the organizing and planning of these activities. Logistics managers combine a general knowledge of each of these functions so that there is a coordination of resources in an organization. There are two fundamentally different forms of logistics. One optimizes a steady flow of material through a network of transport links and storage nodes. The other coordinates a sequence of resources to carry out some project.

logo or logotype The graphic symbol or icon of an organization, trademark or brand, which is set in a special typeface or arranged in a particular way to impart distinctness. The shapes, colours, fonts and images are usually different from others in a similar market. A logo can represent a company, product, event or service, and sometimes even a country (e.g. Canada). It also depicts an organization's personality. In recent times the term 'logo' has been used to describe signs, emblems, coats of arms, insignia, symbols and even flags and pendants.

The uniqueness of a logo is of utmost importance to avoid confusion in the marketplace among clients, suppliers, users, affiliates and the general public. Once a logo is designed, one of the most effective means for protecting it is through registration as a TRADEMARK, so that no unauthorized third parties can use it or interfere with the owner's use of it. If rights in relation to a logo are correctly established and enforced, it can become a valuable INTELLECTUAL PROPERTY asset.

long-range plan A plan that covers a period beyond that normally used for budgeting and control purposes, usually more than one year.

longitudinal study A research design where subjects are assessed at several different times in their lives, usually to assess how they change over time. These studies are often expensive, difficult to conduct and have lots of trouble without dropouts. They also will require more complex statistical analyses. But they provide a wealth of information that could not be obtained readily with other types of research designs.

loose inserts Advertisements distributed separately with a publication and usually inserted loosely within its pages.

loss leader Product or group of products sold by a retailer at a loss in order to increase store flow, turnover and sales of other items. *See also* PREDATORY PRICING.

low-involvement products Products that are purchased frequently and with a minimum of thinking and effort because they are considered of low interest and have no immediate impact on the consumer's lifestyle. *See also* HIGH-INVOLVEMENT PRODUCTS.

loyalty marketing An extension of BRAND LOYALTY in which some additional incentive is offered for doing business with a given supplier, such as joining a club and obtaining some financial benefit as a result.

luxury brand A luxury brand or prestige brand is a brand whose products are mainly LUXURY GOODS. It may also be a brand whose name is associated with luxury, high price or high quality even though few, if any, of its goods are currently considered luxury goods. The French holding company LVMH (Louis Vuitton Moët Hennessy) is one of the largest luxury brand producers in the world with over fifty brands, including Cloudy Bay (New Zealand winery), Louis Vuitton, the brand with the world's first designer label, Hennessy brandy, Moët and Krug champagnes, Glenmorangie whisky, Dior perfumes and Tag Heuer watches.

luxury good Is normally seen as a good or product which increases over and above the rise in general income. Good examples of products that fit into this category include caviar, collections of antiques, art, sculpture and paintings.

M

McCarthy, E. Jerome

Professor at Michigan State University and an internationally known marketing consultant. Since receiving his PhD from the University of Minnesota in 1958, he has taught at the Universities of Oregon, Notre Dame and Michigan State. He received the American Marketing Associations Trailblazer Award in 1987 and was voted one of the top five leaders in marketing thought by marketing educators.

McCarthy focuses upon converting students to marketing and marketing strategy planning and has been deeply involved in teaching and developing new teaching materials to help others do the same. This is why he has spent a large part of his career developing, revising and improving marketing texts to reflect the most current thinking in the field. He is the author of textbooks on data processing and social issues in marketing and co-author (with William D. Perreault) of *Basic Marketing* (now in its sixteenth edition). Besides his academic interests, Dr McCarthy has been involved in consulting for, and guiding the growth of, a number of businesses in the US and overseas.

Machiavelli, Niccolò
(1469–1527)

Italian political philosopher, musician, poet and romantic comedic playwright. He is a central figure of the Italian Renaissance, particularly of its political component, and is most widely known for his treatises on realist political theory (*The Prince*) and republicanism (*Discourses on Livy*). In *The Prince* Machiavelli abandons the moral teachings of the classical and biblical traditions for a new conception of virtue as the willingness and ability to do whatever it needs to maintain what one has acquired. This small book came to be seen as the most notorious and shocking piece of literature of the Italian Renaissance and gave birth to the well-known negative epithet 'Machiavellian', now commonly used in many languages. The primary contribution of *The Prince* to the history of political thought is its fundamental break between realism and idealism. While Machiavelli emphasized the need for morality, the sole motivation of the prince ought to be the use of good and evil solely as instrumental means rather than ends in themselves. A wise prince is one who properly exercises this balance.

The advice offered by Machiavelli to his prince bears a striking resemblance to today's laws of marketing and advertising. As a result he has been referred to as the first saint of marketing, if such a thing exists. He recommends fair and honest trading, because this is the key to success. Today, market economies are in fact based on the trust of the consumers and the stakeholders.

McLuhan, Herbert Marshall
(1911–80)

Canadian professor of English who coined the celebrated phrase 'The medium is the message' as a chapter title in *Understanding Media: the Extensions of Man* (1964). His original argument is very detailed and conceptually difficult. In the marketing communications context, it is usually taken as a reminder that an audience's reaction to a message may be significantly affected by their evaluation of the medium through which it is transmitted. Thus the choice of advertising medium mediates response to an advertisement, or a sales representative's appearance influences the reaction to the sales pitch. His works include *The Gutenberg Galaxy* (1962) – in which he coined the phrase 'the global village' for the worldwide electronic society then emerging – *Understanding Media* (1964) and *The Medium is the Massage* (1967).

Machiavellian marketing A term coined by Harris and Lock ('Machiavellian Marketing: The Development of Political Lobbying in the UK', *Journal of Marketing Management*, 1996) to describe the strategic influencing of decision and policy making in government (LOBBYING) for commercial or organizational gain.

Machiavellianism A term used to describe the ruthless use of power, particularly coercive power, and manipulation to attain personal goals. The name comes from the Italian Renaissance writer and diplomat Niccolò MACHIAVELLI, who some argue condoned questionable tactics for obtaining and holding on to political power.

macro environment Uncontrollable factors that constitute the external environment of marketing including demographic, economic, technological, natural, sociocultural and regulatory forces. *See also* MARKETING ENVIRONMENT; MICRO ENVIRONMENT.

macromarketing The study of marketing processes, activities, institutions and results from a broad perspective such as a nation, in which cultural, political and social, as well as economic, interactions are investigated. The *Journal of Macromarketing* is published by Sage and examines important social issues, how they are affected by marketing and how society influences the conduct of marketing. It is published quarterly and supports an annual international conference which concentrates on these themes. *See also* MICROMARKETING.

macrosegmentation Method of dividing business markets based on such key characteristics as geographic location, type of organization, customer size, and product use. The resultant segments should be accessible, identifiable, measurable, have some predictable responsiveness, and be large enough to be worthwhile.

Madison Avenue An avenue in New York City that was once the address of many of the major advertising agencies. Some of these agencies are still located in New York City but have moved to other addresses or expanded to include offices in Chicago, Los Angeles and other national and international locations. The term 'Madison Avenue', however, still serves as a symbol or metaphor for advertising.

mail order A well established method of buying and selling products or services which is promoted by either Internet and/or media promotion, DIRECT MAIL and/or sales promotion. The potential purchaser is normally invited to order by post and the product is delivered by mail or courier/distribution company such as DHL. The products are typically delivered directly to an address supplied by the customer, such as a home address, but occasionally the orders are delivered to a nearby distribution centre or retail location for the customer to collect. Alternatively an order for goods to be sent by mail.

mail-order catalogue A publication containing a list of general and/or specialist merchandise from a business or organization. Well-known general mail-order catalogues in the UK include Empire Stores, Freemans, Kays and Littlewoods, which were designed to provide nationally low-cost predominantly consumer goods to the mass population paid for in financial instalments. Traditionally the catalogue was passed around friends and family for orders and a percentage commission fee was passed onto the organizer of this sale and ordering process for their work. More recently mail-order catalogues have become increasingly focused on specific needs such as the provision of large size clothing and footwear, meeting specialist leisure activities needs such as hunting, and of course most hobby and interest areas. The catalogue itself is produced in a similar fashion to any magazine publication and distributed through a variety of means, usually the postal service after having been pre-ordered over the Internet.

mail shot A non-requested item sent by post, especially a piece of advertising material or a charity appeal letter or promotion. The term is also used to describe the complete process of sending out a batch of such items to potential customers by post.

mailing list A managed list of names, addresses, postcodes/zipcodes and e-mail addresses of individuals or organizations which is used to send targeted mail communications to. Mailing lists can be bought from specialist agencies that will build up profiles of particular individuals who fulfil particular key characteristics such as age, ethnicity, location, religion, income and/or education level.

make/buy decision A decision by a firm to purchase products, components or services from a supplier rather than make them itself. The buy side of the decision is also referred to as outsourcing.

management **1** The owners, or directors, of an organization. **2** A term employed to designate those executive tasks in a business which ensure that diverse resources are utilized in such a way that pre-planned economic performances are achieved. Management is commonly regarded as comprising the interlocking activities of planning, organizing, staffing, directing, controlling and coordination, using all liaison and communications resources available to achieve these ends.

management audit The systematic assessment of all management functions and techniques to establish the current level of effectiveness, and to lay down standards for future performance.

management by exception A management technique based upon the comparison of performance with set budgets or targets which enjoins action only when large enough variations are recorded.

management by objectives A system whereby each management function is required to define the objectives it is set to achieve. Such objectives are designed to interrelate for maximum efficiency and require an effective feedback system to enable management to be aware of progress and to exercise adequate control.

management development The deliberate formulation of plans to train staff and encourage them to acquire new skills in order to provide an organization with future executives, while at the same time giving staff a sense of purpose.

management information system Software programs deliberately designed to provide managers with the information they need to make decisions.

margin The difference between the selling price and the purchase price of an item usually expressed as a percentage of the selling price.

marginal analysis A method of analysis developed by neo-classical economists such as J. M. Clark, Alfred Marshall and Vilfredo Pareto, founded upon the concepts of marginal utility and marginal productivity. It is an analysis of economic information by examining the results of the value added when one variable is increased by a single unit of another variable.

marginal cost The difference in costs between producing X units for sale and X + 1 units for sale. Marginal revenue is the increase in revenue when one more unit is sold. In some firms at some times marginal cost may be negligible and therefore, when an extra unit is sold, a greater than proportional profit is made. Alternatively, marginal costs may be high, e.g. when maximum output is already achieved. At such times additional sales may have the effect of reducing profit levels.

marginal cost pricing In economics, the setting of a price based on the additional cost to a firm of producing one more unit of output, the marginal cost, rather than the actual average cost per unit. In this way, the price of an item is kept to a minimum, reflecting only the extra cost of labour and materials. Marginal cost pricing is often used by a company during a period of downturn in sales with the additional sales generated allowing it to remain operational without a reduction in the scale of its production and labour force.

marginal propensity to consume (MPC) The proportion of an aggregate rise in pay that is spent on the consumption of goods and services, as opposed to being saved. It is crucial to Keynesian economics (see KEYNES) and is the key variable determining the value of the multiplier.

marginal revenue The additional revenue generated by selling one more unit of output or production.

mark down To reduce a price, as in a sale.

mark-up The amount added to a purchase price to provide a selling price.

market A group of persons and/or organizations identified through a common need and with resources to satisfy that need. Also a place where buyers and sellers gather to do business.

market aggregation The use of an UNDIFFERENTIATED MARKETING strategy which treats all potential customers in the same manner.

market atomization The direct opposite of MARKET AGGREGATION, i.e. a marketing strategy which treats every individual customer as an individual market segment.

market attrition The gradual wearing-away of brand and consequent customer loyalty over time especially following the absence of, or a reduction in, promotion of the product or service to the marketplace.

market coverage Ensuring that the product is made available through appropriate market channel intermediaries so that the potential customer can access it as easily as possible, and that the product is properly displayed, sold and supported within the distribution channel used. Also, the number of available outlets in a given line of retail or wholesale trade, relative to a saturation level, that are selling a manufacturer's brand in a given market area. Manufacturers typically follow one of three forms of market coverage: exclusive distribution, where one retailer only has the right to sell the product (Rolex often adopts this approach); intensive distribution, where the product is distributed widely to a range of retail outlets small and large to cater for all types of consumers (a good example of this is Coca-Cola); or selective distribution, where the product is targeted to certain retailers to supply a focused group of consumers (agricultural equipment and tractors are often sold in this way).

market demand The total demand for a good or service by everyone in the population.

market development The expansion of the total market served by a business, achieved by entering new segments, by expanding the geographic base of the business or by using new channels to reach non-served customers. It is also regularly used to describe the conversion of non-purchasers by offering lower prices or increased and/or specially designed promotions. *See also* PRODUCT PORTFOLIO.

market ecology The study of the cultural, political, economic and social environments of a country together with the effect these have on business methods and trading policy.

market entry The initiation of efforts to sell a new or existing product to a group of consumers not previously targeted by that marketer. The launching of products for market entry requires planning, resources and time to be effective.

market indicators A range of indices that give an indication of the overall direction and strength of the market.

market intelligence The fundamental marketing process of acquiring and analysing information in order to understand the marketplace for both current and potential customers. This enables the marketer to gain an understanding of the needs, preferences, attitudes and behaviour of the market and to assess changes in the business environment that may affect the size and nature of the market in the future.

market leader A company that has achieved a dominant position – either in scale or influence – within its field. This leading position often comes about because the company was the first to market a certain type of product and, with the protection of a patent, has managed to consolidate its position before direct competition was possible. Alternatively, a company may overtake a previous market leader through greater efficiency and the quality use of marketing, especially promotion.

market logistics See LOGISTICS.

market manager The person responsible for coordinating, planning and implementing marketing campaigns. The marketing manager must monitor and meet marketing objectives, goals and targets and analyse, anticipate and exceed competitors' strategies.

market niche A specific market niche which reflects a non-mainstream group of consumers. This could be a group of consumers from an ethnic group, one with specific dietary or specialist clothing needs, age or educational needs amongst many other differentiating consumption patterns. The Pink (gay) Market has often been targeted because of its hedonistic tendencies and high income levels which have benefited many specialist providers of goods and services to this community. See also NICHE MARKETING; SEGMENTATION.

market opportunity analysis The analysis and evaluation of probable future market situations by a variety of techniques to identify commercial opportunities that a company can profitably cultivate.

market penetration The act of a new entrant, either a firm or product, into an existing market. Also obtaining increased market share for a product with no change in the target market. Market penetration is a key issue in assessing the growth prospects for an industry. It is usually fairly straightforward to assess the potential market for a product – i.e. the number of sales it could make if everyone who could reasonably buy it did. However, what proportion of those people actually become paying customers of an industry is another matter. Over-optimistic estimates of eventual market penetration is a common trap for growth investors. Of course, some products do achieve very high penetration – e.g. mobile phones and iPods – but others have not. See also PENETRATION.

market position The position in the marketplace that a particular brand, product and/or organization holds. For instance, Wal-Mart has a dominant market position in the US grocery business and Tesco has the equivalent in the UK.

market price The price commonly asked for a product in the marketplace, described by economists as the value which a purchaser places upon a product or service to satisfy his or her needs. It is related to the LAW OF DIMINISHING MARGINAL UTILITY.

market profile The description of a market in terms of its significant characteristics which must be taken into account when developing an effective marketing plan.

Such a profile may be based upon a summary of the characteristics of a market, including information on typical purchasers and competitors and often general information on the economy and retailing patterns of a specific area.

market research The systematic collection and analysis of information about consumers, competitors and the effectiveness of marketing programmes used to determine the feasibility of a new business, test levels of interest in new products and develop strategies to improve customer service and distribution channels. It is used to monitor and evaluate the marketplace for product placement.

Market Research Society (MRS) The world's largest association representing providers and users of market, social and opinion research and business intelligence. The MRS has members in more than seventy countries and serves individuals and organizations who identify with its core values of professionalism, excellence and effectiveness. It has a diverse membership of individual researchers within agencies, independent consultancies, client-side organizations, the public sector and the academic community at all levels of seniority and in all job functions.

All individual members and company partners agree to self-regulatory compliance with the MRS Code of Conduct. Extensive advice to support this commitment is provided by MRS through its Codeline service and by publication of a wide range of specialist guidelines on best practice. It offers various qualifications and membership grades, as well as training and professional development resources to support them. It is the official awarding body in the UK for professional qualifications in market research.

market sales potential A term that refers to the maximum level of sales that may be available to all organizations serving a defined market over a specific time period.

market segment A group of buyers or potential buyers of products and services that can be characterized by a set of variables. For example, market segments may be demographic or geographic or be based on lifestyle or origin.

market segmentation The theory and practice of dividing a market into definable groups, usually to improve marketing performance. Frequently different segments of a market have individual behaviour patterns and require a different approach for success to be achieved. Because each segment is fairly homogeneous in their needs and attitudes, they are likely to respond similarly to a given marketing strategy. That is, they are likely to have similar feeling and ideas about a MARKETING MIX comprised of a given product or service, sold at a given price, distributed in a certain way and promoted in a certain way. Small segments are often termed NICHE MARKETS or specialty markets.

Marketing opportunities increase when customer groups with varying needs and wants are recognized. Markets can be segmented or targeted on a variety of factors including age, gender, location, geographic factors, demographic characteristics, family life cycle, desire for relaxation or time pressures. Segments or target markets should be accessible to the business and large enough to provide a solid customer base.

A business must analyse the needs and wants of different market segments before determining its niche. A key factor to success in today's marketplace is finding subtle differences to give a business the marketing edge. Businesses that target specialty markets will promote its products and services more effectively than a business aiming at the 'average' customer. The process of segmentation is distinct from targeting (choosing which segments to address) and positioning (designing an appropriate marketing mix for each segment). The overall intent is to identify groups of similar customers and potential customers; to prioritize the groups to address; to understand their behaviour; and to respond with appropriate marketing strategies that satisfy the different preferences of each chosen segment.

The requirements for successful segmentation are:

- homogeneity within the segment;
- heterogeneity between segments;
- segments are measurable and identifiable;
- segments are accessible and actionable;
- segment is large enough to be profitable.

See also CUSTOMER CHARACTERISTICS; SEGMENTATION.

market share A company's share of total sales of a given category of product on a given market. It can be expressed either in terms of volume (how many units sold) or value (the worth of units sold).

market value The price at which the market values a product at any given point in time. *See also* MARKET PRICE.

marketing An organization's prime exchange function and a set of processes for creating, communicating and delivering value to customers and for managing customer relationships in ways that benefit the organization and its stakeholders. It is defined by the American Marketing Association as 'an organizational function and a set of processes for creating, communicating and delivering value to customers and for managing customer relationships in ways that benefit the organization and its stakeholders', and by the Chartered Institute of Marketing as 'the management process responsible for identifying, anticipating and satisfying customer requirements profitably'. Marketing starts in the marketplace with the identification of the customer's needs and wants. It then moves on to determining a means of satisfying these needs and of promoting, selling and supplying a satisfaction. The principal marketing functions might be defined as: marketing information and research; product planning; pricing; advertising and promotion; sales; and distribution.

Marketing is still the subject of much misunderstanding, for it is not just a phenomenon of the twentieth and twenty-first centuries but a whole multi-faceted group of linked phenomena linked to the development of the consumer within society, the evolution of the exchange process and an appreciation of the complexity of inter-organizational buying and selling behaviour and networking.

marketing audit The assessment of a company's marketplace including its size, the competitors' strengths and weaknesses, distribution channels and the company's present marketing activities and the relating of them to what it should be doing.

marketing budget The advance allocation of finance to each of the various marketing functions, e.g. research, sales or advertising. A number of techniques are used to arrive at a budget, the most common and logical of which is related to the MARKETING OBJECTIVES. *See also* BUDGET.

marketing channels The means by which goods are distributed to the ultimate customers. These include the retailers, wholesalers, subsidiaries and agents. *See also* CHANNEL OF DISTRIBUTION; DISTRIBUTION NETWORK.

marketing communications channel The means by which firms are able to communicate with their customers, e.g. press advertising, television and the web.

marketing communications mix Groups of channels available for communication with buyers and prospects.

marketing communications objectives There are many specific objectives, the principal ones being to gain attention for a product or service, to secure and strengthen perception and to generate sales leads. In consumer marketing, the aims also include changing behavioural intent, and then behaviour, i.e. sales. In business marketing, behavioural intent and behaviour are affected by other factors outside the marketing communications remit, e.g. the sales force. But all communications are affected by price and product, and so can be measured only in perceptual terms and not sales. A vital element of the objectives is that they should be quantified in order that their achievement can be measured. *See also* ADVERTISING OBJECTIVES.

marketing communications plan A formal, written-down framework for planning marketing communications campaigns, which can include advertising, sales, public relations and web promotions.

marketing concept The philosophy underlying the application of marketing thought to the operation of a business in all its various activities. The marketing concept suggests that businesses should focus on the needs of their customers and orientate the whole of their business operation to understanding those needs, both now and in the future, to generate profit. The marketing concept is generally held to consist of three major components:

• customer orientation;
• coordinated activities;
• profit orientation.

Thus the marketing concept can be seen as customer orientation, supported by a fully integrated marketing approach designed to generate profits. More recently the marketing concept has been broadened to reflect the changing needs of society and the growth of societal marketing and is now often seen as being made up of the following three factors:

• customer and stakeholder satisfaction;
• organizational profits;

Marketing Concept

• community welfare and CORPORATE SOCIAL RESPONSIBILITY.

marketing controls Procedures and activities involved in checking that marketing action plans are producing the desired results, and the taking of corrective action if they are not. They are used to determine whether the amount spent on sales promotion was excessive and establish performance standards, evaluate actual performance and reduce the differences between desired and actual performance.

marketing cost analysis An attempt to determine the actual costs incurred for marketing and distributing a product.

marketing environment The marketing environment is made up of the actors and forces that directly or indirectly influence the organization's marketing operations and performance. *See also* MACRO ENVIRONMENT; MICRO ENVIRONMENT.

marketing ethics The standards or moral principles governing the marketing profession. Often these standards are based on professional or association codes of ethics.

marketing history The historic development of trading, mercantilism and free trade to allow fair markets and commerce to freely operate underpin the beginnings of what we have come to see as modern marketing. Many brands and practices are established in the nineteenth century, but the academic and systematic study of the subject of marketing becomes significant in the twentieth century. The US business schools have been at the forefront of developing the discipline. The first school to offer courses in marketing was Wharton at the University of Pennsylvania in 1882. Marketing has evolved from a discipline associated with the distribution of manufactured goods to encompass today the management and operation of the exchange process in all aspects of society.

marketing information system (MIS) An organizational section or entity the purpose of which is to gather, organize, store, retrieve and analyse data relevant to a firm's past.

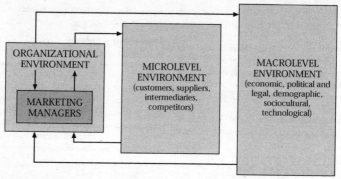

Marketing Environment

marketing intelligence Information or data being gathered or used to aid decision making or to monitor earlier decisions.

marketing management The practical application of marketing techniques and the management of a firm's marketing resources and activities. It is the analysis, planning, implementation and control of programmes designed to create, build and maintain mutually beneficial exchanges with target markets. The marketing manager has the task of influencing the level,

timing and composition of demand in ways that will achieve organizational objectives.

marketing mix One of the pivotal concepts and dominant ideas in modern marketing, the marketing mix is a model of the blending together to form a cohesive whole of the various facets of marketing – ultimately to build a cohesive strategy. The model was originally developed by Neil Borden, who first started using the phrase in 1949. The marketing mix consists of everything the firm can do to influence

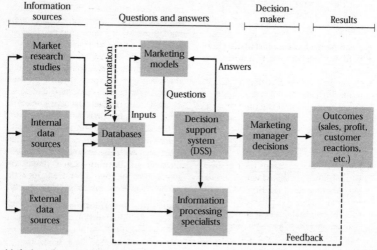

Marketing Information Systems (MIS)

the demand for its products and constitutes the company's basic tactical toolkit for establishing strong positioning in target markets. The prime marketing possibilities are gathered into four groups of variables known as the 'four Ps': product, price, place (distribution) and promotion.

- Product means the totality of 'good and/or services' that the company offers the target market.
- Price is the amount of money customers have to pay to obtain the product.
- Place includes organizational activities that make the product available to target consumers.
- Promotion refers to the activities that communicate the qualities of the product and persuades target customers to purchase it.

There has been debate from the very beginning about the validity of the four P formulation of the marketing mix. In 1981 Bernard Booms and Mary Bitner built a model consisting of seven Ps. In addition to product, price, promotion and place, they included people, physical evidence and process.

- People recognizes the importance of the human element in all aspects of marketing, particularly in services where there is a high degree of intangibility and where service delivery can entail high variability if staff are poorly trained or not adequately motivated to deliver service.
- Process reflects the fact that services, unlike physical products, are experienced as a process at the time that they are purchased. Customers will migrate to other service providers if the process is poorly managed and their expectations are not met.
- Physical evidence means the physical surroundings associated with a service encounter or retail location. Managing physical evidence entails examining every aspect that customers use in their perceptual field to assess such a service. This might include, for a university, its buildings, location, subject notes, lecture theatres, computer labs and audiovisual equipment.

A further P, packaging, has also been added to this list by theorists and commentators. Their argument is that packaging is playing a more significant part of the overall marketing offering as it is invariably the first part of the product seen by a customer and is increasingly becoming a more expensive and intrinsic part of any offering to customers. Is the chocolate box more important than the contents?

marketing myopia The narrow vision of those firms who view themselves in limited, product- or service-centred ways and pay more attention to the specific products they offer than to the benefits and experiences to customers produced by these products. They are so taken with their products that they focus only on existing customer wants and lose sight of underlying customer needs. Consequently they forget that a product is only a tool to solve a customer problem. A manufacturer of quarter-inch drill bits may think that the customer needs a drill bit, but what the customer really needs is quarter-inch holes. These sellers will have trouble if a new product comes along that serves the customer's need better or less expensively. One day firms that make drills will be ousted by firms making laser guns that cut quarter-inch holes with greater precision.

One of the most important marketing papers ever written was 'Marketing Myopia' by Theodore LEVITT, published in the *Harvard Business Review* in 1960. Many consider its publication marked the beginning of the modern marketing movement in general. Its theme was that the vision of most organizations was constricted in terms of what they, too narrowly, saw as the business they were in. It exhorted CEOs to re-examine their corporate vision and redefine their markets in terms of wider perspectives. Organizations found that they had been missing opportunities which were plain to see once they adopted the wider view. George Steiner (*Strategic Planning: What Every Manager Should Know*, 1979) claims that if a buggy whip manufacturer in 1910 had defined its business as the 'transportation starter business', it might have been able to make the creative leap necessary to move into the motor car business when technological change demanded it.

People who focus on marketing strategy, various predictive techniques and the customer's lifetime value can rise above myopia to a certain extent. This can entail the use of long-term profit objectives (sometimes at the risk of sacrificing short-term objectives). One reason that short-sightedness is so common is that people feel that they cannot accurately predict the future. While this is a legitimate concern, it is also possible to use a whole range of business prediction techniques currently available to estimate future circumstances as best as possible.

marketing objective The specific, measurable aims or expected outcomes of marketing activity to be achieved in a given period. This may be broken down into products and territories coupled with sales turnover figures and market share.

marketing organization The structure of the marketing function within the organization. The two historically most commonly used approaches to organizing the marketing effort are a product-based organization and a market-based organization.

marketing orientation A business that has a marketing orientation sees the needs of customers and consumers as vital and is market-oriented when its culture is systematically and entirely committed to the continuous creation of superior customer value. Specifically, this entails collecting and coordinating information on customers, competitors, and other significant market influencers (such as regulators and suppliers) to use in building that value.

marketing plan The part of the business plan outlining the marketing strategy for a product or service. It is a written plan, usually comprehensive, describing all activities involved in achieving a particular marketing objective, and their relationship to one another in both scale and time. Usually it will include short- and long-term sales forecasts, production and profit targets, pricing policy, promotional and selling strategy and staffing requirements as well as the selected MARKETING MIX and expense budgets. *See also* MARKETING STRATEGY.

marketing research The technique of systematically gathering, analysing and interpreting data relating to an organization's customers, competitors and market with the prime aim of improving marketing decision-making. The research provides information on product analysis, brand position analysis, customer surveys, quantitative market and trend analysis, channels of distribution assessment, etc., to marketing and sales departments at client companies.

Marketing research techniques come in a number of guises, including:

- test (or pilot) marketing – a small-scale product launch used to determine the potential acceptance level for the product when it is introduced into a wider market;
- CONCEPT TESTING – the testing of the acceptance rate for a concept by target consumers;
- mystery shopping – an employee or representative of the market research firm anonymously contacts a salesperson and indicates that he or she is shopping for a product. The shopper then records the entire experience. This method is often used for quality control or for researching competitors' products;
- store audit – to measure the sales of a product or product line at a statistically selected store sample in order to determine market share, or to determine whether a retail store provides adequate service;
- SALES FORECASTS – to determine the expected level of sales given the level of demand, with respect to other factors such as advertising expenditure, sales promotion, PR etc.;
- CONSUMER SATISFACTION studies – exit surveys that determine a customer's level

of satisfaction with the quality of the transaction;

- PRICE ELASTICITY testing – to determine how sensitive customers are to price changes;
- SEGMENTATION research – to determine the demographic, psychographic and behavioural characteristics of potential buyers;
- CONSUMER DECISION-MAKING PROCESS research – to determine what motivates consumers to purchase and what decision-making processes they use;
- POSITIONING research – to determine how the target market sees the brand relative to competitors and what the brand stands for;
- brand name testing – to determine what consumers feel about the names of the products;
- BRAND EQUITY RESEARCH – to determine how favourably consumers view the brand;
- ADVERTISING RESEARCH and promotion research – to assess just how effective the ads are and if there is need for modification to strengthen appeal to potential customers. Do potential customers recall the ad, understand the message, and does the ad influence consumer purchasing behaviour? Is there a better form of ad to appeal to these customers. What is the strike rate of the ad?

The organization in addition to primary research will also purchase secondary research and market research reports to check the validity of its own data and ensure it is up to date with current and future market knowledge and trends.

marketing strategy A statement in very general terms of how the marketing objective is to be achieved, e.g. by acquiring a competitive company, by price reductions, by product improvement or by intensive advertising. The strategy becomes the basis of the marketing plan. *See also* MARKETING PLAN.

marketplace The space, actual or metaphorical, in which a market operates. A marketplace is a location where goods and services are exchanged. The traditional marketplace is a city square where traders set up stalls and buyers browse the merchandise. This form of market can be seen around the world and has a long history.

Markov model A model used to explain brand switching and consumer behaviour developed from the Markov process, which relates current values (e.g. brand share) to previous values with the inclusion of a random error term. Markov models are very useful in branding when a problem involves risk that is continuous over time, when the timing of events is important, and when important events may happen more than once. Representing such marketing settings with conventional decision trees is difficult and may require unrealistic and oversimplistic assumptions. Markov models assume that a brand is always in one of a finite number of discrete health states, called brand states. All events are represented as transitions from one state to another. A Markov model may be evaluated by matrix algebra, as a cohort simulation or as a Monte Carlo simulation.

A newer representation of Markov models, the Markov-cycle tree, uses a tree representation of marketing events and may be evaluated either as a cohort simulation or as a Monte Carlo simulation. The ability of the Markov model to represent repetitive events and the time dependence of both probabilities and utilities allows for more accurate representation of marketing settings that involve these issues.

Maslow's hierarchy of needs A theory of human behaviour proposed by Abraham H. MASLOW which contends that people are motivated by six innate needs, and that, as humans meet 'basic needs', they seek to satisfy successively 'higher needs' that occupy a set hierarchy. According to Maslow, although all needs are instinctive, some are more powerful than others. The lower the need is in the pyramid, the more powerful it is. The higher the need is in the pyramid, the weaker and more distinctly human it is. The lower, or basic, needs on the pyramid are similar to those possessed

Marshall, Alfred
(1842–1924)

An English economist who played a major role in the shaping of British and world economics from 1890 until his death in 1924. Marshall's specialty was microeconomics – the study of individual markets and industries – as opposed to the study of the whole economy. His most important book was *Principles of Economics* in which he emphasized that the price and output of a product are determined by both supply and demand: the two curves are like scissor blades that intersect at equilibrium. Modern economists trying to understand why the price of a good changes still start by looking for factors that may have shifted demand or supply. They owe this approach to Marshall.

Maslow, Abraham
(1908–1970)

An American psychologist who is considered the father of humanistic psychology. Maslow was a very inspirational figure in personality theories, and his primary contribution to psychology is MASLOW'S HIERARCHY OF NEEDS, which contends that humans have a number of needs that are innate and that needs are arranged in a hierarchy in terms of their potency.

Maslow received his PhD from the University of Wisconsin in 1934, taught at Brooklyn College from 1937 and was head of the psychology department at Brandeis University from 1951 to 1969. His theory of human motivation led to a therapeutic technique known as self-actualization. His influential works include *Motivation and Personality* (1954) and *Toward a Psychology of Being* (1964).

by non-human animals, but only humans possess the higher needs. If a higher-priority need has not been met, lower-priority needs will have no motivational power.

The first four layers of the pyramid are what Maslow called 'deficiency needs' or 'D-needs': the individual does not feel anything if they are met, but feels anxious if they are not met. Within the deficiency needs, each lower need must be met before moving to the next higher level. Once each of these needs has been satisfied, if at some future time a deficiency is detected, the individual will act to remove the deficiency.

Needs beyond the D-needs are 'growth needs', 'being values' or 'B-needs'. When fulfilled, they do not go away; rather, they motivate further. The diagram shows Maslow's hierarchy of needs, represented as a pyramid with the more primitive needs at the bottom.

Physiological needs

The physiological needs of the organism, those enabling homeostasis, take first precedence. These consist mainly of:

- the need to breathe;
- the need to drink water;
- the need to regulate homeostasis;
- the need to eat;
- the need to dispose of bodily wastes.

Maslow also places sexual activity in this category, as well as bodily comfort, activity, exercise, etc. While several of these activities are important, many are not essential for survival.

Safety needs

When physiological needs are met, the need for safety will emerge. Safety and security rank above all other desires. These include:

- physical security – safety from violence, delinquency, aggressions;

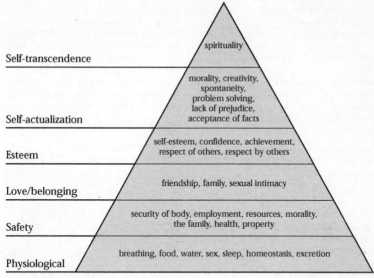

Maslow's Hierarchy of Needs

- security of employment;
- security of revenues and resources;
- moral and physiological security;
- family security;
- security of health;
- security of personal property against crime.

Sometimes the desire for safety outweighs the requirement to satisfy physiological needs completely.

Love/belonging needs
After physiological and safety needs are fulfilled, the third layer of human needs is social. Humans generally need to feel belonging and acceptance, whether it comes from a large social group (clubs, office culture, religious groups, professional organizations, sports teams, gangs) or small social connections (family members, intimate partners, mentors, close colleagues, confidants). They need to love and be loved (sexually and non-sexually) by others. In the absence of these elements, many people become susceptible to loneliness, social anxiety and depression.

Esteem needs
According to Maslow, all humans have a need to be respected, to have self-respect and to respect others. People need to engage in order to gain recognition and have an activity or activities that give them a sense of contribution and self-value, be it in a profession or hobby. Imbalances at this level can result in low self-esteem, inferiority complexes, an inflated sense of self-importance or snobbishness.

Self-actualization needs
Self-actualization is the instinctual need of humans to make the most of their unique abilities and to strive to be the best they can be. In short, self-actualization is reaching one's fullest potential.

Self-transcendence needs
At the top of the triangle, self-transcendence is also sometimes referred to as spiritual needs.

mass communications The delivery of a message to its target audience utilizing traditional mass media such as national press, radio and/or television. The rapidly rising number of electronic media outlets on the Internet, such as information sites and blogging, is transforming mass communication. This and a growing use of public relations as means of communicating both corporate and not-for-profit messages has meant that mass media communications has many more mediums in the twenty-first century and is continuing to evolve.

mass customization A production and service process that allows for a standard mass-produced product, for example, a bicycle, car or motor bike, to be individually tailored to specific customer requirements.

mass market A market for goods that have been mass-produced and covers a substantial part of the population.

mass marketing Mass marketing is used to sell a product to a wide range of customers in large quantities. Mass marketing is the opposite of custom marketing, where a product is made specifically for an individual customer or a consumers group. Mass marketing had a strong beginning after the end of the Second World War, when free market enterprise was allowed to resume in the absence of a state-run economy. An obvious factor contributing to the effectiveness of mass marketing is its use of modern technology, such as radio, television, Internet, mass mailings, etc.

mass-marketing strategy An advertising and media strategy that attempts to target every consumer, rather than targeting a particular market segment. A mass-marketing strategy is effective for products that appeal to a broad cross-section of consumers, for instance, breakfast cereal and chocolate. Mass-market media are usually more expensive than direct marketing media, because they are priced according to the number of consumers who will be reached and must generate a larger return in order to justify the expense.

mass media A term used to describe a class of media which will be seen and/or heard by the whole population of a nation state. The term was developed in the 1920s with the development of broadcast radio and has now been used to cover mass communications media which includes the Internet, television, radio and print. These all lend themselves to using mass communications such as ADVERTISING and PROPAGANDA.

matrix organization An organization structure that is matrix-shaped, with two axes, rather than pyramid-shaped. Typically, but not necessarily, it has product groups on the vertical axis and strategic business units on the horizontal axis. The matrix organization is at the centre of a continuum between purely functional-type organizations and purely product-type organizations. On the functional end of this continuum is the traditional hierarchical structure divided along functional lines such as marketing, production and accounting. On the other end of this continuum is the pure product organization. Here, a separate team is formed, duplicating the functional structure but organized under a product manager.

media Forms of mass communication. Newspapers, magazines, direct mail, billboards, bus signs, radio, television and the Internet are some important media that carry advertising.

media buyer The individual responsible for the purchase of time and space for the delivery of advertising messages in the media. A media buyer may be an employee of an advertising agency who specializes in such purchases, but, technically, a media buyer is any advertiser, advertising manager or individual who buys the commercial time or the advertising space. In some large agencies, the purchase of advertising media has become quite specialized, and there are those who purchase only broadcast time (time buyers), others who purchase only print space (space buyers) and still others who purchase only outdoor space (outdoor space buyers).

media planning The selection of the most appropriate media to deliver the marketing communication message to the target audiences. A media plan sets out the media vehicles to be used and the times and dates when the advertisements will appear.

media reach The size of an audience exposed to an advertisement through a particular medium. It is defined as the size of the audience who listen to, read, view or otherwise access a particular work in a given time period. Reach may be stated either as an absolute number or as a fraction of a population.

media release One of the most frequently used tactics or tools in PUBLIC RELATIONS practice. A media release can either be a news release or feature release. News releases present hard news and feature releases offer human interest stories. Releases are sent to a media GATEKEEPER, such as a print journalist or television producer who determines the stories that appear in a publication or on a broadcast.

media research The collective term for an extremely diverse range of investigations into the size, specification and behaviour of advertising media consumers embracing readers, viewers, listeners and audiences. Media research today is a sophisticated, highly quantitative and somewhat discreet discipline, carried out by media planners. Some research relates specifically to the performance characteristics of individual media vehicles, while some is aimed at improving general understanding of how people consume and use media. Nielsen Media Research (see ACNIELSEN) is the world's leading provider of television audience measurement and related services. Active in more than forty countries, Nielsen Media Research offers television and radio audience measurement, print readership and custom media research services. *See also* ADVERTISING RESEARCH.

media schedule An operational activity which results from media planning designed to achieve particular objectives with respect to reach, frequency and impact. In broadcast media it may include restrictions on limiting the transmission of adult or violent material. *See also* ADVERTISING SCHEDULE.

medium A channel of communication, e.g. television or direct mail.

merchandising All activity associated with selling products once they have reached the point of sale, for instance, packaging, display, stock holding, shelf or aisle positioning, pricing and special offers. This may be carried out by the store's own staff or by the product's owner's specialist sale support people. High quality merchandising staff are normally employed by the leading branded goods companies to ensure their products have the prime position in the stores that they retail through.

merchant An individual or organization which takes title to goods and then resells them. Merchants can be categorized into two types:

- A wholesale merchant operates in the chain between producer and retail merchant. Some wholesale merchants only organize the movement of goods rather than move the goods themselves.
- A retail merchant (commonly known as a retailer) sells commodities to consumers (including businesses). A shop owner is a retail merchant.

merger The combining of two or more entities into one, through a purchase acquisition or a pooling of interests. It differs from a consolidation in that no new entity is created from a merger.

meta-analysis The process of combining the data from a number of independent studies (usually drawn from the published literature) and synthesizing summaries and conclusions addressing a particular issue. It aims to utilize the increased power of pooled data to clarify the state of knowledge on that issue.

meta marketing A method, usually ascribed to Philip KOTLER, of studying marketing and its relationship to every aspect of human life, so establishing a body of knowledge based on experience, and with

Mintzberg, Henry

An acclaimed and iconoclastic management thinker who has advised some of the world's largest corporations. Currently he is Cleghorn Professor of Management Studies at McGill University in Montreal, where he has been since graduating with a doctorate from MIT in 1968. Mintzberg first gained attention with a book, *The Nature of Managerial Work* (1973), based on research carried out for his doctoral dissertation in the late 1960s. He is a prolific writer in the areas of management, strategy formation and forms of organizing and has generated a lot of attention over the years for notable books such as *Mintzberg on Management, The Rise and Fall of Strategic Planning, Inside Our Strange World of Organizations* and *Managers, Not MBAs: A Hard Look at the Soft Practice of Managing and Management Development.* He has received honours including election as an Officer of the Order of Canada and l'Ordre national du Québec and selection as Distinguished Scholar for the year 2000 by the Academy of Management.

every facet, of human personalities and lifestyles.

meta tags The use of meta tags in web pages are often needed by web-based search engines as a source of information to help them to decide how to list and rank websites.

metatheory A theory devised to analyse theoretical systems, i.e. theory about theory. For example, a theoretical account of the epistemological presuppositions of conflict theory and functionalism would be a metatheoretical work.

methodology The basis of a research design application and analysis. It is commonly used as a synonym for 'method', but more properly should apply to a set of methods.

micro environment Elements or activities with which an organization interacts directly. The major aspects of the micro environment are: competitors; suppliers; channels of distribution; customers; and the media. *See also* MACRO ENVIRONMENT; MARKETING ENVIRONMENT.

micromarketing Micromarketing is the practice of tailoring products and marketing programmes to suit the taste of specific individuals and locations. It encompasses the design, creation and manufacture of products, marketing strategies and integrated marketing communication such as advertising campaigns for the benefit of very specific geographic, demographic or psychographic segments of the consumer market. Micromarketing is a relatively new marketing trend created by growing awareness of the diversity of the consumer population and the difficulty in creating a single product that appeals to all groups within the population. In addition, improved technological research abilities, such as data-mining abilities and supermarket scanners, have enabled marketers to pinpoint which specific market segments are buying what products and when. Consequently retailers have come to prefer localized marketing promotions targeted at the specific characteristics of the population in the neighbourhoods of their retail outlets. *See also* MACROMARKETING.

microsegmentation The subdivision of B2B markets on the basis of the characteristics of the buying centre and the individual members of it.

migration The switching from one television channel to another, which may occur as a reaction to television commercials. Or switching attention from a feature or news item in the press to an advertisement.

milking strategy Short-range marketing strategy planned to take the largest possible profit from an item in the shortest amount of time without regard to the item's long-range possibilities for sales. Milking strategies are adopted when budgets are low and the need for funds in other operational areas, such as research and development, is great. The idea behind a milking strategy is to use the profits from one item to develop other products that are believed to have greater future profit potential.

mission statement A mission statement defines the raison d'être, or prime purpose, of an organization over and beyond simply increasing shareholder value and should reflect employees' and stakeholders' motivations for engaging in the organization's work. Effective mission statements are normally short statements of core values, inspiring, long-term in nature and easily understood and communicated.

mixed economy In this form of economy, certain sectors of the economy are left to private ownership and free market mechanisms while other sectors have significant government ownership and government planning.

mixed media Using more than one medium in any advertising campaign, usually where more than one advertising objective has been set for the campaign.

mixed-method research A research approach that combines more than one method. This particular term usually refers to mixed methods that are a combination of QUANTATIVE and QUALITATIVE RESEARCH techniques to achieve a desired research outcome.

mobile advertising Posters on vehicles, or advertising painted directly on to vehicles, e.g. buses or aircraft.

mock-up A facsimile of a package or product for use in photography for television or other visual display form.

model A representation or description of something that aids in understanding or studying it. It can also be a set of assumptions about relationships used to study their interactions, as a computer simulation might model strategic decision-making or as a role-playing might be a model of social interaction.

modem Short for modulator-demodulator, a modem is a device that links computer systems via telephone lines, allowing computers in different locations to exchange and share information. Modems convert telephone impulses to computer-interpretable impulses. There must be a modem at each end of the communications link to either send or receive converted impulses.

modernity A term used to describe the condition of being 'modern'. It is often associated with the rise of capitalism and notions such as progress. Modernity is often seen to be characterized by the liberation of people from ignorance, political tyranny, religious authority and superstition, as well as the mastering of nature through science in order to relieve famine and supply basic necessities. It involved the spread of western bureaucratizing, centralizing and rationalizing practices. In later (twentieth-century) modernity those ideals and practices produced functionalist scientific management involving Taylorism, the Ford Motor Company's assembly line and the mass production of standardized goods with associated ECONOMIES OF SCALE. And individual freedom was enhanced, albeit within a command and control framework, through industrialization with improved living standards, paid employment and the consolidation of parliamentary democracy. *See also* POSTMODERNITY.

modification In product development, to change a product or its presentation in order to effect improvement in performance, characteristics, acceptability, manufacturing procedure or profitability.

modified rebuy *See* BUY PHASES.

monopoly A market where one firm markets all the products that are sold. Often the term 'monopoly' is also applied where one firm controls a very high share of the market. This results in a very low level of competition.

montage 1 An edited succession of scenes

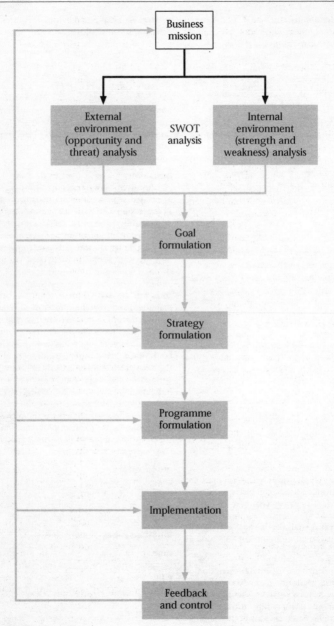

Mission Statement

in television or cinema. **2** The bringing together into one illustration of a number of different materials.

mood advertising Advertising which is deliberately aimed at putting potential customers into a frame of mind conducive to acceptance of the product.

Moore's Law This proposes that the cost of technology declines by 50 per cent every eighteen months. Gordon Moore, in 1965, observed that the number of transistors per square inch on integrated circuits had doubled every year since the integrated circuit was invented. In subsequent years, the pace has slowed down a bit, but data density has doubled approximately every eighteen months. This can equally be applied to most areas of technology advance, most notably computer software and microprocessor power.

morphological analysis A three-dimensional analysis to suggest market segments most likely to produce profit opportunities.

mosaic classification A geodemographic SEGMENTATION system developed by Experian and marketed in over sixty countries worldwide. Each of the nearly one-quarter million block groups were classified into sixty segments on the basis of a wide range of demographic characteristics. It uses a combination of census, electoral roll, housing and financial data (86 variables in all) to classify households into 12 lifestyle groups. These groups in turn break down into 52 subgroups.

MOSAIC is one of the most widely-used geodemographic tools in the corporate and public sector and is the industry standard in finance, insurance, telecoms, retail and The 12 MOSAIC lifestyle groups can be described as follows.

- **High Income Families**. These are found in the more affluent and leafy suburbs, where professionals and wealthy business-people live in large and expensive owner-occupied housing. These are typically family areas, where houses have four or more bedrooms and generous gardens. Such

areas are frequented by two-income, two-car households where children as well as parents are performance and achievement oriented.

- **Suburban Semis** represent the bedrock of middle-brow suburban taste, attracting people whose ambitions are focused on limited and attainable objectives. Living in satellite villages as well as established suburbs, these people live well-organized and agreeable lives and have sufficient time and income to pursue a wide variety of home-based leisure interests.
- **Blue Collar Owners** consist of the less expensive areas of owner-occupier housing, where skilled manual and junior white-collar workers take pride in their homes and gardens. These are unpretentious areas where sensible and self-reliant people have worked hard to achieve a comfortable and independent lifestyle.
- **Low Rise Council** predominantly contains areas of local authority and housing association tenants. There is a relatively high concentration of people who are on low incomes or are unemployed or retired.
- **Council Flats** includes high-rise flats, large municipal overspill estates and smaller developments of local authority maisonettes and mid-rise dwellings. These are commonly areas of very low incomes.
- **Victorian Low Status** contains areas of genuine community feeling, where young families and the childless elderly live in owner-occupied and privately-rented terraces and tenements, often dating from the late nineteenth century. These older-established communities often lie close to the centres of large towns and offer less formal environments than more recently-built suburban areas. There are high levels of local social contact and a wide variety of lifestyles.
- **Town Houses and Flats** are typically areas of lower and middle income housing, often occupied by junior administrative and service employees.

Such areas are found typically in small market towns and service centres, in the older areas of towns where large houses have been divided into small flats and in early turn-of-the-century areas of high density terraced housing designed for clerks and the junior managers in the service industries of large cities. These areas today house people who typically use inter-personal rather than craft skills in their work, and who are well-informed and sociable in their lifestyles.

- **Stylish Singles** includes people for whom self-expression is more important than conformity to any external set of social standards. Typically very well educated and very involved in their work, people are highly interested in the behaviour of different social groups and enjoy living in a diverse, cosmopolitan and sometimes multi-cultural environment. These people prefer the vitality of the large city to the tranquility of outer suburbs.

- **Independent Elders**. As the nation's population ages, this group is rapidly increasing. It includes retired and soon-to-be-retired people who can look after themselves, and who typically own their houses, purpose-built flats or sheltered accommodation. Household income is low, but low expenditure on rent, mortgages and children leads to quite high levels of discretionary expenditure.

- **Mortgaged Families** consists mostly of areas of newly-built private housing, typically lived in by younger households often burdened by high levels of mortgage repayment. Most of these areas contain young families living on the outskirts of towns and cities, but there are an increasing number of young single people, cohabitees and childless couples in this group, often living in in-fill housing in older areas.

- **Country Dwellers** consists of genuinely rural areas beyond the commuter belt of villages with newly-built estates, where houses have names rather than numbers and where agriculture remains

a significant source of local employment. Such areas vary considerably in their levels of affluence, from the gentrified villages of the New Forest and Sussex Weald to the impoverished hamlets of the Celtic fringes.

- **Institutional Areas** do not conform to a typical household pattern. They include military housing, prisons, hospitals, boarding schools and religious retreats.

The basic premise of geodemographic segmentation is that people tend to gravitate towards communities with other people of similar backgrounds, interests and means.

most favoured nation (MFN) A status accorded by one nation to another in international trade. It does not confer particular advantages on the nation but does mean that the receiving nation will be granted all trade advantages, such as low tariffs, that any third nation also receives. In effect, having MFN status means that one's nation will not be treated worse than anyone else's nation. The members of the WORLD TRADE ORGANIZATION (WTO), which include all developed nations, accord MFN status to each other. Exceptions exist for preferential treatment of developing countries, regional free trade areas and customs unions.

motivation The push of mental forces to accomplish an action. Unsatisfied needs motivate. On the biological level basic human needs of food, shelter and survival are powerful motivators. On the psychological level people need to be understood, affirmed, validated and appreciated. On the business level motivation occurs when people perceive a clear business reason for pursuing a transfer of knowledge or practices.

mousetrapping The use of browser tricks in an effort to keep a visitor captive at a website, often by disabling the 'back' button or generating repeated pop-up windows.

Mp3 A standard file format for compressed audio. It is able to reduce the file size while, for the most part, maintaining the integrity of the audio. It is the most favoured file format for podcasting and is a very popular format for iTunes, BBC downloads and file-sharing sites.

multidimensional Having more than one aspect or dimension. Often used to describe attitudes.

multidimensional scaling A research tool used to explore and understand consumer attitudes about the similarities of products and consumers' preferences among those products. Respondents are asked questions about various brands of a product, answers are charted on a scale with an X-axis and a Y-axis, where each axis represents a specific characteristic of a product. Analysis of the scale allows the producer of the product to develop a single product through knowledge of the importance consumers place on different product attributes and features.

multilevel marketing A form of NETWORK MARKETING in which there are a number of levels of distribution, each one passing goods on to the next. The senior distributors split their commission with the 'down-line' distributors. Multilevel marketing has a recognized image problem due to the fact that it is often difficult to distinguish legitimate MLMs from illegal business operations such as pyramid or Ponzi schemes. MLM businesses do operate legitimately in over 100 countries, and new businesses may use terms like 'affiliate marketing' or 'home-based business franchising'. However, many pyramid schemes try to present themselves as legitimate MLM businesses.

multimedia The use of several media (e.g. text, audio, graphics, animation, video) to convey information. Multimedia also refers to the use of computer technology to create, store and experience multimedia content.

multinational corporation A company operating in a number of countries and has production or service facilities outside its country of origin. Multinational corpor-

ations (MNC) are often divided into three broad groups:

- *Horizontally integrated* multinational corporations manage production establishments located in different countries to produce the same or similar products.
- *Vertically integrated* multinational corporations manage production establishments in certain countries to produce products that serve as input to its production establishments in other countries.
- *Diversified* multinational corporations manage production establishments located in different countries that are neither horizontally nor vertically integrated.

Very large multinationals have budgets that exceed those of many countries. Of the 100 largest economies in the world, fifty-one are multinational corporations. They can have a powerful influence in international relations, given their large economic influence in politicians' representative districts, as well as their extensive financial resources available for PUBLIC RELATIONS and political LOBBYING. Multinationals have played an important role in GLOBALIZATION. Given their international reach and mobility, prospective countries, and sometimes regions within countries, must compete with each other to have MNCs locate their facilities (and subsequent tax revenue, employment and economic activity) within them. To compete, countries and regional political districts offer incentives to MNCs such as tax breaks, pledges of governmental assistance or improved infrastructure or lax environmental and labour standards.

multiple regression analysis A means of analysis that attempts to develop a model of the relationship between a dependent variable such as sales and two or more interdependent variables, such as price, promotional expenditure, etc. Multiple regression calculates the relationship that exists between variables and is often used to predict the change in one that will occur from altering one or more of the remaining variables.

multiplex **1** A group of channels in the digital television network, or group of frequencies in the digital radio network. **2** A cinema complex characterized by several salons under one roof, all operating simultaneously and each showing a different programme.

multiplier effect The tendency for an increase in investment or spending to have an effect that grows (multiplies) beyond the original amount spent or invested. The 'multiplier' is a number expressing the extent of the multiplier effect. A multiplier effect occurs when a change in spending causes a disproportionate change in aggregate demand. The local multiplier effect specifically refers to the effect that spending has when it is circulated through a local economy. For example, when the building of a sports stadium or national museum complex is proposed, one of the suggested benefits is that it will raise income in the area by more than the amount spent on the project. The term is used mainly in economics, but the concept of this kind of feedback effect has applications in other fields.

multivariate analysis Any of a number of methods for examining multiple (three or more) variables at the same time – commonly multivariate analysis applies to designs with more than one independent variable or more than one dependent variable or both. Multivariate analysis allows researchers to examine the relation between two variables while simultaneously controlling how each of these may be influenced by other variables.

N

narrow casting Channelling messages into an electronic medium in such a way as to reach small, well-defined specialist audiences.

national account A customer of major 'national' importance, often with several locations throughout a country.

National Readership Survey (NRS) NRS is a non-profit-making but commercial organization which sets out to provide estimates of the number and nature of the people who read Britain's newspapers and consumer magazines. Currently the survey publishes data covering some 250 newspapers, newspaper supplements and magazines. NRS provides an estimate of the number of readers of a publication and the type of people those readers are in terms of sex, age, regionality and many other demographic and lifestyle characteristics. This is used by publishers of newspapers and magazines, advertisers and advertising agencies to plan, buy and sell advertising space in print media. NRS is a common currency of readership estimates for newspapers and magazines, using a methodology agreed by publishers, advertisers and their agencies. It operates at all times to the highest professional standards, in a manner that is cost effective and sufficiently flexible to take account of change and the needs of its users.

nationalization The act of taking assets into public/state ownership. Usually it refers to private assets being nationalized, but sometimes it may be assets owned by other levels of government, such as municipalities. Similarly, the opposite of natio-nalization is usually PRIVATIZATION, but sometimes it may be municipalization. A key issue in nationalization is whether the private owner is properly compensated for the value of the institution. The most controversial nationalizations are those where no compensation or an amount unreasonably below the likely market rate as expropriations is paid.

neck hanger A device fixed around the neck of a bottle and used for sales promotions, e.g. a competition. Commonly found on wine bottles promoting related food and holiday promotions.

need A need is something fundamental to the maintenance of life, such as food, drink, shelter and clothing. The concept of need is often used to refer to things that people 'must' have; they are often contrasted with wants, which are more discretionary. Needs are largely physiological in the sense that they are basic and instinctive drives with which we are born. It is clear, however, that a need may be satisfied by any one of a large number of alternatives, for example thirst may be assuaged by water, tea, coffee, beer, wine, etc. The availability of alternative means for satisfying a need constitutes choice, provision of which is central to the practice of marketing. In the absence of substitute, or alternative, goods there can be choice, and needs and wants become synonymous. Where there is more than one way of satisfying a basic need, physiological drives will be modified by economic, sociological and psychological factors. Variations in these factors will predispose individuals to prefer a specific alternative and this preference constitutes a want.

negative advertising/campaigning A form of campaigning that tries to win an advantage by referring to negative aspects of an opponent or of a policy rather than emphasizing one's own positive attributes or preferred policies. In the broadest sense, the term covers any rhetoric which refers to an opponent, if only by way of contrast, but can also include attacks meant to destroy an opponent's character, which may veer into ad hominem. Negative campaigning can be found in most marketplaces where ideas are contested. In US politics mudslinging has been called 'as American as Mississippi mud'. Some research suggests negative campaigning is the norm in all political venues, mitigated only by the dynamics of a particular contest.

Negative approaches are used in democracies as an element of adversarial policy making and electoral processes. In more unilateral or totalitarian governments the approach is used to suppress opposition. Negative campaign tactics in democracies are often rhetorical, whereas negative campaigns in totalitarian jurisdictions sometimes involve criminal charges and torture to convince constituents of negative aspects of opposition ideas. There are a number of techniques used in negative campaigning, among the most effective of which is running advertisements attacking an opponent's personality or record.

One of the most famous such ads was 'Daisy Girl' by the campaign of Lyndon B. Johnson, which successfully portrayed Republican Barry Goldwater as threatening nuclear war. On 7 September 1964, Johnson's presidential campaign launched 'Peace, Little Girl'. The advertisement shows a sweet young girl plucking the petals from a daisy and counting from one to nine. Then a male announcer counts down from ten. With each successive number the camera jumps to a closer shot of the child's face. At zero, a nuclear blast fills the screen, and President Johnson says: 'These are the stakes – to make a world in which all of God's children can live, or to go into the dark. We must either love each other, or we must die.' The commercial aired just once, but it caused an instant furore. NBC, the network on which the commercial aired, was flooded with phone calls and letters. Senator Barry Goldwater requested equal time from NBC to clarify his position on the tactical use of nuclear warheads. Out of shock and voyeurism, television news programmes on all three networks featured the commercial and the resulting controversy.

Common negative campaign techniques include painting an opponent as soft on criminals, dishonest, corrupt or a danger to the nation. One common negative campaigning tactic is attacking the other side for running a negative campaign. Dirty tricks are also common in negative political campaigns. These generally involve secretly leaking damaging information to the media. This isolates a candidate from backlash and also does not cost any money. The material must be substantive enough to attract media interest, however, and if the truth is discovered it could severely damage a campaign. Other dirty tricks include trying to feed an opponent's team false information hoping they will use it and embarrass themselves.

Campaign organizers who invest their fortunes in negative approaches do so with considerable research to support the merit of their spending. In a 1996 study, researchers concluded that 'the informational benefits of negative political ads possess the capacity to promote political participation, particularly among those otherwise least well equipped for political learning'. Their testing found citizens who were aware of negative advertising were more likely to vote than those who didn't express recollection of such ads.

Negative campaigning can evoke negative responses towards the source of the campaign. Some negative campaign tactics shift focus away from substantive issues or policies and turn attention towards personality. Some strategists say that an effect of negative campaigning is that, while it motivates the base of support, it can alienate centrist and undecided voters from the political process, reducing voter turnout and radicalizing politics. When used by an incumbent, negative ads can increase name recognition for otherwise lesser-known opponents, some sources say. Unless carefully worded, negative campaigns can create an impression that the source of the campaign is mean-spirited.

Negative ads can produce a backlash. Because of the possible harm that can come from being seen as a negative campaigner, candidates often pledge to refrain from negative attacks. This pledge is usually abandoned when an opponent is perceived to be 'going negative', with the first retaliatory attack being, ironically, an accusation that the opponent is a negative campaigner.

In commercial advertising, various regulations prohibit false advertising and broadcast campaigns to promote potentially harmful activities, such as advertising tobacco products. Similar regulations have at times been proposed to limit negative political campaigning on television and radio, where negative claims might not be fully explained due to time constraints, and to expand disclosure requirements in printed political advertising.

negative appeal An advertising copy approach that points out the negative aspects of life without the advertised product. The negative appeal attempts to increase people's anxiety about not using a product or service and stresses the loss they will experience if they do not purchase the product or service.

negative demand Actual avoidance of a product – the refusal even to consider a purchase.

negotiation The process where interested parties resolve disputes, agree upon courses of action, bargain for individual or collective advantage and/or attempt to craft outcomes which serve their mutual interests. Negotiation is usually regarded as a form of alternative dispute resolution. The first step in negotiation is to determine whether the situation is in fact a negotiation. The essential qualities of negotiation are: the exist-

ence of two parties who share an important objective but have some significant difference(s). The purpose of the negotiating conference is to seek a compromise on the difference(s). The outcome of the negotiating conference may be a compromise satisfactory to both sides, a stand-off (failure to reach a satisfactory compromise) or a stand-off with an agreement to try again at a later time.

A skilled negotiator usually serves as advocate for one party to the negotiation and attempts to obtain the most favourable outcomes possible for that party. In this process the negotiator attempts to determine the minimum outcome(s) the other party is (or parties are) willing to accept, then adjusts their demands accordingly. A 'successful' negotiation in the advocacy approach is when the negotiator is able to obtain all or most of the outcomes their party desires, but without driving the other party to break off negotiations permanently.

Traditional negotiating is sometimes called win-lose because of the assumption of a fixed 'pie', that one person's gain results in another person's loss. This is only true, however, if only a single issue needs to be resolved, such as a price in a simple sales negotiation. If multiple issues are discussed, differences in the parties' preferences make win-win negotiation possible. For example, in a labour negotiation, the union might prefer job security over wage gains. If the employers have opposite preferences, a trade is possible that is beneficial to both parties. Such a negotiation is therefore not an adversial zero-sum game. For a negotiation to be 'win-win', both parties should feel positive about the situation when the negotiation is concluded. This helps to maintain a good working relationship afterwards. This governs the style of the negotiation – histrionics and displays of emotion are clearly inappropriate because they undermine the rational basis of the negotiation and because they bring a manipulative aspect to them.

neon sign A sign with a chemically inert gas in a transparent tube that illuminates when electrified; it is also called neon lamp, neon light or neon tube. Any roadside or on-premise painted display, poster panel or non-standardized sign may use neon gas for attention-getting impact and easy visibility during night or day. Neon lights are usually placed in highly trafficked day and night locations to attract the maximum number of passers-by.

net amount In general, the quantity remaining after a deduction from the gross amount, such as the money remaining from a sale after the deduction of expenses.

net margin The excess of sales revenues over cumulative costs, after subtracting fixed costs before taking account of any extraordinary, exceptional or non-product-related issues. *See also* MARGIN.

netiquette Short for network etiquette, the unofficial code of conduct which governs acceptable behaviour when engaging in Internet dialogue, especially in e-mailing, chat rooms and virtual worlds. The politeness conventions vary greatly, and many sites now give guidance about such matters as greeting and leaving a group, addressing messages, the sort of subject matter which is unacceptable and the avoidance of offensive language.

network 1 A distribution system for television content whereby a central operation provides programming for many television stations. The term can also apply to a group of newspapers spread over a wide geographic region the advertising space in which is sold as a unit under one billing.
2 A pathway or pattern of repeated interactions between individuals within a group and between groups in an organization. A network consists of person–person connections by which information is exchanged. Network is also used as a verb to describe the deliberate action by a person to make contact, preferably face-to-face and one-to-one, with other people having similar characteristics or interests or other common features.

network analysis Breaking down a com-plex project into component requirements and recording these in a diagrammatic form which incorporates a critical time scale, so that planning and control can be affected in the most expedient manner. *See also* CRITICAL PATH ANALYSIS.

network effect The phenomenon whereby a good or service becomes more valuable as more consumers use it, thereby encouraging ever-increasing numbers of adopters.

network marketing In popular usage it is a synonym for MULTILEVEL MARKETING and often mistakenly considered the same as a pyramid scheme. The concept of 'network marketing' is often used to describe a marketing paradigm that stresses the interconnectedness of market actors and transactions and can be viewed as the application of systems thinking to marketing. According to network marketing theory other marketing paradigms see the discipline as consisting primarily of dyadic relationships (i.e. one buyer and one seller). Network marketing wishes to overcome this limitation by looking at transactions and relationships from the viewpoint of all those involved.

This perspective originated in industrial marketing, also called B2B marketing, where multiple contact points are typical. It is not uncommon, for example, to have several decision-makers in a company's 'buying centre'. Likewise, the marketer can be organized into a 'selling team'. With multiple actors on each side of the transaction, a complex network is created. This paradigm is further complicated by corollary actors like information GATEKEEP-ERS, influencers, advertisers and intermediaries. This network can expand over time as more people get involved.

The network marketing approach sees marketing as a system of social networks where the relations between each of the links must be understood, including potential feedback loops, while at the same time the system must be comprehended as a whole.

network theory Network theory is the

vital part of systems theory that addresses the pathways of information flow within and between systems. Each pathway is a repeated or potential route for information to flow from person to person, organization to organization, person to organization, organization to person and so on. Network theory features the central premise that people need and want information. How they obtain this information or feel the lack of the desired information can affect their attitude towards, and knowledge about, various topics that are relevant to the goodwill and success of each organization.

new product development (NPD) A function of marketing involving the conceptualization of a new product to satisfy a consumer requirement followed by research and development, design, prototype, consumer testing, test market and campaign launch.

new task *See* BUY PHASES.

news-stand A retail outlet for single-copy magazine and newspaper sales, usually a stall or booth in an area where many consumers are likely to gather or pass by, such as airports, supermarkets, railway stations and sports grounds amongst others.

newsgroup A discussion group on the Internet, similar to an electronic BULLETIN BOARD. Users are presented with a summary of discussion topics and can select from an organized menu and sub-menu structure.

newspaper A well-known communications medium, usually consisting of printed sheets of paper, though newspaper content can now also be viewed via the Internet. Newspapers can be local, regional, national or international in terms of distribution and are normally published daily or weekly. They are a major advertising medium, as they allow mass regular coverage of major target groups, have geographic flexibility and generally have very short lead times. However, newspapers have low regional flexibility and limited opportunities for colour, poor reproduction qual-

IDEA GENERATION
Ideas from:
Customers and users
Marketing research
Competitors
Other markets
Company
    people
Intermediaries, etc.

SCREENING
Strengths and weaknesses
Fit with objectives
Market trends
Rough ROI estimate

IDEA EVALUATION
Concept testing
Reactions from customers
Rough estimates of cost,
    sales and profits

DEVELOPMENT
R & D
Develop model or service
    prototype
Test marketing mix
Revise plans as neeeded
ROI estimate

COMMERCIALIZATION
Finalize product and
    marketing plan
Start production and marketing
'Roll out' in select markets
Final ROI estimate

New Product Development

ity, a short life and are not as intrusive as other media.

newspaper syndicate An organization that sells material to different newspapers for simultaneous publications, on a commission basis. Some newspaper syndicates specialize in editorial copy (columns, feature articles, news, etc.) and/or photography, art, puzzles, or cartoons. A newspaper syndicate usually pays a contributor 40–60 per cent of the gross proceeds, although some firms pay by salary and others purchase material outright.

niche marketing The process of finding and serving small but potentially profitable market segments and designing custom-made products or services for them. For big companies those market segments are often too small to serve profitably as they often lack ECONOMIES OF SCALE. Niche marketers are often reliant on the loyalty business model to maintain a profitable volume of sales. *See also* MARKET NICHE.

Nielsen *See* ACNIELSEN.

Nielsen rating A measurement of the percentage of television households tuned to a network programme for a minute of its telecast, developed by ACNIELSEN.

nixie rate The percentage of undeliverable mail in a mail sample. The nixies are due to illegible or incorrectly addressed mail.

noise The difference between the predicted and observed values of a model due to random error including missing and incomplete data.

nominal scale A scale of measurement in which numbers stand for names but have no order or value. For example, coding female = 1 and male = 2 would be a nominal scale: females do not come first, two females do not add up to a male, and so on. The numbers are merely labels.

non-durable goods Products which are consumed within a short space of time, such as cosmetics and food.

non-governmental organization

(NGO) Organized groups independent of government control set up to accomplish a social goal. NGOs first emerged when many former colonies and territories were undergoing the transition from colonial rule to self-rule. After these countries had achieved independence, NGOs continued to work in solving local problems such as infant mortality and illiteracy. The growth of NGOs reflects a shift away from the beliefs that government is the primary provider of services, that economic growth is the singular key to progress and that leadership is a top-down process. NGOs are not yet institutionalized, but are likely to become so as their efforts become indispensable to society.

non-profit organization (NPO) Incorporated under state law as charitable or not-for-profit corporations, these organizations are distinguished from organizations that focus on either making a profit (the private sector) or serving as an arm of government (the governmental sector). The non-profit organization must focus on making some portion of society better or preventing it from becoming worse. NPOs provide not only welfare services but also social, educational and cultural services.

non-response bias In a piece of research there may be a bias due to certain intended respondents being unavailable or unwilling to be questioned. Thus the sample may become unrepresentative.

normal distribution A statistical term central to sampling theory. On a line chart, it shows the point at which the mean, mode and median averages share the same value and has a characteristic bell-shaped profile.

norms Rules of behaviour adopted by a society which determines what is acceptable or unacceptable within that society.

North American Free Trade Agreement (NAFTA) A commitment between Canada, Mexico and the US to facilitate cross-border movement of goods and services and to protect intellectual property rights. NAFTA became effective on 1

January 1994 and was modelled on MOST FAVOURED NATION policies. NAFTA was agreed upon to enhance participants' competitiveness in global markets in a manner that protects the environment and labour rights. It called for the immediate elimination of duties on half of all US goods shipped to Mexico and Canada and the gradually phasing-out of other tariffs over a period of about fourteen years. Restrictions were to be removed from many categories, including, but not limited to, motor vehicles and automotive parts, computers, textiles and agriculture. The treaty also protected intellectual property rights (patents, copyrights and trademarks) and outlined the removal of restrictions on investment among the three countries. Provisions regarding worker and environmental protection were added later as a result of supplemental agreements.

not-for-profit marketing Marketing activities conducted by individuals and organizations to achieve some goal other than ordinary business goals of profit, market share or return on investment.

NPD *See* NEW PRODUCT DEVELOPMENT.

O

objective A target goal by which one can measure the success or otherwise of one's marketing campaign or plan.

observational research One of a number of research approaches and designs in which the investigator observes subjects but does not interact with them in their role as a researcher. It is used frequently in QUALITATIVE RESEARCH to assess consumer behaviour. It has come to be applied particularly to research where investigators observe in a natural setting, do not identify themselves as researchers and do not participate in what they are observing. On the other hand, virtually all research is observational in one way or another: experimenters observe subjects as much as participant observers do.

observer bias Inaccuracies that occur when observers know the goals of the research or the hypothesis being tested and that acknowledge influences and observations.

observer drift The tendency, especially in lengthy research studies, for observers to become inconsistent in the criteria they use to make and record their observations. This causes a decline in the reliability of the data they collect.

obsolescence In marketing the act where a product or service becomes of no market use or is outmoded by other products or regulation. The planning of product portfolio and their life cycles is at the heart of marketing planning and predicting both factors that will lead to obsolescence and those products that will become obsolete

is an important part of the marketing manager's job and remit.

occupation groups A form of market SEGMENTATION based upon the occupation of the prospective customers. A narrower definition than SOCIO-ECONOMIC GROUPS.

Ockham's razor A philosophical doctrine named after William of Ockham (Occam) (1285–1349) to the effect that theories should be as streamlined as possible. All other things being equal, the simplest theory (e.g. the explanation with the fewest predictions) is the best. The principle is more often called parsimony today.

odd pricing Retail prices are often expressed as odd prices, that is, a little less than a round number, e.g. $19.99 or £6.95. It is a theory in marketing that these prices have a psychological impact that drives demand more than would be expected if consumers were perfectly rational. Interestingly, now that many customers are used to odd pricing, high-end retailers such as Nordstrom psychologically price in even numbers in an attempt to reinforce their brand image of quality and sophistication.

off the page A technique for communication or selling using catalogues to which a buyer/ customer responds directly in person, or by telecommunication. The responses are normally entered into a database, which allows a profile of buyers to be compiled.

offensive warfare A marketing warfare strategy whereby a company in a second or third position will attack a competitive leader in the marketplace. Offensive warfare differs from defensive warfare in that, in the latter, the market leader is protecting its position, whereas in the former the market challenger is launching an attack on the market leader.

offering The total benefits or satisfaction provided to target markets by an organization. An offering consists of a tangible product or service plus related services such as installation, repair, warranties or guarantees, packaging, technical support, field support and other services. Marketing has traditionally differentiated between products and services. The product has been viewed as consisting of a bundle of tangible and intangible attributes and as having several layers, such as: the core, consisting of the essential benefits to the customer; the tangible product, including the colour, taste, design, brand name and packaging; and the augmented product, such as the back-up service, warranty and delivery. The 'product', then, is a set of benefits, many of which can be seen as involving service, offered to the customer

Office of Fair Trading (OFT) A UK government agency established by the Fair Trading Act 1973 to monitor trade and commerce, to ensure compliance with the legislation governing industrial and commercial behaviour and to promote and protect the consumers' interests. The OFT's goal is to make markets work well for consumers. Markets work well when there is vigorous competition between fair-dealing businesses. When markets work well, good businesses flourish. The OFT's activities in pursuit of this goal involve:

- enforcement – of competition and consumer protection rules;
- market studies – into how markets are working;
- communication – to explain and improve awareness and understanding.

As an independent professional organization, the OFT plays a leading role in promoting and protecting consumer interests throughout the UK, while ensuring that businesses are fair and competitive.

oligopoly A market where a small number of firms represent a large proportion of sales. The word oligopoly is derived from the Greek, meaning 'few sellers'.

omnibus In market research, a continuous survey which is used to cover a number of topics at the same time. It is a method of QUANTATIVE RESEARCH where data on a wide variety of subjects is collected during the same interview. Usually, multiple research clients will provide proprietary content for the survey while sharing the common demographic data collected from each respondent. The advantages to the research client include cost savings, as the sampling and screening costs are shared across multiple clients, and timeliness, because omnibus samples are large and interviewing is ongoing. An omnibus survey generally uses a stratified sample and can be conducted either by mail or telephone or over the Internet.

Omnicom The world's biggest marketing services group, controlling an extensive collection of different businesses led by the three global advertising networks of BBDO, DDB and TBWA. An early investor in the Internet economy, Omnicom learned several tough lessons from the subsequent Internet business crash, and since then has almost entirely avoided low-return acquisitions. Instead it has concentrated on filling out gaps in its coverage with selective purchases of niche players. Despite the lack of any transformational acquisitions, Omnicom's overall revenues have continued to rise steadily, mainly through organic growth. Omnicom was the number one ad organization worldwide in 2006 with revenues of $11.4bn.

on-camera A description of the action that takes place in front of the camera and is therefore visible to the viewing audience. An actor, spokesperson or announcer whose face appears in a television programme or commercial is said to have been on camera.

on costs Money spent in producing a product which does not rise with the quantity of the product made. *See also* AVER-AGE VARIABLE COSTS; FIXED COSTS.

on speculation (on spec) A description of work, such as advertising, that is done for a client without a contract or job order, for which the client will pay only if the work is to be used. When a job is done on speculation, the person doing the work takes the risk in the hope of making a profit, gaining a valuable credit or for some other reason. In the advertising business, creative talent will often work on spec in order to establish a name in the industry.

one-shot In advertising, **1** a stand-alone television programme, such as a one-off or one-shot documentary or variety special, in contrast to a continuing series or a programme shown in a limited number of episodes or instalments over time. One-shots are usually heavily promoted before being aired and can give the advertiser greater exposure than a continuing programme. Also, the content of the advertisement can be specially targeted to the context of the programme; **2** a television or motion picture shot of one subject, such as an announcer speaking directly to the camera with nothing in the background.

In direct marketing, a sale completed in one step, such as the sale of a book, as opposed to a sale that involves a series of steps over time, such as the sale of a subscription, which includes renewal of the subscription and delivery of each issue.

one-sided message A persuasive communication that presents only one point of view, also called one-sided appeal. Most mass media advertising messages are one-sided. A one-sided message is more appropriate for an audience that is favourably disposed towards the view being presented or is unlikely to be exposed to the other side. A religious fund-raising appeal is usually one-sided on the assumption that the targeted audience is favourably disposed toward the view being expounded and is unlikely to be receptive to other religious beliefs. With a more sceptical audience, a one-sided message is less effective than a two-sided message, which presents

both points of view and then arguments to counter the opposing view.

one-step flow model The one-step flow model of communications presents mass communication, mainly advertising, as acting directly on each member of the target audience. This model, often called the 'hypodermic needle' model of communications (the communication passing directly to individual members of the audience), contrasts markedly with the two-step flow model, which depicts communications as being filtered through intermediaries called opinion leaders.

one-stop shopping The facility to provide shoppers with a wide range of goods from one retailing centre, usually with parking facilities and good public transport access.

online 1 Connected and turned on, as in a printer when it is ready to receive data from a computer or a computer when it is connected to a computer service through a modem or other electronic connecting device. **2** Information, messages or data that are received through a computer that is connected to a computer service by a modem or other electronic connecting device.

online advertising Advertising messages appearing on a computer screen through a proprietary online service or the Internet's World Wide Web.

online catalogue An Internet-based presentation of a set of items available for purchase, including description, price, quantities available and ordering information. It is also called a cyber catalogue, electronic catalogue, net catalogue or web catalogue.

online database A database provided by an external computer or organization allowing a remote user to connect and interrogate it in real time.

online public relations The use of Internet technologies to manage communications and to establish and maintain mutually beneficial relationships between an organization and its key publics. Organizations have adopted the Internet widely and integrated computer-based delivery into their mix of communications technologies. Particularly valuable is the Internet's ability to allow people and organizations around the world to exchange information on a 24/7 basis.

ontology The study of being or existence. It seeks to describe or posit the basic categories and relationships of being or existence and to define entities and types of entities within its framework. Ontology can be said to study conceptions of reality. Ontology has one basic question: 'What is there?'

Ontology as a branch of philosophy is the science of what is, of the kinds and structures of the objects, properties and relations in every area of reality. 'Ontology' in this sense is often used in such a way as to be synonymous with 'metaphysics'. In simple terms it seeks the classification of entities. Each scientific field will of course have its own preferred ontology, defined by the field's vocabulary and by the canonical formulations of its theories. Traditional (philosophical) ontologists have tended to model themselves on these scientific ontologies, either by producing theories which are like scientific theories but radically more general than these, or by producing theories which represent a regimentation of scientific theories or a clarification of their foundations. Philosophical ontologists have more recently begun to concern themselves not only with the world as it is studied by the sciences, but also with domains of practical activity such as law, medicine, engineering and commerce. They seek to apply the tools of philosophical ontology in order to solve problems which arise in these domains.

open-ended questions Broad questions that require more than a yes/no answer or a one- or two-word response. Open-ended questions develop trust, are perceived as less threatening, allow an unrestrained or free response and may be more useful with articulate respondents. However, they can be time-consuming, may result in unnecessary information and may require more effort on the part of the respondent. *See also* CLOSED-ENDED QUESTIONS.

open source A term developed in 1997 to describe free software. The term was designed to emphasize the freedom of use aspect of the software (the source code is open), without allowing people to assume that 'free' meant no cost (which it did not). Aside from this marketing aspect of the new term, there are also differences in the ideologies of the proponents of the open source movement and those of the free software movement, of which it is a branch. The free software movement believes that all software should be free, and only if all software is free will free software be truly effective. Since all software development relies on previous 'knowledge', and that previous knowledge is in the public domain, then new knowledge, as a derivative, should also be free.

While open source software must have a no-cost alternative (for it to comply with the open source definition), a marketer can sell a version at a price. (Red Hat's version of the Linux operating system is a good example.) The software is released with the source code, which allows the consumer/user to modify the code for their own specific purpose. Users that do modify the code are asked (via the licence) to submit any modifications back to the initiators of the project (known as submitting a patch). This allows any improvements, or resolved bugs, to be included in new releases of the product. The most important developments thus far in the open source and free software movements have been the evolution of the Linux operating system, started in 1991, and the announcement of Netscape's Mozilla project, in 1997. Firefox is a forked iteration of the Mozilla project.

operating costs The day-to-day expenses incurred in running a business, such as sales and administration, as opposed to production. Also called operating expenses. *See also* AVERAGE VARIABLE COST.

operational research The application of mathematical processes to operational problems, having the effect of increasing the proportion of factual data. It is especially useful in helping to resolve questions which are essentially subjective in its absence.

operationalize To define a concept or variable in such a way that it can be measured or identified (or 'operated on'). When you operationalize a variable, you answer the questions 'How will I know it when I see it?' and 'How will I record or measure it?'

opinion The distinction between opinion and ATTITUDE is frequently blurred in marketing usage. Technically, opinions are seen as contributing to the formation of attitudes, which are less subject to change and more likely to influence behaviour. It would seem therefore that, while all attitudes might be classified as opinions, the reverse is not the case. For all practical purposes, however, both attitude and opinion reflect an individual's view about a subject.

opinion-formers Groups of people whose attitudes, access to decision-makers and policy making and use of their own values can lead to actions that are likely to affect those of others.

opinion leader An individual whose behaviour, ideas and opinions serve as a model for others to follow. Opinion leaders communicate messages to a primary group, influencing the attitudes and behaviour change of their followers. Therefore, in certain marketing instances, it may be advantageous to direct the communications to the opinion leader alone to speed the acceptance of an advertising message. For example, advertisers may direct a dental care promotion to influential dentists or a fashion campaign to female celebrities. In both instances, the advertiser is using the opinion leader to carry and 'trickle down' its message to influence its target group. Because of the important role opinion leaders play in influencing markets, advertisers have traditionally used them to give testimonials. Endorsement advertising campaigns by sports and film personalities overlap with this area but is invariably brand re-enforcement of the product.

opinion poll A means by which the views of the general public are ascertained by questioning a representative sample of people.

opinion research Research that gathers together, from a statistical sample of the population, views that are taken to represent those of the entire population.

Opinion Research Corporation International (ORC) A public company founded in 1938 with offices throughout the US as well as in China, Asia, Europe, Latin America and Africa, specializing in market research and business information services. It operates in over 100 countries. The ORC assists clients in monitoring, evaluating and optimizing their marketing and sales strategies. The company conducts commercial marketing research programmes as Opinion Research Corporation in the US and as ORC International outside the US. It also operates through ORC Macro, which specializes in social research programmes for government agencies.

opportunity cost A term used in economics to mean the cost of something in terms of an opportunity forgone (and the benefits that could be received from that opportunity), or the most valuable forgone alternative. For example, if a city decides to build a hospital on vacant land that it owns, the opportunity cost is some other thing that might have been done with the land and construction funds instead. In building the hospital, the city has forgone the opportunity to build a sports centre on that land, or a parking lot, or the ability to sell the land to reduce the city's debt, and so on.

Opportunity cost need not be assessed in monetary terms, but rather can be assessed in terms of anything that is of value to the person or persons doing the assessing. The consideration of opportunity costs is one of the key differences between the concepts of economic cost and accounting cost. Assessing opportunity costs is fundamental to assessing the true cost of any course of action. In the case where there is no explicit accounting or monetary cost (price) attached to a course of action, ignoring opportunity costs may produce the illusion that its benefits cost nothing at all. The unseen opportunity costs then become the hidden costs of that course of action.

Note that opportunity cost is not the sum of the available alternatives, but rather of benefit of the best alternative of them. The opportunity cost of the city's decision to build the hospital on its vacant land is the loss of the land for a sports centre, or the inability to use the land for a parking lot, or the money that could have been made from selling the land, or the loss of any of the various other possible uses – but not all of these in aggregate, because the land cannot be used for more than one of these purposes.

optical character recognition (OCR) An automatic computer input process whereby the computer scanner is able to read printed symbols, numbers and letters and convert them to electronic data. It involves computer software designed to translate images of typewritten text (usually captured by a scanner) into machine-editable text, or to translate pictures of characters into a standard encoding scheme, representing them in ASCII or Unicode. OCR began as a field of research in artificial intelligence and machine vision. Though academic research in the field continues, the focus on OCR has shifted to implementation of proven techniques. Optical character recognition (using optical techniques such as mirrors and lenses) and digital character recognition (using scanners and computer algorithms) were originally considered separate fields. Because very few applications survive that use true optical techniques, the optical character recognition term has now been broadened to cover digital character recognition as well.

opt-in A method of recruitment to a panel whereby members can actively agree to be part of the panel.

orange goods In merchandising, consumer goods, such as clothing, that will last for a period of time but will be replaced, at a moderate rate, because of wear and tear, desire to change or change in season, or at the discretion of the consumer.

ordered metric scale On this scale units of interval are equal, which allows rank ordering of the differences between variables. Zero is relative and arbitrary.

ordinal sampling *See* SYSTEMATIC SAMPLING.

ordinal scale A way of measuring that ranks subjects (puts them in order) on some variable. The differences between the ranks need not be equal (as they are in an interval scale).

organization culture Sets of values, norms and beliefs that are reflected in an organization's structures and systems, including its customs, stories, symbols, traditions and rituals, and the language in which all these facets are expressed. In common parlance, we talk of the differing atmospheres and differing ways of doing things in different organizations ('the way we do things here'). One company may be very sales oriented, another in the same industry may be more profit focused. Others, again, may be more people oriented, or innovation oriented. Intuitively, therefore, organizational culture is easily appreciated, but it is hard to define in a formal sense. It can be described as a system of shared meaning, which ensures everyone is working to the same goals.

All organizations have some sort of culture, and it can be regarded positively or negatively. On the positive side, it differentiates an organization (from other organizations), gives those in an organization a sense of identity and purpose, provides a social fabric and helps to define and enforce the 'rules of engagement' in an organization. However, there may be negative consequences. A strong culture may act as a powerful barrier to change. It may also be unhealthily risk-averse and conformist, e.g. employees hiring only in their own image, rather than thinking about the requirements of the job and who best meets these requirements.

Organization of Petroleum Exporting

Countries (OPEC) An association of oil-producing countries formed in 1960 to control supply for the benefit of its members. By raising prices in the early 1970s they precipitated the energy crisis, which led to the development of many oil fields, including the North Sea, which previously had been uneconomic, as well as encouraging the development of energy-saving devices, more efficient internal combustion engines, etc. OPEC is made up of Algeria, Indonesia, Iran, Iraq, Kuwait, Libya, Nigeria, Qatar, Saudi Arabia, the United Arab Emirates and Venezuela; since 1965 its international headquarters have been in Vienna, Austria.

The principal aim of OPEC, according to its statute, is 'the coordination and unification of the petroleum policies of its member countries and the determination of the best means for safeguarding their interests, individually and collectively; devising ways and means of ensuring the stabilization of prices in international oil markets with a view to eliminating harmful and unnecessary fluctuations; giving due regard at all times to the interests of the producing nations and to the necessity of securing a steady income to the producing countries, an efficient, economic and regular supply of petroleum to consuming nations, and a fair return on their capital to those investing in the petroleum industry'.

OPEC's influence on the market has not always been a stabilizing one, however. It alarmed the world and triggered high inflation across both the developing and developed world through its use of the oil weapon in the 1973 oil crisis. Its ability to control the price of oil has diminished greatly since its heyday, following the much-expanded development of the Gulf of Mexico and the North Sea and the growing fluidity of the market. However, OPEC still has considerable impact on the price of oil. It is still commonly used as a textbook example of a cartel.

organization structure The way in which the interrelated groups of an organization are constructed. From a managerial point of view the main concerns are ensuring effective communication and coordination.

Pre-bureaucratic
Pre-bureaucratic (entrepreneurial) structures lack standardization of tasks. This structure is most common in smaller organizations and is best used to solve simple tasks. They have a very flat hierarchy, and most communication is done by one-on-one conversations.

Bureaucratic
Bureaucratic structures have a certain degree of standardization. They are better suited for more complex or larger scale organizations.

Functional
The organization is structured according to functional areas instead of product lines. The functional-structure groups specialize in similar skills in separate units. This structure is best used when creating specific, uniform products. A functional structure is well suited to organizations which have a single or dominant core product because each sub-unit becomes extremely adept at performing its particular portion of the process. They are economically efficient but lack flexibility. Communication between functional areas can be difficult.

Divisional
Divisional structure is formed when an organization is split up into a number of self-contained business units, each of which operates as a profit centre. Such a division may occur on the basis of product or market or a combination of the two, with each unit tending to operate along functional or product lines, but with certain key functions (e.g. finance, personnel, corporate planning) provided centrally, usually at company headquarters.

Post-bureaucratic
The term post-bureaucratic is often used to describe a range of ideas developed since the 1980s that include Total Quality Management, Culture Management and the Matrix Organization amongst others. None of these, however, has left behind the core tenets of bureaucracy. Hierarchies

O'Shaughnessy, John

John O'Shaughnessy is Emeritus Professor of Business at the Graduate School of Business, Columbia University, New York, and was Senior Associate of the Judge Institute, Cambridge University. He has written thirteen books on business topics and has published in many marketing journals including the *Journal of Marketing*, *Journal of Marketing Science* and the *Journal of Consumer Research*. He has worked in OR/industrial engineering and been a marketing research manager, sales manager and industrial consultant in organization and marketing. His *Competitive Marketing: A Strategic Approach* was an English Language Book Society (ELBS) selection. His *Why People Buy* was the first book in marketing to employ hermeneutics in interpreting what consumers say before, during and after buying. A major interest lies in the philosophy of social science and linguistic philosophy indicated by his *Explaining Buyer Behaviour: Central Concepts and Philosophy of Science Issues*.

still exist, and the organization is still rule bound.

organizational behaviour The study of how and why people behave within organizations with a view to improving organizational structures and performance. Organizational behaviour is the study of what people think, feel and do in and around organizations. It explores individual emotions and behaviour, team dynamics and the systems and structures of organizations. Organizational behaviour seeks to provide an understanding of the factors necessary for managers to create an organization that is more 'effective' or 'successful' than its competitors.

organizational buyer behaviour 1 The way in which organizations, as contrasted with individuals, identify, evaluate and choose the products they buy. A car manufacturer, for example, buys hundreds of components from accessory suppliers. The company's negotiations with such suppliers may start at the early stages of research and development of a new product and continue right through until that model or variant is replaced. Organization buying decisions can be seen in terms of a problem-solving activity with identifiable decision stages. **2** The study of the motives and actions of, and the influences upon, organizations while engaged in purchasing goods and services. *See also* ORGANIZATIONAL PURCHASING.

organizational marketing The marketing of all goods and service between one organization and another. The key concept is that the marketing concentrates on the nature of demand. Whereas consumers are perceived as buying frequently for personal satisfaction, organizations are seen as buying deliberately, usually with quantifiable benefits in view. Marketers are thus required to vary their approaches accordingly. *See also* B2B MARKETING.

organizational purchasing The process of how companies or organizations buy goods and services. Many of these purchases will be straight rebuys, in which case reordering can be automated or delegated to a single procurement/purchasing officer. Other purchases are complex, one-off, high-involvement decisions that may occupy a team of people and require wider consultation. In these circumstances, the decision-making process can be involved and protracted, with perhaps several suppliers asked to pitch or tender for the business. *See also* CORPORATE PURCHASING; ORGANIZATIONAL BUYER BEHAVIOUR.

organizational segmentation The goal of organizational segmentation is to divide a large organizational market into smaller components that are more homogeneous with respect to product needs.

original equipment manufacturer (OEM) The manufacturer of goods and components that are subsequently sold to be included within the products of another company (often called a value-added reseller, or VAR). An OEM will typically build to order based on designs of the VAR. For example, a hard drive in a computer system may be manufactured by a corporation such as Seagate which is separate from the company that markets and sells the PC.

outbound link A link to a website outside of one's own website.

outdoor advertising Any outdoor sign that publicly promotes a product or service, such as a billboard or telephone kiosk, and advertising space at railway stations, airports, health and leisure centres etc.

outer wrap An advertising message that is printed on the plastic bag that wraps the entire newspaper. An advertiser may also distribute lightweight items (such as a CD) to all home-delivery subscribers via the outer wrap.

outlier A subject or other unit of analysis that has extreme values on a variable. Outliers are important because they can distort the interpretation of data or make misleading a statistic that summarizes values (such as a mean). In most samplings of data, some data points will be further away from their expected values than what is deemed reasonable. This can be due to systematic error or faults in the theory that generated the expected values, or it can simply be the case that some observations happen to be a long way from the centre of the data. Outlier points can therefore indicate faulty data, erroneous procedures or areas where a certain theory might not be valid. However, a small number of outliers is expected in normal distribution.

outsourcing The activity of purchasing goods or services from external sources, as opposed to internal sourcing. It is often defined as the delegation of non-core operations or jobs from internal production within a business to an external entity (such as a subcontractor) that specializes in that operation. Outsourcing is a business decision that is often made to lower costs or focus on competencies.

outwork Work that is farmed out to people working at home and thus with reduced overheads.

over-run An additional number of copies printed of a magazine or publication over and above the quantity strictly needed. A contingency to allow for an unexpected demand.

oversampling A procedure of stratified sampling in which the researcher selects a disproportionately large number of subjects from a particular group (stratum). Most often, researchers oversample in a stratum that has a large variance or in a stratum that would yield too few subjects if a random sample were used.

overselling 1 Persuading a distributor or customer to order more goods than they can reasonably handle or consume. **2** Overstating the case for buying a product or service.

own branding The process whereby a product or service name is developed for or by a retailer for its exclusive use. Own-brand goods are often positioned in the marketplace to compete directly with manufacturers' brands. In other cases some stores only stock their own brands, e.g. The Body Shop.

own label This is the practice of retailers branding products using their own private brand label, as opposed to branding by a manufacturer or a distributor, e.g. Marks and Spencer, Boots, Sainsbury. This practice is widely used by supermarkets and chain stores where their own-label products are intended to enhance the store's image and encourage customer loyalty.

ownership transfer When the legal right to possess something is transferred to another person or entity.

packaging The enclosing of a physical object, typically a product that requires protection from tampering, for instance, bottled water. Packaging has seven key objectives:

- protection against physical impact – the objects enclosed in the package may require protection from, among other things, damage caused by physical force, rain, heat, cold, sunlight, pressure, airborne contamination, automated handling devices or any combination of these;
- protection against dust and dirt;
- agglomeration – small objects are typically grouped together in one package for reasons of efficiency. For example, a single box of 1,000 pencils requires less physical handling than 1,000 single pencils. Alternatively, bulk commodities (such as salt) can be divided into packages that are a more suitable size for individual households;
- information transmission – information on how to use, transport or dispose of the product is often contained on the package or label;
- marketing – the packaging and labels can be used by marketers to encourage potential buyers to purchase the product. Package design has been an important and constantly evolving phenomenon for decades.
- reducing theft – some packages are made larger than they need to be so as to make theft more difficult. An example is software packages that typically contain only a single disc even though they are large enough to con-

tain dozens of discs. These packages may also be deliberately difficult to open, to hamper thieves from removing their contents without drawing notice. Packages also provide opportunities to include anti-theft devices, such as dye-packs or electronic article surveillance tags, that can be activated or detected by devices at exit points and require specialized tools to deactivate. Using packaging in this way is a common tactic for loss prevention;
- prevention of pilferage and tampering – products are exposed to many contacts in the supply chain. Persons handling could steal products (pilferage), replace full products with empty ones or add unwanted contaminants to the contents (tampering). Packaging that cannot be reclosed or gets physically damaged (shows signs of opening) is very helpful in the prevention of these acts. The flaps of corrugated and cardboard boxes are therefore glued in such a way that any opening irreversibly damages them. The over packaging of certain objects has led to a phenomenon known as wrap rage.

page proofs The typeset composition of uncorrected pages before formatting into a book, allowing the reader to detect errors. A proof copy can be inexpensively bound and sent to reviewers before publication.

page traffic The number of readers of a particular page in a publication expressed as a percentage of the total readership of that publication.

pagejacking The theft of a page from the

Packard, Vance
(1914–1996)

An American journalist, social critic and author. He wrote a number of books popularizing social issues, including *The Hidden Persuaders* (1957), *The Naked Society* (1964), and *The People Shapers* (1977). His million-selling book *The Hidden Persuaders* examined media manipulation of the populace in the 1950s and the use of consumer motivational research and other psychological techniques, including depth psychology and subliminal tactics, by advertisers to manipulate expectations and induce desire for products, particularly in the post-war era in America. The book questioned the morality of using these techniques.

Packard's discussion of advertising in politics showed especial foresight; he predicted the way image and personality would rapidly come to overshadow real issues in the age of televised elections. His writings on PLANNED OBSOLESCENCE by the producers of consumer goods are still relevant. Packard's work, though it sold well, was sometimes criticized as being poorly thought out, light on facts, high on supposition and frivolous relative to the seriousness of his topics. One thing the critics could not argue with, however, was the success of his 'pop science' books and their value in bridging a gap between the highly educated classes and the less educated ones.

original website and the publication of a copy (or near-copy) on another website.

palletization A system of transporting goods on a platform, on which the goods remain throughout the journey. The advantage of the platform (pallet) is that it can accommodate mechanical handling methods (e.g. forklift trucks, etc.), thus reducing handling costs. A pallet may be no more than two strips of wood separated by two blocks, but more sophisticated versions in cardboard, plastic or metal, which are recyclable or reusable, are most frequently used.

palming off To misrepresent inferior goods of one producer as superior goods made by a reputable, well-regarded supplier in order to gain commercial advantage and foster further sales. The term derives from an ancient conjuring trick.

panel A sample of retail establishments or consumers specially recruited to provide information on buying, media and consumption habits and sometimes to test potential new products. It requires careful supervision and maintenance in order to preserve an effective data basis.

panel data Information, usually quantitative, gathered from a group of people specially commissioned to provide a continuous flow. It is the major type of data used in the marketing of consumer goods and services.

Pantone colours *See* PMS (PANTONE MATCHING SYSTEM) COLOURS.

paradigm From the Greek word *paradeigma*, the term paradigm was introduced into science and philosophy by Thomas Kuhn in his landmark book *The Structure of Scientific Revolutions* (1962). Essentially, a paradigm is simply the predominant worldview in the realm of human thought. For instance, today we would say that we live within an *evolutionary paradigm*, since evolution is the predominant worldview regarding origins, having replaced creation as the explanation for the origin of the universe. A *paradigm shift* occurs when cultures transform their way of thinking from one thought system to another. For instance, prior to Copernicus and Galileo (*c.* 1600), most people believed that astral bodies revolved around the earth (*geocentrism*), but after the Copernican Revolution, it became obvious that the earth revolved around the sun (*heliocentrism*). In marketing a paradigm shift is seen as a major change in market activity and related theory. The move from MARKETING MIX approaches to the use of RELATIONSHIP MARKETING in modern business is often cited as a paradigm shift.

parameter Most broadly, a parameter is either (a) a limit or boundary; (b) a characteristic of a population; or (c) a distribution of scores, described by a statistic such as a mean or a standard deviation. For example, the mean (average) score on the midterm exam in International Marketing is a parameter.

Pareto effect (or law) Where a small proportion has a disproportionate effect on the whole. The term is often used to refer to the so-called 80/20 rule, whereby 20 per cent of customers may take 80 per cent of production and vice versa. The effect is more commonly observed in industrial than in consumer goods marketing, though examples can be found in both sectors.

Parfitt-Collins model A model for predicting the market share of a new product, based on early sales results derived from research panel data. The model views market share as the product of three quantities: the brand's penetration level (i.e. the proportion of buyers of this product class who try this brand); the brand's repeat purchase rate (i.e. the proportion of repurchases going to this brand by consumers who once purchased this brand); and the buying-rate index of repeat purchasers of this brand. This index shows the extent to which the consumer is a relatively heavy buyer or light buyer of the product category. Panel data is used to make a projection over time for each of these quantities, from which the ultimate market share is calculated.

parsimony Generally, frugality or thriftiness. It is used in methodological writing to mean a principle for choosing among explanations, theories, models or equations: the simpler the better, less is more. Of course, applying this standard makes most sense when the explanations one is choosing among are equally good except for their degree of simplicity. *See also* OCKHAM'S RAZOR.

participant observation A form of investigation in which a researcher participates as a member of the group that he or she is studying. Sometimes the researcher informs the group that he or she is observing as well as participating and sometimes the researcher pretends to be an ordinary member. Ethical dilemmas most often arise in the latter case, that is, when one is researching 'under cover'. *See also* ETHNOGRAPHIC RESEARCH.

partnership In common law, a partnership is a type of business entity in which partners share with each other the profits or losses of the business undertaking in which they have all invested. Partners may have a partnership agreement or a declaration of partnership, and in some jurisdictions such agreements may be registered and available for public inspection. There are two types of partners:

- A general partner has an obligation of strict liability to third parties injured by the partnership. General partners may have joint liability or joint and several liability depending upon circumstances. The liability of limited partners is limited to their investment in the partnership.
- A silent partner, also known as a sleeping partner, is one who shares in the profits and losses of the business but is uninvolved in its management and/or whose association with the business is not publicly known.

party selling The selling of goods through agents operating from the homes of customers, each of whom, in succession, holds a party for friends offering goods for sale and earning a commission on sales achieved.

passing off The name given to a legal action brought to protect the 'reputation' of a particular trademark/brand/get-up. In essence, the action is designed to prevent others from trading on the reputation/

goodwill of an existing trademark/brand/get-up.

patent The exclusive right, granted by the government, to make use of an invention or process for a specific period of time, usually 14 years.

Pavlovian learning model One of four basic models of buyer behaviour proposed by Philip KOTLER in his book *Marketing Management* (1972) and derived from the Russian psychologist Ivan Pavlov's learning model, which contains four central concepts: drive, cue, response and reinforcement. Drives may be inherited or learned – hunger is a basic physiological drive, for example; ambition is learned – but they are usually latent or passive until stimulated by a cue. In the case of hunger, this may be internal (being physiologically hungry) or external (the sight or smell of food), but either way a response is called for. When the Pavlov Dog model is applied in marketing, it suggests that consumers are trained to respond to cues such as advertisements on TV for major products. Just like Pavlov's dog creating an emotional connection between a bell and the anticipation of food, people are constantly creating emotional cues as they go through their days linking stimulus to response. And only if the outcome is satisfactory will reinforcement occur and the new learned behaviour become habitual, or, as Pavlov would have termed it, a conditioned response.

payback period The length of time required to recover the cost of an investment. It is calculated as the cost of the project divided by the annual cash flow. All other things being equal, the better investment is the one with the shorter payback period. For example, if a project cost £100,000 and was expected to return £20,000 annually, the payback period would be 100,000/20,000, or five years.

There are two main problems with the payback period method. Firstly, it ignores any benefits that occur after the payback period and, therefore, does not measure profitability. Secondly, it ignores the time value of money. Because of these reasons, other methods of capital budgeting like net present value, internal rate of return or discounted cash flow are generally preferred.

pay per sale (PPS) An online advertising payment model in which payment is based solely on qualifying sales.

pay TV Cable television to a community who pay for the service by subscription.

payload 1 Cargo or freight producing revenue or income, usually expressed in weight. Any kind of merchandise that a carrier transports and that will be sold for profit is considered a payload.
2 Returned merchandise transported by truck to a wholesaler, while en route to another merchandise delivery. Since the truck did not have to make an extra trip to return the unwanted products, its trip was not considered unprofitable.
3 A virus carried by mutant software.

payment method The means of payment employed by a customer, such as cash, cheque, money order or credit card, with order or upon invoicing. It is also called payment type.

payment transfer When payment for something is transferred to another person or entity. This usually entails the electronic transfer of funds via a bank or financial institution.

peak time The period of the day when television and radio audiences are at their highest and the contracting companies can therefore charge the highest price for advertising time. The American term is prime time.

pedagogy The art or science of teaching. The word comes from the ancient Greek *paidagogos*, which was the name used for slaves who took children to and from school. *Paida* refers to children, which is why some like to make the distinction between pedagogy (teaching children) and andragogy (teaching adults). The Latin word for pedagogy, education, is much more common, and the two words are often used interchangeably. The dominant pedagogy within marketing education continues to be the 4Ps, although recent developments in SOCIAL and RELATIONSHIP MARKETING and the evolution of SERVICE DOMINANT LOGIC may see this hegemony challenged.

peer group A group of people of approximately the same age, social status and interests. A peer group will have common values, beliefs and/or behaviour. The peer group may be either formal – colleagues at work, etc. – or informal – friends or members of social groups.

PEEST PEEST is an acronym for Political Economic, Environmental, Scientific and Technological. It is a marketing research framework widely used for assessing the effects of the macro environment on a business. It is also still widely known by its earlier acronym, PEST, which has been modified to be more explicit about the environment, reflecting societal concerns.

penalty A loss or forfeit imposed for failure to complete an exchange on the terms agreed between parties, e.g. if a bill is not paid in the agreed span of time a financial penalty is usually incurred.

penetration The extent to which a product or an advertisement has been accepted by, or has registered with, the total of possible users. It is usually expressed as a percentage.

penetration pricing A pricing method used to introduce a new product to market that involves pricing low and promoting heavily in order to gain a large market share and associated economies of scale as quickly as possible before competition builds. This method assumes that consumers are price sensitive, that product awareness is low and that competition will build quickly.

per capita income The average level of income of each member comprising a population. The per capita income for a group of people may be defined as their total personal income divided by the total population. Per capita income is usually reported in units of currency per year. Per capita income is often used as a measure of

the wealth of the population of a nation, particularly in comparison to other nations.

per diem A daily allowance, usually for travel, entertainment, employee compensation or miscellaneous out-of-pocket expenses while conducting a business transaction. The sum of money is always calculated on a daily basis and may be paid in advance or after the expense is incurred. Employees are sometimes paid on a per diem basis.

perceived risk The element of risk perceived by an intending buyer when faced with a purchase opportunity. It is a subjective state, specific to the individual and may vary over time according to changing circumstances. The lower the perceived risk the more likely the consumer is to act positively and vice versa.

perceived value The benefits that a consumer or end user perceives they will gain from the purchase of particular product or service. The perceived value of a product has direct impact on the price and must be built into any pricing plan.

perception The process of acquiring, interpreting, selecting and organizing sensory information into a meaningful picture of the world. A fundamental aspect of perception is that it represents the receiver's effort to organize received stimuli into meaningful structures and understandings of their environment. In doing so two major groups of factors are involved – stimulus factors and functional factors. By structural factors we mean those factors deriving solely from the nature of the physical stimuli and the natural effects they evoke in the nervous system of the individual. The functional factors of perception, on the other hand, are those which derive primarily from the needs, moods, past experience and memory of the individual. On receiving information the brain organizes the incoming stimuli into patterns following four basic tendencies: similarity, proximity, continuity and context. Perception refers both to the experience of gaining sensory information about the human behaviour, things and events and to the psychological processes by which this is accomplished. *See also* BELIEFS.

perceptual mapping A QUANTATIVE RESEARCH tool used to understand what customers think of current and future products. Consumers' product perceptions and preferences are visually represented as points on a map or graph. Typically the position of a product, product line, brand or company is displayed relative to their competition.

perfect competition A term used by economists to describe an open-market situation, where free trade prevails without restriction, where all goods of a particular nature are homogeneous and where all relevant information is known to both buyers and sellers. Such conditions rarely, if ever, exist in totality, but the hypothesis has been found useful in analysing the forces governing the operation of supply and demand factors in real-life conditions.

performance evaluation An analysis undertaken at a fixed point in time to determine the degree to which stated objectives have been reached. This is generally used as a basis for decision-making, including updating plans.

permanent income hypothesis The theory that people spend in line with the average income they expect to receive in their lifetime. *See also* ABSOLUTE INCOME HYPOTHESIS; RELATIVE INCOME HYPOTHESIS.

permission marketing A form of online direct marketing that involves gaining the recipient's permission to contact them. This type of marketing usually involves sending promotional material via e-mail to an opt-in list of subscribers. The term was popularized by the marketing author and evangelical entrepreneur Seth Godin who has authored such popularist classic marketing books and original thinking as *The Guerrilla Marketing Handbook* (1994), *Permission Marketing* (1999), with Jay Conrad Levinson, *Unleashing the Ideavirus* (2000), *The Big Red Fez* (2002), *Survival is not Enough* (2002), *Purple Cow* (2004), *Free*

Prize Inside (2004), *The Big Moo* (2005), *All Marketers are Liars* (2005), *Small is the new Big* (2006), *The Dip* (2007), and *Meatball Sundae* (2008). Godin has a very interesting personal blog at http://sethgodin.typepad. com/ which is full of thought provoking comment and ideas for marketers.

personal marketing Any marketing initiative that directly impacts upon individuals as opposed to groups of people.

personal selling The process of making oral commercial representations in a buyer–seller interview situation. It is colloquially referred to as face-to-face selling and sometimes known as the buyer–seller interface. *See also* CALL PLANNING.

personality 1 A term which attempts to aggregate that combination of traits, behaviours and experiences which may indicate what a person will do, or how an individual will behave when placed in given or differing situations. **2** A well-known person such as may be used to feature in an advertisement or a campaign.

persuasion A process with the aim of changing a person's attitude or behaviour with respect to some object. In marketing, the development in a person of a desire to purchase a product or service or, more properly, to acquire the perceived benefit.

phenomenology The study of phenomena, the way things appear to us in experience or consciousness. Immanuel Kant (1724–1804) used the term to distinguish between the study of objects and events (phenomena) as they appear in our experience and objects and events as they are in themselves (noumena). Friedrich Hegel (1770–1831) used the term to describe the science in which we come to know *mind* as it is in itself through the study of the ways in which it appears to us.

Phenomenology differs from the various human science approaches such as ethnography, symbolic interactionism and ethnomethodology in that it makes a distinction between appearance and essence. This means that phenomenology always asks the question of what the nature or meaning

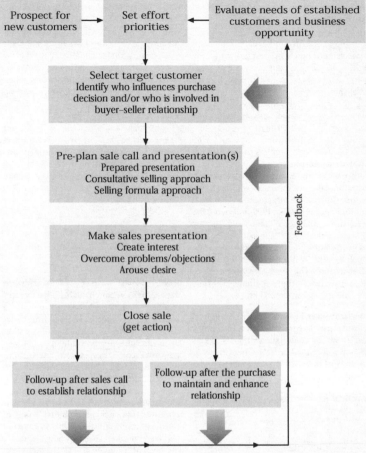

Personal Selling

of something is. Phenomenology demands of us that we relearn to look at the world as we meet it in immediate experience, and it requires of us an awareness and will to seize the meaning of the world as that meaning comes into being. In other words, phenomenology does not produce empirical or theoretical observations or accounts. Instead, it offers accounts of experienced space, time, body and human relations as we live them.

A phenomenological approach is widely adopted in contemporary marketing practice and theory and underpins much of its conceptualization in buying and consumer behaviour and knowledge of the exchange process.

Phillips curve A curve that shows a relationship between inflation and unemployment.

phishing Creating a replica of an existing web page, usually belonging to a major company, with the intention of fooling

Peters, Tom

An American writer and expert on business management practices, best known for co-writing the classic book *In Search of Excellence* with Robert H. Waterman, Jr. First published in 1982, it is one of the best-selling and most widely read business books ever, selling 3 million copies in its first four years and being the most widely held library book in the United States from 1989 to 2006. The book explores the art and science of management used by leading 1980s companies with records of long-term profitability and continuing innovation. It was named by the US organization National Public Radio (NPR) in 1999 as one of the 'top three business books of the century', and ranked as the 'greatest business book of all time' in a poll by Britain's Bloomsbury Publishing (2002).

Peters followed *In Search of Excellence* with a string of international best-sellers including: *A Passion for Excellence, Thriving on Chaos, Liberation Management, The Tom Peters Seminar: Crazy Times Call for Crazy Organizations* and *The Circle of Innovation: You Can't Shrink Your Way to Greatness.* Peters has done much to enliven and shake up management thinking, and his message is delivered with enthusiasm, passion and a genuine anger directed at dull or wrong thinking.

---

someone into passing on sensitive data (such as a password or personal financial information). The term derives from 'fishing' and refers to the way the perpetrators are 'angling' for information.

physical distribution The tasks involved in planning and implementing the physical flows of materials and final goods from points of origin to points of use or consumption to meet consumer needs at a profit.

physical product Also referred to as the tangible product. It is the PRODUCT MANAGER'S job to turn a core product into a physical product. Tangible products may possess up to five identifiable characteristics: a quality level, features, styling, a brand name and packaging.

piggy-back promotion Where a product is accompanied by another product or a voucher for one, e.g. a free sample.

piggy-backing Adding an additional mailing piece to a mailing which is already programmed to take place.

pilot testing Initial small-scale testing of a product concept or draft survey questionnaire. Feedback from the pilot test can be used to refine product concept or questionnaire and gain more appeal or improved responses.

PIMS (Profit Impact of Marketing Strategies) A data bank initiated by General Electric in the 1960s which provides a source of cross-sectional and time-series data. The database contains information on a number of environment-, strategy-, performance-, competition- and firm-related variables. Data from the study are used to craft strategies in STRATEGIC MANAGEMENT and MARKETING STRATEGY. The study identified several strategic variables that typically influence profitability. Some of the most important strategic variables studied were market share, product quality, investment intensity and service quality.

PIMS seeks to address three basic questions: what is the typical profit rate for each type of business? Given current strategies in a company, what are the future operating results likely to be? And what strategies are likely to help improve future operating results? PIMS yields solid evidence in support of both commonsense and counter-intuitive principles for gaining and sustaining competitive advantage. It was developed with the intention of providing empirical evidence of which business strategies lead to success within particular industries.

ping A message sent from one computer to another to see if it is active and accessible. Pinging allows you to notify other sites that your blog has been updated.

pirated products The use of another's TRADEMARK, trade name or COPYRIGHT to gain the benefit of that established name or reputation.

pitch A colloquial term describing an agency presentation before a prospective client. It is also used in the term 'sales pitch' – a presentation by a salesperson to a buyer. *See also* PRESENTATION.

place One of the elements of the four Ps (see MARKETING MIX). It relates to the outlets and channels of distribution in marketing and also to delivery time in the B2B sector.

place marketing Activities designed to encourage people to locate in or visit a particular city, region or physical place, e.g. 'The Cornish Riviera'.

placebo In an experiment, the control treatment in which the control group is treated in a harmless but unhelpful way, without knowing that the treatment is really not meant to elicit a change in the dependent variable. An example of a placebo is a sugar pill which resembles the real medication used in the experiment.

planned economy *See* CENTRALLY DETERMINED ECONOMY.

planned obsolescence The somewhat controversial practice of designing products with a short lifetime, either because they go out of date or they cease to function as they should. Planned obsolescence has great benefits for a producer in that it means a consumer will buy their product repeatedly, as their old one is no longer functional or desirable. It exists in many different products from vehicles to light bulbs, from buildings to software. There is, however, the potential for backlash if consumers become aware of such obsolescence; such consumers can shed their loyalty and buy from a company that caters to their desire for a more durable product.

Planned obsolescence was first developed in the 1920s and 1930s, when mass production had opened every minute aspect of the production process to exacting analysis. Estimates of planned obsolescence can influence a company's decisions about product engineering; there is little business reason to make a product that lasts longer than anyone is expected to use it. Therefore the company can use the least expensive components that satisfy product lifetime projections.

planning A pervasive human activity by which we seek to exercise some degree of control over the future. As a process it will vary enormously depending upon a number of variables, foremost among which will be the complexity of the activity and the degree of uncertainty concerning the future situation in which the activity will take place. Fundamentally, however, all planning seeks to arrive at a present decision concerning future action – the more complex the activity and the more uncertain the future, the greater the need for formal, systematic planning procedures, etc.

planning style Everyone has a particular way, form or technique of planning. These different planning styles have strengths and limitations and are suited to different situations. Individuals and organizations routinely use one planning style regardless of the situation rather than tailoring their approach to suit the problem.

PLC *See* PRODUCT LIFE CYCLE.

PMS (Pantone Matching System) colours Industry standards for various shades of ink colour created by printing specified proportions and densities of primary colour on paper. For example, a particular shade of blue may be 50 per cent cyan and 5 per cent magenta on a white surface. A printer's customer may request a particular shade, using a PMS identifying number taken from a PMS colour chart.

podcast A digital media file, or a series of such files, that is distributed over the Internet using syndication feeds for playback on portable media players and personal computers. Podcasting allows listeners to be in control when they view or listen to TV or radio programmes.

point of presence (POP) POP is a service provider's location for connecting to users. Generally, POPs refer to the location where people can dial into the provider's host computer. Most providers have several POPs to allow low-cost access via a telephone line.

point-of-purchase The place at which a product is purchased by the customer. The point-of-sale can be a retail outlet, a display case, a checkout counter in a shop or a variable location where a transaction occurs.

point-of-purchase (POP) displays Advertising display material located at the retail store, usually placed in an area where payment is made, such as a checkout counter.

point-of-sale The place at which a sale is made, usually a retail sales outlet. The term is also applied to publicity material used there, e.g. posters, show cards, display units, dispensers and leaflets.

political advertising Advertising the central focus of which is on the marketing of ideas, attitudes and concerns about public issues, including political concepts and the policies of political candidates.

political environment This aspect is concerned with political developments such as new and proposed legislation as well as attempts to influence such regulatory developments through lobbying and disseminating information. The political environment is one of the elements of the marketing environment.

political factors An important aspect of the external environment which needs to be taken into account when making a marketing audit or developing a marketing strategy.

political marketing Political marketing is broadly seen to both include political campaigning for elections and referenda and more covert campaigning in support of LOBBYING, pressure group and PUBLIC AFFAIRS work. Political marketing was born

and has developed as an inevitable consequence of the development of the mass electorate, the mass media and global government institutions.

It has been argued that the main factors responsible for the early development of the phenomenon in the US were the presidential system, the tradition of election for all public offices and the rapid expansion of modern mass media. The US also provides good examples of the early usage of typical marketing tools such as the adoption of DATABASES, DIRECT MAIL, political advertising and publicity stunts in political communication.

In the UK, although it has also been suggested that major political parties have been engaged in marketing-related activities for most of the twentieth century, political marketing as a phenomenon became firmly established in the 1980s under the party leaderships of Margaret Thatcher and Neil Kinnock, who aimed to integrate all political communications and control the news agenda. It has been argued that there has been a greater focus on the packaging and presentation of leaders, partly as a result of centre-left politicians' and parties' attempts to gain the centre ground, such as Bill Clinton in 1992 with his 'third way', which was replicated by Tony Blair's UK Labour Party. As in the USA, television is the most significant medium of political communication, and the factor which dominates all other considerations by party strategists is the battle to dominate the television agenda.

In order to obtain clarity and order in the presentation of the various tools used in political marketing and to illustrate analogies with mainstream marketing, the classic division of MARKETING MIX into the 'four Ps' of product, place, price and promotion has been adopted.

Place is represented by the electoral system and the associated network which is at grassroots level and is at the heart of a placement strategy. Local electioneering takes the form of traditional activities such as canvassing and leafleting and 'getting the vote out' on polling day. In the modern marketing era of political campaigns it is more important to identify and contact potential supporters than to persuade them.

Some researchers discount the pricing element of the political marketing mix; others justify the relevance of price and see it as comprising voters' feelings of national, economic and psychological hope or insecurity. Discussing the price aspect of voting behaviour, two aspects emerge: one resulting from negative campaigning, which is designed to build voters' fears, and the other resulting from the voters' 'feel-good factor'.

Promotion plays the crucial role in the political marketing mix. It comprises various elements and techniques such as ADVERTISING, PUBLIC RELATIONS, direct mail and pseudo-events planned to gain publicity and attention. Innovations in computers, television and direct mail have directly affected the way the campaigns are run. Some of the applications of technological advances include database marketing and new methods of fund-raising and polling and enable the candidates to go directly to the voter. Moreover, political marketers are provided with new opportunities because of computer, video and Internet development, e.g. with the possibilities of new types of advertising or direct mailing, and also with new challenges connected with the development of digital television and reaching target voters.

Televised advertising has become important because it reaches the voters, and at the same time the party or candidate fully controls the message. Contrary to popular belief that political ads are solely concerned with image, it has been found that most political advertising is concentrated on issues or contains issue-based information. Although there are contradictory theories on the effects of political advertising, most researchers agree that it acts mostly to reinforce the existing image.

Televised debates are increasingly regarded as the capstone of the election campaign even though there is no evidence that they can dramatically change the outcome of the campaign. Debates, like other pseudo-events, are meant to look spontaneous but in fact are carefully staged and they continue to attract the attention of the media and gain publicity for the political players.

Direct mail is used to pre-test the market, personalize and concentrate the message, raise funds, promote issues and candidates and recruit volunteers. It has been argued that the real potential of direct mail is that it offers the opportunity to personalize one's basic message so as to convince voters that a party which can campaign so efficiently might actually be up to the job of running the country.

Political marketing has been criticized from the ethical standpoint as undermining democracy because of its ability to promote people with media abilities and the right appearance and to manipulate and mislead the voter. There is also a strong debate about ETHICS in conducting political campaigns. Some draw attention to the need to introduce financial regulation, while others point out the impracticality and difficulties in enforcing ethical standards in campaigns.

Political marketing has emerged as a major area of research, which has begun to reflect the growing internationalism and professionalism of political campaigning. The focus was initially on image and use of the marketing mix and its adoption, but has since moved on to segmentation of voters, strategy, buyer/consumer behaviour and exchange processes in political lobbying. The subject had its origins in the US but has more recently become established in Europe, with leading theory and research being developed in the UK.

poll A poll is either an election or a survey of a particular group. The word often refers to the election itself, as the place where voters cast their ballots is called a polling station. However, polls may also be surveys that merely canvass opinions and have no binding force. In this sense, a poll is often assumed to relate to politics, but it may simply refer to any survey of popular opinion.

pop-up advertisements Pop-up advertisements are a form of Internet advertisement that appear in a separate window, either as a full screen or partial screen. These advertisements, similar to some interstitial advertisements, require the user to take some form of action (even if it is to simply close the window). The benefits are that the user can simply continue to browse the web without being interrupted yet still engage with the advertisement if desired at a later time. Balancing this, they do create another window in the user's screen that the user did not request, and that can be considered somewhat annoying.

population A group of persons (or institutions, events or other subjects of study) that one wants to describe or about which one wants to generalize. To generalize about a population, one often studies a sample that is meant to be representative of the population. *See also* GENERALIZABILITY; SAMPLING.

population parameter A characteristic of a population described by a statistic, such as a mean or a correlation.

population validity A type of external validity or representativeness. A population with overly narrow selection criteria may lack validity. For example, results of studies in which the samples are comprised solely of first-year university students might not be validly generalizable to the population of all adults.

portable document files (PDF) A file format developed by Adobe Systems for representing documents in a manner that is independent of the original application software, hardware and operating system used to create those documents. A PDF file can describe documents containing any combination of text, graphics and images in a device- and resolution-independent format.

portal A web page that works as a starting point for a user's session on the Internet. Portals typically include a directory of websites, access to web services and shopping sites and a search functionality powered by a search engine provider. Example of por-

tals are AOL, Netscape, CompuServe and EarthLink.

Porter's generic strategies The three strategies identified by Michael Porter in his work on COMPETITIVE ADVANTAGE, namely cost leadership, differentiation and focus.

portfolio analysis 1 Analysing elements of the MARKETING MIX. **2** Analysing product performance within the product range.

portfolio management The arrangement of investments so as to achieve a balance of risks and rewards acceptable to the investor. The term can be applied to a global product portfolio.

position *See* MARKETING MIX.

positioning The method by which marketers position their product to attract certain consumers. Product positioning is a pivotal concept of modern marketing which attempts to maximize demand for a product.

positive appeal Advertising copy approach that attempts to alleviate a person's anxiety about buying and using a particular product. The positive appeal stresses the attractive aspects of a product and the positive gains for a person who consequently purchases the product.

positivism A philosophy developed by Auguste Comte at the beginning of the nineteenth century that stated that the only authentic knowledge is scientific knowledge, and that such knowledge can only come from positive affirmation of theories through strict scientific method. The approach is influenced by the researcher's ontological and epistemological positions, in other words, their views on reality and the independence of the researcher in relation to knowledge. It is one of the fundamental scientific and marketing research tenets used in understanding consumption and the exchange process.

post-test A procedure for evaluating advertising effectiveness, during or after an advertising campaign. *See also* ADVERTISING EFFECTIVENESS.

postcode The postcode is a combination of between five and seven letters/numbers which defines four different levels of geographic unit. It is part of a coding system created and used by the Royal Mail across the United Kingdom for the sorting of mail. Postcode systems operate in many countries, including Australia and New Zealand, and operate on similar principles but may take the form of numeric combinations. Postcodes are abbreviated forms of addresses which enable a group of delivery points (a delivery point being a property or a post box) to be specifically identified.

There are two types of postcode, these being large- and small-user postcodes. A large-user postcode is one that has been assigned to a single address due to the large volume of mail received at that address. A small-user postcode identifies a group of delivery points. On average there are fifteen delivery points per postcode; however this can vary between one and 100.

Each postcode consists of two parts. The first part is the outward postcode, or outcode. This is separated by a single space from the second part, which is the inward postcode, or incode. The outward postcode enables mail to be sent to the correct local area for delivery. This part of the code contains the area and the district to which the mail is to be delivered. The inward postcode is used to sort the mail at the local area delivery office. It consists of a numeric character followed by two alphabetic characters. The numeric character identifies the sector within the postal district. The alphabetic characters then define one or more properties within the sector. *See also* ZIP CODE.

postcode analysis All direct marketing analysis is focused on postcodes. The wide use of geodemographic modelling and targeting could not exist without postcode geography. To give an idea of the variations in detail that can emerge, the lowest postcode level in the UK represents, on average, approximately fifteen households. In other countries, the lowest level can denote anything up to 1,000 households. Therefore any idea of a pan-European direct marketing campaign has to be very carefully thought out. *See also* ZIP CODE ANALYSIS.

posters The principal medium for outdoor advertising. Posters have high visibility, cover a high percentage of the population, are highly flexible and provide repeat exposure at a relatively low cost. However, they are not suitable for complex advertising, and audience selectivity is limited.

postmodernity Accounts of postmodernity put its start somewhere between the atomic bomb explosions of the 1940s and the oil crisis of the 1970s. As its name suggests, postmodernity is connected to MODERNITY and comes after it. From a postmodern vantage point the modernist road to freedom is seen to have led to concentration camps, ethnic cleansing and mass unemployment. Postmodernity is characterized as more democratic, more fragmented and more mediated, as well as multi-ethnic, post-colonial, post-Fordist, post-industrial and, in terms of knowledge, poststructural. Based less in material production, it adds value through a new economy of intangibles by managing meanings, brands and perceptions in ways that combine NICHE MARKETS with dispersed global production, global sales and flexible global workforces. *See also* BROWN.

pre-test In a pre-test a questionnaire is tested on a statistically small sample of respondents before a full-scale study in order to identify any problems such as unclear wording or the questionnaire taking too long to administer. A pre-test can also refer to an initial measurement before an experimental treatment is administered and subsequent measurements are taken.

predatory pricing The tactic of selling a product at a very low price to drive competitors out of a particular market or to ensure new suppliers do not enter it.

preprint A page or section that is printed in advance of the actual publication date. It is later inserted into a particular issue or section of the paper. Preprints are often referred to as 'FSIs', i.e. free-standing inserts.

presentation A meeting in which proposals are put to an audience in a planned and usually formal manner. Originally used primarily by advertising and market research agencies but has increasingly been adopted as a means of putting forward information and a strategic appeal in most businesses. *See also* PITCH.

press relations The part of PUBLIC RELATIONS and/or marketing communications activity aimed at establishing and maintaining favourable relationships both with and through the press. Not to be confused with PUBLIC RELATIONS.

press release A written statement describing an event or item which is considered to be of sufficient interest to readers for an editor to publish some reference to it. It is sometimes referred to as a news release – a more appropriate term as it includes the use of broadcasting media.

price The amount of money which is asked in consideration for the transfer of legal title to a product or service. By custom and practice 'price' may be used to define the value of other goods or services, as in a barter transaction, and so need not always be expressed in monetary terms. *See also* MARKETING MIX.

price bundling Where a group of products is sold to a customer for less than the total of their individual prices. This is frequently done where a seller feels that a bundle of particular products has more appeal than the products individually. Good examples are cosmetic or personal hygiene products offered as bundles at a discount by producers such as Molton Brown amongst others.

price controls The regulation of prices by government order. In times of scarcity price controls may be used to slow down inflation, but if there is a severe imbalance between supply and demand (e.g. in wartime) rationing may be necessary also. Many or most macroeconomists oppose the use of these controls because, since controls interfere with the price mechanism, encouraging inefficiency, they lead to shortages and a decline in the quality of goods on the market, while requiring large government bureaucracies for their enforcement.

price cutting Reductions in price below the commonly accepted level for a particular product or commodity designed to undercut competitors and secure increases in market share. In the absence of significant cost advantages, the price-cutter may not be able to sustain this tactic for long, particularly as other sellers are likely to reduce their prices too in the short term in order to protect their own market share. *See also* PREDATORY PRICING.

price–demand elasticity The relationship between the selling price of a product and the volume of demand that will be generated as a result. High elasticity is indicative of a product for which demand will be very sensitive to changes in price. This is often to be found in highly competitive markets and is more closely associated with non-essential commodities. Low elasticity will apply to essentials, particularly in a monopolistic situation. Price–demand elasticity should never be taken to imply that reducing prices will inevitably lead to increasing demand or that increasing prices will result in a reduction in demand; the reverse may actually occur in both cases.

price discrimination The practice of charging some customers a lower price than others for an identical good or of charging an individual customer a lower price per unit on a large purchase than on a small one, even though the cost of servicing all customers is the same.

price effect The change in consumption that results from a change in the price of a good or service, other things remaining the same.

price elasticity The effect on demand of changes in price. It is similar to the concept of price sensitivity.

price fixing An agreement between business competitors selling the same product or service regarding its pricing. In general, it is an agreement intended ultimately to push the price of a product as high as possible, leading to windfall profits for all the sellers. Price fixing can also involve any agreement to fix, peg, discount or stabilize prices. The principal feature is any agreement on price, whether expressed or implied. Generally, price fixing is illegal, but it may nevertheless be tolerated or even sanctioned by some governments at various times, especially those whose countries are developing economies.

price index A measure used to illustrate the changes in the average level of prices, where price changes are expressed relative to a base year, usually with a baseline figure of 100.

price leadership A situation when one company, usually the dominant competitor, is able to exert considerable influence over its rivals' pricing decisions.

price point The ideal price of a product, set at a level where demand is relatively high. Finding out which price point to set is important for profit maximization.

price promotions The advertising of a price for a product or service. Usually, the price being promoted is a reduction from a previously established price and may take the form of a lower price, a coupon to be redeemed or a rebate to be received.

price-sensitive The tendency for product demand to vary in direct relation to movements in price. Some products are more price-sensitive than others, for instance petrol.

price structure Detailed prices and discounts, the amount of detail depending on whether the price structure is prepared for trade, the final user or the consumer.

price war The attempt by a market competitor to drive one or more other competitors out of the market by pricing relatively lower.

pricing mix The policy adopted in setting prices of particular products to meet competition.

pricing strategies The deliberate planning of the pricing structure in relation to factors such as consumer wants, product attributes and competition in such a way as to ensure overall profitability. Until recently only two broad strategic approaches to prices have been recognized, namely skimming and penetration. As the name suggests, skimming recognizes that in almost all markets there is a 'hard core' of demand for whom the product in question has a particular importance. Because of the strength of their perceived need such users tend to be relatively insensitive to price, and this insensitivity can be exploited through a policy of setting a very high price and thus 'skimming the cream off the market'. By contrast, a penetration strategy is based on the assumption that if you can produce a similar product to your competitor's and underprice him then you will take away some or all of his market share. As a result of ECONOMIES OF SCALE and EXPERIENCE EFFECTS, the strategist using a penetration policy hopes to reduce his initial cost structure to a point at which he can support the penetration price profitably. More recently, a number of authors have begun to suggest an alternative value-based strategy, which is based on the PERCEIVED VALUE held by the customer.

primary advertising Also known as generic advertising, this is advertising for a general product category, as opposed to advertising for a specific brand in that category.

primary buying motive The motive that induces an individual to buy a general class of article or service, as opposed to that underlying the selection of brands within a class.

primary colours The three hues (red, yellow, blue) that together constitute all the colours in the visible spectrum. In four-colour-process printing, the primary colours are commonly referred to as magenta (red), yellow and cyan (blue), the fourth 'colour' being black.

primary data *See* DATA.

primary demand The total demand for all products in a given category such as washing machines or vacuum cleaners.

primary research Research that collects data specifically to address a particular research issue. Both QUALITATIVE and QUANTITATIVE RESEARCH methods can be used. *See also* DATA.

prime time *See* PEAK TIME.

principal component analysis Principal component analysis attempts to represent the interrelationships within a set of variables; it tries to reduce the number of variables required to represent a set of observations. It is associated with factor analysis, and the two are multivariate techniques.

prisoner's dilemma A popular GAME THEORY model. It is a game between two players that is designed to see how one player reacts to another player's decision. This classic problem of game theory sheds light on many of the problems that have plagued ethical and political philosophers throughout history. It addresses that class of situations in which there is a fundamental conflict between what is a rational choice for an individual member of a group and what is rational for the group as a whole. It helps us to understand how such dilemmas can be resolved for the greater good and is used extensively in decision-making in SOCIAL MARKETING.

private brand A retailer's or wholesaler's own brand.

private sector The private sector of a nation's economy consists of those entities which are not controlled by the state – i.e., a variety of entities such as private firms and companies, corporations, private banks, non-governmental organizations, etc.

privatization The return of nationalized industries into private ownership through the sale of shares in the company or the transfer of the management of a service or activity from the government to the PRIVATE SECTOR. The UK Conservative government privatized a number of nationalized industries during the 1980s, such as British Airways, British Telecom and British Steel. Privatization is sometimes known as denationalization or, especially in India, disinvestment.

probability The likeliness or chance of an event occurring. Probability is the basis of sampling theory; providing sufficient history of an event is known, then the probability that it will occur again is calculable.

probability sampling A method for drawing a sample from a population such that all possible samples have a known and specified probability of being drawn. *See also* CONVENIENCE SAMPLE; JUDGEMENT SAMPLING; RANDOM SAMPLE; REPRESENTATIVE.

procurement The overall process of acquiring a product or service. Depending on the circumstances, it may include some or all of the following: identifying a need; specifying the requirements to fulfil the need; identifying potential suppliers; soliciting bids and proposals; evaluating bids and proposals; awarding contracts or purchase orders; tracking progress and ensuring compliance; taking delivery; inspecting and inventorying the deliverable; and paying the supplier.

product In marketing, a product is anything that can be offered to a market that might satisfy a want or need. However, it is much more than just a physical object. It is the complete bundle of benefits or satisfactions that buyers perceive they will obtain if they purchase the product. It is the sum of all physical, psychological, symbolic and service attributes. *See also* MARKETING MIX.

product attributes The positive features of a product from which the 'benefits' are selected for promotion. These must be chosen to match customer requirements.

product benefits Factors which go towards satisfying the requirements of a customer. Fundamentally the purchasing decision is based upon the perceived product benefits rather than the product itself or its specification or performance.

product champion An individual who has a commitment to, or belief in, a new product, which is strong enough to overcome organizational resistance to a new product idea. Product champions are key in the NEW PRODUCT DEVELOPMENT process.

product concept A product concept is a brief statement that explains the product a manufacturer intends to make and describes the product attribute, benefit and value to a customer. It may include an approximate description of the technology, working principles and form of the product. It should include a concise description of how the product will satisfy customer needs. It has a well-defined form, including both a written and visual description that includes its primary features and customer benefits combined with a broad understanding of the technology needed.

product deletion The process of eliminating a product that does not perform at a level considered adequate, according to certain criteria. There are two categories of product deletion: product replacement, where the product is phased out and replaced with something new, and product elimination, which involves the removal of a product without replacing it with a substitute.

product development The overall process of strategy, organization, concept generation, product and marketing plan creation and evaluation and commercialization of a new or existing product. Such developments range from generating an entirely new concept to meet a newly defined consumer 'want' to the modification of an existing product or indeed its presentation and packaging. The process has to be continuous to arrest the decline intrinsic within the life cycle of any existing product.

product differentiation The distinguishing of products from one another by advertising and the like. Whereas buyers of a homogeneous product regard the output of any particular seller as identical in all respects to that of all other producers of that product, the seller of a 'differentiated'

product enjoys a favoured position over its rivals in that the buyers consider it a superior product and are willing to pay a 'premium' price for it rather than accept the substitutes offered by those rivals.

product elimination In marketing this refers to the elimination of products from the product portfolio once they have reached the decline stage of the cycle. Products can either be gradually phased out, killed instantly or sold off to be managed by another organization if it is no longer considered core business.

product innovation A change, or the introduction of something new, or the first successful application of a new product. Product innovation occurs when an idea is made into a commercial success.

product life cycle (PLC) The course of a product's life in terms of sales and profitability from its development to its decline. A marketing theory in which products or brands follow a sequence of stages including:

1 New product development stage:
   - very expensive;
   - no sales revenue;
   - losses.
2 Market introduction stage:
   - cost high;
   - sales volume low;
   - no/little competition – competitive manufacturers watch for acceptance/ segment growth;
   - losses.
3 Growth stage:
   - costs reduced due to ECONOMIES OF SCALE;
   - sales volume increases significantly;
   - profitability;
   - public awareness;
   - competition begins to increase with a few new players in establishing market;
   - prices to maximize market share.
4 Mature stage:
   - costs are very low as one is well established in market and there is no need for publicity;

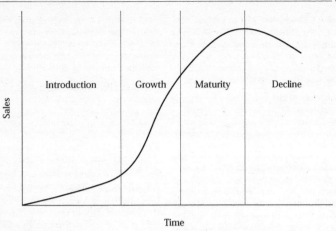

Product Life Cycle

- sales volume peaks;
- increase in competitive offerings;
- prices tend to drop due to the proliferation of competing products;
- brand differentiation, feature diversification, as each player seeks to differentiate from the competition with 'how much product' is offered;
- very profitable.

5 Decline or stability stage:
  - costs become counter-optimal;
  - sales volume declines or stabilizes;
  - prices, profitability diminish;
  - profit becomes more a challenge of production/distribution efficiency than increased sales.

See also LIFE CYCLE.

product line analysis Analysis of the product line to determine the relative strengths of the firm's individual products compared to each other and those of their competitors. Such an analysis is an essential input to PRODUCT PORTFOLIO analysis.

product manager The individual within an organization responsible for the day-to-day management and welfare of a product or family of products at all stages of their product life cycle, including their initial development.

product market A product market comprises all those products and/or services which are regarded as interchangeable or substitutable by the consumer by reason of the products' characteristics, their prices and their intended use.

product mix The range of products which, when viewed as a whole, provides a more than proportionate return than the sum of the individual items if marketed in isolation. Such a return can be achieved by adding complementary products to an existing range and selling them to the same market without significant additional expense. Alternatively, existing products with minor modifications involving little further expense can find a demand in different market segments. A product mix can be such that seasonal demands for one are offset by those of another, thereby maintaining continuity of production and distribution resources. Yet again, the mix can be so structured as to embrace products in each of the stages of the PRODUCT LIFE CYCLE. *See also* SYNERGY.

product orientation An approach to business that centres its activities on being focused on continually enhancing, extending its range and improving and refining its products, making the base assumption that customers simply want the best possible quality for their money.

product placement Securing one's own product as part of the set or scenery in a television, film-making or theatrical production.

product planning Evaluating and determining the products to be produced including the design features, quantities, pricing strategies and MARKET NICHE(S) to be served.

product portfolio Based upon the BOSTON CONSULTING GROUP MATRIX, which categorizes all products into one of four classifications. These are commonly shown in the diagrammatic form of a box with the horizontal axis representing market share and the vertical market growth. Products having high market share in a market with high growth are referred to as stars; those with high market share and low market growth are cash cows; low market share and high market growth are problem children (or wildcats or question marks); finally the products with both low market share and growth are classified as dogs.

product positioning Examining the perception of a product in relation to its competitors in terms of a series of predetermined criteria, e.g. consumer benefits, and then taking such communications actions as are necessary to move it to a stronger or more desirable perception and to change its position in relation to its competitors.

product range The full list of available products made by any one firm.

production contract Broadly speaking, a contract is a written or oral agreement between parties involving an enforceable promise to do or refrain from doing something. In agriculture, production contracts are agreements between farmers and companies or other farmers that specify conditions of production and/or marketing of an agricultural product. Contracts can specify not only quality requirements but also price and quantities. The form of the con-

tract, specific provisions and terms can vary greatly among commodities, and among producers of the same commodity.

The distinguishing characteristic of production contracts is that they specify in detail the production inputs supplied by the contractor (processor, feed mill, other farm operation or business), the quality and quantity of a particular commodity and the type of compensation to the grower (contractee) for services rendered. Since contractors control the amount produced and the production practices that are used, they tend to dominate the terms of the contracts. One advantage of production contracts is that the grower and contractor share risks of both the production and the marketing of the commodity. Another advantage of the production contract arrangement is that financing is available either directly from the contractor or indirectly through other lenders who are more assured of loan repayment.

profile analysis A short description of a person, particular form of media or group in terms of a number of specific parameters which allows the marketer to make an assessment of how they can be best used as part of the marketing process.

profit A company generates a profit when its revenues and gains are greater than its expenses and losses. Profits increase a company's retained earnings and generally an owner's equity value.

profit and loss account A financial breakdown showing what net profit or loss the business has made within an accounting period after deducting all expenditure from the income. A net profit is earned if total expenditure is less than the sales figure and a net loss is made if it is greater than income.

profit centre An accountable unit or centre of activity in an organization through which profits are accrued.

profit earnings ration The number of years' earnings by which a company is valued according to its quoted share prices.

Profit Impact of Marketing Strategies
See PIMS.

profit maximization The standard neo-classical assumption is that a business seeks to maximize profits from producing and selling an output in a market. However, there are other objectives firms might decide to pursue, and this has implications for price, output and economic welfare. A second point is that it is difficult for firms to identify their profit-maximizing output, as they cannot accurately calculate marginal revenue and marginal costs.

Traditional economic theory assumes there is a single goal. Behavioural economists argue differently. Any corporation is an organization with various groups including employees, managers, share-holders and customers. Each of these groups is likely to have different objectives or goals. The dominant group at any moment in time can give greater emphasis to their own objectives – for example the main price and output decisions may be taken at local level by managers, with shareholders taking only a distant view of the company's performance and strategy.

profiteering The act of making a profit by methods considered corrupt and unethical. Business owners may be accused of profiteering when they raise prices during an emergency (especially a war) or during a perceived oil shortage. The term is also applied to businesses that play on political corruption to obtain government contracts.

progressive obsolescence The gradual periodic restyling of goods in order to update established models. *See also* PLANNED OBSOLESCENCE.

projective techniques A QUALITATIVE RESEARCH method that is useful when it is felt that a typical direct questionnaire may not be appropriate in providing the information sought. Projective techniques include word association tests, sentence completion and story completion. *See also* SALES PROMOTION.

promotion under friendly fire This is where the finance director or the board slashes a firm's promotional budget. Coined by A. Smithee.

prompt 1 To provide a number of alternative answers in a questionnaire to enable a respondent to select the one most appropriate to his/her beliefs. 2 A masthead or magazine cover used in readership research to help respondents remember the titles they have read, or the product they have seen advertised.

proof Preliminary printing to facilitate checking and approval prior to final electronic or mechanical printing.

proof of purchase Evidence that a product has actually been purchased, such as the package, label, receipt etc.

propaganda The word propaganda comes from the Latin word meaning to propagate or sow. In its most neutral sense it means to disseminate or promote particular ideas. Propaganda has been defined in many ways, most of which centre on words such as lies, deceit, psychological warfare, brainwashing and more recently spin. Propaganda has been associated with mass communication, mass persuasion, mind control and mass brainwashing. It has a history of being used to promote an ideology and way of life that benefits some to the disadvantage of others. People often see tactics they don't like as propaganda.

The relationship of propaganda to PUBLIC RELATIONS has always been a contentious one. Both of these practices stem from a common desire to affect the attitudes and perceptions held by people, collectively defined as publics, crowds, citizens or consumers, towards a variety of subjects in order to shift opinion and beliefs in a desired direction. Propaganda in particular has been defined in largely negative terms because of its close historic association with religion, warfare and political practices. Public relations has managed to establish itself as a legitimate activity that enhances the images and perceptions of a wide variety of institutions.

propensity to buy An attitude of mind which directs and supports an inclination to buy one product as against another. This can be as a result of having a positive perception of the company which, in turn, may be the outcome of a PUBLIC RELATIONS campaign.

proposal A formal sales proposition which is presented to the customer to make the case of purchase. The typical proposal will attempt to analyse the problems of the customer and seek to show how the seller's product or service can meet the customer's needs effectively and better than the competition.

proposition The selling or advertising platform upon which an advertising campaign will be based.

prospect A potential customer identified as having an effective demand for a good or service.

protectionism Government policies fostering home industries by protecting them from the competition of foreign goods, the importation of these being checked or discouraged by the imposition of duties (tariffs) or otherwise.

protocol A formal document or plan that describes the objective(s), design, methodology, statistical considerations and organization of an experiment or research activity.

prototype The first working model or initially constructed version of a product. To all intents and purposes, the prototype is the product in appearance, characteristics and performance. Its existence facilitates numerous judgements, tests and management decisions regarding future developments.

psychographic analysis 1 A technique that investigates how people live, what interests them, and what they like; it is also called lifestyle analysis or AIO because it relies on a number of statements about a person's activities, interests and opinions. **2** A technique that investigates how people live and what interests them.

psychographic segmentation The breaking-down of markets into smaller groups of people (segments) on the basis of consumer lifestyles, e.g. interests, activities and opinions. It can also apply to personality or consumption patterns.

psychographics A term that describes people's psychological, as distinct from physical, characteristics. Psychographics identify personality characteristics and attitudes that affect a person's lifestyle and purchasing behaviour.

psychological drives Those drives that are not based on the fundamental biological needs of the individual but rather are social in origin. The need for self-actualization, status and belongingness are examples.

psychometrics A group of techniques depending on the theory that particular psychological measurements can be used to divide consumers into groups, each of which has sharply different purchasing behaviour in a number of product fields and also in media usage. Several systems of psychological classification have been advocated. The application of these to respondents by applying attitude scales is usually lengthy enough to restrict their use to panels from which the brand and media information is obtained later. Psychometry is primarily concerned with differences between individuals and employs statistical tools such as normal distribution and factor analysis.

public Any group of people of relevance or importance to an organization with whom it may wish to communicate.

public affairs A term used usually to describe PUBLIC RELATIONS activities in relation to government, pressure groups and sometimes financial affairs at a corporate level, i.e. excluding customers, PROSPECTS and probably employees. Public affairs has now become a much-discussed topic in continental Europe's political and economic circles, including Germany and Austria. The problem is that few people really understand just what the term means.

Many people have the impression that public affairs is another way of describing LOBBYING. Others perceive it as classic public relations. Lobbying still tends to have a negative image, and although almost everyone is attempting to do it, few organizations claim that they are professional lobbyists.

Perhaps the most concrete definition of the term comes from Austrian lobbyist Peter Koeppl. He says:

The key task of public affairs is to represent the interests of enterprises and organizations within the context of international, national or regional governments, local political administrations, the public sector, politicians or public officials. The objective is to build up constructive relationships within specific and selective areas of interests and to look after those interests on behalf of the organization concerned. How the interests of an organization are officially represented is always linked to the decision-making process.

There are significant cultural differences in the day-to-day operation of public affairs in the US and Britain on the one hand and in Germany and Austria on the other, most notably its more overt and transparent nature in the Anglo-Saxon countries, especially the US, as against the more integrated societal approach adopted in the latter two countries. Brussels operates as a centre for both styles to mix and appreciate one another. German public affairs consultants have now realized that a country of 80 million has huge market potential, and many international companies are setting up a base in Berlin and expanding their staff to cope with the demand. Because of its political and economic importance, Germany must be viewed as the most relevant development market for public affairs. Similarly, big companies such as Hill and Knowlton and Shandwick also consider Austria as relevant. Major market players are currently testing the waters in Eastern Europe, well aware of the enormous differences between countries like the Czech Republic, Hungary and the Ukraine.

Washington, DC, must be recognized as the 'headquarters' of public affairs, with Brussels now gaining in importance. Berlin is currently developing into the third metropolis. It is in these three cities that exchange with policy-makers tends to dominate, while New York, Frankfurt and London are more significant because of their economic influence. Many of the big public affairs companies have now set up offices in all these cities.

US companies often say that having no public affairs consultant is like having no company lawyer: the concept is almost unthinkable. In Europe, the benefits of using professional public affairs consultants can be summarized as follows:

- The time it takes to implement political decisions either at European or national level is time that saves money and creates competitive advantage. It can be put to very effective use.
- Recognizing trends prevents meaningless activities. It is essential to take decisions based on the multicultural and multinational environment. To interpret issues purely from a national perspective can be damaging, but it can be avoided.
- Communications management nurtures relationships. Political decisions can alter the market and affect competition, just as those decisions now increasingly depend on public opinion and public sentiment. Companies can now win a clear competitive advantage if they practise good communications and issue management and set up a strong network.
- The ability to take advantage of public funding and partnerships: EU funding is available to help achieve a coherent internal market and to ensure a powerful position in the global market. It is essential to be informed about these resources and to take advantage of them.

Many decision-makers in the business world lack a specific knowledge of policy making; however, until now just a few such executives have taken advantage of the real opportunities opened up by using the services of professional public affairs consulting. Communications companies in Europe are now offering public affairs consulting as part of their services, with increasing success.

Public Affairs Council Launched in 1954 at the urging of President Dwight D. Eisenhower, the Public Affairs Council is the leading association for PUBLIC AFFAIRS professionals. Thousands of member-company employees take advantage of its programmes and services each year. The Council provides unique information, training and other resources to its members to support their effective participation in government, community and PUBLIC RELATIONS activities at all levels. More than 600 member corporations, associations and consulting firms work together to enhance the value and professionalism of the public affairs practice and to provide thoughtful leadership as corporate citizens.

public domain The body of knowledge and innovation, especially creative works such as writing, art, music and inventions, in relation to which no person or other legal entity can establish or maintain proprietary interests.

public opinion The majority view held by members of a given POPULATION, usually the adult population of a country, concerning a particular topic.

public relations The art and science of managing communication between an organization and its key publics – whether employees, customers, shareholders, local communities or trade unions – to build, manage and sustain its positive image. Not to be confused with PRESS RELATIONS. See also CORPORATE COMMUNICATIONS; PUBLIC AFFAIRS; PUBLICITY.

public relations consultant A consultant specializing in the public relations field. Agencies and practices of public relations consultants can vary significantly in size from one-person businesses to large multinational organizations. The public relations consultant will in many cases provide skills to an organization that it does not have amongst its staff or provide specialist knowledge to benefit the organization. Recent growth areas for public relations consultants have been as crisis management and healthcare spokespersons.

Public Relations Consultants Association (PRCA) In the UK the PRCA acts as a forum for government and other public bodies and associations to talk to PUBLIC RELATIONS CONSULTANTS and represents the views of its members to the Department of Trade and Industry and other bodies. It also aims to represent the sector in the media. The trade association was set up in 1969 and members now represent 70 per cent of fee income for UK public relations consultancies.

public relations officer (PRO) An employee of an organization who is charged with responsibility for PUBLIC RELATIONS.

Public Relations Society of America (PRSA) The world's largest professional organization for PUBLIC RELATIONS professionals, headquartered in New York City. PRSA offers members research and job referral services and sponsors relevant seminars and symposia. Members agree to adhere to a code of professional standards. The PRSA offers an accreditation programme that entitles participating members to use the initials APR after their name. The PRSA presents a Silver Anvil award for public relations excellence.

public sector The sector of the economy which comprises the central government, local authorities, nationalized industries and public corporations.

public sector borrowing requirement (PSBR) The budget deficit of the government and public corporations.

public sector debt repayment (PDSR) The budget surplus of the government and public corporations.

public service advertising Non-commercial advertising, sometimes provided by media at reduced rates or free of charge, and concerned with the welfare of the community in general.

publicity The deliberate attempt to manage the public's perception of a subject. The subjects of publicity include people (for example, politicians and performing artists), goods and services, organizations of all kinds and works of art or entertainment. From a marketing perspective, publicity is one component of promotion. The other elements of the promotional mix are ADVERTISING, SALES PROMOTION and PERSONAL SELLING.

Publicity is also a tool of PUBLIC RELATIONS. Whereas public relations is the management of all communication between the client and selected target audiences, publicity is the management of product- or brand-related communications between the firm and the general public. It is primarily an informative activity (as opposed to a persuasive one), but its ultimate goal is to promote the client's products, services or brands. A publicity plan is a planned programme aimed at obtaining favourable media coverage for an organization's products – or for the organization itself, to enhance its reputation and relationships with stakeholders.

puffery An exaggerated advertising claim that would be generally recognized as such by potential customers. Good examples are the world's softest mattress or quietest vacuum cleaner.

pull-out section A section of consecutive pages printed inside the newspaper that, when removed, becomes a stand-alone section.

pupilometrics A method of advertising research in which a study is conducted on the relationship between a viewer's pupil dilation and the interest factor of visual stimuli. The more dilated the pupil (or black centre of the eye) the more pleased is the receiver of the stimulus, so the theory suggests.

purchase decision The final stage in the buying process which has culminated in the decision to buy a particular product/service from a particular supplier.

purchaser In general, a purchaser buys goods and services for use by their company or organization. Purchasers determine which commodities or services are best, choose the suppliers of the product or service, negotiate the lowest price and award contracts that ensure that the correct amount of the product or service is received by the company at the appropriate time. Purchasing managers and agents evaluate suppliers on the basis of price, quality, service support, availability, reliability and selection. To assist them in their search for the right suppliers, they review catalogues, industry and company publications, directories and trade journals.

purchasing (procurement) The professional activity of buying goods and services on behalf of organizations.

purchasing department A departmentally-based grouping of individuals within an organization who are involved in the procurement of the company's purchased components or services. Often alternatively referred to as the buying or procurement department.

purchasing patterns Individual, or collective, purchasing behaviour within a market.

purchasing power The extent to which an organization, group of people or a geographical area with funds available, whether committed or otherwise, has the ability to make purchases during specified time periods.

purchasing process Webster and Wind (*Organizational Buying Behaviour*, 1972) provided a general model of organizational buying behaviour. They explicitly characterized organizational buying as a purchasing process involving several people, in contrast to the earlier conception of buying as the purchasing act, carried out by a purchasing executive.

The influences on the buying process were categorized by Webster and Wind as environmental factors, organizational factors, social factors and individual factors. The buying process, and ultimately the buying decision, will vary depending on the business environment and the organization within which it takes place and will vary with the social group involved in the process and the characteristics of the individuals within that group. At the environmental level factors such as the level of competition and general economic conditions will affect a purchase decision. For example, an economic recession may cause buying organizations to be more cost-conscious and to emphasize price as a decision-making criterion more than they would if the economy were booming. At the organizational level factors such as business strategy, purchasing policy and corporate ownership can make a difference to purchasing decisions. For example, a company that has a marketing strategy designed to achieve differentiation through highly innovative product design will want to do business with suppliers who can contribute towards this objective – purchase price will be a secondary criterion. Corporate ownership can affect buying decisions in a number of ways. Large Japanese manufacturing firms (such as Toyota) have well-established policies of building long-term relationships with suppliers and offering them practical support to develop new products and quality systems. Comparable American firms have traditionally been less supportive, and less loyal, towards their suppliers.

Going beyond the environmental and organizational levels, the Webster and Wind model suggests that group dynamics within the purchasing team and the individual characteristics of those involved in the decision-making process will influence the outcome of the buying decision. This means that it is not enough, in formulating business-to-business (B2B) marketing strategy, to look at the relatively tangible factors associated with the buying organization and the purchasing environment – one must also consider the less tangible factors associated with the people making the decision.

At the group level, commonly five roles are identified within the 'buying centre'.

- The USER, who will put the purchased item to work. For example, the estates or facilities manager would adopt the role of user if a new barrier system for the car park were being procured.

- The INFLUENCER, who is considered to have relevant expertise and therefore to have a valuable opinion on the purchase.

- The DECIDER, who has the ultimate decision-making authority. If it is an important and costly purchase, then this will probably be a senior manager. For minor items decision-making authority may be delegated to junior management.

- The BUYER, who is the individual responsible for organizing the buying process and ultimately dealing with the contractual detail once a decision has been made. Large organizations usually have a purchasing department staffed by professional buyers.

- The GATEKEEPER: this is anyone who controls the flow of information to the buying centre. Often it will be the purchasing department representative, who has an overall responsibility for managing the purchasing process and who decides what is relevant information to be circulated to members of the buying centre.

A sixth buying centre role of 'initiator' has also been suggested – someone who is responsible for identifying the need for a purchase in the first place. In many cases the initiator would be the same as the user.

The buying centre, also often referred to as the 'decision-making unit' or simply 'DMU', may have five or more roles within it, but this does not mean that there are always five or more people in it. Clearly one person can fulfil more than one role. For example, often the purchasing department representative will fulfil the roles of buyer and gatekeeper. Equally, there may be more than one person fulfilling a single role. Suppose that a public utility company, such as a gas or electricity business, is purchasing a computerized billing system, which it will use to monitor customer usage, to generate periodic bills to be sent to customers and to check that customer payments are correctly received. The accounts department, the 'user department', responsible for customer billing, may well want to involve more than one representative in the purchasing process. For example, one representative might focus on ensuring accuracy in the billing process, while another might focus on the customer relations aspects of billing, making the bills easy to understand, dealing with visually impaired customers and so on.

In considering the group and individual buying influences, it is useful to remember the distinction made by Webster and Wind between 'task-related' and 'non-task-related' factors in the buying decision. Task-related factors are decision criteria that are directly related to the explicit purpose behind the purchase. Examples that are frequently cited include purchase price, product quality and reliability, after-sales service and speed of delivery. Non-task-related factors are decision criteria that are not directly related to the explicit purpose behind the purchase. Members of the buying centre might be motivated to make a 'safe' decision rather than objectively the 'best' decision; for example, choosing a better-known supplier

over one less well known simply because the decision will be easy to justify. It should also be remembered that the members of the buying centre are human beings, as well as managers. Therefore they may carry their own personal prejudices, for example, against suppliers from a particular country, educational level, gender, social class or religion, and preferences into the organizational buying process. Although the processes in the purchasing arena are rational, frequently the final decision may come down to personal relationships and prejudices. *See also* ORGANIZATIONAL BUYING BEHAVIOUR.

pyramid selling The sale of or the right to sell products or services to distributors who in turn recruit other distributors and frequently ending with no final buyer, pyramid selling is a form of multilevel marketing and often uses a system of franchises. It has similarities with network selling but in many cases no end products are sold. The initiators of such a scheme take profit from the initial fees paid to them by distributors in advance of promised sales income. It has been reported that on average 95 per cent of investors never get their money back. Pyramid schemes and selling are banned throughout Europe, USA, Australia, New Zealand and many other developed markets. *See also* MULTILEVEL MARKETING; NETWORK MARKETING.

qualifying The process of checking whether or not a particular PROSPECT is genuine in terms of wanting the product in the foreseeable future and has some means of paying for it.

qualitative research Research that deals with data frequently difficult to quantify. Results are often expressed as value judgements by individuals from which any collective general conclusions are difficult to draw. Such research usually involves group discussions or interviews. *See also* QUANTITATIVE RESEARCH.

quality control Those actions necessary to assess, control, evaluate and verify the features and characteristics of a material, process, product, service or activity to meet specified requirements. The aim of quality control is to provide quality that is satisfactory, adequate, dependable and economic.

quality of life The level of enjoyment and fulfilment gained by people from their daily lives within their own local economic, cultural, social and environmental conditions. The well-being or quality of life of a population is often cited as an important concern in economics and political science and indicator of standards of civilization by others. There are many components to well-being. A large part is the standard of living, the amount of money and access to goods and services that a person has; these factors are fairly easily measured. Others, like civil liberties, freedom from crime, happiness, art, environmental health, innovation and personal security are far harder to measure and could be more important. This has created an inevitable imbalance as programmes and policies are created to fit the easily obtainable and measurable economic targets while ignoring the other more environmental and social targets, which are very difficult to plan for or assess.

quantitative research Numeric research that deals with facts, figures and measurements and produces data which can be readily analysed. Measurable data is gathered from a wide range of sources, and it is the analysis and interpretation of the relationships in this data that gives the information researchers are looking for. These data are collected using numbers, perhaps through answers to questionnaires. The numbers are then examined using statistical tests to see if the results have happened by chance. *See also* QUALITATIVE RESEARCH.

quantity discount A price reduction given on the basis of the quantity bought: the greater the quantity bought, the cheaper the unit price to the buyer. It is frequently the basis on which a manufacture/distributor bases his 'scaled' price list. Also the logic that lies behind the economy pack sold to consumers: the bigger sizes being pro-rata cheaper than the smaller.

quanxi The Chinese word 'quanxi' (pronounced *quanshe*) is a pervasive network of personal relationships based on trust and mutual benefit, which is not officially acknowledged but runs deep. Having quanxi working for the company is essential. This does not necessarily come at a high price. A friendly, sincere relationship established over a period of time and based on mutual respect is an integral part of Chinese culture. The foreign business person is well advised to establish such relationships.

quasi-experiment A form of research design for conducting studies in field or real-life situations where the researcher may be able to manipulate some independent variables but cannot randomly assign subjects to control and experiment groups. For example, one cannot cut off some people's unemployment benefits to see how well they could get along without them or to see whether an alternative job-training programme would be more effective, but one could try to find volunteers for the new programme. One could compare the results for the volunteer group with those of the people in the regular programme. The study is quasi-experimental because one was unable to assign subjects randomly to treatment and control groups.

question-and-answer format 1 A meeting or interview format where information is given in the form of replies to questions. **2** A technique for writing copy where the advertiser or a spokesperson for the advertiser replies to questions posed by the customer or prospective customer.

question mark *See* BOSTON CONSULTING GROUP MATRIX.

questionnaire A questionnaire (also known as self-administered survey) is a type of statistical survey handed out in paper form usually to a specific demographic to gather information in order to provider better service or goods. Question-naires have advantages over some other types of surveys in that they are cheap, do not require as much effort from the questioner as verbal or telephone surveys and often have standardized answers that make it simple to compile data. However, such standardized answers may frustrate users. Questionnaires are also sharply limited by the fact that respondents must be able to read the questions and respond to them. Thus, for some demographic groups conducting a survey by questionnaire may not be practical.

quota 1 A predetermined goal in a sales programme expressed as a total financial figure, as a percentage of increase over sales from a previous time or as quantities of products sold. **2** A predetermined target to be achieved in a media plan established in terms of money to be spent, gross rating points to be achieved or the number of ads, insertions and spots to be bought. **3** The quantity of goods of a specific kind that a country permits to be imported without restriction or imposition of additional duties.

quota sampling A technique where the population is first segmented into exclusive subsets (as in stratified sampling) and then a certain number (quota) of subjects selected for each category. Although it has resemblance to stratified random sampling, quota sampling is less reliable for drawing inferences about a population. Quota sampling when used in electoral polling results often has generated poor forecasts of election results.

R

radio A broadcast communications medium which depends for its value on the spoken word. Radio advertising has the advantages of: local and regional flexibility; cheap production; short LEAD TIMES; and the ability to reach people on the move. However, it has limited creative opportunity, being focused on sound, although via digital radio programming there are technology crossover possibilities that downloaded programming can include visual material hence this limitation may erode.

random error The result of a measurement minus the mean that would result from an infinite number of measurements of the same measure and carried out under repeatability conditions. The distribution of random errors follows a Gaussian-shape 'bell' curve. The precision is described by statistical methods such as a standard deviation or confidence limit and used extensively in market research.

random sample A sample in which each member of a population has the same chance to be selected, for the sample and sample points are independent of each other in that the selection of a point does not depend on the previously chosen points. Sampling bias occurs when some members of the population are more likely to be selected than others. *See also* CONVENI-ENCE SAMPLE; JUDGEMENT SAMPLING; PROBABILITY SAMPLING; REPRESENTATIVE.

Rasch modelling An item response model with one parameter set for item difficulty is known as a Rasch model. Georg Rasch (1901–1980), a Danish statistician, invented the model in the 1960s. Rasch models are one of the dominant models for binary items (e.g. success/failure on test items) in psychometrics which are widely used in marketing to assess consumer responses.

rate card A listing of a publication's prices for running ads of various sizes and at various frequencies. It generally also includes some mechanical specifications such as ad sizes, preferred source materials and closing dates.

ratio analysis An approach to the analysis of financial information which allows management to monitor changes in the performance of their company from one period to the next or to compare it with other companies. Typical ratios which are calculated and compared include profit/capital employed or current assets/current liabilities. More detailed evaluation of ratios such as production costs/sales turnover, administration cost/sales turnover and selling costs/sales turnover can be used to indicate the relative efficiency of the company in each functional area and changes in that efficiency over time.

rationalization In reference to products, the elimination of items in the range which bring in the minimum return and call for a disproportionate effort to sustain demand. Rationalization leads to a concentration of resources into those products from which a maximum return can be expected.

raw materials The term 'raw materials' is often used to describe the physical goods used in manufacturing, without distinguishing between natural raw materials and semi-manufactured or fabricated materials. For example, the raw materials used in the packaging industry – paper, plastics, fibreboard, etc. – are the finished goods of other manufacturers in the chemical industry. Natural raw materials include both those such as coal, iron ore and oil which occur in a natural state and are non-renewable and those which occur in a natural state but have been 'adopted' and cultivated by man, which are renewable and the supply of which can be increased or decreased through man's efforts – wheat, rubber, wool, etc.

RBV (resource-based view)   The resource-based view (RBV) argues that organizations hold resources, part of which allow them to achieve competitive advantage, and a proportion of these resources can be used long term to maintain superior advantage. Resources that are difficult to obtain or are rare and in short supply can create a distinct competitive advantage. That advantage can be sustained over longer time periods to the extent that the organization is able to protect against resource imitation, transfer, or substitution.

reach   The application of statistics to advertising and media analysis, reach is defined as the size of the audience who listen to, read, view or otherwise access a particular work in a given time period. Reach may be stated either as an absolute number or as a fraction of a population.

reach and frequency   Refers to a metric used extensively in the advertising industry that shows how many people saw your ads and how many times they saw them over a certain period of time. *See also* ADVERTISING IMPACT.

readership   A general term referring to the number of people who read a particular publication. This includes both the individual that purchased the publication and the persons other than the purchaser who have read the publication.

realism   **1** A philosophical doctrine holding that abstract concepts really exist and are not, as nominalism would have it, just names. **2** A philosophical doctrine holding that the external world can be fairly directly known by sensory experience.

Realism is an approach often used in marketing to understand the complexity of changing markets.

rebate   A sum of money returned to a customer following payment for goods or services. A reduction from the original sales price.

recall   **1** Spontaneous: where an informant's memory is allowed to suggest information without guidance or assistance. **2** Prompted or assisted memory: where an informant is shown possible alternatives, or part of the actual subject matter, as a memory stimulus.

recession   Usually taken to mean two consecutive quarters of a year where an economy or market shrinks. A recession normally refers to a serious economic downturn; a longer period of economic downturn is referred to as a depression. In a recession the first aspects of the market economy to contract are normally non-essential household goods, new vehicle and house sales.

reciprocity   Refers to an arrangement in the marketplace between two suppliers or buyers of products. Often used as a term in RELATIONSHIP MARKETING to refer to the linkages in long-term relationships in sharing costs, markets and resources to sustain each partner's or organization's businesses.

red goods   Consumer goods, such as food products, that are consumed and replaced at a fast rate and have a low profit margin.

redemption   The process of trading in or redeeming coupons, vouchers, special offers and the like in exchange for a stated product or benefit.

reductionism   The term refers to the basic theory that complex things or ideas can always be reduced to something more simple and straightforward. It also follows that theory building should be based upon hard scientific knowledge rather than supposition. In marketing, reductionism is an approach which is often used to focus debate and resources to the realities of the market and what the customer wants.

reference groups A group of consumers or an organization which an individual respects, identifies with, or aspires to join, for instance, the Lords Cricket Club, Reform Club or Harley Davis Bike drivers group. Particular reference groups are often seen as major consumers of certain products and may be targeted by certain organizations marketing their products.

referral The use of a person's or company's name as an endorsement of a product or service. Of all the message sources that may persuade a PROSPECT to become a customer, probably the most powerful is 'third party endorsement'.

refusal rate The percentage of contacted people who decline to cooperate with the research study or break off an interview.

regionalization In national politics, regionalization is a process of dividing a political entity – typically a country – into smaller regions and transferring power from the central government to the regions. The opposite process is called unitarization. The growing need of regions to promote themselves in the world has led to an increase in place marketing and associated cultural competition, for example, activity focusing on gaining events such as European City of Culture for cities such as Cork, Liverpool, etc.

regression analysis A mathematical technique for explaining or predicting the variability of a dependent variable using information about one or more independent variables. Regression analysis attempts to answer the question 'What values in the dependent variable can we expect given certain values of the independent variable(s)?' The regression equation indicates the nature and closeness of the relationship between two or more variables, specifically, the extent to which one can predict some by knowing others (that is, the extent to which some are associated with others). The equation is often represented by a regression line, which is the straight line that comes closest to approximating a distribution of points in a scatter plot. *See also* BIVARIATE ANALYSIS.

Reilly's law A model used in trade-area analysis to define the relative ability of two cities to attract customers from the area between them.

relational database A database system in which different types of data are linked for analysis.

relationship marketing Starting from the mid-1980s the concept of relationship marketing originally applied by Berry (1983) to services marketing and Jackson (1985) to industrial marketing emerged in the marketing literature. The traditional view of marketing as a specialist function was increasingly questioned as a proper basis for strategic and operational marketing planning. As an example, Gummesson (1987) argues for what he calls 'new marketing', an approach emphasizing business relationships and interaction out of new theories of services marketing, industrial marketing and also out of practical experience and observation. The old marketing concept based on the marketing mix is perceived as too transactional, functionalist and prescriptive as business moves from a structured manufacturing paradigm to a more service-orientated and holistic approach. Gummesson argues that the four Ps (product, promotion, price and place) and their extensions will always be needed, but the paradigm shift develops their role from that of being founding parameters of marketing to one of being contributing parameters to relationships, networks and interaction.

The observable weakness of existing business theories in predicting or discovering vital aspects of changing business reality can be pointed to as the major reason for a shift in approach to the study of business disciplines. The significance of the interaction approach (Häkansson, 1982) and network theories in providing a new way to understand business disciplines can also be seen to apply to political lobbying which can also be viewed in terms of the new theoretical and empirical assumptions approach.

Borg (1991) argues that the interactional approach to market relationships is one of several shifts in approach to markets which accommodate an understanding of business relationships, especially in industrial markets. The search for alternative business theory which interaction and network-related theories represent can be regarded as a series of problem shifts rather than a change in fundamental aspects of market-related theory building. The growing use of network theories in 'business to business marketing' provides a relevant example of problem shifts in business research without at the same time abandoning a pluralist view of science. The observable weaknesses of existing business theories in predicting or discovering vital aspects of changing business reality can be identified as the major reason for a shift in approach to the study of business disciplines.

It is for these reasons that relationship marketing is suggested as the area where lobbying and political marketing belong, within the management discipline.

Core Features of Relationship and Business to Business Marketing

The interaction, network and relationship marketing research shows that similar features of relationships recur and are typically characterized by four core features: mutuality, long-term character, process nature, and context dependence.

1. Mutuality

According to Holmlund and Törnroos (1997), a number of factors may be at work within the feature of mutuality:

- Degree of mutuality – here, relationships continue because of different types of bonds between business actors – these include technical, economic, planning, social, knowledge and legal bonds. Mutuality between the partners may be expressed with concepts such as trust and commitment, as well as conflicts and conflict resolution.

- Symmetry – a relationship may be balanced in terms of the ability of each counterpart to be able to influence the relationship, or else one of the partners may dominate the relationship.

- Power-dependence structures – large and small firms may have distinct power positions which change over time. However, no partner is assumed to have absolute control over their relationships, although their roles may differ.

- Resource dependence – firms develop some resources internally but most are gained through relationships with others in a business network. The resources might constitute financial, human or technological assets. Complementary skills and heterogeneous resources may be a major strength of business networks.

2. Long-term character

Two features emerge as features of a long-term character of a relationship (Hakansson and Snehota, 1995):

- Continuation – here, relationships evolve over time and therefore temporality is a vital component of a relationship. Relationships can be long-lasting although it can take some time before a sequence of interactions can be labelled an effective relationship. Both the past and future expectations related to business relationships influence the present state, and in this sense, time is a relational factor. Continuity can also be a competitive tool, where creating long-term relationships becomes an asset.

- Strength can increase over time as partners learn to work with each other and create bonds, make necessary investments and enhance the relationship through commitment between interacting actors.

3. Process nature

A further core feature of a relationship in business networks is its process nature, which can have a number of dimensions and include:

- Exchange and interaction – where

relationships are composed of different interactions, consisting of a multitude of exchanges and adaptations between organizations. The content of this exchange can be products, personnel, money, social contacts or information.

- Dynamics – relationships are also characterized by change because of their dynamic nature. Processes and events within a relationship as well as in the surrounding network produce change and dynamics in relationships.
- Potential – relationships are valuable to firms because they provide access to resources and may enable further opportunities. On the other hand, relationships may function as burdens for firms as they can also limit future options and entail large unexpected costs.

4. Context dependence

A fourth core feature of a relationship is that it is context dependent, with embeddedness (Granovetter, 1985) within the network a core factor:

- The concept of embeddedness relates to the fact that economic action and outcomes, like all social action and outcomes, are affected by the actors' dyadic relations and by the overall structure of network relations (Strandvik and Törnroos, 1995). Relationships are embedded in a network and connected to other relationships in that particular network. Relationships are therefore highly context-bound, with their features dependent on their particular setting.

Although these four core features of relationships in business networks may go some way towards generating an understanding of a relationship, the notion of a business relationship still remains difficult to grasp (Halinen, 1997). There are many potential facets and elements to a relationship and the concept has rarely been defined explicitly in the marketing. When considering what makes dealings with two companies in a market become a relationship, or what makes a relationship cease to

exist, researchers have approached the problem in at least two different ways, using to a greater or lesser extent the four core characteristics outlined above. They have either tried to classify and characterize different relationships or have sought to identify the necessary conditions for a relationship to exist (Halinen, 1997).

Finally 'network marketing' extends beyond a narrow definition of relationship marketing to encompass a much wider range of potential business relationships. This is akin to Morgan and Hunt's proposition that in order to compete successfully in global markets the firm must be a member of an effective network of partnerships, including supplier partnerships, buyer partnerships, internal partnerships, and lateral partnerships (Morgan and Hunt, 1994) developing a theory of relationship marketing using commitment and trust as the core concepts. They argued that to be an effective competitor in a global market requires the firm to be a trusted collaborator, which has given rise to the axiom 'collaborate to compete'. Global competition is conducted between networks of competing firms, and in order to succeed it is as important to build strong relationships within the network as it is to outperform the rival network. Relationship commitment exists where an exchange partner believes that an ongoing relationship with another firm is so important that maximum effort will be exerted to maintain it. Relationship trust is defined as having confidence in an exchange partner's reliability and integrity.

Commitment is the glue that binds the relationship together. Trust is the key factor that enables commitment to develop. Where we trust an exchange partner we expect them to behave in a manner that promotes our interests. When we believe this to be the case, we can take the risk of making a tangible commitment to the relationship. *See also* INTERNAL MARKETING AND SERVICE – DOMINANT LOGIC.

References and Sources

Berry, L.L. (1983), 'Relationship Marketing' in L. Berry, L. Shostack and G. Upah (eds),

Emerging Perspectives on Services Marketing (pp.25–8). Chicago: American Marketing Association.

Borg, E. A. (1991), 'Problem Shifts and Market Research: The Role of Networks in Business Relationships'. *Scandinavian Journal of Management* 7. 4, pp. 285–95.

Granovetter, M. (1985), 'Economic Action and Social Structure: The Problem of Embeddedness'.*American Journal of Sociology* 91, pp. 481–510.

Gummesson, E. (1987), 'The New Marketing – Developing Long Term Interactive Relationships'. *Long Range Planning* 4, pp. 10–20.

Häkansson H and the IMP Group. (1982), *International Marketing and Purchasing of Industrial Goods*. Chichester: Wiley.

Häkansson H. and Snehota I. (1995), *Developing Relationships in Business Networks*, London: Thompson.

Halinen, A. (1997), *New Relationship Marketing in Professional Services*, London, Routledge

Holmlund, M. & Törnroos, J. (1997), 'What are relationships in business networks'. *Management Decision* 35, pp. 304–9.

Jackson, B. B. (1985). 'Build Customer Relationships that Last'. *Harvard Business Review*, 63. November–December, pp. 120–8.

Morgan, R M and Hunt, S D (1994), 'The Commitment-Trust Theory of relationship Marketing', *Journal of Marketing*, 58 (July), pp. 20–38.

relative income hypothesis This hypothesis states that an individual's attitude to consumption and saving is guided more by his or her income in relation to others than by an abstract standard of living. In other words, 'keeping up with the Joneses' may be a more powerful incentive than the pursuit of wealth for its own sake. *See also* ABSOLUTE INCOME HYPOTHESIS; PERMANENT INCOME HYPOTHESIS.

relativism A philosophy that espouses the view that there are no universal truths and that there is no objective knowledge. It is suggested that human beings evaluate their behaviour and beliefs only in terms of their cultural and historic context. In marketing,

relativism is often used in strategy development and individual judgements and is grounded in experience and the marketer's own cultural perceptions.

relaunch Repeating the LAUNCH of a product usually with some new feature – often a product which has failed or which is in need of being revitalized.

repeat visitor A unique visitor who has accessed a website more than once over a specific time period.

repertory grid technique A market research technique in which a test is first run to discover what the respondents' main criteria are in judging product brands, followed by another test in which the respondents evaluate brands on the basis of these established criteria.

repetition One feature of a media schedule. It is intuitively obvious that the probability of an acceptable proportion of the target audience seeing an advertisement depends on the number of repetitions over a period of time. Media planners furthermore assume that individuals need to see it more than once before taking it in fully. The challenge is to work out a pattern of repetition that will maximize opportunities-to-see without either costing too much or running the risk that some of the audience will react negatively to perceived over-exposure.

replication Research that tries to reproduce the findings of other investigators so as to increase confidence in (or refute) those findings. Repeating studies with different subjects or in different settings is especially important for experimental laboratory research because it helps increase external validity. Despite the undeniable importance of replication, it is not done as often as it might be, largely because it is not considered high-status work. On the other hand, almost all studies that build on past research are replication studies to some extent. Thus replication is more a matter of degree than of kind.

repositioning The modification of consumer perception of a product or service relative to competitive products or services. Repositioning is necessary when the preferences of the market shift. For example, a premium brand of shampoo sold at a relatively high price with advertising that emphasizes its superior performance may need to be repositioned as consumers become more price-sensitive. One way would be to position it as the best-value brand with price cuts and advertising that emphasizes that a little bit goes a long way. The costs associated with repositioning a brand, in terms of product, price or promotion modifications, must be weighed against the added revenue potential.

representative Said of a sample that is similar to the population from which it was drawn. When a sample is representative, it can be used to make inferences about the population. The most effective way to obtain a representative sample is to use random methods to draw it. *See also* PROBABILITY SAMPLING; REPRESENTATIVENESS.

representativeness The extent to which a study's results can be generalized to other situations or settings. Another term for external validity. *See also* REPRESENTATIVE.

resale price maintenance The practice of a supplier who sells to an intermediary conditional upon the setting of a resale price, at the wholesale and/or retail level. This is now legal only for the pharmaceutical trade.

research and development (R&D) The functions within a business geared up to researching and developing new and existing products for the organization's customers. This process can involve invention, design, production and packing developments, process engineering, training of scientific and technical staff and the creation of improved products in support of the business. Quality marketing and profitability are all linked to sustaining good R & D.

research design The systematic planning of research, usually including: the formulation of a strategy to resolve a particular question; the collection and recording of the evidence; the processing and analysis of these data and their interpretation; and the publication of results.

research ethics The principles of good and bad conduct that (should) govern the activities of researchers.

research proposal The submission prepared by a research agency for a potential client specifying the research to be undertaken, its methodology, sample design, project time-scale and costs. On the basis of the research proposal, the client will select an agency to undertake the research. The proposal then becomes the contract between the agency and the client company.

research question The broad question that the experiment is supposed to answer, which acts as the guiding force behind the experiment. The research question poses the problem of the relationship between the objective(s) and the purpose, between the specific experimental procedure and the reason why that procedure is being carried out in the first place.

reserve price A minimum but usually undisclosed price which is the least a seller is willing to accept for the object on offer, e.g. an item in an auction, property, etc.

respondent An individual who takes part in a market survey or piece of research.

respondent error A type of non-sampling error caused by respondents intentionally or unintentionally providing incorrect answers to research questions.

response bias The bias that can appear in survey data garnered from respondents who have been given loaded questions or an ill conceived questionnaire or sampling procedure.

response mechanism A part of any advertisement or promotional item which sets out deliberately to generate some action, e.g. an inquiry or sales order.

response rate The proportion of those people originally drawn at random from the population who actually end up taking part in a survey. This will help indicate whether the data being collected accurately reflects the views of the population being interviewed. If the response rate is low it is important to examine the profile of the sample and assess whether weighting or other methods would help to improve the quality of the data.

results The focus of an academic or scientific paper in which the researcher reports the outcomes of an experiment. Results should not contain any explanations of the experimental findings or in any other way interpret or draw conclusions about the data. The results section typically consists of both visual representations of data (tables and graphs and other figures) and written descriptions of the data.

retail audit An assessment of an organization's total retailing capability. The prime reasons for a retail audit are to ensure that targeted customers' needs are being met by the retail marketing strategy of an organization. Given changing consumer demand patterns and the rapid evolution of Internet-based shopping, it is critical that retail groups regularly review their retailing provision.

retail buying The acquisition by retailers of a suitable range of product stock from suppliers for sale within their outlets.

retail distribution channels The end of the manufacturer–wholesaler–retailer DIS-TRIBUTION CHANNEL. These channels serve consumers directly and include both store and non-store selling media such as MAIL ORDER CATALOGUES. These channels are viewed as being critical to the success of a retail business.

retail franchise Selling rights within a given geographical area for certain products and services. The franchising company provides a recognized brand name, goods, equipment and services, such as training in merchandising and management, receiving in return a fee or a percentage of turnover or both. Facilitating rapid and reduced risk expansion opportunity, franchising has assisted national and international network development for retailers such as

Blockbuster Video, The Body Shop, Kentucky Fried Chicken, McDonald's; Pizza Hut and Starbucks.

retail hierarchy A retail hierarchy is the organization of stores within a chain according to size or sales per unit of area. The larger stores within the chain (in terms of selling-floor space or total sales) would appear higher up the hierarchy than those with lower sales or less selling-floor space. Larger stores may offer an extended range of goods and services. Two-tier or multi-level store formats can effectively add a new dimension to the portfolio of stores within a retail business or chain and permit merchandise categories to be split between floors.

retail image The way in which the retailer is perceived by the public. It has become essential for retailers to develop, maintain and communicate a compelling, positive image to foster and sustain competitive advantage. Retail image can thus create a point of difference between one retailer and its major competitor or competitors.

retail location Location is considered one of the most important decisions that a retailer faces as by moving locations a retailer can alter its position in the marketplace. Hence, the location of a store is seen as influencing the RETAIL IMAGE of the retailer.

retail merchandising Primarily the merchandise mix, the store space allocation and the placement of products within it.

retail outlet The physical point or premises at which goods are retailed.

retail park A planned retail development, usually on the outskirts of a major suburb, with easy access and ample parking with a wide variety of different outlets often linked in an enclosed shopping mall.

retail positioning The differentiation of a retailer from its competitors through a retail offering that appeals to and is readily identifiable by its specific target markets.

retail price index More often termed the 'cost of living index', this index measures changes in the prices of a representative 'shopping basket' of household goods. The composition of the shopping basket is determined from the government's family expenditure survey and is varied on a seasonal basis; the individual items are weighted to reflect their relative importance to the basket as a whole. Sampling of prices is undertaken on a regional basis, enabling comparison to be made between different areas in the UK and the UK national index.

retail pricing The process for deciding the price to be charged to the customer for a product or service. The pricing technique most commonly used by retailers is cost-plus pricing. This involves adding a mark-up amount (or percentage) to the retailer's cost. Another common technique is suggested retail pricing. This simply involves charging the amount suggested by the manufacturer, which is usually printed on the product by the manufacturer or supplier.

In developed countries, retail prices are often little less than a round number, for example £9.95; these are known as psychological or odd prices. In Chinese markets, prices are generally either a round number or sometimes a lucky number. This creates PRICE POINTS.

retail product range The assortment of goods and services offered for sale by a retailer. The particular range offered may be tailored closely to the needs of target customers.

retail promotion This involves the retailer communicating with its target customers. It may take one or several forms and usually includes ADVERTISING, PERSONAL SELLING, PUBLIC RELATIONS, PUBLICITY or SALES PROMOTION.

retailer Any establishment engaged in selling merchandise for personal or household consumption and rendering services incidental to the sale of such goods.

retailing All activities concerned with selling goods or services to the final consumer or another person acting on his or her behalf. Retailing consists of the sale of goods or merchandise for personal or household consumption either from a fixed location, such as a department store or kiosk, from a vehicle, for instance an ice cream van, or from a website and includes related subordinated services. In commerce, a retailer buys goods or products in large quantities from manufacturers or importers, either directly or through a wholesaler, and then sells individual items or small quantities to the general public or end-user customers, usually in a shop, also called a store. Retailers are at the end of the supply chain. Marketers see retailing as part of their overall distribution strategy.

There are three major types of retailing. The first is the market, a physical location where buyers and sellers converge. Usually markets take place on town squares, pavements or designated streets and may involve the construction of temporary structures (market stalls). The second form is shop or store trading. Some shops use counter-service, where goods are out of reach of buyers and must be obtained from the seller. This type of retail is common for small expensive items (e.g. jewellry) and controlled items like medicine and alcohol. Self-service, where goods may be handled and examined prior to purchase, has become more common since the twentieth century. Store owners are discovering that, in the competition with the Internet, mail-order companies and other retail stores, one of their most valuable tools is dramatic and fun store design and visual graphics. Customers want to visit stores with ambience, where shopping is an enjoyable experience rather than a simple visit to pick up product. A third form of retail is virtual retail, where products are ordered via mail or telephone or online without having been examined physically but only viewed in a catalogue, on television or on a website. Sometimes this kind of retailing replicates existing retail types – hence online shops or virtual marketplaces such as eBay.

retention strategy The basis of

Rossiter, John

An international expert in advertising management and advertising research and Research Professor of Marketing at the University of Wollongong, Australia. Rossiter is the author of a number of books and numerous journal articles and is currently the most-cited Australian marketing academic in the international Social Sciences Citation Index. His book with Larry Percy, *Advertising Communications and Promotion Management*, is used as a textbook at many of the leading business schools worldwide and has become a useful reference for marketing managers.

RELATIONSHIP MARKETING, which exploits to the full the existing customer base to encourage further purchases, or larger and/or more frequent purchases. Existing customers take more interest in, and read more frequently, the suppliers' advertisements and direct mail shots. Also, the cost per purchase is many times lower than that of a new customer. *See also* CONQUEST STRATEGY.

return In a direct mail campaign the return is the number of replies to a mailout, expressed as a percentage of the total number of mailings sent out.

return link A URL that is used to direct web traffic to an originating site.

return on investment (ROI) 1 The benefit gained in return for the cost of an ad campaign. Although exact measurement is nearly impossible, click-through rate and conversion rate combined with advertising costs can help to assess the ROI of a campaign. **2** The amount, expressed as a percentage, that is earned on a company's total capital calculated by dividing the total capital into earnings before interest, taxes or dividends are paid.

reverse engineering The process of taking something (a device, an electrical component, a software program, etc.) apart and analysing its workings in detail, usually with the intention of constructing a new device or program that does the same thing without actually copying anything from the original.

reverse pricing model A pricing model that allows a buyer to establish their needs and then offer these requirements to suppliers to competitively bid for.

RFID tag An RFID (Radio Frequency Identification) tag is a microchip with an antenna in a small compact component form that can be attached to goods and/or packing and can allow the product to be tracked. Tags can be minute and are often the size of grain of rice. It is used extensively in retailing as a security device, a provider of product purchase information and a stock-holding and logistics inventory-providing system. It is not always deactivated by the supplier and has been used to track individual purchases in certain situations.

risk A purchase of a product has two elements which combine to create a certain level of perceived risk: the consequences which follow from a wrong choice, and the certainty or uncertainty about the likelihood of this product choice being a wrong choice. A consumer's tolerance for risk taking varies amongst individuals and is related to personality and education.

rival brands Competing brand choices, often of nearly homogeneous goods.

robot A program that runs automatically without human intervention. A robot is typically endowed with some artificial intelligence, so it can adjust to the various situations it may encounter. Two common types of robots are agents and spiders. Also known as a bot. Some bots also implement a specialist function to harvest e-mail addresses.

roll-out The regional or national

expansion of a new product from its initial area of introduction.

Rosenthal effect This occurs in situations in which students perform better than other students simply because they are expected to do so. The psychologist Robert Rosenthal tested the hypothesis that biased expectancies can essentially affect reality and create self-fulfilling prophecies as a result. He predicted that, when given the information that certain students are brighter than others, elementary school teachers may unconsciously behave in ways that facilitate and encourage the students' success.

royalty A payment to the owner of a copyright or trademark for its use by another seller. This is usually an agreed percentage of sales revenue.

S

Sale of Goods Act 1979 (UK) The Sale of Goods Act 1979, amended in 1994 to the Sale and Supply of Goods Act, says that when you buy goods from a trader they must fit the description, be of satisfactory quality – which includes lasting a reasonable length of time – and be fit for their purpose. If goods aren't of satisfactory quality buyers are entitled to compensation, which could be a refund, replacement or repair. The retailer, not the manufacturer, is legally obliged to sort out a problem if the goods don't meet these requirements. The Sale of Goods Act holds true for second-hand goods as well, but takes into account that the quality should simply be what you could reasonably expect from that product, given its age and how much it has been used.

sale or return A guarantee that the price of the goods sold will be returned if they are returned in good order within an agreed time. A condition of sale regularly offered by online sales organizations such as Amazon and book clubs.

sales The function of selling a good or service. One caricature of the sales process is the 'hard sell', where the salesperson heavily pushes a product (even when the consumer is evidently reluctant to buy) and where inducements such as price cuts are very readily given (even if they harm revenues and margins in the short run and undermine the brand image in the longer term). Aggressive selling is found in discount retailing and, in the past at least, in some consumer sectors, e.g. door-to-door selling, insurance, cars. However, this is a partial and unhelpful view of sales in general. Far from 'pushing' the product, the astute salesperson will listen carefully to the customer, finding out what he/she wants and what reservations he/she might have. Only after having done this will the salesperson direct the customer to specific products and in doing so show how the product meets his/her needs and overcome any reservations. This approach is more likely to result in sales without costly inducements and ensure that the customer is satisfied.

Selling has long suffered from a tarnished image. Dubious selling practices may occasionally result in a sale if the customer is particularly gullible. But it is arguable that, even then, only good marketing (which encompasses a far wider range of skills, with an almost diametrically opposed motivation) will lead the customer to buy again from the same company. Organizations seldom profit from single purchases made by first-time customers. Normally they rely on repeat business to generate the profit that they need.

Selling is a practical implementation of marketing; it often forms a separate grouping in a corporate structure, employing separate specialist operatives. The successful questioning to understand a customer's goal and the creation of a valuable solution by communicating the necessary information that encourages a buyer to achieve his/her goal at an economic cost is the responsibility of the salesperson.

sales agent A person or organization operating independently to sell products or services on behalf of a company or a third party.

sales analysis The gathering, classifying, comparison and detailed analysis of an organization's sales data. It may simply involve the comparison of total sales in two different time periods, for instance annual sales for 2007 and 2008, or it may entail subjecting thousands of component sales (or sales-related) figures to a variety of comparisons among themselves, with external data and market research and with like figures for earlier periods of time.

sales budget Usually the sum of money required over a specified time to run a sales department. It is a term also often used to include all marketing expenditures of which selling is only a part.

sales call cycle A pattern of activity in which the field salesperson is involved in the process of calling on their customers. Primarily, such a cycle is determined by (a) the targeting of customers and their geographical distribution; (b) the frequency of calls required per customer; (c) the cost-effectiveness of calling; and (d) the sales history and pattern of sales with the specific customer. Some flexibility is required in establishing a sales call cycle in order to allow the sales representative the discretion to deal with, for example, the unexpected demands of customers.

sales campaign The implementation of the selling strategy. It sometimes refers to a specific selling operation for a product, a market segment or a geographical area in isolation from the normal sales activity.

sales conference A meeting normally organized for the purpose of educating, motivating, new product launch, reviewing and setting targets with sales and related personnel.

sales conversion rate The percentage of sales achieved against visits made or customer leads followed up.

sales coverage The distribution of selling agents or sales outlets reaching potential markets.

sales effectiveness test Test designed to assess the ability of a targeted advertising, promotion or communications campaign to sell a particular product over a given time period.

sales force Staff within the organization responsible for selling products or services via direct contact with the customers.

sales forecasts Projections of likely sales, given certain defined criteria and making defined assumptions. Often based upon historical data.

sales incentive The offering of a bonus, remuneration or some other incentive to motivate salespersons to increase their efforts and sales.

sales lead When a salesman is given basic information or a contact which may help him focus his selling efforts and possibly result in a sale. Sales leads may come from an INQUIRY in response to advertising, by referral from an existing customer or by following up other information, e.g. offering catering services, mortgages, etc. to couples announcing their engagement.

sales management The organization, direction, control, recruitment, training and motivation of the field selling effort within the planned marketing strategy.

sales maximization The philosophy that businesses try to maximize sales and revenue rather than profit.

There are several motives for such a stance:

- to grow or sustain market share;
- to ensure survival;
- to discourage competitors;
- to build up the prestige of senior management;
- to achieve bonuses if they are based on volume rather than profit.

sales orientation Where the selling of a product is regarded as the primary task as against the satisfying of the customer's requirements. *See also* MARKETING ORIENTATION.

sales-orientated   Orientation towards

the selling function as the key organizational activity. One of a triumvirate of company orientations which identify, chronologically, the history of business attitudes towards marketing: (a) production (manufacturing) orientation; (b) SALES ORIENTATION; (c) MARKETING ORIENTATION.

sales penetration The extent to which total market potential has been realized, i.e. the proportion of people in that market who have become users or consumers of a product or service.

sales pitch The content and style of salesperson's presentation to prospective customers.

sales planning Determining sales objectives and selling activity quotas in an effort to achieve pre-set targets.

sales promotion Sales promotion refers to any activity designed to boost the sales of a product or service. It may include an advertising campaign, increased PUBLIC RELATIONS activity, a free-sample campaign, offering free gifts or vouchers, arranging demonstrations or exhibitions, setting up competitions with promotional prizes, temporary price reductions, door-to-door calling, telephone-selling, personal letters, Internet advertising or other methods. *See also* PUBLICITY.

sales quota A sales assignment, goal or target set for a salesperson or a territory in a given accounting period. Commonly used types of sales quotas are pound or euro volume quotas, unit volume quotas, gross margin quotas, net profit quotas and activity quotas.

sales reports Written information feedback to sales management on sales performance and a salesperson's activities.

sales representative A person who represents his or her organization in a selling capacity. Sales representatives are product or company specialists who spend their time contacting customers and prospective customers and attempting to obtain sales. Sales representatives are the front-line selling operators of an organization and they typically work in a particular geographical territory, although the size of the territories can vary considerably between different types of products. In the last decade the term has been modified to such titles as sales executive, relationship development manager and senior sales agent amongst many others.

sales territory The segment of the market for which a salesperson is responsible. Territory assignments can be exclusive or non-exclusive. Territory may be defined in terms of geographic or market segments, product lines or the size of customer.

sample 1 A trial offer designed to encourage potential buyers to test the product without risk in the hope that they will then adopt it. **2** A group of people or amount of data that can be used to provide market information via quantitative or qualitative research techniques.

sampling The process of selecting a subgroup of a POPULATION of interest for the collection of information which may be generalized to the whole population, as opposed to a census, in which information is regularly collected from the entire population.

sampling distribution A theoretical frequency distribution of the scores for, or values of, a statistic, such as a mean. Any statistic that can be computed for a sample has a sampling distribution. A sampling distribution is the distribution of statistics that would be produced in repeated random sampling from the same population. It is all possible values of a statistic and their probabilities of occurring for a sample of a particular size.

sampling error The inaccuracies in inferences about a POPULATION that come about because researchers have taken a sample rather than studying the whole population. Sampling error is an estimate of how a sample statistic is expected to differ from a population PARAMETER in a random sample drawn from across the whole of the population.

sampling frame A list or other form of

record of the POPULATION from which the sampling units are drawn. It is an operational definition of the population.

sampling units Items from a POPULATION selected for inclusion in a sample.

satellite television Delivered by means of communications satellites in comparison to cable TV which is via fixed cable and conventional terrestrial television which is broadcast conventionally over UHF or VHF airwaves. The five largest pay TV satellite operators in Europe are: BSkyB (UK), Canal Plus (France), Sky Italia (Italy), Premiere (Austria and Germany), and Sogecable (Spain).

satisficing Seeking or achieving a satisfactory outcome, rather than the best possible outcome. This contrasts with the optimizing behaviour outcome usually assumed in economics, general management and international trade theory.

SCA (sustainable competitive advantage) A long-term competitive advantage of an organization. This can be a particular competency like Proctér and Gamble's ability to manage brands or alternatively the fact that an organization owns a particular brand such as Nestlé owning KitKat.

scanner A digital device used to translate visual information, pictures or typed text into a pattern of dots which can be understood and stored by a computer.

scanner data Retail purchase information (such as price, brand product size, discounts, amount purchased) gathered at the point of purchase by an electronic device that reads a BARCODE on or attached to the product through the use of an electronic reader over which the product passes. This information can be gathered and used to build a range of consumer behaviour profiles and propositions to be offered by marketing and retail groups.

scatter diagrams Diagrams that show the correlation between variables but not necessarily the cause-and-effect relationship. They show the relationship between two variables – as one increases so does the other. Analysis should allow for possible intervening variables which may be the 'drivers'.

scenario In the context of marketing business planning a scenario (in Italian, that which is pinned to the scenery) depicts a particular combination of the interdependent issues, factors or forces (social, economic, competitive, technological and political) that define the future. A scenario depicts a possible future state and should not be taken as a forecast. It does so in a logical and internally consistent manner. A scenario will, therefore, describe the course of events, combination of factors or evolution of trends that is expected to realize one of several plausible alternative futures. Additional scenarios can be constructed to describe a range of possible combinations of the pertinent variables, for example, from optimistic to pessimistic. Multiple scenarios provide a vehicle for environmental analysis and strategic planning.

scientific method A process that is the basis for scientific inquiry. The scientific method follows a series of steps: **1** identifying a problem to be solved; **2** formulating a hypothesis; **3** testing the hypothesis; **4** collecting and analysing the data; **5** making conclusions.

screening The second stage in the NEW PRODUCT DEVELOPMENT process. Once a firm has generated a portfolio of ideas for new products, it is essential that these be screened to ensure that only the most promising are subject to thorough analysis. Screening is an essentially subjective procedure in which managers use their knowledge and experience to weed out obvious non-starters. Managers tend to be most confident when applying their knowledge of internal constraints and will eliminate many ideas as being inconsistent with the firm's product policy and objectives, with the existing skills and resources and so on. In the same way, ideas that are incompatible with the firm's existing markets and its knowledge of its current users and customers are likely to be screened out at this phase as the firm seeks to build upon its existing strengths.

search engine A programme that indexes documents, then attempts to match documents relevant to the user's search requests. Internet search engines (e.g. Google, AltaVista, MSN, Yahoo!) help users find web pages on a given subject. The search engines maintain databases of websites and use programmes (often referred to as 'spiders' or 'ROBOTS') to collect information, which is then indexed by the search engine. Similar services are provided by WEB DIRECTORIES, which maintain ordered lists of websites, e.g. Yahoo!

search optimization The process of choosing clear and focused keyword phrases related to a website and ensuring that the site uses them well when these are part of a web search. These tactics and techniques make it easier for spiders to find the page, contributing to higher ranking on a list of search engine results. Basic optimization starts with listing relevant keywords in META TAGS and building clear and descriptive words into page copy, title, text hyperlinks and image file names. It is also important to design a site on a logical link structure and follow standard HTML conventions, avoiding the use of frames, dynamic URLs, image maps and JAVASCRIPT for navigation.

seasonal demand Demand which varies according to the season of the year. For example, more soup is consumed during the winter months and more ice cream during the summer.

secondary data *See* DATA.

segment The process by which one segments the market into particular groupages of behaviours and consumption patterns.

segmentation The dissection of the market into distinct parts by the uniformity of behaviour in that segment. At the core of marketing and focuses the supplier or user on customer groups and preferences. *See also* MARKET NICHE; MARKET SEGMENTATION; TARGETING.

segmentation variable A factor which can be used as the basis for segmenting a market.

selection bias In marketing refers to the distorting nature of the way the evidence for research has been collected, producing bias and requiring moderation or the sample group changing.

selective distribution *See* EXTENSIVE DISTRIBUTION.

selective exposure The avoidance of stimuli which may not be congruent with the receiver's self-perception. The changing of TV channels, or ZAPPING, is a form of selective exposure in that the viewer switches from the communication they wish to avoid to another channel.

selective retention The tendency to recognize and retain only that information that is congruent and consistent with one's existing values and beliefs.

self-image A psychological term referring to individuals' concepts of themselves and their roles in relation to others.

self-selection bias A major problem in market research where groups or individuals self-select and this has not been factored into the research. Norming can happen and the results from the research can skew results. In human interaction it is a known phenomenon that left to their own devices good students will select each other to work with whilst the less able individuals will also form a group.

self-service A retail arrangement which allows shoppers direct access to merchandise, which is then carried by the customer for payment to a POINT-OF-SALE or service unit. It is effective in reducing store labour costs, but can lead to an increase in theft.

sell-by date A date printed or stamped on perishable produce indicating the date by which it should be purchased for consumption.

seller's market A market in which more people want to buy than sell. These exist when there are shortages of goods and services for general consumption and have been particularly evident in certain housing markets where buyers want property in a given area, but it does not become available often. In wartime conditions and in periods of rationing an economy is said to be operating as a seller's market. Where such basic items as food, clothing and fuels are in short supply, customers buy whatever is available. Fashion is of little importance when you are cold in winter and you just need a warm coat and there is little variety to choose from. Thus, where seller's markets exist, producers do not have to take heed of consumers' wishes, as they are capable of selling all they can make. Thus in a seller's market there is little need for marketing activities, as competition between producers is non-existent. The opposite of a seller's market is a BUYER'S MARKET, where consumers have a wide choice, as is the case of Western society today. Manufacturers have to differentiate their products in an attempt to win customers, and so marketing activities become important.

selling The process of offering a product for sale to a customer. This may be face-to-face, via phone or the Internet. The quality of the salesperson is normally related to the cost and value of transactions.

selling agent An individual making sales of a product or service to a consumer. The sales agent may not be employed by the organization and may be operating on a commission basis.

semi-variable costs Costs that are composed of two cost components – a fixed component and a variable component. Such costs vary with activity, but not in direct proportion to it. Maintenance, supervision and store-keeping are typical examples of semi-variable costs. For instance, maintenance can be both monthly or annual (preventative maintenance), the costs of which are independent of activity and therefore fixed, or activity-based (e.g. a 5,000-mile service for vehicles, replacement of worn-out parts), the costs of

which are wholly dependent on product use and therefore variable.

semiotics The study of signs and symbols both individually and in groups to project images and memories that belong to a particular place, person or product. Semiotics are normally classified by the way they are transmitted, so it could be voice, picture or sometimes the smell associated with an image, which may reinforce a figure.

Semiotics is used substantially in branding and of course has played a major role in propaganda.

service characteristics Services can be distinguished from physical goods by their main attributes: intangibility, inseparability, variability and perishability.

Service intangibility means that services cannot be handled, smelled, tasted, heard or seen before they are purchased. Because the quality of a service cannot be assessed before consumption consumers will look for clues about service quality. These can come from the physical premises, equipment, people, price and the communications they can see and experience prior to buying the service.

Service inseparability means that services cannot be separated from the service provider whether it is a person or a machine. This interaction between provider and customer is a special feature of services marketing and can influence service quality and outcome.

Service variability often depends on the actions of individuals and consequently the quality and delivery of services can be more variable than physical products. In particular, personal contact between the service provider and the customer can influence customers' reactions to the service. Technology is increasingly used in service provision to reduce variability and costs; however, used inappropriately it can alienate customers and/or introduce new complexity to the service process.

Service perishability means that services cannot be stored for later use or sale. For example, airplane flights are unable to be used once the plane has departed and similarly sales for theatre seats end at a certain point. When demand is steady perishability is not a problem; however, when demand fluctuates service providers can experience problems.

service delivery This is dependent upon people, equipment and processes. Many service businesses are reducing their reliance upon people-reliant service delivery by using technology and specialized equipment to reduce costs and variability, improve quality and deliver services to customers more quickly.

service design Design management is relevant in the context of the service product and also relates to other elements of the MARKETING MIX, in particular the extended marketing mix for the services sector. A particular aspect of service design is service blueprinting, which is basically a flow chart of the service process in which all the elements or activities, their sequencing and interactions can be visualized.

service distribution The term covers the whole area of services and the way that they are delivered to the customer whether it be individually or across an organization or sector. Services typically have been delivered in person to customers, i.e. a customer must be present to receive a haircut. A feature of a number of service organizations is also multiple outlets which provide convenient access to customers. Increasingly, web-based technologies are delivering services to customers without the need for them to be physically present; for example, most banks allow their customers to perform online banking activities without them needing to be present at a branch. This allows the bank to better meet the needs of customers while reducing the capital required for multiple outlets.

service-dominant logic An approach to a unified understanding of the purpose and nature of organizations, markets and society, developed by Steve Vargo and Bob Lusch in 'Evolving to a New Dominant Logic for Marketing', *Journal of Marketing* (January 2004). The foundational proposition of SDL is that organizations, markets and society are fundamentally concerned with exchange of service – the applications of competences (knowledge and skills) for the benefit of a party. That is, service is exchanged for service; all firms are service firms; all markets are centred on the exchange of service; and all economies and societies are service-based. Consequently, marketing thought and practice should be grounded in service logic, principles and theories.

SD logic says that customers create value through service experiences and relationships, especially in the co-creation and sharing of resources with suppliers, including skills and knowledge. What a supplier firm does essentially is offer value propositions (promises) and marshal resources together for customers. The difference in the logic is subtle but it has profound practical implications. Rather than firms marketing to customers, emphasis is placed on marketing with customers (an interaction process). In this the customer is the arbiter of value co-created in direct service interaction and, most importantly, the arbiter of value-in-use of any goods sold. Put another way, goods are service appliances which offer the customer value-in-use. Ultimately service is exchanged for service.

Of course, SD logic could be seen as just another restatement of ideas from earlier phases in the development of marketing thought, such as SERVICES MARKETING, RELATIONSHIP MARKETING, market orientation, network perspectives, INTEGRATED MARKETING COMMUNICATIONS and the resource-based view of the firm. But this would miss the point. Vargo and Lusch's special contribution to the marketing debate is in bringing these ideas together in a new way in a new pattern – a 'service logic' for marketing practice as a whole.

A goods-dominant marketing logic arguably limits the mind-set for seeing the opportunities for co-creation of value with customers and other stakeholders of the firm. In a similar way, a transactional exchange view ignores customer loyalty and puts constraints on developing the lifetime value of the customer to the firm. It is the broadened possibilities for value exchanges over time, both social and economic, that excites thinking about SD logic and its role in rethinking marketing innovation at the edge.

service encounter The direct interaction between a service provider and its customers in the service-delivery process is referred to as a service encounter, moment of truth or critical incident. A service encounter may take varying forms. For example, a bank customer wishing to make account inquiries may choose between an interaction with an ATM or online banking service or with a bank employee by telephone or letter or face to face in a branch. Every time the customer comes into contact with an aspect of the bank and its employees there is an opportunity to form an impression and make an evaluation of the bank and its service(s). Service encounters, in particular those involving employees, have a high impact on consumers, and the quality of the encounter is an essential element in the overall quality of service experienced by the customer.

service environment The service environment plays a key role in almost all service production and delivery; exceptions would include remote services such as communications and utilities. The service environment includes consideration of the physical environment (both physical design and access aspects and emotional or atmospheric impact) and also distribution of goods and their promotion – all of which influence consumers' (and employees') judgements of a service-marketing organization. The physical design comprises aspects of space, colour, furnishings, temperature, noise, music, layout and employee dress and provides an atmosphere within which the consumer buys and consumes services. Access includes hours, availability, convenience of location and privacy and security. Closely integrated with these are the distribution and promotion of goods utilized by service organizations to create awareness of, and interest in, their offerings and to differentiate themselves from competitors. Sometimes the tangible aspects are essential to the provision of the service (e.g. aircraft);

sometimes they are much more peripheral and/or of no independent value.

service guarantee A written assurance that the service will be provided or will meet certain specifications. Some aspects of service and customer satisfaction cannot be guaranteed, e.g. unconditional on-time arrival of planes, and so promises and guarantees have to be realistic. A good service guarantee should be unconditional, easy to understand and communicate, easy to invoke and easy to collect on. It should also be meaningful, especially with respect to payout, which should be a function of the cost of the service, representing the seriousness of failure and a perception of what is fair.

service industries Suppliers of services not directly involved with manufacturing, e.g. travel, entertainment, health, insurance, professional and personal treatment.

service price The pricing of a service is usually based on a combination of expertise, time taken and speed of delivery. Price forms are also very different; for example, entertainment services are usually priced through admission tickets with all kinds of variables; personal care services are priced based upon skill levels and time; estate agents take commission based on sale value; buses, taxis, trains and planes take fares based upon length of travel; professional services charge fees based on expertise by the hour or day; financial services charge interest based upon the amount of debt or service; governments charge taxes for services, locally and nationally; employees are paid salaries, wages and bonuses for their labour and skill level.

service product An activity of an intangible nature that normally, but not necessarily, takes place in the interrelationship between the customer and service employees and/or physical resources or goods and/or systems of the service provider, which are provided as solutions to customer needs. The distinction between services and products is not clear-cut, in that there are few pure services and products.

For example, a car is a physical object and an airline provides a service, but transport is common to them both. Another view is proposed by Christian Grönroos (*Strategic Management and Marketing in the Service Sector*, 1983), who has developed a concept of the service product – the service offering – which is geared to the concept of perceived service quality. First there is the basic core service package, such as a hotel, which includes facilitating services that are required to assist consumption of the service (e.g. reception), together with supporting services that are not required but which enhance the service and differentiate it from competition (e.g. restaurants and bars, leisure and conference facilities). *See also* SERVICE-DOMINANT LOGIC.

service promotion A particular activity that is intended to promote a service. The promotion of services presents some significant problems, in particular because of the intangibility and variability in their delivery and production due to the part played actively by human beings in the form of service personnel. The key means of promotion in the services sector is PERSONAL SELLING, as there is a high level of contact between the service organization's employees and its customers. This area is increasingly becoming more regulated to satisfy consumer demands.

service quality The relative inferiority/ superiority of an organization's services in terms of the consumer's overall impression and judgement. Customers require organizations to perform consistently to their expectations and in today's highly competitive climate they are unlikely to accept less. When an organization fails to meet customer expectations or deliver on its promises, it diminishes the customer's faith in the organization and reduces its chance of being seen as a quality service provider. High-quality service is defined as delivery of service that meets or exceeds customers' expectations.

service recovery No organization can deliver 100 per cent service all of the time. Consequently service failure and the subsequent complaints from customers are inevitable in most businesses. The rapid, effective handling of service failures is a key business strategy and has proven to be vital in maintaining customer satisfaction and loyalty as well as in developing relationships with new customers. Service recovery refers to the actions a service provider takes in response to service failure with the intention to return dissatisfied customers to a state of satisfaction.

services marketing The marketing of intangible products, such as hairdressing, cleaning, insurance and travel.

services sector The services sector of an economy is generally considered to include all industries other than those involved in manufacturing.

servicescapes The concept of a servicescape was developed by B. Booms and M. Bitner ('Marketing Strategies and Organization Structures for Service Firms', in J. Donnelly and W. George (eds.), *Marketing of Services*, 1981) to develop an appreciation of the impact of the physical environment in which a service process takes place. A good example would be the difference a customer encounters between a branch of a fast food chain and that of an up-market restaurant. Booms and Bitner defined a servicescape as 'the environment in which the service is assembled and in which the seller and customer interact, combined with tangible commodities that facilitate performance or communication of the service'.

SERVQUAL (service quality) A tool used to assess SERVICE QUALITY developed by the marketing research team of Berry, Parasuraman and Zeithaml. They identified the five dimensions (tangibles, reliability, responsiveness, assurance, empathy) that were consistently ranked by customers to be most important for service quality, regardless of the service industry. Based on these five dimensions, a survey instrument was developed which measures the gap between customers' expectation of excellence and their perception of actual service delivered.

Sheth, Jagdish

Internationally renowned scholar of marketing, particularly in the areas of customer satisfaction, global competition and strategic thinking. Sheth has worked for numerous industries and companies in the United States, Europe and Asia, both as a consultant and as a seminar leader, and is currently the Charles H. Kellstadt Professor of Marketing at the Goizueta Business School, Emory University. He is rated as one of the ten top marketing professors in America, and his many books and articles are among the most frequently cited publications in marketing.

Sheth is one of only four Americans ever honoured with the Viktor Mataja medal from the Austrian Research Society in Vienna for his contributions to advertising and consumer research. In 1989 he was awarded the Outstanding Marketing Educator award by the Academy of Marketing Science and in 1991 he received the Outstanding Educator Award by the Sales and Marketing Executives International (SMEI). He was also awarded the P. D. Converse Award for his outstanding contributions to theory in marketing in 1992 by the American Marketing Association. Among his more influential scholarly books are *Marketing Theory: Evolution and Evaluation* and *Consumption Values and Market Choices* and a text book, *Customer Behaviour: Consumer Behaviour and Beyond.*

---

share of voice A relative portion of inventory available to a single advertiser within a defined market sector over a specified time period.

shopper typologies A classification that identifies shoppers based upon their purchase behaviour, motives and attitudes, e.g. the convenience shopper, the leisure shopper, the price-conscious shopper and the store-loyal shopper.

shopping cart Software used to make a website's product catalogue available for online ordering, whereby visitors may select, view, add/delete and purchase merchandise.

shopping centre/mall A building or set of buildings that contains stores and has interconnecting walkways that make it easy for people to walk from store to store. The walkways may or may not be enclosed. In the UK and Australia these are called shopping centres or shopping arcades.

shotgun approach Sales messages sent to a very general range of PROSPECTS without any degree of targeting, either in the choice of media or the message.

shrinkage The difference between phys- ical stock takes and book stocks. Could be due to theft or product going out of date.

skimming pricing A pricing policy where the supplier charges the highest price possible to those consumers who want a particular product thus 'skimming the cream' before reducing the price to gain more sensitive customers.

skyscraper A tall, thin advertisement that runs down the side of a web page. A skyscraper is usually 120 x 600 pixels or 160 x 600 pixels.

sleeper effect Studies have shown that even after factual information within an advertisement has been forgotten, attitudes may still have shifted in favour of the advertisement. This is known as the sleeper effect.

slogan A short, memorable phrase used in advertising. Examples include: 'Designed to save lives', used to promote the Volvo S40 range of cars; 'Hand-built by Robots', for the Fiat Strada; and 'Coke is it'. When a product or company uses a slogan consistently, the slogan can become an important element of message identification in the public's perception of the brand or product. Slogans can also be used in political, religious and other contexts as a repetitive

Smith, Adam
(1723–1790)

The great Scottish moral philosopher and a pioneering political economist who is often seen as the modern founder of economics and ethical trading. Smith is the first great contributor to our modern perception of free market economics. A leading figure, with David Hume, of the intellectual movement known as the Scottish Enlightenment, he is known primarily as the author of two great works: *The Theory of Moral Sentiments* (1759) and *An Inquiry into the Nature and Causes of the Wealth of Nations* (1776). The former is regarded as one of the best treatises on moral philosophy whilst the latter is one of the earliest attempts to systematically study the historical development of industry and commerce in Europe as well as a sustained attack on the doctrines of mercantilism. *The Wealth of Nations* has become so influential because it did so much to create the subject of political economy and develop it into an autonomous systematic discipline. In the developed world, it is one of the most influential books on the subject ever published. Smith's work became the basis for classical economics and provided one of the best-known intellectual rationales for free trade, capitalism and libertarianism.

expression of an idea or purpose. 'Labour isn't working' was a memorable campaign phrase used by the Conservatives against the Labour government in the 1979 UK general election to highlight unemployment policy.

Slogans vary from the written and the visual to the chanted and the vulgar. Often their simple rhetorical nature leaves little room for detail, and as such they serve perhaps more as a social expression of unified purpose than as a projection for an intended audience. The word 'slogan' comes from *sluagh-ghairm* (pronounced slogorm), which is Scottish Gaelic for 'battlecry'.

Slow Food Slow Food is a non-profit, eco-gastronomic member-supported organization that was founded in 1989 to counteract fast food and fast life, the disappearance of local food traditions and people's dwindling interest in the food they eat, where it comes from, how it tastes and how our food choices affect the rest of the world. It began in 1986, in Rome, when Carlo Petrini organized a demonstration in which he and his followers brandished bowls of penne as weapons of protest. Soon after, he founded the International Slow Food Movement and issued a manifesto, a response to fast food, fast life, non-sustainable farming and the eroding of local economies. By the mid-1990s, Slow Food had grown phenomenally and had become politically active, lobbying the European Union on trade and agricultural policy and working to save endangered foods. Today, the movement has over 80,000 members throughout the world and has become accepted as an international advocate for the production and consumption of artisan, quality food.

smart card A card that includes an imbedded chip that can store data. Since smart cards can store data, they can be used in transactions that allow the consumer to remain anonymous (data storage is in the hands of the consumer, not the company), which is a key benefit for those concerned with their privacy. Smart cards have not reached full adoption at this point, though are more commonly used in Europe than in the US. The Smart Card Alliance is an alliance of industry leaders working for the widespread acceptance of smart card technology.

snowball sampling A technique for finding research subjects. One subject gives the researcher the name of another subject, who in turn provides the name of a third, and so on. This is an especially useful technique when the researcher wants to contact people with unusual experiences or characteristics who are likely to know each other – members of a small religious group, for example.

social class The stratification of members of a society into a hierarchy of classes, such as upper, middle and lower classes, which was seen as the bedrock of British society for much of the nineteenth and twentieth centuries.

social group A number of individuals who share specific characteristics and who are bound to a unified group through shared expectations and obligations.

social indicators Statistics describing variables that reflect social conditions, that is, that 'indicate' something about the nature and quality of life in a society, often as it changes over time. Examples of social indicators include PER CAPITA INCOME, average life expectancy, median years of education and infant mortality rate.

social marketing The application of marketing to persuade the citizen to modify their actions and behaviour in particular circumstances and situations to benefit themselves and society. Campaigns have covered anti-smoking, drink driving prevention, contraception and preventive medicine especially in the cancer and heart health areas. Major social marketing campaigns have now moved into areas such as responsible driving, daily physical fitness and community care. Measurement of effectiveness in the area is still not widespread as many campaigns appear to be politically motivated and not tested for effectiveness, thus they look good but do not achieve what they were supposedly commissioned to achieve.

Although social marketing is often seen as the application of commercial business marketing techniques to societal issues this can often be an oversimplification. It is true that monetary profit for the organization sponsoring the effort may not necessarily be a prime goal. Government sponsorship of public health initiatives, though maintaining an awareness of budget concerns, may not aim at commercial returns at all. But commercial returns may be a central aim if the sponsor of the marketing effort is a non-profit organization intending to raise funds. Also, whereas commercial marketing often aims at a comparatively simple influence over its target market, social marketing goals can be far more subtle and complex. For instance a number of social marketing campaigns are now using social network websites such as Facebook to get over complex messages to younger users of the need for nutritional and physical health care.

A commercial marketer selling a product may only seek to influence a buyer to make a product purchase. Social marketers, dealing with goals such as reducing cigarette smoking or reducing alcohol consumption or encouraging condom usage, have more difficult goals: to make potentially difficult and long-term behavioural change in target populations.

It is sometimes felt that social marketing is restricted to a particular spectrum of clients – the non-profit organization, the health services group, the government agency, and so on. Indeed, these are often the prime clients of social marketing agencies, but the goal of stimulating social change is not restricted to governmental or non-profit charitable organizations; it can be argued that corporate PUBLIC RELATIONS efforts such as funding for the arts or the sponsorship of the Portman Group by the brewing industry to promote sensible drinking and avoiding alcohol abuse are also good examples of this work in the private sector.

social mobility The extent to which a person, during their lifetime, can move up or down in social status in a given society.

social responsibility In marketing this is taken to mean the belief that businesses, whether they be private sector, not-for-profit or public sector organizations, should make a contribution to the welfare of their local community and society irrespective of their desire to maximize profit.

social responsibility audit An

evaluation or assessment of the policies and practices of an organization to establish how and to what extent it is behaving in a socially responsible manner, e.g. in terms of employment practices, relationships with its local community, environmental protection, etc.

societal marketing *See* SOCIAL MARKETING.

socio-economic groups A census classification of groups based on employment status and occupation (or former occupation), bringing together people with jobs of similar social and economic status, e.g. professional workers, skilled manual workers. *See also* DEMOGRAPHY.

soft sell The technique of using low-pressure appeals in advertisements and commercials. *See also* HARD SELL.

sole agent Someone who represents another on an exclusive basis in relation to a specific product or service, or for a particular region.

sole trader One-person trading concern, representing the simplest and earliest form of business organization.

sound bite Technically, the information given in a ten- or twenty-second time period within a news broadcast. In common usage, any short pithy statement summarizing a point of view but without elaborating on it. As the context of what is being said is missing, the insertion of sound bites into news broadcasts or documentaries is open to manipulation and thus requires a very high degree of journalistic ethics.

source effect The effect that the source of marketing communications message has upon the target audiences' perceptions of it and their reactions to it.

spam a) In Internet usage the term refers to unsolicited and particularly unwanted bulk e-mail messages. Generally spam is e-mail advertising for some product sent to a mailing list or newsgroup. Spam messages are neither requested nor wanted by recipients. Unwanted e-mail messages consume a vast amount of consumers' time and can clog up mail boxes and bandwidth. Most online service providers, businesses and public institutions have instituted policies to prevent spammers from spamming their customers.

b) Well-known luncheon meat product popularized by the Monty Python song 'SPAM' and more recently the musical *Spamalot*. SPAM, which is believed to have been derived from the 'Shoulder of Pork and Ham', was introduced in 1937 and was used as a basic foodstuff during and after the Second World War. It is still produced by Hormel Foods Corporation worldwide. Largest consumers of SPAM worldwide by quantity are the US, the UK and South Korea. *See also* E-MAIL; E-MAIL MARKETING.

specialty goods Goods not always available in conventional outlets and sold direct to the home from leads obtained by advertising, such as double glazing, encyclopaedias, insurance.

specialty salesperson A salesperson who is usually confined to one product or at most a limited range of products. Specialty salespeople are frequently used where there is a once-only selling opportunity or at least little likelihood of a repeat sale in the immediate future.

specifier A member of the decision-making unit and an individual involved in the technical specification of purchasing requirements.

spider A programme that automatically fetches web pages and feeds them to search engines. (It is called a 'spider' because it 'crawls around the web'.) Because most web pages contain links to and from other pages, a spider can start almost anywhere. As soon as it recognizes a link to another page, it goes off and collects it. Large search engines have many spiders working simultaneously. It is also known as a crawler.

spin In PUBLIC RELATIONS and POLITICAL MARKETING, spin is usually taken to mean putting a nice or nasty edge to a media story for personal and/or strategic political gain. A pejorative term signifying a heavily biased portrayal in one's own favour of an event or situation that is designed to bring about the most positive result possible. It is uniform amongst those that practise spin to deny they are spin doctors until their memoirs appear.

spin doctor A PUBLIC RELATIONS or POLITICAL MARKETING person who tries to forestall negative publicity by publicizing a favourable interpretation of the words or actions of a company, political party or famous individual. Alternatively, they can of course trawl negative stories, but these are done more subtly or brutally to ensure success and that the spin doctor is not outed. Another area of activity is where the spin doctor leaks out low-key bad news when something else has gripped the media and public's attention. In working life, spin doctors come under a number of titles such as communications advisor, strategic media advisor and information officer amongst others.

splash page A page on a website that the user sees first before being given the option to continue to the main content of the site. Splash pages are used to promote a company, service or product or are used to inform the user of what kind of software or browser is necessary in order to view the rest of the site's pages. Often a splash page will consist of animated graphics and sounds that entice the user into exploring the rest of the website. It usually does not have much actual information on it – like a title page in a book.

sponsor An organization that finances sporting or other activities in order to gain coverage and prestige from its association with them.

sponsorship A business or professional arrangement where an individual or group acquires the right to associate their name, products or services with a sponsored event, activity, person, or an organization's services, products or activities by providing money or other resources of value. This is usually in return for benefits such as publicity and advertising. Adidas,

Air China, Coca-Cola, Johnson & Johnson, McDonald's, Omega, Samsung, Volkswagen and Visa were all prime sponsors of the 2008 Beijing Olympics.

sports marketing Marketing products through the SPONSORSHIP of sporting events or of teams or equipment for sporting events.

spot A single television advertisement.

spot lengths Standard times for television commercials, e.g. fifteen, thirty, forty-five and sixty seconds, thirty seconds being the base time.

spot market A market in which a commodity is bought or sold for immediate delivery or delivery in the very near future.

spread Two facing pages in a publication over which one advertisement may be printed.

stable market A market where the volume of sales shows very little change when prices vary.

stakeholder marketing Marketing to discrete and identifiable groups of people to whom a corporate image is to be projected and whose goodwill is important to an organization in the achievement of its overall objectives. Such audiences will include shareholders, employees, customers, government, local community and opinion formers, all of which go to form the audience for a marketing campaign. A stakeholder orientation implies that the ultimate objective of a business is to create value for all of its stakeholders beyond just value to customers.

Stakeholder RELATIONSHIP MARKETING involves creating, maintaining and enhancing strong relationships with customer, employee, supplier, community and shareholder stakeholders with the goal of delivering long-term economic, social and environmental value to all stakeholders in order to enhance sustainable business financial performance.

stakeholder theory The doctrine that businesses should be run not for the financial benefit of their owners, but for the benefit of all their stakeholders. It is an essential tenet of stakeholder theory that organizations are accountable to all their stakeholders, and that the proper objective of management is to balance stakeholders' competing interests.

standard costing A system of costing an item over a period of time by forecasting probable changes of such costs and averaging these out to provide a 'standard' cost. Such as system avoids the hazard that sharp, short-term fluctuations in costs make it difficult to compare financially consecutive periods of company activity or arrive at sensible price-change decisions. The system requires a back-up control system that ensures that this forecast of cost changes is accurate.

standard deviation (SD) A measure of the variability of a distribution of scores. The more the scores cluster around the mean, the smaller the standard deviation. In a normal distribution, 68 per cent of the scores fall within one standard deviation above and one standard deviation below the mean, and 95 per cent within two standard deviations.

Standard Industrial Classification (SIC) A numbering system established by the US Office of Management and Budget that identifies companies by industry. It is used to promote the comparability of economic statistics from various sectors of the US economy. SIC was intended to promote greater uniformity and comparability in data presentations by government, industry and research institutions.

SIC is the closest thing we have to a classification of goods system in marketing. There is a SIC scheme in both the UK and the US, and, though not identical, they are very similar, both based on a decimal code. For example, in the US a pair of pliers would be coded SIC 342311. The first two digits identify the basic industry: the numbers from 19 to 39 indicate manufactured goods, the number 34 specifying fabricated metal products. The rest of the digits are as follows:

3rd	Industry group	2 = cutlery, hand-tools, hardware
4th	Specific industry	3 = hand and edge tools
5th	Product class	1 = mechanic's hand service tools
6th	Product	1 = pliers

All government statistics relating to industrial production in both countries are published under SIC codes and are therefore a valuable secondary data (see DATA) source for marketing researchers.

standardization The process of establishing a technical standard among competing entities in a market, where this will bring benefits without hurting competition. It can also be viewed as a mechanism for optimizing economic use of scarce resources such as forests, which are threatened by paper manufacture. As an example, all of Europe now uses 230 volt 50 Hz AC mains grids and GSM mobile phones and measures lengths in metres.

standout test In consumer goods marketing, a test that places a package on a shelf in a store to determine how well the designed package shows up when compared with competitive offerings displayed in close proximity.

star *See* BOSTON CONSULTING GROUP MATRIX.

Starch rating A technique developed by Daniel Starch in 1923 and used to test the effectiveness of print advertising. Readers are asked to recall magazines or papers they have read and then asked to recall particular ads. Depending upon the answers given, readers are then placed in one of three categories: noted, read-most, seen/associated. *See also* ATTENTION VALUE.

Statistical Package for the Social Sciences (SPSS) A popular package of computer software used to analyse data, including data obtained in marketing research surveys.

statistical test Another term for test statistic, that is, any of several tests of the statistical significance of findings. Statistical tests provide information about how likely it is that results are due to random error.

stickiness This is a form of TRACKING on the Internet and measures the average amount of time spent by a user at a particular website. It is normally measured in pages viewed, downloads made, hours and minutes spent viewing the site and number of visits made. Using this data assists the proposal and setting of advertising rates.

stock 1 The fund invested in goods used in trade, or in raw materials to be processed and used in trade. **2** All the goods held by a merchant ready for trading. **3** A capital sum to trade with. The term tends to be more widely used in the UK than in the US, and with a greater range of meaning.

stockist An organization which acts as a holder and distributor of goods from stock.

stocktaking A physical count of products actually held in STOCK as a basis for verification of the stock records and accounts, held periodically.

storyboard A visual cartoon-like mock-up of a series of sketches on boards designed to show the key episodes and events from a storeyline for a film, Internet or television commercial. Used to get over basic concepts and ideas with clients and creatives when selling promotion ideas.

straight rebuy *See* BUY PHASES.

strapline A short statement or SLOGAN incorporated into all of a firm's advertising. Its purpose is to emphasize a phrase that the company wishes to be remembered by, particularly for marketing a specific corporate image or in connection to a product or consumer base, e.g. 'Guinness is good for you'.

strategic alliance Recent research and thinking on strategic alliances is dominated by joint ventures and mergers; however, there is also much that can be said about marketing agreements and acquisitions in looking at corporate competitive edge.

To realistically comprehend what strategic alliances are we need a reasonably robust definition to fully encompass what has become a very broad international corporate term. Borys and Jemison (1989) make a good starting point in categorizing strategic alliances, seeing them as hybrids, and define five main types of inter-company agreements:

i) Mergers are the complete unification of two or more organizations into one entity.

ii) Acquisitions involve the purchase of one organization by another, enabling one buyer to assume control over the other.

iii) Licence agreements involve the purchase of a right to use an asset for a particular time and offer rapid access to new technology and product innovations.

iv) Supplier arrangements (of which partnering is one specific example) represent contracts for the sale of one firm's output to another.

v) Joint ventures result in the creation of a new organization that is formally independent of the parents; control over and responsibility for the venture varies greatly among specific cases.

These points all warrant different levels of organizational commitment from the acquisitive or alliance-forming organizations; for instance, a merger can stretch management to the limit as they are forced to grapple with building a new organizational structure, merging the two businesses and developing a single organization. One of the most significant developments in the global economy in recent years has been the growth and spread of strategic alliances which have developed in response to the changes that have been happening to the world economy, for example, acceleration of technological change and the increased costs of developing, producing and marketing new products. Collaborative ventures between firms and across firms is not new as Devlin and Bleackly (1988) have pointed out. What is different is the scale, which has dramatically increased, with many firms forming not just one alliance but networks of alliances. These relationships, as Dicken (1992) has highlighted, 'are increasingly polygamous rather than monogamous'.

Very few organizations have only one

single alliance. Instead, they form a series of alliances and clusters, each with partners that have their own web of collaborative arrangements. For example, Nokia, Philips, Toyota and Toshiba are at the heart of what are often overlapping alliance networks which frequently include a number of fierce competitors.

Global competition is frequently found as a key feature in why alliances are formed. Devlin and Bleackly (1988) state, 'Probably the greatest stimulus to alliance formulation has been the emergence of global competitors and those corporations wishing to become global.' This view has been echoed by Ohmae (1989) who has commented that, 'To compete in the global arena, you have to incur and defray immense fixed costs. You need partners.'

Thus the necessity to effectively compete in the new global market is driving companies into forming strategic alliances, and the most competitive companies in the new global market have a network of alliances covering all aspects of their business. An excellent example of the network of alliances can be seen in Gugler's (1992) work on alliance networks in the semiconductor industry and Philips international network. This diagrammatically outlines the complex network of alliances, joint ventures and dependencies that are in operation in these ultra competitive and interdependent electronics and information technology markets.

Lorange and Roos (1991) argue that, 'For many multinational firms, strategic alliances have become increasingly important tools for ensuring speed and flexibility in arguing out multinational strategies.'

Sources and References

Borys, B. and Jemison, D. B. (1989), 'Hybrid arrangements as strategic alliances: theoretical issues in organisational combinations', *Academy of Management Review*, Vol. 14, No. 2, pp. 234–49.

Devlin, G. and Bleackly, M. (1988), 'Strategic Alliances Guide-lines for Success', *Long Range Planning*, Vol. 21, No. 5, pp. 18–23.

Dicken, P. (1992), *Global Shift*, London: Paul Chapman Publishing, p. 213.

Gugler, P. (1992), 'Building Transnational Alliances to create Competitive Advantage', *Long Range Planning*, Vol. 25, No.1, pp. 90–9.

Kindleberger, C. P. (1969), *American Business Abroad*, Newhaven, CT: Yale University Press.

Lorange, P. and Roos, J. (1991), 'Why some strategic alliances succeed and others fail', *The Journal of Business Strategy*, Vol. 12, No. 1, pp. 25–30.

Ohmae, K. (1989), 'The Global Logic of Strategic Alliances', *Harvard Business Review*, March/April, pp. 143–54.
See also JOINT VENTURES.

strategic business units (SBUs) A business unit within the overall corporate identity which is distinguishable from other businesses because it serves a defined external market where management can conduct strategic planning in relation to products and markets. An SBU can encompass an entire company, or can simply be a smaller part of a company set up to perform a specific task. The SBU has its own business strategy and objectives, and these will often be different from those of the parent company.

strategic control A periodic assessment of the effectiveness of the corporate strategy, business strategy or marketing strategy. The concern will be to ensure that strategic objectives are being achieved as planned. More broadly, the aim might be to assess the current strategy in light of competitors' performance and the demonstrated ability of the company to capitalize on opportunities. Such assessments may be part of an annual strategic planning cycle with the results feeding into the next annual review or cycle.

Effective strategic control will involve assessing whether or not, amongst other things, the organization is effectively capitalizing on opportunities and will highlight the importance of taking remedial action where there are significant deviations from plan or there is inadequate performance relative to competitors.

strategic decisions Decisions primarily focused on the external marketing environment rather than the internal effectives and associated processes of the organization. Strategy will be very much built around the marketing mix and how this can be used to underpin product positioning in the marketplace.

strategic gap analysis A process by which gaps in the marketplace are assessed and evaluated for potential product development and extension. Strategic management will need to perceive that there is a sufficient gap in the market to allow room for product development and that such an initiative will fully meet costs and returns necessary for reinvestment. It is critical in gap analysis that all potential options are costed and market entry ease and difficulties fully assessed. 'Can the gap be filled?' and 'Is it worth it?' are useful questions to ask before entering the gap, as well as evaluating a time period both for entry and return.

In 1956 Malcolm McLean spotted a major gap in the transportation market; he is credited as the inventor of the simple but revolutionary idea of a standard-sized shipping container that could be loaded onto ships, railway carriages and lorries. Containerization changed cargo shipping from a labour-intensive enterprise to an equipment-intensive enterprise and stimulated the development of worldwide container shippers such as Maersk.

strategic group A concept used in strategic management and marketing to refer to clusters of organizations that either operate in a similar way, are positioned in a particular quadrant of the market (low cost for example) or have similar marketing strategies (for instance Procter and Gamble and Unilever).

strategic innovation The development and design of products to meet the aspirations and needs of a particular organization and its long-term plans to meet its customers' needs profitably enabling it to continue to renew its business and capital base. In pharmaceutical marketing, with lead times being more than twelve years on average in developed markets from the conception of the product idea to market entry primarily due to scientific and regulatory needs, the need to innovate is led by human demand which in those markets is ageing and has led to those drugs dealing with the diseases of age being promoted. Also, in the insurance market traditional not-for-profit suppliers of support for the older consumer, such as Age Concern in the UK, who have moved from being a provider of basic burial insurance to becoming an endorser of ethically benchmarked insurance and assurance products for the elderly, this was a strategic innovation in line with the organization's ethos which has generated significant profit to strengthen its core activities: the support of the elderly. The term also covers NEW PRODUCT DEVELOPMENT, MARKET DEVELOPMENT or DIVERSIFICATION policies in the search of profitable markets.

strategic management The totality of management decisions that determine the purpose and direction of an organization. It involves strategic planning, operational abilities and implementation and control. The selected strategy will determine the organization's raison d'être, direction, its goals and the activities it pursues to achieve its objectives. The strategies adopted will establish the internal character of the organization, how it relates to the external environment, the range of products and services, and the markets in which it operates. An example would be Aldi or Lidl, the European supermarket groups whose prime mission is to be low-cost but profitable suppliers of quality goods to consumers – this is their key strategic management approach.

strategic marketing The long-term planning of an organization's products and position in the marketplace. The organization has either planned for continuous growth or has built into its strategy market planning cycles declines in consumer demand that result in consumers moving to alternative projects or reducing their demand in the marketplace.

strategic objectives Broadly stated, they are what an organization must achieve to remain or become competitive and ensure the organization's long-term sustainability. Strategic objectives are generally focused both externally and internally and relate to significant customer, market, product, service or technological opportunities and challenges (strategic challenges). They set an organization's longer-term directions and guide resource allocations and redistributions.

strategic planning A structured approach to the formulation of corporate or business strategy, involving a series of stages which include: STRATEGIC OBJECTIVES; a SWOT ANALYSIS; the identification of strategic options, the selection of the optimum strategic option and the implementation of the strategy. A disciplined effort to produce fundamental decisions and actions that shape and guide what an organization (or other entity) is, what it does and why it does it. Strategic planning requires broad-scale information gathering, an exploration of alternatives and an emphasis on the future implications of present decisions. It can facilitate communication and participation, accommodate divergent interests and values and foster orderly decision-making and successful implementation.

strategic styles It has been suggested that organizations can be categorized according to their broad strategic style. Henry Mintzberg, in *The Nature of Managerial Work* (1973), suggests there are three main approaches to strategy making, these being adaptive, entrepreneurial and planning styles. In addition, how centralized and devolved the organization is can reflect both the operation and style of the organization: does the regional or national headquarters have autonomy to make key decisions or is it just an adjunct of its whole operating company? Is the style of the organization Anglo-Saxon, Japanese or German in its management and orienta-

tion? Is it a small business, family concern, trust or not-for-profit organization?

stratified sampling A method of SAMPLING from a POPULATION. When sub-populations vary considerably, it is advantageous to sample each sub-population (stratum) independently. Stratification is the process of grouping members of the population into relatively homogeneous subgroups before sampling. The strata should be mutually exclusive: every element in the population must be assigned to only one stratum. The strata should also be collectively exhaustive: no population element can be excluded. Then random or systematic sampling is applied within each stratum. This often improves the representativeness of the sample by reducing sampling error. It can produce a weighted mean that has less variability than the arithmetic mean of a simple random sample of the population.

structural equation modelling (SEM) A technique which effectively subsumes a whole range of standard multivariate analysis methods, including regression, factor analysis and analysis of variance. Hypothetical relationships between variables are represented in a network of causal and functional paths. Whilst being a sophisticated theoretical tool, and certainly not easy to implement, SEM actually underlies much of what practising market researchers do on a daily basis. That is, on the basis of things we can measure, we attempt to make predictions for things we cannot measure.

For market research SEM provides an opportunity (in fact, a requirement) to hypothesize models of market behaviour and to test or *confirm* these models statistically.

structure-conduct-performance paradigm The dominant paradigm in industrial organization from 1950 till the 1970s, it was made up of the following:

• structure: the market structure, defined mainly by the concentration of market share in the market;

• conduct: the behaviour of firms –

competitive or collusive (pricing, R&D, advertising, production, choice of technology, entry barriers, etc.);
• performance: social efficiency, mainly defined by extent of market power.

The paradigm was based on the following hypotheses:

Structure influences conduct: the lower the concentration, the more competitive the behaviour of firms.

Conduct influences performance: more competitive behaviour leads to less market power (i.e., greater social efficiency).

Structure influences performance: lower concentration leads to lower market power

(a), (b) and (c) imply that, directly and indirectly, structure determines performance.

stuffer A piece of publicity matter intended for general distribution with other material such as outgoing mail or goods.

style obsolescence The deliberate restyling of goods in an attempt to make models already on the market out of date. *See also* OBSOLESCENCE; PLANNED OBSOLESCENCE.

subliminal advertising Signals or messages embedded in another object, designed to pass below the normal limits of perception. These messages are indiscernible to the conscious mind but are alleged to be perceptible to the subconscious or deeper mind: for example, a single frame in a film, visible for only a fraction of a second. Subliminal techniques have occasionally been used in advertising and propaganda. The purpose, effectiveness and frequency of such techniques is debated. See also PACKARD.

subsidiary A company legally controlled by another company.

substitute products A different product that can be substituted for an existing product, that satisfies the needs of the particular consumer or user. Thus in fuels, coal for wood; in foodstuffs, butter for margarine; and in colas, Coca-Cola for Pepsi.

supermarket 1 A self-service store of over 2,000 square feet and having three or more checkout points, primarily selling a wide range of fast-moving consumer goods, including a high proportion of preprepared foodstuffs, usually at premium prices. **2** A site where many traders operate their business on their own account under the same roof.

supplier An individual, company or other organization which provides goods or services to a recognizable customer or consumer.

supply chain management The management process associated with the operations of all the companies and organizations involved in the total sequence that leads from supply of a particular product to the ultimate user or consumer. The process can incorporate raw material sourcing, manufacturing process and design, packaging, distribution systems, transport, storage facilities, warehousing and information systems to support such a process that contribute to the creation and delivery of a product or service. The supply chain for petrol will run from the refinery through to the petrol pump but will also include heavy linkages back into crude oil production and downstream to customer promotions.

survey The collection of information from a common group through interviews or the application of questionnaires to a representative sample of that group.

survey methods A generic term that embraces all the methods that may be used in collecting data by means of a survey.

swatch a) A small sample of fabric, metal, ink, paint, paper, plastic, fabric or other material for the purposes of colour matching. b) One of the great modern Swiss iconic wristwatch companies; many of its early models are very sought after by collectors.

SWOT analysis A mnemonic for Strengths, Weaknesses, Opportunities, Threats, a SWOT analysis is a strategic planning tool used to evaluate a project or a business venture. One of the most

STRENGTHS	WEAKNESSES
Relative to key competitors, what differential strengths does the organization have?	Relative to key competitors, what differential weaknesses does the organization have?
OPPORTUNITIES	THREATS
On the basis of an analysis of the organization's external business environment, what are perceived to be the key opportunities open to the organization during the plan period?	On the basis of an analysis of the organization's external business environment, what are perceived to be the key threats facing the organization during the plan period?

SWOT Analysis

commonly used market-positioning assessment techniques used in marketing. Strengths and weaknesses are internal to an organization and can cover such features as product quality, marketing and operations, staff and organizational abilities. Opportunities and threats originate from outside the organization and can include competitors, the impact of new technologies and global changes in the environment.

A SWOT analysis is usually performed early in the project development process, helping organizations evaluate the environmental factors and the internal situation facing a project. *See also* EXTERNAL AUDIT.

symbolic association An association of ideas, relating ideas or symbols to other functional or abstract things.

synectics A creative problem-solving approach used in advertising and the integrated communications industry, similar to brainstorming and sometimes known as 'blue skies thinking' or 'out of the box'. It consists of four prime principles: **1** the identification of a specific leader to focus the group; **2** detailed knowledge and common understanding of the issue or situation; **3** the common belief that all ideas have some good qualities; and **4** the equal importance and value of all participants and their ideas. Idea generation is kept confidential and the best solutions are then ranked in order of the ability to resolve the problem or issue.

synergy The term synergy is taken from the Greek *syn-ergo*, meaning working together. It refers to the direct gain in incremental savings, revenue growth and organizational effectiveness that can be gained when one combined business or enterprise is created from two or more separate parts. The merger of Audi and Volkswagen generated incremental revenues from co-branding and new products while reducing operating costs through the rationalization of excess capacity and elimination of redundant activities. It also allowed the new group to focus on brand building and developing a global capability rather than being European car manufacturers that exported.

systematic sampling A sample obtained by taking every 'nth' subject or case from a list containing the total population (or sampling frame). The size of n is calculated by dividing the desired sample size into the population size. This makes systematic sampling functionally similar to simple random sampling. Its advantage to the researcher is it is much more efficient and much less expensive to carry out.

systems marketing In many B2B markets, for example those for integrated computer technology or chemical and oil production and processing, the supplier sells not only the product itself but also a broader set of benefits to the customer. The product is sold as part of an overall 'system' that will solve the company's problems. In the case of a chemical plant this may be a computer system to run an integrated inventory and distribution system. Systems marketing is the adoption of a marketing approach aimed at providing better service and satisfaction to customers through the design of well-integrated groups of interlocking products, together with the implementation of a system of production, inventory control, distribution and other services, to meet a major customer's needs for a smooth-running twenty-four-hour operation.

systems theory The development of marketing can be modelled within the paradigm of general systems theory. Using this approach, marketing thought can be described in terms of the attempt by organizations to become more aware of, and their ability to react to, their relevant external publics or users. Systems theory is one of several methodologies, such as operations research, systems analysis and systems dynamics, which use a systems approach to analyse and explore complex phenomena and problems. Systems theory focuses on structure rather than function and proposes that all complex systems share some basic structural commonalities and that these can be modelled mathematically. Systems theory was introduced by the Austrian biologist Ludwig von Bertalanffy (1901–1972).

T

tachistoscope testing A research method employed in advertising, packaging and product recall testing. It uses the different lighting and exposure techniques of a tachistoscope, a device that projects an image at a fraction of a second, to measure a viewer's recognition and perception of various elements within an ad, especially subliminal messages and perceptions.

target audience The term usually used to describe groups in the community selected as being the most appropriate (e.g. primary purchasers, users or influencers) for a particular advertising campaign or schedule. The target audience may be defined in DEMOGRAPHIC or PSYCHOGRAPHIC terms, or a combination of both.

target costing The disciplined process of designing a product with a specified functionality at a particular cost to gain a profit. Target costing involves setting the planned selling price and subtracting the desired profit as well as marketing and distribution costs, thus leaving the required manufacturing or target cost.

target market A defined segment of the market that is the strategic focus of a business or a marketing plan. Normally the members of this segment possess common characteristics and a relatively high propensity to purchase a particular product or service. Because of this, the members of this segment represent the greatest potential for sales volume and frequency. The target market is often defined in terms of geographic, DEMOGRAPHIC and PSYCHOGRAPHIC characteristics.

target marketing Marketing to a particular group or groups of consumers commonly called segments with similar characteristics, within a broader group of consumers who purchase this type of product. MARKET SEGMENTATION is the process of target marketing. Once target market(s) are identified, the organization develops a product offering (MARKETING MIX) that is positioned to be attractive to that segment.

target pricing The setting of a price based on costs plus the required rate of return on investment for a particular production run or quantity of product or service.

targeting Choosing a medium which will direct an advertising message at a narrowly defined market segment. *See also* SEGMENTATION.

tariff a) Usually takes the form of a government tax imposed on imports designed to protect a particular market or raise revenue for the home administration. b) Also commonly used as the standard term for the rate for a hotel room or restaurant meal.

teaser campaign An advertising or promotional campaign aimed at stimulating consumer interest in a particular product. A good example would be Singapore Airlines' promotional campaign for the Airbus 380: ' "Be part of history: Bid to be the first to fly on the A380" First A380 flight to be sold for charity.'

technology transfer The process of converting scientific or technical knowledge into viable products for the business sector.

tele-marketing An alternative term for

telephone selling. It also includes use of a telephone for research purposes. In tele-marketing, marketers contact the customer via telephone calls. One of the original attractions of tele-marketing was the speed with which marketing campaigns could be executed or research from respondents collected. While DIRECT MAIL is cost-effective, it is relatively slow, since marketing pieces must be shipped by mail. Tele-marketing also lends itself well to products and services that are complex to buy, such as when a customer wants to switch to another telephone company or purchase a financial service. Certain types of transactions may also be subject to government regulation; tele-marketing permits a company representative to walk the customer through the purchase, while ensuring compliance with laws.

While not as varied as direct mail, tele-marketing can take several forms:

- outbound tele-marketing: calls made to customers. By using autodialers and predictive dialers, call centres can call a large number of customers;
- inbound tele-marketing: promotions and offers made when a customer calls the centre;
- voice messages: a number of firms employ special technology to call customers' answering machines;
- telecanvassing: to illicit voters' preferences in electoral and referenda campaigns. When applied effectively it has been shown to have a very high rate of accuracy.

In the last decade there has been some decline in the use of tele-marketing as a result of the rise of mobile phones over house or landline telephones. Mobile phone numbers and associated addresses are not freely available to marketers, and this inaccessibility erodes the integrity of the process and negate some of the effectiveness of conventional tele-marketing. *See also* DIRECT MAIL; DIRECT MARKETING.

tele-shopping Although originally associated with purchasing by telephone following a promotion on the TV, this term has now increasingly come to encompass Internet retailing.

teletext An information-retrieval service provided by television broadcast companies. Teletext pages can be viewed on television sets with suitable decoders. They offer a range of text-based information, usually including national, international and sporting news, weather and TV schedules. Subtitle (or closed-caption) information is also transmitted in the teletext signal.

telethon A marathon television programme aimed at giving support to a charity or political candidate. The term originated in the United States and is simply a combination of the words 'television' and 'marathon'. The format of a telethon usually consists of performances by singers, musicians, comedians or other entertainers interspersed with pitches for donations. The BBC's annual *Children in Need* campaign is one of the largest telethons in the world and raised £19,089,771 in 2007. Telethons have been replicated across the world and are a regular feature of media and personality charity fundraising.

television Often abbreviated to TV and sometimes called the telly, tube or box, television has become the prime household-based telecommunication system for broadcasting and receiving moving pictures and sound over a distance. The word is derived from the Greek *tele*, meaning far, and Latin *visio*, meaning seeing.

Since it first became commercially available in the late 1930s, the television set has become a common household communications device in homes and institutions, particularly in the first world, as a source of entertainment and information. Since the 1970s, video recordings on VCR tapes and, later, digital playback systems such as DVDs, have enabled the television to be used to view recorded films and other programmes.

Television is a major advertising medium and has the advantage of being able to provide both national and selective coverage and variable time slots. Awareness can be built quickly and the effectiveness of the promotion can be assessed easily thanks to the availability of accurate audience audit and market research data. Television broadcasters such as ABC, BBC, CNN, NBC and SkyFOX have become major brands within the industry and are internationalizing their services, particularly sport, travel and news, which can attract lucrative and targeted commercial advertising and sponsorship.

television marketing Television shopping programmes are used to market goods and services to the consumer through various means, including: DIRECT SELLING via television; lead-generation (encouraging the consumer to ask for more information via mail or the Internet); or traditional retail (suggesting that the consumer visit a retail location).

Television shopping programme formats include:

- spots or short-form commercials (up to two minutes in duration);
- INFOMERCIALS or long-form commercials (fifteen to thirty minutes in duration)
- Shopping channels, which can be either live or pre-recorded (up to twenty-four hours per day).

Each of the above formats can be interactive (where customers can contact the programme directly) or non-interactive (simply providing information, telephone numbers, text numbers or web addresses).

television ratings (TVRs) A measure of television programme popularity based on survey research. Sophisticated equipment is attached to sets in selected homes (a quota sample) to record which channel the set is tuned to. Diary panels are used to determine how many people are watching the set. Ratings are calculated as a minute-by-minute programme audience and expressed as a percentage of total households which can receive TV. Advertisers measure the coverage of their advertising campaigns in TVRs, the percentage of a target audience (housewives, teenagers, men) having the television on during the spot (commercial). Audience research is undertaken in the USA by ACNIELSEN and in the UK by BARB.

terms of trade The policies, facilities and other arrangements that characterize the trade between one country or group of countries and another.

test marketing A method of testing a marketing plan on a limited scale, simulating as nearly as possible all the factors involved in a national campaign; usually carried out in a restricted but representative location, often a particular TV region. This procedure enables a marketing company to obtain an indication of likely market acceptance without the full commitment and expense of a national launch. It also exposes the product and the plan to competitors, and consequently the results of the test can seldom be regarded as absolutely conclusive.

testimonial A statement, often given by a celebrity, affirming the value of a product, event or service. The authority, glamour, character or special knowledge of a celebrity can reflect on the advertised product. Michael Jordan, perceived as an expert on sports footwear, speaks for Nike. Customer testimonials are also commonly used.

text messaging The sending of short written messages from a mobile phone to other mobile phone users using the SMS standard. This is becoming an increasingly popular form of communication. Text messaging has the advantage over E-MAIL that it doesn't require access to a computer, and it is less intrusive and less expensive than a phone call.

theory of demand The branch of economic theory concerned with the determinants of choice, involving the selection of sets of purchases from among the many available. It involves the study of conflict between incomes, prices and marketing interactions in order to make predictions on likely future behaviour patterns. *See also* ELASTICITY OF DEMAND.

theory of reasoned action This theory basically states that a person's behaviour is determined by their behavioural

Thompson, J. Walter
(1847–1928)

The founder of the pioneer advertising agency JWT in New York in 1867. At that time, American magazines carried almost no advertising, and Thompson succeeded in persuading the publishers of general periodicals and women's magazines that the sale of advertising space would greatly subsidize their production costs. Having done so, he bought it all up and resold it in lots to potential advertisers. He was thus a classic case of the entrepreneurial space broker, acting as a sales agent for the media owners. At the turn of the century, his agency still controlled the sale of almost all the magazine advertising space available.

During the early twentieth century, JWT became established as the largest and most important advertising agency in the world, by steadily opening offices overseas. In the 1970s, in a strong echo of the founder's business ethics, it led an industry-wide boycott in America against buying advertising time in unacceptably violent television programmes. That action is credited with being the single most influential factor in the eventual reduction of the level of violence on American television screens. JWT remained the undisputed leader in virtually every country where it operated, until falling victim to a dramatic resurgence in British advertising by losing a takeover battle in 1987 against the WPP Group (owner of Young and Rubicam and Ogilvy and Mather) led by Martin Sorrell. JWT now lives on as one of the constituent agencies of the world's second-largest advertising group and had reported turnover of $1.3 billion in 2006.

intentions. Thus a person's behaviour can be predicted by their attitude toward a particular behaviour and how they think other people would view them if they did the actual behaviour. Both of those factors determine a person's behavioural intentions, which determine whether the behaviour is done or not.

thumbnail A small version of an image that is used to give the viewer an idea of what the full-sized image is like or used in order to display multiple images on the same web page at the same time. Typically, clicking on the thumbnail image will cause the full-sized image to download.

time series analysis The branch of quantitative forecasting in which data for one variable, measured typically at successive times and spaced apart at uniform time intervals, are examined for patterns of trend, seasonality and cycle.

time-sharing a) Term used in real estate marketing referring to a process where a property in a particular location, usually a holiday destination, is sold in weekly blocks over a time period of normally

twenty-five years to a number of users. b) Also an approach in network computing in which a single computer is used to provide simultaneous interactive general use computing to multiple users who share processor time.

time to market The average length of time from the conceptual idea for a product to the date it becomes commonly available for purchase by consumers in the particular marketplace. Pharmaceutical development can require between twelve and seventeen years from the start of the research programme to the final approval by the FDA in the US.

tipping point The critical point in an evolving situation that leads to a new and irreversible development. This term was popularized by Malcolm Gladwell in 2002 when he published his book *Tipping Point: How Little Things Can Make a Big Difference.* The term is said to have originated in the field of epidemiology to describe the point where local controls become inadequate to prevent the spread of an infectious disease. The term is now used in many fields. Journalists apply it to social phenomena, demographic data and almost any change that is likely to lead to additional consequences. Marketers see it as a threshold that, once reached, will result in additional sales. In some usages, a tipping point is simply an addition or increment that in itself might not seem extraordinary but that unexpectedly is just the amount of additional change that will lead to a big effect. A tipping point can also refer to the nature of the market, and how its balance turns to favour one company over another. In the butterfly effect of chaos theory, for example, the small flap of the butterfly's wings that in time leads to unexpected and unpredictable results could be considered a tipping point. However, more often the effects of reaching a tipping point are more immediately evident. A tipping point may simply occur because a critical mass has been reached.

token In online marketing, token refers to a tag or tracer mechanism attached to the receiving server of the address (URL) of a page requested by a user. A token normally lasts through a series of requests by a user, regardless of the length of the interval between requests.

top-level domain (TLD) The name which occurs at the top of the Internet domain name hierarchy and is displayed as the last letters at the end of the online address. Examples include country codes such as au for Australia and org for not-for-profit organizations such as org in www.icann.org. In the 1980s, seven TLDs (.com, .edu, .gov, .int, .mil, .net and .org) were created. Domain names can be registered in three of these TLDs (.com, .net and .org) without restrictions; the other four have specific and restricted purposes. TLDs with two letters (such as .de, .mx and .jp) have been established for over 240 countries and external territories and are referred to as 'country-code' TLDs or 'ccTLDs'. They are delegated to designated managers, who operate the ccTLDs according to local policies that are adapted to best meet the economic, cultural, linguistic and legal circumstances of the country or territory involved. For more details, see the ccTLD web page on the IANA website. For a full list of top-level domain names, please see page 280.

total quality management (TQM) A management strategy aimed at embedding awareness of quality in all organizational processes. This approach to quality assurance emphasizes a thorough understanding by all members of a production unit of the needs and desires of the ultimate service recipients, a viewpoint of wishing to provide service to internal, intermediate service recipients in the chain of service and a knowledge of how to use specific data-related techniques to assess and improve the quality of their own and the team's outputs.

tracking Term used extensively to track advertising responses throughout the duration of a campaign, whether it be online or via traditional media. Tracking and reporting tools such as the use of focus groups, polling and market research can aid organizations in modifying their campaign to bring about the desired result such as increased sales or votes in an election. The publisher of online ads usually provides reports on ad impressions and CLICK-THROUGH. For additional analysis of traffic and actual customer conversion rates, tracking mechanisms are built into a website. It is widely known that a number of promotional campaigns for consumer products and political campaigns were not adequately tracked and did not give the desired result.

trade counter The sales point in a retail or wholesale outlet where provision is made to supply 'the trade' – i.e. professionals rather than the general public. It is often used in the building trade.

trade cycle The pattern of periodic oscillations (of about eight to ten years) in the level of business activity ranging from booms or peaks to depressions or troughs. Due to government action after the Second World War, the extremes of the trade cycle have been considerably reduced, permitting more steady growth, but the phenomenon has reappeared in recent times under the pressure of inflationary increases in the costs of energy and materials created not only by the action of producers but also as a response to fears of resource exhaustion. No government has found it easy to control the resulting barriers to continued growth and the diminution of employment prospects. An upturn in trade would appear to await discovery and exploitation of alternative sources of supply. *See also* BUSINESS CYCLE.

trade discount A discount given by a manufacturer to a retailer/wholesaler, or a company to another company in the same trade.

trade fair An exhibition of goods and services for the benefit of individuals or companies involved in a particular trade. Generally, a trade fair is held in an exhibition hall, and each exhibitor is allowed to rent space to display goods and services. Many trade shows are accompanied by seminars and lectures, where the newest trade information can be presented and new trade ideas and concepts may be exchanged.

trade journal A publication aimed at a specific industry or professional association and made available to its members as part of their membership package. Trade journals provide a publication vehicle to a clearly defined target audience for both advertising and publicity. Now rapidly being augmented by member- or user-only trade or profession websites such as that operated by CIM and CIPR.

trade magazine A magazine with editorial content of interest only to persons engaged in a particular industry, occupation or profession, e.g. *Farmers Weekly*, *Management Today*, *PR Week*. It is also called business publication.

trade press *See* TRADE MAGAZINE.

trademark The term trademark is a logo, sign or symbol that distinguishes organizations and/or products from one another. It is a form of intellectual property right, which endorses a particular product or organization in order to protect consumers from counterfeit, fake or substitute goods

that are not produced by the trademark holder.

The protection of the trademark strengthens the image and perceived quality of the brand in the eyes of the consumer or user. It is seen as a surety of quality and made to a perceived and agreed specification. Trademarks are normally obtained nationally and then protected by WTO agreements which regulate against infringement of trademark agreements.

Trademark-holders have realized the importance of protecting their rights to their respective domain names. CYBERSQUAT-TING is the deliberate attempt to acquire specific domain names with the hope of reselling them at a higher price, often to the trademark-holder. Trademark law is typically implemented at the national level, which creates problems for the global Internet. However, harmonization via bodies like the WORLD TRADE ORGANIZATION (WTO) helps with cross-national dispute resolution.

transaction cost analysis An approach to costing transactions to establish whether it is more economic to perform functions oneself or sub-contract them to other members of the system.

transfer pricing The pricing of goods and services within a multi-divisional organization. Goods from the production division may be sold to the marketing division, or goods from a parent company may be sold to a foreign subsidiary. The choice of the transfer prices affects the division of the total profit among the parts of the company. It can be advantageous to choose them such that, in terms of book-keeping, most of the profit is made in a country with low taxes.

transnational A term applying to companies transacting or managing business across national boundaries on a large scale.

treatment group The item or subject that is manipulated during an experiment.

trend 1 A move in price characterized by a series of higher lows and higher highs (an uptrend) or lower highs and lower lows (a downtrend). **2** In market research the movement in one direction of the values of a variable over a period of time and the general drift or tendency to drift in a set of data. **3** A move in attitudes by the consumer or user. An example would be the growing trend for young consumers to become vegetarians.

trend analysis The systematic analysis of market research data that shows an upward or downward pattern that is not due to seasonality or random factors such as the closure of a major production unit such as an oil refinery for environmental maintenance checks. The analysis of trends plays a leading role in the ability to be able to predict packaging demand types, production patterns and future demand for products. In marketing, trend analysis is used extensively as a form of market demand forecasting.

trendline A line drawn through successive maximum price movements. These can be a series of two or more successively lower peaks as in a downtrend, or successively higher troughs in an uptrend. Trendlines can also be drawn through closing levels. The more instances of contact, the more reliable the trend.

triad economies The three largest economic blocs of the world: the NORTH AMERICAN FREE TRADE AGREEMENT (NAFTA), the EUROPEAN UNION and industrialized Eastern Asia (Japan, Taiwan, South Korea, Hong Kong, Singapore). It is in this triangle that the global consumer with similar lifestyles, needs and desires is based.

triangulation A means of establishing the accuracy of information in a study of a phenomenon or construct by comparing three or more types of independent points of view on data sources, for example, interviews, observation and documentation; different times and their bearing on the same findings.

trick banner A BANNER AD that pops up on the user's Internet system that attempts to persuade people into clicking onto the site, often by imitating an operating system, error message or by leaving a intriguing message.

trickle-down An economic theory that suggests that as wealth is created it will trickle down to all sectors of society. In marketing, the term is usually applied to a group of consumers who trade down to buy lower priced goods and specifically brands.

trojan An Internet programme that appears realtively harmless and hides a malignant and often spying virus, such as a password programme that secretly records the passwords entered and e-mails them to the author of the virus.

turn-key operations A product or service which can be acquired and utilized by the buyer with very limited work by the purchaser, thus by just 'turning the key'. A business that is being sold as a turn-key business would include tangibles such as equipment stock and order book and intangibles such as the brand, goodwill and reputation. The most common type of business sold as a turn-key business is a FRANCHISE. In the case of franchises, a turn-key business often includes a building that has been constructed to the franchise's brand's livery style and specifications, corporate promotions of the franchised brand, training of staff and right to sell exclusively in a particular territory. Subway, the sandwich maker founded in the US in 1965, is a high-quality mass franchise operation that utilizes these techniques.

turnover, rate of The number of times the average value of stock is sold during a fiscal year or some designated period. The formula for calculation is:

$$\frac{\text{value of sales at cost}}{\text{average stock at cost}} \times 100$$

Care must be taken to ensure that the average inventory and net sales are both reduced to the same denominator; that is, inventory at cost should be divided into sales at cost or inventory at selling price should be divided into sales at selling price – cost price and selling price should not be confused. The turnover, when accurately calculated, is one measure of the efficiency of a business.

TVR *See* TELEVISION RATINGS.

U

ultimate consumer The person who actually consumes a product or service, as distinct from the shopper or buyer, who may be no more than a purchasing agent, such as a housewife.

umbrella strategy When an organization has a been given a clear definition of strategic goals, and even the general strategic direction, by the chief executive, but the detail of how these goals are to be achieved has yet to be decided.

uncertainty Used in marketing as a fear appeal where information provided to the marketplace makes a consumer concerned about the quality, reliability or supply of particular product, thus leading to an alternative choice being purchased.

undifferentiated marketing One of the three key marketing strategies, undifferentiated marketing ignores market segment differentiation and aims to appeal to the maximum of potential customers with a single basic product that is mass promoted. The other marketing strategies are concentrated marketing and differentiated marketing. *See also* CONCENTRATED MARKETING; DIFFERENTIATED MARKETING.

Unfair Contract Terms Action, 1977 (UK) An Act that allows consumers to challenge any term in a contract they have signed or entered into if that term seems unfair or unreasonable. The Act applies to both consumer and business contracts and to both standard form terms and individually negotiated terms. The Act relies on aggrieved individuals to take action and does not contain any process for dealing with unfair terms in a systemic manner.

uniform resource locator (URL) The specific web address of a web page, which can be either the domain name or a specific file or web page on a website.

unique selling proposition (USP) The unique benefits that a particular firm's products or services offer consumers, and that competing firms do not; in other words, what gives the firm its COMPETETIVE ADVANTAGE.

unique user A single individual or browser who accesses a site or is served unique content and/or ads. Unique users can be identified by user registration or cookies; they are also known as unique visitors.

unit pricing Price information presented on a per-unit weight or volume basis, so shoppers can compare prices across brands and across package sizes within brands.

univariate analysis The analysis of single variables as distinct from relationships among variables for purposes of description (e.g. averages, or the proportion of cases falling into a given category among the entire sample). *See also* MULTIVARIATE ANALYSIS.

universe The total POPULATION of the audience being measured.

unloading Disposing of goods in a market at a low or concessionary price.

unstructured interview *See* DEPTH INTERVIEW.

up-market Market segment where higher prices dominate the buying behaviour.

upwardly mobile A term that describes people who aspire vigorously to move upwards towards a higher socio-economic position.

Uruguay Round The multilateral negotiations between the member countries of GATT that were held in Uruguay from the mid-1980s to 1993.

use-by date The date up to and including which the food may be used safely (e.g. cooked, processed or consumed) if it has been stored correctly. In large supermarkets and shops the normal practice is that shelves are stacked with the products with older dates at the front so that customers are more likely to buy them first. It is also known as best-before date, though it is gradually replacing this term as consumers find it less confusing.

users In marketing theory users are normally the members of the decision-making unit and are those individuals working in an organization who are directly involved in the use of the goods or services purchased by the organization.

utilitarianism A moral philosophy, utilitarianism accepts the existence of ethical conflicts and the legitimacy of some ethical dilemmas and proposes ethical analysis based on the question 'Which act will result in the greatest good for the greatest number of people?' It entails the balancing of greater and lesser goods and is useful for unravelling complex ethical problems. It generally operates on the principle that the utility (happiness or satisfaction) of different people can not only be measured but also meaningfully summed over a period of time and that utility comparisons between people are meaningful. That makes it possible to achieve a well-defined societal optimum in allocations, production and other decisions and achieve the goal utilitarian British philosopher Jeremy Bentham described as 'the greatest good for the greatest number'. Utilitarianism is widely used in the measurement of ethical evaluations of marketing activities.

utility the usefulness of a particular product, which can lead to satisfaction in the user and purchase of the product.

V

validation A term used in market research whereby a sample of interviewees or respondents is contacted to confirm that initial contact has been made, and in the right manner. This confirms the accuracy of the research programme and also gives an indication of the extent to which the interviewers are acting properly.

validity The extent to which a piece of research or test has proved what it has set out to assess or not. The validity of a piece of research can prove whether or not a campaign or product offer will work. This is important in marketing as products and concepts may look good but often do not work in the marketplace for valid reasons.

value-added The additional value created at a particular stage of manufacture by improved production, packaging and re-packaging and/or service delivery. Adding value by improved service delivery or by faster delivery times can be a vital part of the product mix in gaining improved margins for the business.

value added tax (VAT) A sales tax levied on the value of the goods sold, whether they be physical products or services, which was first introduced to France as *taxe sur la valeur ajoutée* (TVA) in 1954 and has subsequently become the prime indirect tax form offered in the EU and the rest of the world. In Singapore, Australia, New Zealand and Canada, this tax is known as 'goods and services tax' or GST. VAT is an indirect tax in that the tax is collected from the retailer or supplier of products rather than the end user. It is seen as a regressive tax as all consumers of products carrying VAT pay the same amount of tax irrespective of income level.

value analysis In manufacturing, an analysis to determine the most economical method of manufacturing, taking into account the cost and the process capability of alternative manufacturing systems under consideration, their degree of variation, the benefits of the resultant product and desired quality and production quantity and rate.

value-based pricing A pricing strategy in which a product's price is actively dependent upon its demand. This method of pricing allows companies to take advantage of highly demanded products by charging a premium for the product. Good examples are how refreshments generally cost more at sporting events and flight bookings at critical times and during high season activity are charged at a premium to the consumer.

value chain An organization's set of linked, value-creating activities, ranging from securing basic raw materials and energy to the ultimate delivery of products and services to the customer's benefit. There are two main types of activity: primary activities, which include operations, logistics, marketing, sales and service; and support activities, which can include infrastructure, human resource management, technology development and the purchasing function. The concept argues that a firm can deliver more value to its customers through performing these activities more efficiently than its competitors or by performing the activities in a unique way that

van Riel, Cees

Professor of Corporate Communication at the Business School at Erasmus University, Rotterdam, in the Netherlands. He is director of the Corporate Communication Centre, a research institute at the same university, and has worked as a communication strategy consultant for a range of companies in Europe. He has published numerous books and articles, with recent publications focusing on reputation management. Van Riel is the editor-in-chief (together with Charles Fombrun of Stern Business School, New York University, USA) of the *Corporate Reputation Review*. He also founded the Master of Corporate Communication (degree) programme at Erasmus University Rotterdam and the RFN, the Dutch reputation forum. He is the managing director of the Reputation Institute in New York and a member of the Branding Steering Committee of ING Group.

creates greater differentiation. It allows for each step of the chain to be analysed so that an assessment can be made of whether it is making a positive or negative contribution to customer value. The concept has often been used to assess businesses' potential and to strengthen and/or rationalize particular aspects of the business operation.

value engineering An analytical approach to assessing the costs versus the benefits of a new acquisition or cost of raw material as part of the manufacturing process. 'Does the additional cost lead to improvements in output, lower cost production and/or increased margin?' or 'Does it lead to a decline in profit?' are the questions that can be asked in assessing the cost/benefit ratio.

value proposition The promise that a company or organization makes to customers to deliver a particular combination of values. Thus many organizations have moved away from an internal focus to being focused on customer-orientated, market-driven processes, looking towards a form of value delivery. Three types of value propositions have been commonly indicated, these include:

- operational excellence: these organizations provide the middle of the market with products at the best price with the least inconvenience;
- product leadership: these organizations offer products that push performance boundaries; the proposition to the customer is the best product in the best time;
- customer intimacy: these companies specialize in delivering not just what the market wants but what specific customers want by building relationships designed to satisfy the unique needs of their clients.

variable costs Costs that vary with the volume of output, such as labour hours, energy and raw materials. These costs rise as production increases and conversely decline as output is reduced. These variable costs can include other items such as plant and buildings as these can be transferred to leasehold agreements to ensure that they are not always considered a fixed cost. Variable costs are subject to day-to-day management of costs as against fixed costs which have to be factored into financial planning over a longer time period.

variance A measure of the spread of scores in a distribution of scores, that is, a measure of dispersion. The larger the variance, the further the individual cases are from the mean. The smaller the variance, the closer the individual scores are to the mean. Specifically the variance is the mean of the sum of the deviations from the mean score divided by the number of scores. Taking the square root of the variance gives the standard deviation. The concept is used widely in marketing analysis.

VBM (value-based management) A management approach that places shareholders and investors as the key consideration. The object of the firm, its systems, strategy, processes, analytical techniques, performance measurements and culture have as their guiding objective shareholder wealth maximization.

vehicle A particular publication or channel used to carry advertising messages.

venture capital A term to describe the financing of start-up and early-stage businesses which exhibit potential for above-average growth, as well as businesses in 'turn-around' situations. Venture capital investments generally are high-risk but offer the potential for above-average returns. Venture capital is typically raised by venture capital firms, which, in return for this investment, receive significant ownership of the company and seats on the board.

verisimilitude The state of being close to or similar to the truth. Scientific theories are sometimes thought of as having different degrees of verisimilitude. In the philosophy of science verisimiltude refers to the attempt to articulate how a false theory could be closer to the truth than another false theory. This usage was mostly popularized by Karl Popper. Verisimilitude has been used to explore the relevance of different communications and messages in marketing.

vertical integration The operational system linking upstream suppliers to downstream buyers. It is very evident in many industries such as chemicals where the producing organization, such as Bayer (the makers of aspirin), may both convert raw materials into intermediate products and supply these via wholly owned subsidiaries to end buyers who are in turn owned by the company and who will supply the consumer. Control upstream is usually referred to as backward integration (thus towards suppliers of raw material), while control of activities downstream (thus towards the eventual buyer) is referred to as forward integration. A good example of a company with both upstream and downstream activities would be an oil company such as Shell,

BP or Exxon. *See also* HORIZONTAL INTEGRATION.

vertical market This term refers to a particular industry sector made up of similar businesses supplying products and services using comparable marketing methods and distribution systems. Good examples of vertical markets are: the chemical and oil industry; mineral extraction businesses; financial services; local, regional and national government services; retailing; pharmaceuticals; media; distribution and shipping; education and health care. *See also* HORIZONTAL MARKET.

viral marketing A very rapidly developing form of marketing whose prime aim is to encourage consumers to pass on a promotional message or idea, whether it be a statement, video clip or e-mail. Viral marketing is dependent upon fast and high pass-along rates from consumer to potential consumer and is reliant upon friends and acquaintances sharing information, ideas and of course video clips which are most frequently placed on YouTube. A number of viral campaigns have used billboard ads or pictures of celebrities reading certain items in the press which are then sent as an attachment to friends to comment on; this can lead to substantial commentary about the particular product or concept raised. Highly successful campaigns have been Firefox's viral ad campaign and Hotmail which is widely regarded as the first true viral marketing campaign.

virtual reality Software and hardware which attempts to simulate real-life scenarios without the risk (physically or financially) of making mistakes.

vision statement A vision statement 'paints a picture' of ideal future outcomes. Whereas a MISSION STATEMENT provides immediate guidance, describing the organization as it currently exists, a vision statement provides inspiration by presenting an image of where the organization might be in ten or twenty years' time.

voice-pitch analysis (VOPAN) An

advertising effectiveness research technique which measures a respondent's voice, describing their perceptions of promotional appeals, to judge their feelings and responses to a particular ad.

voiceover (VO) The technique of using the voice of an unseen speaker during film, slides or other visual material.

volume discount A reduction in the overall charges for a product based upon staged increases in purchases by the user or customer. Used extensively in large industrial contracts such as petrochemicals or other intermediates where a staged discount is offered for increases in volume purchased thereby rewarding loyalty.

volunteer bias Any of several problems in drawing valid conclusions from research that arise because participation in the research is voluntary. Volunteers may exhibit exposures or outcomes which may differ from non-volunteers (e.g. volunteers tend to be healthier).

VPN (Virtual Private Network) This type of network is used to communicate in private over a public network like the Internet and may be used by a company or a group of companies.

Wall Street The name of the street in lower Manhattan, New York City, running from east from Broad Hill to East River where the New York Stock Exchange, AMEX and many banks and brokerages are located. The name is also used as a metonym to refer to the New York financial district and to the investment community in general. Interestingly, most New York financial firms are no longer located in Wall Street but in lower or midtown Manhattan.

want A desire by a person to possess a product or a service. It is usually a prerequisite to a purchase, but not always so, since a consumer may buy a product which he/she needs even though he/she may not want it.

war room A room in which strategic decisions, especially for a military or political campaign, are made. The term was popularized within political marketing by the 1993 film of the same name which was a behind-the-scenes documentary on the Clinton for President campaign. Tony Blair's New Labour replicated the idea of the war room in the Labour election campaign of 1997.

warranty A written guarantee by a producer or supplier on a particular product to a customer, which is normally given as part of the purchase. The warranty will normally agree to replace defective parts or put right any problems with the product over a given period.

web browser An application that provides a way to view and interact with all the information on the World Wide Web which was designed by Marc Andreessen et al. in 1993 when they launched the first browser, MOSAIC. The software interprets the mark-up of files in HTML and formats them into web pages and displays them to the user. The most popular web browsers are Internet Explorer, Firefox and Safari.

web directory A directory on the World Wide Web. It specializes in linking to other websites and categorizing those links. Web directories often allow site owners to directly submit their site for inclusion and have editors review submissions for accuracy, readability and quality of content.

web page A single-page document on the Internet which is usually written in HTML and invariably accessible via HTTP, the World Wide Web protocol that transfers information from the website's server for listening, reading and/or watching in the user's web browser.

web survey A market research survey that is hosted on a particular website. Potential respondents are invited to participate in a questionnaire on a particular subject, such as recent purchases (by a BANNER AD or other message) and are given a direct link to a website where they complete an online survey form. The survey is completed online and can be set up so that initial answers cannot be amended, building in spontaneity of response.

webcast Derived from the combination of the terms 'web' and 'broadcast', a webcast is the transmission of audio and/or video content over the Internet. In essence, webcasting can be thought of as broadcasting over the Internet. A webcast uses streaming media technology to take a single content source and distribute it to many simultaneous listeners/viewers. The largest 'webcasters' include existing radio and TV stations who 'simulcast' their output, as well as a multitude of Internet-only 'stations'. The term webcasting is usually reserved for referring to non-interactive linear streams or live events.

Webcasting is also used extensively in business for financial and shareholder relations presentations (such as annual general meetings), in e-learning (as a platform for online seminars and specialist workshops), and for related specialist communications such as keynote addresses by CEOs. Webcasting is distinct from web conferencing which is designed for a multi-member interactive event such as a symposium whereas webcasting tends to be one-dimensional.

The ability to webcast using low cost and easily accessible technology has allowed independent media to flourish. There are many notable independent shows that broadcast regularly online. Often produced by members of the general population in their homes and cover a range of topics and interests from the common to the obscure. YouTube has increasingly become a platform for both low-cost and high-fidelity broadcasts which is open to all. Webcasts are used extensively to bring together leading edge thinkers and businesses in marketing to discuss and review complex issues.

website A site (location) on the World Wide Web. Websites are owned and managed by an individual, company or organization and are typically focused on one or a range of topics or purposes. Each website opens with a home page, which is the first document users see when they enter the site. The website will usually contain additional documents, files and links and is often called a portal if it links to a number of different subsections and closed sections on the site. The URLS of the web pages on the site organize themselves into a hierarchy, although the hyperlinks between them control how the reader perceives the overall structure and how the traffic flows between the different parts of the site. Some websites require a subscription to access some or all of their content. Examples of subscription sites include many Internet pornography sites, parts of many news sites, gaming sites, message boards, web-based e-mail services, and sites providing real-time stock-market data. In addition, many websites are partially closed to non-members of the community that owns and manages a particular website; this is very much used by professional associations to allow members entry to restricted areas, and similar arrangements are frequent in public, not-for-profit and private organizations, where access is restricted to seniority and essential users. Any website can contain a hyperlink to any other website, so the distinction between individual sites, as perceived by the user, may sometimes be blurred.

Websites are written in, or dynamically converted to, HTML and are accessed using a software program called a WEB BROWSER, also known as an HTP client. Web pages can be viewed or otherwise accessed from a range of computer-based and Internet-enabled devices of various sizes, including desktop computers, laptop computers, PDAs and mobile phones. A website is hosted on a computer system known as a web server, also called an HTTP server, and these terms can also refer to the software that runs on these systems and that retrieves and delivers the web pages in response to requests from the website users.

website traffic The number of visitors and visits a website receives.

weighting A mathematical process which allows individual values in a data set to be multiplied by a particular number or weight, usually employed to make the data comparable to other variables or to compensate for some perceived phenomenon.

wheel of retailing An American theory of retailing based on the fact that retailing is constantly changing. Even over a short period of time it is possible to observe this

Weitz, Barton

The J. C. Penney Eminent Scholar Chair and Executive Director of the David Miller Center for Retailing Education and Research at the University of Florida. Weitz was Chair of the American Marketing Association and a member of the Board of Directors of the American Marketing Association, the National Retail Federation and the National Retail Institute. He was also editor of *Journal of Marketing Research* and is presently the co-editor of Marketing Letters. He is the co-author of the text books *Retailing Management* and *Personal Selling: Building Relationships*, which are used in more than 200 colleges and universities in the United States and have been translated into Spanish, Portuguese and Mandarin. In 1998, Professor Weitz was the recipient of the American Marketing Association/Irwin Distinguished Marketing Educator Award for lifetime contribution to the marketing discipline.

Professor Weitz's current research interests focus on the development of long-term relationships among firms in a channel of distribution (retailers and vendors), between firms and their employees, and between salespeople and their customers, as well as retailing and sales-force management issues. His research has been recognized with two Louis Stern Awards for research publications that make the greatest contribution to the understanding of channel issues and the Paul Root Award for research that makes a significant contribution to management practice. Professor Weitz has been involved in consulting, expert testimony and executive education assignments in retailing, sales-force management and marketing strategy.

Wensley, Robin

The director of the ESRC/EPSRC Advanced Institute of Management Research and Professor of Policy and Marketing at the Warwick Business School. He was co-editor of the *Journal of Management Studies* from 1998 to 2002. His research interests include marketing strategy and evolutionary processes in competitive markets, investment decision-making, the assessment of competitive advantage and the nature of choice processes and user engagement in public services.

He has published a number of articles in the *Harvard Business Review*, the *Journal of Marketing*, and the *Strategic Management Journal* and has twice won the annual Alpha Kappa Psi Award for the most influential article in the *US Journal of Marketing* as well as the Millennium Prize for the best article in the *UK Journal of Marketing Management*. He has worked closely with other academics and practitioners both in Europe and the US. His books include *Handbook of Marketing* and *Rethinking Marketing: Towards Critical Marketing Accountings*.

happening on every high street or in every shopping centre: some retail shops are opening and others are closing. The 'wheel of retailing' theory states that most new retailers start this as low-status, low-margin, low-priced operators, and as they prosper they move up-market, leaving opportunities for new entrants. The theory has some explanatory value. Many discount stores started after the Second World War in the way described by the theory. Some, as they prospered, moved up-market into more expensive locations and became as a result higher-status, higher-priced operators.

white goods Washing machines, refrigerators, freezers and cookers. The term derives from the fact that at one time these durable goods were always covered in white enamel paint. *See also* CONSUMER DURABLES.

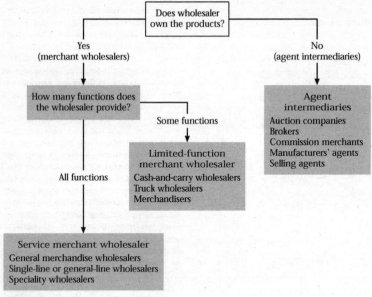

Wholesaler

wholesaler A middle person or distributor who sells mainly to retailers, other merchants and industrial, commercial and institutional users as opposed to consumers.

wiki An online environment network that allows readers to add content to a subject or topic; typical uses include campaign group sites, causes, dictionaries, encyclopedias, manuals, product documentation and help systems. Most have a system to record changes so that, at any time, a page can be returned to any of its previous states. A wiki system may also include various tools designed to provide users with an easy way to monitor the constantly changing state of the wiki, as well as a place to discuss and resolve the many inevitable issues over content. Although not directly related to blogs, the social interaction and dialogue strength is very evident. Organizations that use blogs often develop wikis for internal and especially communications purposes; this is very common in techno-

logically-based industries such as software, bio science, chemicals and pharmaceutical industries.

Wilcoxon test A non-parametric alternative to the t-test (which compares the means of two samples) for dependent samples. It is designed to test a hypothesis about the location (median) of a population distribution. It often involves the use of matched pairs, for example, 'before' and 'after' data, in which case it tests for a median difference of zero.

Wilks' Lambda A widely employed test statistic used for the equality of group means in a MANOVA (multivariate analysis of variance) and in other multivariate tests. It outlines whether there are differences between the means of identified groups of subjects on a combination of dependent variables.

window dressing 1 Displaying goods in a shop window to best advantage to attract customers. **2** Arranging products or a presentation in such a way as to impress another party; sometimes used to describe an artificial situation where the intention is to mislead.

Woolworth's The F. W. Woolworth Company (often referred to as Woolworth's or affectionately as Woolies) is a major retail company that was one of the original US five-and-dime stores. The first Woolworth's store was founded, with a loan of $300, in 1878 by Frank Winfield Woolworth. Despite developing into one of the largest retail chains in the world through most of the twentieth century, Woolworth's went into a steady decline beginning in the 1980s owing to increased competition. As a result, in 1997 the F. W. Woolworth Company converted itself into a sporting retailer, closing its remaining retail stores operating under the Woolworth's brand name and renaming itself Venator Group. By 2001, the firm focused exclusively on the sporting goods market, changing its name to the present Foot Locker Inc. Chain stores using the Woolworth name still operate in the United Kingdom, Germany, Austria, Mexico and South Africa, owned by a range of holding companies. The similarly named Woolworth's supermarkets in Australia and New Zealand are operated by Woolworths Limited, a separate company with no historical links to the F. W. Woolworth Company.

word of mouth The communication of information between potential users in an informal manner normally by verbal means, especially recommendations, but also general information, in a person-to-person manner. Word of mouth is typically considered a spoken communication, although phone conversations, texts and dialogue via SMS (short message service), via web discussions on social marketing websites such as Facebook, blogs, bulletin and message boards and e-mails are often now included in the definition. Given the rapid changes in communications technology this is not surprising as a number of mobile phone operators can take down a verbal message and send it via a text to the user.

word-of-mouth marketing (WOMM) The marketing that can be gained by actively engaging customers to freely share insights with each other either in a retail store situation or over the Internet (stimulating an interest in a product that becomes 'viral'). WOMM has been a core facet of marketing since its inception, as all consumers are looking for advice and pointers from other users or observers of what is a good product and will/does work for the individual consumer. It has gained significant parlance with the growth of the Internet, and the ease with which customers can share their stories on Web 2.0 technologies such as BLOGS, bulletin boards, specialist mailings, company testimonial notices and news readers. DISCUSSION BOARDS, as used by Amazon for instance, have helped customers form communities. Good WOMM relies on quality products that consumers evangelize and proselytize to other potential users.

Conceptually it is possible to see marketing initiatives on the Internet as three concentric circles: the inner circle represents traditional promotional marketing; the middle circle represents an organization's direct activities at engaging with consumers (hosting a blog, a discussion or bulletin board, etc.), or WOMM; the outer circle represents the broader web, where the organization's product offering is being discussed in the wider web domain by the public at large.

World Bank The World Bank was created in 1945 as a sister organization to the INTERNATIONAL MONETARY FUND (IMF) as a result of the Bretton Woods conference. Its purpose, after initially emphasizing the reconstruction of Europe after the Second World War, was to lend funds at commercial rates and to provide technical assistance in order to facilitate economic development in its poorer member countries.

Officially called the International Bank for Reconstruction and Development, its activities are focused on developing countries, in fields such as development (e.g. education, health), agriculture and rural development (e.g. irrigation, rural services), environmental protection (e.g. pollution reduction, establishing and enforcing regulations), strategic infrastructure (e.g. roads, urban regeneration, electricity) and good governance (e.g. anti-corruption, legal institutions development). It provides finance at preferential rates to member countries, as well as aid and grants to the poorest countries. Loans or grants for specific projects are often linked to wider policy changes in the sector or the economy.

World Trade Organization (WTO)
Established on 1 January 1995 as a result of the URUGUAY ROUND of the GATT negotiations, the WTO replaced the GATT as the legal and institutional foundation of the multilateral trading system of member countries. It sets forth the principal contractual obligations determining how governments frame and implement domestic trade legislation and regulations and it is the platform on which trade relations among countries evolve through collective debate, negotiation and adjudication.

World Wide Web (WWW) A rapidly expanding interconnected and interactive collection of information within the Internet that allows users (browsers) to view images, video clips, music, spoken word and sound recordings and, via the advanced search engines and growing sophistication of users, find, if screened properly, quality and reliable information about almost all subjects. Is widely used by the leading professions, governments and foundations to share high-quality information over closed sections of the Internet. Although it is difficult to outline the precise size of the WWW, WorldWideWebSize. Com, the independent Dutch website based at Tilburg University, estimates that in July 2008 the Indexed Web 2007 contained at least 27.78 billion pages of information, with the majority of these being in the English language. It is a very rapidly evolving platform and communications network for marketing activity. It provides marketing businesses the opportunity to create interactive brochures and virtual storefronts as well as offering consumers an information clearing house and online customer service. The term is often mistakenly used as a synonym for the Internet, but the web is actually a service that operates over the Internet.

XML Extensible Markup Language is used to enable the sharing of data across different sites on the World Wide Web. A popular use of XML is to subscribe to news feeds and BLOGS.

Yellow Pages advertising Advertisements for products or services placed in a business telephone directory. The cost for advertising depends upon the type of listing or advertising space you contract for as well as the circulation size of the book you will be listed in. A large metropolitan Yellow Pages book commands a much higher rate per ad than does a small-town book, for instance.

Young & Rubicam's Brand Asset Valuator WPP Group's lead advertising agency, Young & Rubicam (Y&R) has developed a multiple-criteria method to assess brand equity growth. The company has used its Brand Asset Valuator to assess the brand equity of 450 global brands and over 8,000 local brands in twenty-four countries. Each brand has been examined using a thirty-two-item survey that included, in addition to a set of brand personality scales, four distinct measures:

- differentiation: measures how distinctive the brand is in the marketplace;
- relevancy: measures whether a brand has personal relevance for the potential customer;
- esteem: measures whether a brand is held in high regard and considered the top in its class. Closely related to perceived quality and the extent to which the brand is growing in popularity;
- familiarity: measures the degree to which potential customers understand what the brand stands for.

According to this approach to brand equity, brand differentiation is the core of a successful brand proposition with a distinctive position in the marketplace that will promote long-term growth. Y&R defines it as the power of a brand to express its uniqueness and reach top-of-mind status with target consumers. Once consumers are aware of the brand, it needs to be relevant to their needs, satisfying and exceeding their expectations. The way that the brand manager is able to express that relevancy in a language consumers appreciate will determine its success. Once consumers understand what the brand can do for them, they need to aspire to own it, or have esteem for it. Finally, when the brand has communicated its unique, relevant and aspirational message, it will be able to achieve familiarity through repurchase and reuse. These four measures form the basis of two equations:

- differentiation x relevance = brand strength (or vitality)
- esteem x familiarity = brand stature

The equations represent an attempt to overcome issues with other methods that assess brands solely in terms of present and estimated earning power. They suggest that scores relating to brand differentiation and relevance indicate the potential for growth, while those relating to brand esteem and familiarity indicate its present stature. The results, however, are dependent on the analysis of the four criteria in relation to the market, the consumer and the company.

yuppie An acronym for young urban professionals which became synonymous with the aspiring population in the 1980s with thirty-year-olds and their lifestyles. Typical paraphernalia of the then yuppie was considered to be a filofax and a Walkman. Yuppie became a popular word used to suggest greed, self-gratification and a lack of a social conscience by a particular group within society. More recently, the term seems to have undergone a revival with a new socially-caring yuppie being seen to have emerged who is very green, wears expensive outdoor clothing and quality recycled trainers, owns an iPod and drinks sustainable coffee.

zapping The act of using a remote control to change television channels when an advertisement begins. Advertisers are concerned that this will be harmful, but it is still unclear what effect zapping will have on advertising effectiveness.

zero defects A condition in which a production unit makes every product without defect. It is usually only a theory or a reference point, but it is actually sought in such categories as aerospace, serums and others.

zero-sum game A game or more broadly social situation in which one person (alternatively social actor) can gain only at the expense of another and losses and gains are equal amongst partners. The term zero-sum game is derived from the fact that if you deduct one's losses from your winnings, the final result or sum is zero.

ZIP code A Zone Improvement Plan (ZIP) code is the numerical code used by the US Postal Service to denote a local area or entity for the delivery of all forms of mail. ZIP codes are made up of numeric formulas which can consist of five, seven, nine or eleven digits, and can refer to a street, a block of streets, an organization, a building or a group of post office boxes. The term 'ZIP' was also used and developed for its resonance with the consumer of speed and efficiency. *See also* POSTCODE.

ZIP code analysis A US postcode analysis technique used by marketers to determine where their best and worst prospects are and also to assess the impact of how a message or promotion has performed according to a five-digit ZIP CODE or ZIP+4 area; the practice is also referred to as a ZIP code count. Direct marketers take the view that ZIP code-based purchase or support patterns can be identified as consumers and electors with similar consumption patterns tend to reside close to each other. ZIP code analysis is also now linked to very advanced market research techniques used to assess political activist and voter support and donation potential in the US – this was used to great effect by Barack Obama in 2008. *See also* POSTCODE ANALYSIS.

zipping The act of fast-forwarding through commercials while watching a previously taped show on a VCR. Advertisers are concerned about the effect of zipping on advertising effectiveness, but any effect is not yet known. In fact, viewers may pay more attention to advertising while zipping in order to be able to stop fast-forwarding in time when the show restarts.

List of Abbreviations and Acronyms

AAA	American Academy of Advertising
AAAA	American Association of Advertising Agencies
ABC	Australian Broadcasting Corporation
ABC	Audit Bureau of Circulations
ACORN	a classification of residential neighbourhoods
ACP	African, Caribbean and Pacific (countries which are former colonies of member states of the EU)
ACR	Association of Consumer Research
AEBF	Asia–Europe Business Forum
AIB	Academy of International Business
AIDA	attention, interest, desire and action
AIDS	acquired immune deficiency syndrome
AM	Academy of Marketing (UK)
AMA	American Marketing Association
AMI	Australian Marketing Institute
AMS	Academy of Marketing Science (US)
ANZMAC	Australian and New Zealand Marketing Academy Conference
ANOVA	analysis of variance
AOM	Academy of Management (US)
APEC	Asia-Pacific Economic Co-operation
ASEAN	Association of Southeast Asian Nations
ASEM	Asia–Europe Meeting
B2B	business-to-business
B2C	business-to-consumer
BA	British Airways
BAe	British Aerospace
BAM	British Academy of Marketing
BARB	Broadcasters' Audience Research Board
BBC	British Broadcasting Corporation
BCG	Boston Consulting Group
BHS or BhS	British Home Stores
BMW	Bayerische Motoren-Werke; in English, Bavarian Motor Works
BP	British Petroleum
BRAD	British Rate and Data
BRITE	Basic Research in Industrial Technologies for Europe
BSI	British Standards Institute
BSE	Bovine Spongiform Encephalopathy

BTO	build-to-order
C2B	consumer-to-business
C2C	consumer-to-consumer
CAD	computer-aided design
CAP	Common Agricultural Policy
CBI	Confederation of British Industry
CCP	Common Commercial Policy
CCPA	Centre for Corporate Public Affairs (Australia)
CCT	Compulsory Competitive Tendering
CCTV	closed-circuit television
CEE	Central and Eastern Europe
CEN	Comité Européen de Normalisation (European standards body)
CENELEC	Comité Européen de Normalisation Electronique (European standards body for electrical equipment)
CEO	Chief Executive Officer
CET	common external tariff
CIM	Chartered Institute of Marketing
CIPD	Chartered Institute of Personnel and Development
CIPR	Chartered Institute of Public Relations
CIS	Commonwealth of Independent States; in Russian, Sodruzhestvo Nezavisimykh Gosudarstv
CJD	Creutzfeldt-Jakob Disease
CMEA	Council for Mutual Economic Assistance (also known as COMECON)
COD	cash on delivery
CO-OP	co-operative
COR	Committee of the Regions
COREPER	Committee of Permanent Representatives (permanent Civil Servants in the Council of Ministers)
CPA	cost per action
CPC	cost per click
CPCA	cost per contact analysis
CPI	cost per inquiry
CPT	cost per thousand
CRM	Customer Relationship Management/Marketing
CSR	Corporate Social Responsibility
CSS	Cascading Style Sheets
CTR	click-through rate
D1	German Telecom
D2	Mannesmann Mobilfunk
DAGMAR	defining advertising goals for measured advertising results
DCC	digital compact cassette
DCI	compact disc interactive
DFI	direct foreign investment
DIY	do it yourself
DMA	Direct Marketing Association
DMU	Decision Making Unit
DOW	Dow Jones Index (US)
DTH	direct to home

DTI	Department of Trade and Industry (UK)
DTV	digital television
DVD	digital video disc
EAGGF	European Agricultural Guidance and Guarantee Fund (the funding for the CAP and for the reconstruction of the agricultural sector)
EASA	European Advertising Standards Alliance
EBRD	European Bank for Reconstruction and Development
EC	European Communities
ECB	European Central Bank
ECE	United Nations Economic Commission for Europe
ECJ	European Court of Justice
ECPA	European Centre for Public Affairs
ECR	Efficient Consumer Response
ECSC	European Coal and Steel Community
ECU	European Currency Unit
EEC	European Economic Community
EFA	European Food Agency
EFA	European Fighter Aircraft
EFSA	European Food Safety Authority
EFTA	European Free Trade Association
EFTPOS	electronic funds transfer at point of sale
EIB	European Investment Bank
EIS	executive information systems
ELM	elaboration likelihood model
ELMAR	electronic marketing: it is a virtual community for marketing professors and others interested in the study and teaching of marketing
EMS	European Monetary System
EMU	European Economic and Monetary Union
·Eni	Ente Nazionale Idrocarburi
EP	European Parliament
EPA	Environmental Protection Act
EPOS	electronic point of sale
ERDF	European Regional Development Fund
ERM	European Exchange Rate Mechanism
ERR	expected rate of return
ESC	Economic and Social Committee
ESCB	European System of Central Banks
ESF	European Social Fund
ESOMAR	worldwide organization for enabling better research into markets, consumers and societies
ESPRIT	European Strategic Programme for Research and Development Technology
EU	European Union
EURAM	European Research in Advanced Materials
EURATOM	European Atomic Energy Community
EV	expectancy value
EVC	European Vinyls Corporation
FAS	free alongside ship

FC	football club
FCC	Federal Communications Commission
FDA	Federal Food and Drug Administration (US)
FIFO	first in first out
FMCG	fast-moving consumer goods
FOB	free on board
FTC	Federal Trade Commission
G8	group of eight industrial nations
GATS	General Agreement on Trade in Services
GATT	General Agreement on Tariffs and Trade
GDP	gross domestic product
GDR	German Democratic Republic
GE	General Electric Company
GM	General Motors
GMO	genetically modified organism
GMS	global system for mobile communication
GNP	gross national product
GOP	Grand Old Party (the Republican Party)
GSP	Generalized System of Preferences
GST	goods and service tax
HDI	Human Development Index
HTML	hypertext mark-up language
IAA	International Advertising Association
IABC	International Association of Business Communicators
IBRD	International Bank for Reconstruction and Development
ICC	International Chamber of Commerce
ICT	information and communication technology
IDM	Institute of Direct Marketing
IE	Institute of Export
IMC	Integrated Marketing Communications
IMF	International Monetary Fund
IMP	Industrial Marketing and Purchasing Group
INFORMS	Institute for Operational Research and Management Science
IP	Internet Protocol
IPO	initial public offering
IS	information systems
ISBN	International Standard Book Number
ISDN	Integrated Services Digital Network
ISP	Internet Service Provider
ISSN	International Standard Serial Number
ISTAT	Istituto Nazionale di Statistica
ITV	Independent Television (UK)
JIT	just in time
JV	joint venture
KISS	keep it simple stupid
KPI	key performance indicator
MBO	management buyout
MEP	Member of the European Parliament

MFA	Multi Fibre Arrangement
MFN	most favoured nation
MHS	Meat and Hygiene Service
MIS	marketing (or management) information system
MITI	Japanese Ministry of International Trade
MLC	Meat and Livestock Commission
MNC	multinational corporation
MOD	Ministry of Defence
MP	Member of Parliament (UK)
MPC	marginal propensity to consume
MRS	Market Research Society
NAFTA	North American Free Trade Area/Association
NAP	North American Philips
NATO	North Atlantic Treaty Organization
NBC	National Broadcasting Corporation (US)
NFC	National Freight Corporation
NFP	not for profit
NGO	non-governmental organization
NIC	newly industralized countries
NPD	new product development
NPV	net present value
NRS	national readership survey
NTA	New Transatlantic Agenda
NTB	non-tariff barrier
NUTS	Nomenclature of Territorial Units for Statistics
NZDB	New Zealand Dairy Board
OCR	optical character recognition
OECD	Organization for Economic Co-operation and Development
OEM	Original Equipment Manufacturer
OFT	Office of Fair Trading
OPEC	Organization of Petroleum Exporting Countries
ORC	Opinion Research Corporation
OTMS	Over Thirty Months Scheme
PDF	portable document files
PEEST	political, economic, environment, social and technological factors
PHARE	Poland and Hungary: Assistance for Restructuring their Econimies
PIMS	Profit Impact of Marketing Strategies
PLC	product life cycle
PLC	public limited company
PMS	Pantone matching system (colours)
POP	point of purchase
PPS	pay per sale
PR	public relations
PRCA	Public Relations Consultants Association
PRO	public relations officer
PRSA	Public Relations Society of America
PSB	public service broadcasters
PSBR	public sector borrowing requirement

PSDR	public sector debt repayment
PVC	polyvinyl chloride
QA	question and answer session
RBV	resource-based view
R&D	research and development
REC	Regional Environmental Centre for Central and Eastern Europe
ROI	return on investment
SBU	strategic business unit
SCA	sustainable competitive advantage
SD	standard deviation
SEA	Single European Market
SEP	Single European Programme
SERVQUAL	service quality
SIC	standard industrial classification
SME	small- and medium-sized enterprise
SPSS	statistical package for social sciences
SWOT	strengths, weaknesses, opportunities and threats
TABC	Transatlantic Business Dialogue
TACD	Transatlantic Consumer Dialogue
TLD	top-level domain
TQM	total quality management
TUC	Trades Union Congress
TVR	television ratings
UNCTC	United Nations Centre on Transnational Corporations
UNICE	Union of Industrial and Employers' Confederations of Europe
UPS	United Parcel Service
URL	uniform resource locator
USMEF	United States Meat Export Federation
USP	unique selling proposition
USSR	Union of Soviet Socialist Republics
VAT	value-added tax
VBM	value-based management
VCM	vinyl chloride monomer
VCR	video cassette recording
VO	voice over
VOPAN	voice-pitch analysis
VW	Volkswagen
WTO	World Trade Organization
WWW	World Wide Web
XML	extensive mark-up language

Good Website and Journal Resources

General Marketing Resources

American Marketing Association (AMA)

http://www.marketingpower.com/

The website of the Chicago-based AMA contains a wide range of information for the academic and professional marketer. The site contains an extensive glossary of marketing terms and has access to a wide range of resources, including the global marketing and consumer behaviour academic special-interest group sites.

ANZMAC

http://www.anzmac.org/

The website of the Australian and New Zealand marketing academics' organization.

Australian Marketing Institute (AMI)

http://www.ami.org.au/

The AMI was founded in 1933 and represents professional marketers throughout Australia, including practitioners from all marketing functions and industries. This site has some very useful material on marketing metrics.

Chartered Institute of Marketing (CIM)

http://www.cim.co.uk

The website of the largest international professional body for the discipline, based at Moor Hall, Cookham. The site has a knowledge hub on marketing and links to extensive resources and courses in the discipline.

Chartered Institute of Public Relations (CIPR)

http://ipr.org.uk/

The CIPR is the UK's leading public relations industry professional body. Founded in February 1948, today it has over 9,000 members.

China Marketing Academy

http://www.ecm.com.cn/

One of the prime academic organizations for marketing in China.

CIA World Fact Book

https://www.cia.gov/library/publications/the-world-factbook/index.html

Great source of market information on most countries in the world, key resources and economic and human trends.

European Marketing Academy

http://www.emac-online.org/

The prime professional body for marketing academics in Europe.

Institute of Marketing and Management
http://www.immindia.com/
The Indian teaching and research body based in New Delhi.

International Association of Business Communicators (IABC)
http://www.iabc.com/
The IABC provides a network of more than 14,000 business communication professionals in over 70 countries.

KnowThis
http://www.knowthis.com/
Well-regarded marketing information site.

Korean Academy of Marketing Science
http://www.kams.org/
The Korean Academy of Marketing Science is an international professional organization for practitioners, professors and students involved in various areas of marketing.

MarketingProfs
http://www.marketingprofs.com/
MarketingProfs is a very usable, US-based professional marketing support website, with over 300,000 members and 300 contributors.

New Zealand Marketing Association
http://www.marketing.org.nz/
The Association's purpose is to encourage and develop the highest standards of measurable marketing in New Zealand.

Specialist Marketing Resources

Adbusters
http://www.adbusters.org/home
Based in Vancouver, *Adbusters* is a not-for-profit, reader-supported magazine with a circulation of 120,000, which is concerned with the erosion of the physical and cultural environment by commercial forces. Very much a counter-culture organization that challenges non-responsible marketing.

Advertising Age
http://adage.com/Advertising Age
Advertising Age magazine contains news, analysis, information and data on advertising, marketing and media, and the site includes news, demographics, columns, blogs, podcasts and research papers.

Advertising Principles
http://www.advertisingprinciples.com/
A website developed by Scott Armstrong that provides useful knowledge about persuasion through advertising as a set of evidence-based principles. The principles draw upon typical practice, expert opinion, factual evidence and empirical studies.

Advertising World
http://advertising.utexas.edu/world/
A marketing communications directory maintained by the department of advertising at the University of Texas, Austin; a well-organized directory of websites related to everything, from account planning to actors and models to website promotion and word of mouth.

Association for Consumer Research (ACR)
http://www.acrwebsite.org/
The website and resources of the internationally regarded ACR.

Bookmarket
http://www.bookmarket.com/
A website established by John Kramer, which provides a list of self-help sites for those involved in marketing, publishing and writing books and electronic texts. Very interactive and a mine of useful sources for the entrepreneurial author.

Brand Channel
http://www.brandchannel.com/
Established in 2001 by Interbrand, this website is a major international resource and discussion forum for all aspects of branding.

CSR Europe
http://www.csreurope.org/
CSR Europe is the leading European business network for corporate social responsibility, with around 70 multinational corporations and 25 national partner organizations as members.

Ethicsweb
http://www.ethicsweb.ca/resources/
A California-based applied ethics resource.

European Academy of Business in Society
http://www.eabis.org/
EABIS is an alliance of companies, business schools and academic institutions that is, with the support of the European Commission, committed to integrating business-in-society issues and the heart of business theory and practice in Europe.

Fairtrade Labelling Organization International
http://www.fairtrade.net/
A non-profit, multi-stakeholder association involving 23 member organizations that are focused on fair trade. The site includes traders, external experts and links to national organizations.

Intelligent Giving
http://www.intelligentgiving.com
Independent UK-based, charity-advisory organization, which rates best practice in charities.

Marketing Terms
http://www.marketingterms.com/
Includes extensive resources on Internet marketing, including a list of acronyms and dictionary of terms.

Phil Harris
http://www.Phil-Harris.com
Author's website with corporate communication, political marketing and public affairs papers, plus a number of links to international research sites.

Polmark

http://www.polmark.org/

The political marketing website.

PRWeek

http://www.prweek.com/

The website of the largest internationally circulated magazine on public relations.

Scott Armstrong

http://www.jscottarmstrong.com

The website of Scott Armstrong of Wharton Business School contains a range of information on forecasting and predicting outcomes, and a list of useful papers and ideas.

Sfxbrown

http://www.sfxbrown.com

The website of Professor Stephen Brown, who has been called 'the Antichrist of Marketing' and 'a postmodern provocateur', and who is invariably thought-provoking.

Slow Food

http://www.slowfood.com/

A non-profit, eco-gastronomic member-supported organization that was founded in 1989 to counteract fast food. It is now a worldwide pressure group, with support throughout Europe, North America, Australia and New Zealand.

Web Marketing

http://www.wilsonweb.com/

A website that includes e-commerce, e-mail, Internet marketing; annotated links to articles and resources; and articles from current and past issues of *Web Marketing Today*.

Word of Mouth Marketing Association

http://www.womma.org

A consumer-to-consumer and consumer-to-marketer communications site that has a library of information, including case studies, and among its related concepts are viral, buzz, grassroots, street team and other types of marketing in which the consumer takes on an active role.

Social Networking Websites

Bebo

http://www.bebo.com

Based in San Francisco with over 30 million users, who are primarily teenagers and young adults. In 2007 it was rated the most used social networking website for the UK, Ireland and New Zealand.

Facebook

http://www.facebook.com

The second-most significant social networking site on the US web, with a significant emphasis on college students. In the top ten of sites visited in the world, and often referred to as a marketer's dream because of its availability to use advertising to target potential customers.

MySpace
http://www.myspace.com
The largest social networking site on the web, with a reported 200 million members in 2007. Bought in 2005 by Rupert Murdoch's NewsCorp, stable mate of Fox TV, the *Wall Street Journal*, *The Times*, Sky TV and the *Sun*.

Zebo
http://www.zebo.com
A social networking site for learning what brands your friends own, judging photos of products and being able to trade. Free to use, since Zebo sell products in their online shop. As a member you can also sell your own products.

International Marketing Resources

Globaledge
http://globaledge.msu.edu/ibrd/ibrd.asp
A website maintained by the Center for International Business Education and Research (CIBER), located at Michigan State University. It provides a comprehensive glossary of business concepts and has access to a range of websites that provide data on trade and investment flows.

Research Resources

ACNielsen
http://acnielsen.com/site/index.shtml
Renowned marketing information provider; part of the Nielsen group of companies.

BBC
http://news.bbc.co.uk/
The British Broadcasting Corporation website is very interactive and full of data and links.

Coalition Against Unsolicited Commercial Email
http://www.cauce.org/
The anti-commercial spam site with major branches in the USA, Canada and Australia.

Executive Planet
http://www.executiveplanet.com
The site maintained by Executive Planet Inc. provides basic information on business culture in many developed and developing countries, and it links to sites with further information on this subject.

Google
http://www.google.com
No marketing resources would be complete without the services of Google to search the web, usernet and images. It also includes specialist research facilities such as Google Scholar and Google Maps.

Guardian Unlimited
http://www.guardian.co.uk/
Home of the *Guardian*, the *Observer* and the *Guardian Weekly* newspapers, plus special-interest websites, it has a regular special on advertising, marketing and public relations.

The New York Times
http://www.nytimes.com/
Nicknamed the 'Gray Lady' for its staid appearance and style, it is seen as the US national paper of record, its stable mate being the *International Herald Tribune*.

NewsNow
http://www.newsnow.co.uk/
Monitors breaking news in 22 languages from the Internet's key online publications, including international, national and regional titles, newswires, magazines, press releases and exclusively online news sources spanning 139 countries.

Quintura
www.quintura.com
a visual search engine that extracts keywords from search results and builds a word cloud. By clicking words in the cloud you refine your query. A very good site for creatives, it is based in Russia to give breadth to the marketing mindset.

Wikipedia
http://www.wikipedia.org
An online encyclopaedia written by users. Provided one has a critical perspective, Wikipedia can often be an excellent source for background on a subject. Currently the largest multilingual free-content encyclopaedia on the Internet.

International Institutions

Websites of international organizations containing information on policies, programmes, statistics, papers and other data connected to marketing.

APEC
www.apec.org
A website with information on the aims and objectives of APEC, and data relating to trade and investment flows.

European Union
www.europa.eu.int
Access to all the institutions, policies and programmes of the EU, Eurostat (the statistical agency of the EU), and to the text on all legislation issued by the EU.

Food and Agriculture Organization for the United Nations (FAO)
www.fao.org
Papers, reports and data on global issues connected to food and agriculture.

International Labour Organization (ILO)
www.ilo.org
Papers, reports and data on global issues connected to labour and employment, including labour market conditions in developed and developing countries, and employment practices by multinational corporations (MNCs).

International Monetary Fund
www.imf.org
Access to data, papers, reports and comments on international monetary and investment matters, including country studies, and developments in financial and banking conditions in many developed and developing countries.

International Telecommunications Union (ITU)
www.itu.int
Papers, reports and data on global issues connected to telecommunications and information, technology and communication (ITC).

Mercosur
www.mercosur.org
Information on legal texts and other data on Mercosur; some of the material is in Spanish.

NAFTA
www.nafta-sec-alena.org; www.sice.oas.org/trade/nafta/naftatce.asp
Information on legal texts and other data on NAFTA; in English, French and Spanish.

Organization for Economic Co-operation and Development (OECD)
www.oecd.org
Papers, reports and comments on matters connected to many areas of international business, and codes of conduct for MNCs.

United Nations Conference on Trade and Development (UNCTAD)
www.unctad.org
Papers, reports and data on matters connected to trade, investment and development in developing countries.

United Nations Economic Commissions
Papers, reports and data matters connected to trade, investment and development.

United Nations Economic Commission for Africa (UNECA)
www.uneca.org

United Nations Economic Commission for Europe (ECE)
www.unece.org

United Nations Economic Commission for Latin America and the Caribbean (ECLAC)
www.eclac.org

United Nations Economic and Social Commission for Asia and the Pacific (ESCAP)
www.escap.org

United Nations Economic and Social Commission for Western Asia (ESCWA)
www.escwa.un.org

United Nations Environmental Program (UNEP)
www.unep.org
Papers, reports and data on matters connected to sustainable development and environmental protection in a global economy context.

United Nations Industrial Development Organization (UNIDO)
www.unido.org
Papers, reports and data on matters connected to industrial policies and competitiveness in a global economy context.

United Nations Organizations
www.unsystem.org
This site provides web access to all United Nations agencies and programmes.

World Bank

www.worldbank.org

Access to data, papers, reports and comments on developing country issues, including access to the World Business Environment Survey (WBES), a global survey of business environment conditions. This includes information on ownership, location, size, exports, government regulations and measures of corruption, as well as other indicators on the characteristics of business culture.

World Trade Organization

www.wto.org

Papers, reports and data on trade issues, including trade disputes, rules for trading and access to material on general agreement on trade and tariffs (GATT), general agreement on trade in services (GATS), trade-related intellectual property (TRIPS) and trade-related investment measures (TRIMS).

Websites of Central Banks

Bank of England

www.bankofengland.org

Access to data, papers, reports and comments on economic and business issues in the UK.

Bank of International Settlements

www.bis.org

Access to data, papers, reports and comments on matters connected to international capital flows and international banking.

Bank of Japan

www.boj.or.jp/en/

Access to data, papers, reports and comments on economic and business issues in Japan.

European Central Bank

www.ecb.int

Access to data, papers, reports and comments on economic and business issues in the EU.

Federal Reserve Bank of America

www.frb.org

Access to data, papers, reports and comments on a host of economic and business issues that affect both the US and world economy.

Websites of financial and business newspapers, magazines and media providers

Bloomberg

www.bloomberg.com

Information services, news and media company site.

Business Week

www.businessweek.com/globalbiz/index.html

Site provides limited free access (unlimited to subscribers), articles and commentary on global business issues.

Economist

www.economist.com

Site provides limited free access (unlimited to subscribers), articles and surveys on matters connected to international business.

Financial Times
www.ft.com
Site provides limited free access (unlimited to subscribers), articles, surveys and statistics on companies and matters connected to international business.

Infoworld
www.infoworld.com
Electronic publication on global issues connected to information, technology and communication (ITC).

Reuters
http://www.reuters.com/
Provider of information on current affairs, finance and technology.

Leading Service Market Resources

Boston Consulting Group
www.bcg.com
Limited free access to material on strategic issues affecting marketing.

Ernst & Young
www.ey.com/global/content.nsf/international/home
Good site from this leading accountancy and service provider, particularly on international and growth markets.

IBM
www.ibm.com/e-business
Limited free access to material on strategic issues affecting marketing.

JointVentures
www.jointventures.org
Limited free access to material on joint ventures affecting a part of strategic marketing.

KPMG
http://www.kpmg.com
Accountancy and service provider who is a leader in corporate social responsibility initiatives in the UK; also has good materials on countering corruption and access to free background reports on key marketing sectors.

McKinsey
http://www.mckinsey.com/
Good access materials, especially on the development of Chinese business and marketing.

PriceWaterhouseCoopers
www.pwc.com
Limited free access to material on strategic issues affecting marketing.

Academic Journals with Articles On Marketing (selected)

Australasian Marketing Journal
European Journal of Marketing
Industrial Marketing Management
International Journal of Research in Marketing
International Management Review

International Marketing Review
Journal of Advertising Research
Journal of Advertising
Journal of Business and Industrial Marketing
Journal of Consumer Research
Journal of Global Marketing
Journal of International Business Studies
Journal of International Management
Journal of International Marketing
Journal of Macromarketing
Journal of Marketing
Journal of Marketing Communications
Journal of Marketing Management (UK and US versions)
Journal of Marketing Research
Journal of Non-profit and Public Sector Marketing
Journal of Political Marketing
Journal of Public Policy and Marketing
Journal of Research in Marketing
Journal of Retailing
Journal of Services Marketing
Journal of Strategic Marketing
Journal of the Academy of Marketing
Journal of World Business
Management International Review
Marketing Theory
Psychology and Marketing
Public Relations Review

Other Journals with Some Marketing Articles

Academy of Management Journal
Academy of Management Review
California Management Review
European Management Journal
Harvard Business Review
Journal of Public Affairs
Organizational Studies
Sloan Management Review
Strategic Management Journal

Area Studies Journals

Asian Economic Journal
Asian Studies Review
China Economic Review
EuroMed Journal
European Business Journal
European Business Review
International Journal of Asian Management
Journal of African Business

Journal of Asian Economies
Journal of Asian-Pacific Business
Journal of East–West Business
Latin American Business Review
Pacific Economic Review

Other Journals with Some Articles Related to Marketing

Annals of Tourism
British Journal of Management
International Journal of Human Resource Management
International Journal of the Economics of Business
Journal of Business Research
Journal of Common Market Studies
Journal of Management Studies
Journal of Small Business Management
Long Range Planning

List of Top-level Domain Names

The top-level domain names in alphabetical order and abbreviation:

TLD	Domain	TLD	Domain
ad	Andorra	br	Brazil
ae	United Arab Emirates	bs	Bahamas
aero	Air transport industry	bt	Bhutan
af	Afghanistan	bv	Bouvet Island
ag	Antigua & Barbuda	bw	Botswana
ai	Anguilla	by	Belarus
al	Albania	bz	Belize
am	Armenia	ca	Canada
an	Netherlands Antilles	cc	Cocos (Keeling) Is
ao	Angola	cf	Central African Republic
aq	Antarctica	cg	Congo
ar	Argentina	ch	Switzerland
arpa	old-style Arpanet	ci	Ivory Coast
as	American Samoa	ck	Cook Is
at	Austria	cl	Chile
au	Australia	cm	Cameroon
aw	Aruba	cn	China
az	Azerbaijan	co	Colombia
ba	Bosnia-Herzegovina	com	USA commercial
bb	Barbados	coop	cooperatives
bd	Bangladesh	cr	Costa Rica
be	Belgium	cs	former Czechoslovakia
bf	Burkina Faso	cu	Cuba
bg	Bulgaria	cv	Cape Verde
bh	Bahrain	cx	Christmas Island
bi	Burundi	cy	Cyprus
biz	business	cz	Czech Republic
bj	Benin	de	Germany
bm	Bermuda	dj	Djibouti
bn	Brunei Darussalam	dk	Denmark
bo	Bolivia	dm	Dominica

TLD	Domain	TLD	Domain
do	Dominican Republic	in	India
dz	Algeria	info	unrestricted
ec	Ecuador	int	international
ac & edu	educational	io	British Indian Ocean Terr.
ee	Estonia	iq	Iraq
eg	Egypt	ir	Iran
eh	Western Sahara	is	Iceland
es	Spain	it	Italy
et	Ethiopia	jm	Jamaica
fi	Finland	jo	Jordan
fj	Fiji	jp	Japan
fk	Falkland Is	ke	Kenya
fm	Micronesia	kg	Kyrgyzstan
fo	Faroe Is	kh	Cambodia
fr	France	ki	Kiribati
fx	France (European Terr.)	km	Comoros
ga	Gabon	kn	Saint Kitts & Nevis Anguilla
gb	Great Britain	kp	North Korea
gd	Grenada	kr	South Korea
ge	Georgia	kw	Kuwait
gf	French Guyana	ky	Cayman Is
gh	Ghana	kz	Kazakhstan
gi	Gibraltar	la	Laos
gl	Greenland	lb	Lebanon
gm	Gambia	lc	Saint Lucia
gn	Guinea	li	Liechtenstein
gov	Government	lk	Sri Lanka
gp	Guadeloupe (French)	lr	Liberia
gq	Equatorial Guinea	ls	Lesotho
gr	Greece	lt	Lithuania
gs	S. Georgia & S. Sandwich Is	lu	Luxembourg
gt	Guatemala	lv	Latvia
gu	Guam (USA)	ly	Libya
gw	Guinea Bissau	ma	Morocco
gy	Guyana	mc	Monaco
hk	Hong Kong	md	Moldavia
hm	Heard & McDonald Is	mg	Madagascar
hn	Honduras	mh	Marshall Is
hr	Croatia	mil	USA military
ht	Haiti	mk	Macedonia
hu	Hungary	ml	Mali
id	Indonesia	mm	Myanmar
ie	Ireland	mn	Mongolia
il	Israel	mo	Macau

TLD	Domain	TLD	Domain
mp	Northern Mariana Is	qa	Qatar
mq	Martinique (French)	re	Reunion (French)
mr	Mauritania	ro	Romania
ms	Montserrat	ru	Russian Federation
mt	Malta	rw	Rwanda
mu	Mauritius	sa	Saudi Arabia
museum	museums	sb	Solomon Is
mv	Maldives	sc	Seychelles
mw	Malawi	sd	Sudan
mx	Mexico	se	Sweden
my	Malaysia	sg	Singapore
mz	Mozambique	sh	Saint Helena
na	Namibia	si	Slovenia
name	name	sj	Svalbard & Jan Mayen Is
nato	NATO	sk	Slovakia
nc	New Caledonia (French)	sl	Sierra Leone
ne	Niger	sm	San Marino
net	network	sn	Senegal
nf	Norfolk Island	so	Somalia
ng	Nigeria	sr	Suriname
ni	Nicaragua	st	São Tomé & Principe
nl	Netherlands	su	former USSR
no	Norway	sv	El Salvador
np	Nepal	sy	Syria
nr	Nauru	sz	Swaziland
nt	Neutral Zone	tc	Turks & Caicos Is
nu	Niue	td	Chad
nz	New Zealand	tf	French Southern Terr.
om	Oman	tg	Togo
org	non-profit organizations	th	Thailand
pa	Panama	tj	Tadjikistan
pe	Peru	tk	Tokelau
pf	Polynesia (French)	tm	Turkmenistan
pg	Papua New Guinea	tn	Tunisia
ph	Philippines	to	Tonga
pk	Pakistan	tp	East Timor
pl	Poland	tr	Turkey
pm	Saint Pierre & Miquelon	tt	Trinidad & Tobago
pn	Pitcairn Island	tv	Tuvalu
pr	Puerto Rico	tw	Taiwan
pro	professionals	tz	Tanzania
pt	Portugal	ua	Ukraine
pw	Palau	ug	Uganda
py	Paraguay	uk	United Kingdom

TLD	Domain	TLD	Domain
um	USA Minor Outlying Is	vu	Vanuatu
us	United States	wf	Wallis & Futuna Is
uy	Uruguay	ws	Samoa
uz	Uzbekistan	ye	Yemen
va	Vatican City State	yt	Mayotte
vc	Saint Vincent & Grenadines	yu	Yugoslavia
ve	Venezuela	za	South Africa
vg	Virgin Is (British)	zm	Zambia
vi	Virgin Is (USA)	zr	Zaire
vn	Vietnam	zw	Zimbabwe

PENGUIN POCKET REFERENCE

PORTABLE   **DESIRABLE**   **INDISPENSABLE**

Penguin Pocket Babies' Names

Penguin Pocket Book of Facts

Penguin Pocket Crossword Finisher

Penguin Pocket Dictionary of Quotations

Penguin Pocket English Dictionary

Penguin Pocket Famous People

Penguin Pocket French Dictionary

Penguin Pocket German Dictionary

Penguin Pocket Italian Dictionary

Penguin Pocket Jokes

Penguin Pocket Kings and Queens

Penguin Pocket On This Day

Penguin Pocket Rhyming Dictionary

Penguin Pocket Roget's Thesaurus

Penguin Pocket School Dictionary

Penguin Pocket Spanish Dictionary

Penguin Pocket Spelling Dictionary

Penguin Pocket Thesaurus

Penguin Pocket Writer's Handbook

Our Penguin Pockets are part of the extensive Penguin Reference
Library – a resource that draws on over 70 years of experience bringing
reliable, useful and clear information to millions of readers around the
world. We want to make knowledge everybody's property.